CENTRAL AND LOCAL FINANCE
IN GERMANY AND ENGLAND

CENTRAL AND LOCAL

FINANCE

IN GERMANY AND ENGLAND

MABEL NEWCOMER

NEW YORK
COLUMBIA UNIVERSITY PRESS
1937

FOREIGN AGENTS

OXFORD UNIVERSITY PRESS
HUMPHREY MILFORD, AMEN HOUSE
LONDON, E.C.4, ENGLAND

KWANG HSUEH PUBLISHING HOUSE
140 PEKING ROAD
SHANGHAI, CHINA

MARUZEN COMPANY, LTD.
6 NIHONBASHI, TORI-NICHOME
TOKYO, JAPAN

OXFORD UNIVERSITY PRESS
B. I. BUILDING, NICOL ROAD
BOMBAY, INDIA

PREFACE

This study has been undertaken in the hope that an account of the financial relations of central and local governments in other countries will be of value to students of the problem in the United States. Germany and England were selected as the countries in which post-war developments had made local governments markedly dependent on the central government for support. At the time the study was begun the writer was impressed by similar developments in this country, although it was not expected that, with our decentralized government, we should follow very closely in the footsteps of Germany or England. Today, however, it is apparent that local financial systems in the United States are as incapable of coping with the exigencies of a severe depression as local financial systems in other countries. In the later years of the depression our local governments have depended on Federal and state support to almost the same extent as the local governments of Germany and England; and there are many striking parallels— as well as important differences—in the manner in which central support has been given to local authorities here and abroad.

The pitfalls that await the investigator who attempts to describe the intricacies of the financial structure of a country with which he has only a limited acquaintance are many. The work has been greatly facilitated by the extensive statistical data dealing with local finances published in government reports in both countries —documents which have no counterpart in the United States. There is available, also, in the case of Germany, an extensive literature discussing central-local fiscal problems under the Weimar Constitution. This published material has been supplemented by interviews with central and local government officials and with others acquainted with the problem, during a sojourn of several months in each country. Nevertheless, the writer is very conscious of the limitations on her knowledge, and it is with some misgivings that the study is offered for publication.

To all those who have aided in this study the writer makes grateful acknowledgment. The many officials and students of the problem in both countries from whom information has been sought have given invaluable assistance and have been unfailing in their courtesy. The writer is also deeply indebted to friends and students of finance in this country for advice and encouragement and to the several assistants who have helped in gathering the statistical data and in preparing the manuscript for publication and in reading the proof. Finally, she gladly acknowledges a grant-in-aid from the Social Science Research Council, which has made possible the extensive statistical analysis on which the study is based; and the co-operation of Vassar College in giving a leave of absence.

MABEL NEWCOMER

Vassar College
September 15, 1936

CONTENTS

Introduction

The Fiscal System of Germany

The Fiscal System of England and Wales

Conclusions

CHARTS AND TABLES

Charts

Tables

INTRODUCTION

I

THE PROBLEM

THE division of the public revenues among the different governmental authorities covering the same geographic area offers an increasingly difficult problem as the tax burden grows. As long as revenue demands are small in proportion to resources, no serious difficulties arise. It is even possible for two or more tax authorities to exploit the same base without great hardship to the taxpayer and without undue friction among the authorities concerned. Thus state and local governments in the United States have shared the general property tax, depending on it in some instances for nine-tenths of state and local tax needs; and, except for occasional tax limits, all the participating authorities have been free to fix their own rates. In much the same way the state and local governments of pre-war Germany shared the income tax, the local governments determining, often without check, the rate they wished to add to the state base, or even levying independent taxes. This tax was used in Germany, as the property tax has been used in the United States, as the principal source of state and local revenues, and it supplied more than half of all tax income in the majority of states.

With the growth of governmental expenditures this comparatively peaceful and rather casual sharing of the same sources is no longer possible. A heavy tax burden is not to be endured unless its weight is equitably distributed; and substantial equity can be achieved only through uniform taxes and an integrated tax system. This, in turn, demands extensive central control of the tax system, if not actual central administration. Few tax bases are sufficiently localized to permit their exploitation at the discretion of local authorities.

The same forces which are promoting centralization of tax administration foster the centralization of other governmental functions. An ever widening jurisdiction is required to curb crime or disease. The operations of a single business unit are too widespread to be controlled by local, or even state, governments. Moreover, many citizens earn their living in a different community from that in which they reside and have important interests in the government of both communities.

The powers and functions of central governments have tended to increase rapidly in recent years. In most instances this increase has occurred without any diminution in the duties of local governments, although local obligations may have grown more slowly than would otherwise have been the case. Occasionally important functions have been transferred from local to central administration. But in the process revenues have been taken over by the central government faster than the support of governmental functions.

This lag in the transfer of other functions may be attributed partly to the fact that local governments cling tenaciously to their inherited functions. It is also partly due to the fact that central governments have tended to impose obligations on local governments more readily than they have delegated the means of support. The central government is apt to balance its own budget at the expense of the local governments. If taxes shared by both become too high, it is usually the local tax rates which are limited. If central government expenditures outrun revenues, sources formerly available to local authorities may be taken over for the exclusive use of the central government, or central government obligations may be shifted to local governments in the form of mandatory expenditures. Then, when local administration becomes too ineffectual or local protests too vigorous, the situation is alleviated by a grant-in-aid or the distribution of a substantial slice of some specific tax. Thus a complex system of revenue transfers grows up between the superior and inferior governments; and the situation becomes more involved if the number of layers of government is multiplied.

All governments are pyramided, with some kind of local authority at the base and some form of national government at the peak. Between these two extremes there are commonly one or more layers of government. The exact number tends to vary with the form of government and with the size of the country; but it varies also within a single country. In the United States, for instance, a consolidated city and county government may reduce the number of governmental layers within the area of the city to three, whereas in a New York village there are six layers, and if special districts exist within the village, seven or eight. All these jurisdictions are engaged in more or less costly activities, and all have more or less financial authority in consequence. Most of them are fixing their own tax rates. The English citizen may be burdened with only two or three layers of government, but the ordinary American taxpayer may count himself fortunate if he is paying taxes to no more than four different taxing jurisdictions. The Prussian taxpayer is contributing to no less than five. Probably he is supporting six or seven.

This subdivision of government has developed partly as a result of necessity. But in many cases there are overlapping functions and consequent waste; and administrative machinery has grown out of all proportion to the work to be done. This has been so frequently emphasized that it need not be dwelt on here. Thoroughgoing reorganization of local government has been achieved here and there. The financial problem is not solved, however, by the abolition of excessive administrative machinery and of duplication of government activities. Simplification of government reduces costs and also reduces the number of claimants to the same tax source, and to that extent it simplifies the problem. But if government were to be reorganized to meet the approval of the experts and functions could be properly allocated, there would still be two or three layers of government to be supported from public funds, and the problem of dividing the sources of revenue to meet the needs of these different authorities would remain.

The usual approach to the problem of a satisfactory distribution of governmental functions and revenues among overlapping jurisdictions is to assume that functions should be distributed among the different authorities regardless of their ability to support such functions, and that revenues should then be adjusted to needs. In view of the fact that the final objective of government is presumably the satisfactory performance of certain functions, and the administration of the revenue system is incidental to that end, this would seem to be the reasonable approach. If a local government can adapt a service to peculiar local needs better than the more remote central government, then the administration of that function should be in the hands of local officials. If uniform administration over a wide area is essential to the success of some governmental activity, then the function should be assigned to central authorities. Adjustment in revenues can be made, if necessary, by the transfer of funds from one jurisdiction to another.

Nevertheless the possibility of adjusting functions to revenues cannot be ignored. The fact that central governments are in a better position to obtain large revenues than the smaller underlying jurisdictions has undoubtedly facilitated the transfer of functions from local to central authorities and has probably caused the transfer of functions in some instances when local administration would have been preferable. Moreover, there are limitations to the amount of revenues that can be transferred efficiently. If the local spending authority is in no way responsible for the amount of its revenue and the money does not come obviously, at least, from the pockets of local taxpayers, there is little check on the amount and manner of expenditure. Many believe that welfare work, for instance, can be administered best by local authorities in close touch with local needs; but the community with the heaviest welfare burden is usually, also, the community least able to support it. The necessary funds may be contributed by the central government; but this removes all local demand for an accounting. Because local officials are in a position to administer certain activities more effectively than state officials, it does not follow that they will do so when pressure is lacking. Under these conditions central administration may be preferable. Responsible local administration might be more effective, but responsibility is difficult to achieve when support comes from elsewhere. Thus, while for the most part the allocation of functions will be made without consideration of resources and revenues will then be adjusted to needs, resources cannot be disregarded entirely, and the allocation of functions will be modified to some extent by revenue possibilities.

Three distinct methods are available for the adjustment of revenues to needs among the different jurisdictions covering the same geographic area: separation of sources, sharing of specific sources, and grants-in-aid.

Separation of sources has been the usual practice in the early history of federal governments, the federal government being allotted the customs and certain other indirect taxes, and the state and local governments retaining the direct taxes. This is a natural division since the customs almost inevitably fall to the lot of the federal government, and the states are loath to cede more than the minimum of financial power to this superimposed authority. Even unitary governments, when not too highly centralized, have sometimes assigned to local authorities important independent revenues and maintained strict separation of sources, although they have not ceded the whole field of direct taxation to the underlying jurisdictions. Thus English local authorities have been left in sole possession of the "rates."

Separation has not ordinarily been complete, however. There has often been overlapping in the case of minor taxes; and federal governments have usually had the privilege of levying on the states in proportion to population, and by this means have been able to share, indirectly, in state tax revenues. This right was regularly exercised in Germany until after the world war. Germany was, however, the last federal state to employ it. Switzerland and the United States abandoned the practice before Germany adopted it, and in most other federal states it had found only occasional use and has long since been discontinued.

Separation of federal and state revenue sources has never been satisfactory to federal authorities and has been abandoned by most of them. The national governments of both the United States and Germany had invaded the field of direct taxation before the world war: with the adoption of a federal income tax in the United States in 1913, and with the adoption of several small national direct taxes in Germany in the decade preceding the war. During the war Canada, Switzerland, and Australia introduced direct federal taxes, and recently Brazil has adopted a federal income tax. Separation of state and local sources has only occasionally been tried, and for the most part unsuccessfully.

Complete separation of sources tends to disappear as the cost of government grows. The burdens of the different governments cannot readily be adjusted to the chance yield of the taxes that fall to their lot; and the increasing necessity for central administration of most of the important tax revenues results in an increasing share of the income falling to the central government. Nevertheless, partial separation of sources exists in almost every government. Even highly centralized governments leave some revenue sources for the exclusive use of local governments and also appropriate some for their own exclusive needs.

The second method of distributing revenues among the different governments is the sharing of specific sources. This may take the form of independent levies on the same revenue sources or of a uniform tax levied by the central government and shared in fixed proportions with the underlying governments. The wholly separate federal and state income taxes in the United States represent one extreme, whereas the single German income tax, which is shared in fixed proportions by Reich, state, and local governments, represents the other extreme. Between these extremes many variations are to be found. In place of two separately administered taxes there may be a single administration in the hands of either the state or local government, but with independent levies. Thus, in the highly centralized governments of France and Italy the central authorities have tended to monopolize all important revenue sources and have permitted local governments to levy additions to some of them. Within limits the local authorities have been free to determine the amount of such local additions. Comparable arrangements are to be found in the sharing of the property tax in the United States. Here, however, the administration is local and the additions are made by the state government. This is not, of course, the only method of administering this tax. Collections are frequently separate for the different local subdivisions, and sometimes independent assessments are made. Also, the property included in the base may differ for state and local levies. Only the comparative wealth of the United States makes such duplication of administration possible.

Independent taxes on the same base were exceptional in Europe, even before the war. Taxes were frequently administered by local governments as agents of the state, but there was a uniform base and a single levy, even though local additions might vary in amount. Today, with greater pressure on resources, even this limited freedom has been abandoned in many countries. Rates do not vary with local needs; administration is central; and local governments receive a fixed percentage of the yield.

A third method of sharing revenues is through grants-in-aid from the superior to the inferior government, or "levies" if the procedure is reversed and the revenue goes from the inferior to the superior government. In either case the amount paid is determined by the central government. This method differs from the sharing of sources discussed above, in that the amount paid comes from no specific tax source and bears no definite relation to the yield of specific taxes. The grant is usually for the support of a specified function, whereas the distribution of a given tax usually originates as compensation for a source of revenue which the central government has taken from the local government. But the grant may be for general use, as in the case of the block grant in England, and the expenditure of a specific tax may be limited, as in the case of the motor vehicle taxes returned to local governments in the United States.

In actual practice all three methods of apportioning revenues among central and local governments are to be found in the tax systems of different countries. Separation of sources is playing a decreasingly important part in most tax systems, but it is to be found to some extent even in highly centralized governments. Sharing of sources prevails in most countries, including the United States and Germany, but whereas in Germany the sharing is achieved largely by the division of centrally administered taxes, in the United States it is accomplished for the most part by levying more or less independent taxes on the same base. The third method of sharing the same sources, local percentages added to state taxes, formerly characteristic of many of the systems of continental Europe, survives, in part, in France and Italy, but in a number of countries it has been replaced by the centrally administered tax at a uniform rate. The grant-in-aid is to be found in all these tax systems, but it is most characteristic of the English system.

Separation of source and independent taxes levied on the same source are both giving way, even in the United States, to uniform and centrally administered taxes, which the local governments share directly through the distribution of fixed percentages or indirectly through grants-in-aid. There are already several states in this country which are turning back to local governments in one way or another more than half of the tax revenue that they collect. The federal government, also, is rapidly developing an important system of grants-in-aid. Centralization of the tax system is inevitable, and if any important functions are to be retained by local governments they will be supported increasingly by central government funds. It is only a question of how far and how fast centrally administered taxes should replace independent local taxes; to what degree local independence must be sacrificed to efficiency and economy; and whether once the transfer of revenues has been made the local governments will function better with grants-in-aid or shared taxes, or with some combination of the two. And the possibility that the ultimate solution may be the transfer of local functions themselves must always be kept in mind.

Germany and England have been selected for special study of this problem because both have gone much farther in the centralization of the tax system than in the centralization of other governmental functions. Thus they are faced with the distribution of revenues to underlying governments on a large scale. In the highly centralized governments of France and Italy the national governments spend a larger part of their income directly, and only comparatively small sums are redistributed for local use. In the United States, while the underlying governments are responsible for the bulk of public expenditures, they still have at their disposal important revenue sources, and for the most part do not depend on subventions or redistributed revenues for a large part of their income.

Germany and England offer sharp contrasts in the methods of dealing with this problem. With resources seriously impaired and with unprecedented financial burdens following the war, Germany attempted to meet her obligations by centralizing the tax system in the hands of the Reich. To win the consent of the states it was necessary to compensate them with substantial shares of the taxes they were giving up. The financial provisions of the Weimar Constitution and the tax legislation immediately following were frankly compromises in time of emergency. A "permanent" system based on sound financial principles has been promised; but the time for establishing this system has not yet come. During the eighteen years which have elapsed since the adoption of the Weimar Constitution, Germany has passed from one crisis to another. The early legislation was nullified by inflation, and while inflation wiped out the heavy internal debt it brought burdens of its own. Heavy reparation payments came simultaneously with stabilization. A brief period of prosperity followed stabilization, but it was hardly adequate for the task before it; for in addition to war burdens the country had an ambitious program of housing and social insurance. The reduction of reparation payments came only with depression. Each new emergency has brought new compromises, and while elaborate plans have been made for the final system, the introduction of this system has been indefinitely postponed.

In spite of many variations in the different German states and the frequent changes which have been made in both the Reich and state systems since the adoption of the Weimar Constitution, the distribution of revenues has been based almost exclusively on the principle of sharing fixed percentages of specific, centrally administered taxes. That such a system would work more smoothly under more favorable conditions can scarcely be questioned, but both the strength and the weakness of such a system are more sharply outlined by the strain to which it has been subjected.

In marked contrast to the German system, the English system is the outgrowth of well considered plans and is regarded as permanent in spite of the fact that the Local Government Act of 1929 was in part a recovery measure. England, too, has suffered from war burdens and depression, but the financial situation has never been as acute as in Germany. England has at least been spared loss of territory, inflation, and reparations. Moreover, the existence of a unitary government has simplified the problem.

Fewer compromises have been found necessary; there are fewer layers of government; and there is one system in place of eighteen systems. Division of centrally administered taxes plays no part in the English plan. The system is based entirely on grants-in-aid, apportioned according to various measures of need. The "block grant" provided by the Local Government Act of 1929 offers a new departure of particular interest.

It is believed that the experience of England and Germany may throw some light on the advantages and shortcomings of the different systems of revenue distribution which will be helpful in developing systems of aid to local governments in the United States. It is recognized that the political and economic structure of the United States differs in many important respects from that of either Germany or England. But the central problem of retaining some measure of local self-government and at the same time achieving local efficiency and responsibility in the expenditure of tax revenues for which local authorities are not responsible to their constituents is the same in all countries.

THE FISCAL SYSTEM OF GERMANY

II

THE GERMAN POST-WAR PROBLEM AND ITS HISTORICAL BACKGROUND

THE problem of allocating available revenues among the different claimants has offered peculiar difficulties in Germany. In the first place the fact that Germany was a federal state complicated the problem.[1] Not only was there one more layer of government to be considered than there would be in a unitary state, but the division of power between federal and state governments led to bargaining and compromises which were hardly conducive to a clear-cut solution of the financial problem. In the second place, the diverse origin of the constituent states, their varying economic interests, and the great differences in their size necessarily have caused friction. At one extreme, Prussia has more than three-fifths of the area, population, and wealth of the Reich; at the other extreme, Schaumburg-Lippe has less than one one-thousandth part of the area, population, and wealth. And the smaller states, some of which are entirely surrounded by Prussian territory, have not submitted willingly to Prussian domination.

The administrative problem has been complicated by the fact that the states do not always cover contiguous territory. Not only are many of the small states completely surrounded by Prussia, but a single small state may represent several disconnected fragments. Oldenburg is in three widely separated parts. Anhalt and Brunswick have scattered bits of territory within Prussia;

[1] All legislative powers of the German states were abolished in January, 1934, as the final step in the process of subordinating the states to the Reich. Thus Germany is no longer a federal state and the *Länder* have been reduced to mere administrative districts. The boundaries of the old states have not yet been changed, however (July, 1936), and the varying state tax systems of the former states continue. Consequently the *Länder* are referred to as states in this discussion, and the present tense is used in so far as the specific conditions referred to still apply.

and Prussia itself is divided by the Polish corridor and possesses enclaves in the southern states. Political unity is difficult under such conditions, and the economic unity essential to an effective tax system is clearly impossible. Moreover, the local subdivisions are many,[2] and the ultimate commune, which is the most important local unit, is extremely small.[3]

Some efforts have been made to remedy these difficulties. The

TABLE 1

SIZE OF COMMUNES IN THE GERMAN STATES

State	Population (In thousands)[a]	Area (In square miles)	Number of Communes[b]	Average Population of Communes	Average Area of Communes (In square miles)
Prussia	39,934	113,036	42,857	932	2.6
Bavaria	7,682	29,343	8,025	957	3.6
Saxony	5,197	5,789	2,975	1,747	1.9
Württemberg	2,696	7,532	1,887	1,429	4.0
Baden	2,413	5,819	1,557	1,550	3.7
Thuringia	1,660	4,535	1,964	845	2.3
Hesse	1,429	2,970	987	1,448	3.0
Mecklenburg	805	6,196	1,991	404	3.1
Oldenburg	574	2,480	224	2,562	11.0
Brunswick	513	1,418	447	1,148	3.2
Anhalt	364	890	298	1,221	3.0
Lippe	176	469	174	1,012	2.7
Schaumburg-Lippe	50	131	83	602	1.6
Hamburg	1,218	160	32	38,063	5.3
Bremen	372	115	17	21,882	6.8
Lübeck	136	99	38	3,579	2.6
Total	65,218	180,982	63,556	1,026	2.8

[a] 1933.   [b] 1928.

[2] In Prussia the *Provinz, Regierungsbezirk, Kreis* and *Gemeinde* are to be found throughout, although the latter two are usually combined, in larger cities, in the *Stadtkreis.* Rural circles (*Landkreisen*) are subdivided into administrative districts (*Amtsbezirke*) for certain purposes, and often a number of communes will join together for some specific purpose in *Zweckverbände.* The smaller states have fewer subdivisions.

[3] See Table 1. In Prussia rural communes (outside cities of 5,000 population and more) have an average area of between two and three square miles and an average population of about four hundred. In contrast, the average area of the New York rural town, which is generally considered to be too small for efficient administration, is 51 square miles, and the average population is 2,600.

number of states has been reduced from 26 to 16 since the war;
Saxony and Thuringia traded enclaves in 1928; and the Rhine-
land and Westphalia have been reorganized, reducing the number of circles from 52 to 38, and combining communes, and even
large cities, so that Essen, Dortmund and twelve other cities, each
with a population in excess of 50,000, form one continuous territory with no intervening communes.[4] Berlin was consolidated
into a single commune in 1920, whereas before that year it had
comprised 94 communes. The local governments of Oldenburg
were completely reorganized in 1933, with a resulting reduction
in the number of jurisdictions and a redistribution of functions.
Other instances can be found, and agitation for super-counties
(*Grosskreisen*) has made some headway. But the largest part of
the territory continues under the old, complex, needlessly pyramided, and hopelessly small political subdivisions.

This study is concerned primarily with the revenue system
under the Weimar Constitution, but the Weimar Constitution was
only one step in the long struggle of the central government for
financial power, which culminated with the *Gleichschaltung*
under the National Socialist regime. The Weimar Constitution
insured the fiscal supremacy of the Reich over the states, and the
Gleichschaltung removed the last vestige of state financial power.

The first important step in undermining the fiscal independence of the German states was taken with the formation of the
Customs Union of 1834, when the participating states agreed
to abolish interstate customs duties and establish a uniform, ex-
ternal tariff. No serious loss of revenues resulted from this step.
The entire amount of customs duties collected was returned to
the states concerned, and any losses occasioned by the abolition
of interstate tolls were soon offset by growing foreign trade. But
the distribution of these revenues among the several states in
proportion to their population involved a radical reallocation of
revenues, which operated to the disadvantage of those states,

[4] O. Most, *Die Finanzlage der Ruhrgebietsstädte*, Jena, 1932, Pt. 1, p. 6.

notably Prussia, with the greatest per capita imports.[5] Other uniform taxes were added to the customs duties in later years, namely, a tax on beet sugar, a salt tax, and a tobacco tax.[6] All these taxes were distributed with the customs on a per capita basis, and the proceeds were used to meet state expenditures for defense and foreign affairs. The North German Federation of 1867 appropriated all these revenues, in so far as they belonged to the states comprising the Federation, for the federal treasury and added taxes on beer and spirits and a stamp tax.[7]

With the foundation of the Empire in 1871 no radical change was made in this system. The Reich took over the revenues of the North German Federation and added a small stamp tax.[8] The other members of the Customs Union gave up their per capita shares in customs, sugar, salt, and tobacco taxes in return for the Reich's assumption of the cost of national defense. The southern states retained their beer and spirits taxes, making special contributions to the Reich in payment for this privilege. The federal government was given the power of imposing per capita levies (*Matrikularbeiträge*) on the states to meet any deficit,[9] a privilege of which the government availed itself in the first year of the Empire and did not abandon until 1919.

It was generally accepted that the Reich should be permitted to develop the field of indirect taxation and that the state and local governments should depend mainly on direct taxes,[10] thus establishing a separation of tax systems which would abolish overlapping and friction between the two jurisdictions. In this respect the new federation conformed to the usual practice of

---

[5] Prussia's per capita income from customs duties was 2.31 marks in 1821, whereas Bavaria's per capita income from this source, in 1820, was only .90 mark. A. Wagner, *Finanzwissenschaft*, Leipzig, 1901, IV, 62, 182.

[6] The sugar tax came with the renewal of the Customs Union on June 8, 1841; the salt tax was imposed by law of October 12, 1867; and the tobacco tax by law of May 26, 1868.

[7] Laws of July 8, 1868, and June 10, 1869.   [8] Law of June 8, 1871.

[9] This, too, was taken over from the financial system of the earlier federation.

[10] Statements to this effect appear in practically every account of this period. See, especially, Wagner, *op. cit.*, IV, 648 *et seq.*

federal states. The state and local governments were not required, however, to abandon their indirect levies until such time
as they came into direct conflict with Reich taxes; and the Reich
had the power [11] to levy direct as well as indirect taxes, although
no direct tax was in fact levied by the Reich for forty years.
Duplication of taxes by the two jurisdictions was scrupulously
avoided.

Bismarck had a somewhat different aim. He was eager not to
separate the two systems but rather to reverse the financial position of the Reich and the states, making the states dependent on
the Reich for revenue instead of the Reich on the states. To this
end he urged the further development of federal indirect taxes,
nationalization of the railways, and monopolies of tobacco,
sugar, spirits, and other articles of consumption. This policy had
a double purpose: first, and most important, the increase in the
power of the Reich; and second, a diminution of direct taxes, to
which he was relentlessly opposed.[12]

Bismarck met with only limited success at first. Of his earlier
tax program only a paltry tax on playing cards was enacted
into law,[13] but in 1879 increases in the customs duties were
coupled with the provision that any excess over 130 million
marks from the customs and tobacco taxes should be returned to
the states on a per capita basis.[14] Since the *Matrikularbeiträge*
remained, this did not in any way impair the fiscal position of
the Reich. If the Reich needed more than the 130 million marks
allotted to it from the customs and tobacco taxes, it recaptured

[11] Under the so-called Miquel clause, "*solange Reichssteuern nicht eingeführt
sind*," Article 70 of the 1871 constitution. This clause originally specified only indirect taxes, but this modification was stricken out by Miquel. (See W. Markull,
Kommentar zum Gesetz über den Finanzausgleich, Berlin, 1923, p. 4, and A. Hensel,
Finanzausgleich im Bundesstaat, 1922, p. 115.) This clause disappeared with the
amendment of Article 70, May 14, 1904, but the right of the federal government to
levy common (*gemeinsamen*) taxes was definitely stated.

[12] "*Sie wissen von mir dass ich ein Gegner der direkten, ein Freund der indirekten
Steuern bin.*"—Reichstagrede vom 22 Februar, 1878, quoted in W. Gerloff, *Finanz-
und Zollpolitik des Deutschen Reiches*, Jena, 1913.

[13] Law of July 3, 1878.   [14] Law of July 15, 1879.

whatever excess it needed through the *Matrikularbeiträge;* and if
the entire yield of these customs and tobacco taxes proved inadequate, the Reich could levy contributions in excess of the sums
nominally distributed to the states. Thus the Reich seemed to
be insured equally against deficits and surpluses.

In the twenty years that followed, the Reich received a net contribution from the states in six years and made a net contribution
to the states in the other fourteen years, the net contributions to
the states amounting to six times as much as the net contributions
from the states. The gain to the states was between four and five
hundred million marks. While this system simplified the balancing of the imperial budget and in the long run benefited the
states, a system which distributed large sums of money one year
and made heavy demands on state treasuries the next year [15] was
hardly conducive to the reduction of state direct taxes or the
balancing of state budgets. These alternate donations and requisitions did not bulk large enough, however, in most of the state
budgets to create serious disturbances; and while state taxes,
direct and indirect, were for the most part rising, the large and
growing surpluses from public domains, state railways, and
other state industries during this period kept taxes as a whole
comparatively low.[16]

The federal government did not rest with the 1879 changes.
On the contrary the development of the financial independence of
the Reich had just begun. In furtherance of Bismarck's policies a
series of stamp taxes was adopted in 1881,[17] the entire net proceeds of which were to be added to excess customs duties and
tobacco taxes for distribution to the states. In 1887 a new tax on
spirits was imposed,[18] extending over the entire Reich and super-
seding the state spirits taxes, which the southern states had re-

[15] See Table 2.

[16] Wagner estimates Reich and state taxes in Prussia, at the end of the nineteenth
century, at 23.8 marks per capita, compared with 32.4 in Italy, 50.5 in Great Britain
and 61.6 in France. See Wagner, *op. cit.,* IV, 790-91.

[17] Law of July 1, 1881.   [18] Law of July 24, 1887.

TABLE 2

NET GAINS AND LOSSES TO THE STATES FROM IMPERIAL LEVIES
AND TAX DISTRIBUTIONS, 1880-1919 [a]

(IN MILLIONS OF MARKS)

Year (Beginning April 1)	Levies[b] on States	Distributions to States	Difference	Year (Beginning April 1)	Levies on States	Distributions to States	Difference
1880........	64	38	—26	1900........	528	509	—19
1881........	85	68[c]	—17	1901........	571	556	—15
1882........	85	84	— 1	1902........	580	556	—24
1883........	74	85	+11	1903........	566	542	—24
1884........	64	105	+41	1904........	220	196[e]	—24
1885........	103	116	+13	1905........	213	189	—24
1886........	119	137	+18	1906........	230	206	—24
1887........	171	176[d]	+ 5	1907........	227	195	—32
1888........	208	278	+70	1908........	220	195	—25
1889........	215	355	+140	1909........	169	121[f]	—48
1890........	301	379	+78	1910........	228	180	—48
1891........	316	383	+67	1911........	212	164	—48
1892........	316	353	+37	1912........	247	195	—52
1893........	369	339	—30	1913........	255	203	—52
1894........	385	382	— 3	1914........	246	194[g]	—52
1895........	383	400	+17	1915........	246	194	—52
1896........	399	414	+15	1916........	246	194	—52
1897........	420	433	+13	1917........	246	194	—52
1898........	455	468	+13	1918........	246	194	—52
1899........	490	477	—13	1919........	48[h]	30[h]	—18

[a] 1880 to 1911 from W. Gerloff, *Finanz- und Zollpolitik, op. cit.* p. 522; 1912 to 1919 from *Statistisches Jahrbuch für das deutsche Reich.*

[b] These figures do not include the special payments by the southern German states for the privilege of retaining beer and spirits taxes and the postal and telegraph service.

[c] Stamp taxes added.   [d] Spirits tax added.

[e] Distribution of customs and tobacco tax discontinued.

[f] Distribution of stamp taxes discontinued.

[g] Spirits tax distribution fixed.   [h] Discontinued August 14, 1919.

tained at the time that the Empire was founded. The net proceeds of this, also, were to be distributed to the states on a per capita basis. These changes benefited the Reich treasury, as well as the treasuries of the states, since increases in *Matrikularbeiträge* did not meet with the same opposition when they did not come from revenues already in the hands of the states. The *Matrikularbei-*

träge increased more than sixfold between 1883, the year of the first distribution of net surplus to the states, and 1898, the year of the last such distribution.

Unfortunately for the states, Reich expenditures grew very rapidly with increasing armaments during the nineties; and with Bismarck no longer controlling and the needs of the central government pressing, the imperial surpluses [19] distributed to the states gave way to increasing deficits, which were met once more by net requisitions on the states.

The years just preceding the war were marked by rapid expansion of federal taxes. In 1902 a new tax on sparkling wines was imposed for the benefit of the Reich,[20] and customs duties were increased,[21] but this did not reduce the net levy on the states. In 1904 the nominal distribution of surplus customs and tobacco taxes was discontinued.[22] The only effect of this was to reduce both levies and allotments, since no net income had been derived by the states from this source since 1898. In a renewed effort to give the Reich adequate income of its own a series of new taxes was introduced in 1906: a cigarette tax, taxes on freight and passenger traffic and automobiles, and taxes on directors' fees and on inheritances.[23] Also, postal rates and the tax on beer were increased. The inheritance tax bordered on the field of direct taxation and definitely infringed on existing state tax systems. By way of compensation the states, which administered the tax, were allowed to keep one-third of the proceeds and were guaranteed, in addition, against any loss of revenue from this change. A further concession was made to the states by limiting

---

[19] It should be noted that during the entire period in which these "surpluses" were being distributed the indebtedness of the Reich was increasing so rapidly that in only one year, 1889, was the "surplus" revenue distributed to the states greater than the increase in the debt. The Reich debt in 1898, the last year in which the states received a net payment from the Reich, was approximately ten times as much as it had been in 1880, the first year in which the Reich undertook to distribute excess customs duties and tobacco taxes, i.e., 2,182 million marks as compared with 218 million marks. W. Gerloff, *Finanz- und Zollpolitik, op. cit.* p. 521.

[20] Law of May 9, 1902.   [21] Law of December 25, 1902.

[22] Law of May 14, 1904.   [23] Law of June 3, 1906.

the net *Matrikularbeiträge* to forty *pfennig* per capita. No direct
compensation was offered, however, for the taxes on freight and
passenger traffic, which must to some extent have cut into state
revenues in so far as the states owned the railways.

The Reich found even these new sources of revenue inadequate, and in 1909, alarmed by a debt which had more than
doubled in eight years, imposed a series of new taxes.[24] These
included new stamp taxes, a new tax on matches and lamps, and
increases in the beer tax and tea and coffee duties. The Reich
encroached further on state tax income by cutting the states'
share of the inheritance tax to one-fourth, discontinuing the distribution of the stamp taxes altogether, and increasing the net
contributions of the states to eighty *pfennig* per capita, where
they remained until they were finally discontinued in 1919.

In 1911 the Reich imposed an unearned increment tax, this
time invading the field of local taxation.[25] In compensation the
municipalities were allotted 40 percent of the proceeds. The
states were allowed 10 percent, in return for the work of administering the tax, and the Reich received the remaining 50 percent.
This tax was replaced in 1913 by a periodical property increment
tax (*Besitzsteuer*), the first recurring direct tax to be levied by
the Reich. Also in 1913 some new stamp taxes were added, and
the *Wehrbeitrag*, a single direct tax on property and income, was
imposed. Finally, the inheritance tax was increased, and the
states' share in this tax was reduced to one-fifth.[26]

Thus, in the years prior to the war, the growing cost of armaments and popular preference for direct taxes led to a wide expansion of Reich taxes and definite encroachment on state and
local taxing powers. The Reich did not achieve separation of
central and state tax systems; nor did it develop its own tax
sources rapidly enough to keep abreast of rising expenditures. It
never freed itself completely from state contributions; much less

[24] Laws of July 15 and August 15, 1909.
[25] Law of February 14, 1911.   [26] Law of July 3, 1913.

did it make the states financially dependent upon it; and it accumulated a debt of nearly five billion marks.[27]

The constitutional power of the Reich to tax was practically unlimited, but political pressure from the states was strong. Nevertheless, independent Reich taxes had largely replaced the *Matrikularbeiträge*, which declined from 22.5 percent of the tax income of the Reich in 1878 to 3 percent in 1913.[28] Thus the Reich strengthened its financial position materially, since taxes once taken over were no longer subject to the same opposition as varying annual requisitions.

The states, too, probably gained. While there might be a certain amount of rivalry between the two governments, the citizens and the taxable wealth of Reich and states were one and the same. The Reich was performing useful functions, which would otherwise have fallen on the states, and the only question could be as to the appropriateness of the division of functions between the two jurisdictions. Assuming that this was satisfactory and that the Reich must be supplied, in consequence, with a certain income, the advantage of uniform Reich taxes over per capita requisitions from general state revenues can hardly be questioned, although the benefit accrued primarily to the poorer states.

When the Reich entered the field of state and local taxes it did not duplicate these taxes; it replaced them. There was no real double taxation.[29] Thus the states lost in independent taxing powers; but in view of the gains accruing from uniform taxation it seems probable that their actual revenues were impaired less by the loss of certain taxes than they would have been by per capita levies of equal size. In any case, the financial position of most of the states was more than satisfactory. Surplus revenues

[27] 4,802 million marks, or 74 marks per capita, March 31, 1913.
[28] W. Gerloff, "Der Staatshaushalt und der Finanz-system Deutschlands," *Handbuch der Finanzwissenschaft,* Tübingen, 1929, III, 27.
[29] No express prohibition was placed on state taxation of directors' fees (1906) and matches and lamps (1909), but no important state taxes, if any, existed on

from state industries almost equalled tax revenues in Prussia, and in some of the smaller states such earnings exceeded taxes. Only Hesse suffered serious losses from its property and industries.[30] Some of the states had substantial surpluses at the end of the fiscal year 1913-14, and only Hesse and Bremen had any important deficit.

Local governments, too, were for the most part in a satisfactory financial condition. They obtained 12.8 percent of their net revenue (defining net revenue to be that from taxes and net earnings of municipal property and industries) from excess earnings of municipal properties and industries in 1913-14; and at the end of the year surpluses overbalanced deficits by appreciable amounts. State and local taxes combined amounted to a little less than 43 marks per capita. Debts were growing but for the most part were not excessive, and a substantial part of the proceeds of loans was applied to productive industries.

The growing centralization of financial power and the increasing co-ordination of tax systems which accompanied it were reflected in state and local fiscal relations as well as in the federal and state adjustments. Wide variations were still to be found among the different state and local systems of pre-war Germany. Even within a single state, local authorities were often granted a generous range of tax bases and rates. Nevertheless, the process of centralization is apparent, and a certain degree of regimentation of local taxes is to be found toward the end of the pre-war period.

Both the diversity of tax systems and the tendency toward

---

these. The law of 1906 expressly permitted state fees for identification of freight and regulation of automobiles. Also state surtaxes on inheritances (1906), and local surtaxes on property increments (1911), were permitted within definite limits. These are not, however, strictly duplicate taxes. For the rest, state taxes on the same bases as Reich taxes were expressly prohibited. Hensel, *op. cit.*, pp. 125-28.

[30] The percentage of surplus earnings and taxes combined represented by earnings was as follows for 1913-14: Prussia 45.3, Bavaria 29.5, Saxony 21.5, Württemberg 18.7, Baden 15.7, Thüringia 39.0, Mecklenburg-Schwerin 61.1, other states (excluding Hesse and the Hanseatic cities) 44.9. Computed from data in *Einzelschrift zur Statistik des deutschen Reichs*, No. 10.

centralization and uniformity can be illustrated by a brief account of the systems in the three most important states. Saxony, at one extreme, gave the local governments wide powers of taxation. Bavaria, at the other extreme, tended to limit the local authorities to additions to state taxes. And Prussia developed a mixed system of independent local taxes and local additions to state taxes.[31] Saxony, a comparatively wealthy and densely populated industrial state, had the highest per capita taxes and the highest per capita taxpaying ability of any of the three states. Bavaria, a relatively poor agricultural state, had slightly higher taxes per capita than Prussia, but lower taxpaying ability than either Prussia or Saxony. This in indicated by the figures in Table 3.

TABLE 3

COMPARATIVE FIGURES OF POPULATION, INCOME, PROPERTY, AND TAXES FOR PRUSSIA, BAVARIA AND SAXONY, 1913

| State | Percentage of Population[a] | Density of Population (Per qkm)[a] | PERCENTAGE OF DEFENSE LEVY | | Per Capita State and Local Taxes (In marks) |
			From Income[b]	From Property[b]	
Prussia	61.9	115	60.0	62.0	40.4[c]
Bavaria	10.6	91	6.4	8.2	40.7[c]
Saxony	7.4	321	9.9	8.8	42.4[c]
All states	100.0	120	100.0	100.0	41.4[d]

[a] *Statistisches Jahrbuch für das deutsche Reich.* Figures are for 1910.
[b] A. Jessen, "Der deutsche Finanzausgleich in Theorie und Praxis," *Vierteljahresschrift für Steuer- und Finanzrecht,* 6 Jahrg., 1932, Pt. 3, p. 695.
[c] Computed from data in Sonderbeilage zu *Wirtschaft und Statistik,* 9 Jahrg., 1929, No. 1, p. 4.   [d] Jessen, *op. cit.,* p. 666.

In the early part of the nineteenth century the principal direct taxes in Saxony were taxes on land and buildings for property owners, and personal and trade taxes for others.[32] These taxes were supplemented by a large number of consumption taxes and

[31] Markull, *op. cit.,* p. 8.
[32] See Wagner, *op. cit.,* IV, 97 *et seq.,* for an account of the nineteenth-century tax system of Saxony.

a salt monopoly, which, combined, yielded more revenues than the direct taxes. An income tax was introduced in 1874.[33] This income tax was revised in 1878 and made the principal tax of the state system,[34] yielding more than half of all state tax revenues in the year following. The state tax on land was reduced at the same time to four-ninths of the former rate,[35] and it produced only 15 percent of state tax revenues in 1879. The substantial yield of the income tax enabled the state to give up or to reduce other taxes in the years that followed, and by 1896 the state was obtaining more than two-thirds of its tax revenues from this source. The income tax was revised in 1900, and again in 1902,[36] but its importance as the central tax of the state system continued. It was supplying four-fifths (82.0 percent) of all state tax revenues in 1913.

No serious attempt was made to unify local tax systems, or to co-ordinate them with state taxes until just before the war. Local governments were permitted to levy surtaxes on the state income tax and on the other state direct taxes almost at will. Or they might levy independent taxes on property and income if they preferred. State consent was sometimes required for new taxes or for higher rates for old taxes, but very few real restrictions were imposed. In 1890, 59 of the 142 cities levying income taxes were levying them on the state base, while the remaining 83 cities had independent taxes.[37] In 1910 only 27 cities are reported as levying additions to the state base.[38] All the large cities had independent taxes. Some of these independent taxes were combined with a poll or property tax; others were not. Among the rural communes there was similar variation. About two-fifths of such communes imposed income taxes in 1890.[39] Of

[33] Law of December 22, 1874.   [34] Law of July 2, 1878.
[35] Law of July 3, 1878.   [36] Laws of July 24, 1900, and July 2, 1902.
[37] Wagner, op. cit., p. 132. Quoted from J. Neumann, Zur Gemeindesteuer Reform in Deutschland, Tübingen, 1895.
[38] "Begründung zum sächsischen Gemeindesteuergesetzentwurf vom 30 November 1911." Finanz-Archiv, XXXI (1914), 779.
[39] Wagner, op. cit., IV, 132.

these, the larger number, nearly two-thirds, took advantage of the
state base and the remainder levied independent taxes. In 1901
more than half the communes, including most of the larger ones,
were levying income taxes, and three-fourths of such taxes were
imposed on the state base.[40]

There was no greater uniformity in the local land and building
taxes. Rural communes tended to take advantage of the state
base, as in the case of the income tax, and cities tended to levy
independent and widely differing taxes. Taxes on real estate and
business were not used, however, to the same extent as income
taxes. Indirect taxes offered wide scope for individual initiative,
but among these only the beer tax was in general use.[41]

Nor was this the end of local financial anarchy. There was
complete separation of the finances of overlapping local jurisdictions. Rates for general local government, poor rates, school
rates, church rates, and occasionally fire rates were levied independently. Sometimes these were all pyramided upon the same
base. Sometimes the separate administrations exploited exclusive
sources of revenue. Entertainment and dog taxes, for instance,
were often reserved for poor districts; but taxes on transfer of
property were available to poor, school, church, and fire districts
alike.[42] Only the facts that the state was comparatively wealthy
and that taxes as a whole were not especially burdensome made
this variegated local tax system possible.

Municipalities, in practice, obtained most of their revenue
from the income tax and made little use of the multiplicity of
other taxes at their disposal. In 1913, 78 percent of all local
taxes came from this single source. Some cities were depending
on it for more than 90 percent of their tax revenue.[43] The state's
attempt to substitute income taxes for other direct taxes had been
far too successful; and a thorough revision of local tax systems,
not unlike that in Prussia twenty years earlier, resulted.

[40] "Begründung zum sächsischen Gemeindesteuergesetzentwurf," *op. cit.*, p. 779.
[41] Wagner, *op. cit.*, IV, 130.   [42] Wagner, *op. cit.*, IV, 128.
[43] "Begründung zum sächsischen Gemeindesteuergesetzentwurf," *op. cit.*, p. 808.

The commune taxation law of 1913 [44] endeavored to check this excessive dependence on the income tax by specifying that not more than 85 percent of local tax revenues might be obtained from this source; that the land and building taxes must be used in every commune levying direct taxes; and that the proceeds of such taxes should equal at least 7.5 percent (or 30 percent if no income tax is levied) of the commune's tax revenues. It also required the levy of a tax on the sale of real estate at a rate of one or two percent of the value of land.[45] This was to replace any existing local taxes on the transfer of real estate. The law specified, further, that unless the public interest were endangered the cost of communal industries, including interest and amortization, should be covered from the income of such industries and provided for optional taxes on local industries. Finally, it provided that no new poll taxes should be introduced and that beginning in 1918 the old ones should be discontinued. These provisions applied to church and school districts, as well as to other local tax authorities. Even these restrictions left the municipalities with a large measure of financial independence, although they did insure a certain balance of taxes in every jurisdiction.

The state gave local governments substantial aid toward the cost of local functions, either through subventions or through direct state expenditure. Small subventions were introduced for highways in 1870,[46] and for teachers' salaries in 1873.[47] Other school subventions followed, and beginning in 1886 the state turned over to the school districts half the proceeds of the state land tax.[48] In 1913-14 state taxes amounted to 46 percent of state and local taxes combined, approximately the same percentage as in Bavaria (with 44 percent), but a much larger proportion than in Prussia, where state taxes amounted to only 29

[44] Law of July 11, 1913.
[45] The rate might be reduced below one percent in case the yield of the tax exceeded 15 percent of the communal tax needs.
[46] Law of January 12, 1870.
[47] Law of April 26, 1873.
[48] Law of March 27, 1886.

percent.[49] This same year the state was meeting approximately one-third of the cost of common schools, police, highways, health, and welfare and approximately two-thirds of the cost of higher education.[50] Much of this was direct state expenditure, however, rather than subventions to local governments. The state was exercising comparatively little control over local finances, and it was not using state aid in any marked degree to control other local functions.

Bavaria, a predominantly agricultural state, was poorer than either Saxony or Prussia. It obtained a considerable income from its forests, however, in the pre-war period; and, thanks largely to this fact, it relied on taxes for a slightly smaller proportion of state and local income than did Saxony.[51]

When the new Kingdom of Bavaria was established, at the beginning of the nineteenth century, it inherited a diversity of taxes.[52] Unification began almost at once. Uniform state taxes on land and houses and a class tax on trade were established in 1808.[53] These taxes were revised from time to time, and new taxes on capital and general income were added in 1848.[54] The latter was converted into a classified income tax in 1856,[55] and the general income tax was not re-established until 1912.[56]

Space cannot be given here to the many additions and revisions of state taxes, but one distinctive feature of the Bavarian tax system, as contrasted with those of Prussia and Saxony, should be noted. When the Reich was formed, Bavaria retained her tax on beer; and while she paid a substantial sum to the Reich for

[49] Computed from data in *Einzelschrift zur Statistik des deutschen Reichs*, No. 10.

[50] Sonderbeilage zu *Wirtschaft und Statistik, op. cit.*, pp. 23-25.

[51] Bavaria obtained from state and local property in 1913-14, 22 percent of its income from taxes and surplus property earnings combined. Saxony obtained only 20 percent from this source. Prussia, however, obtained 26 percent. *Einzelschrift* No. 10., *op. cit.*

[52] Wagner states that there were 607 different direct taxes, including 114 different land taxes. Wagner, *op. cit.*, IV, 139.

[53] Laws of May 13 and November 25, 1808.

[54] Law of June 4, 1848.   [55] Law of May 31, 1856.

[56] Law of August 14, 1910, effective January 1, 1912.

this privilege, she kept about two-thirds of the yield for her own use. This amounted to about three-fifths as much as the state income tax in 1913 and almost half as much as all the state direct taxes combined.

The local tax system was very closely tied to that of the state. In 1913, 90 percent of local tax revenues came from local additions to state taxes. Most of the independent local taxes were consumption taxes, the beer tax overshadowing all the others. Except for small "paving" taxes, independent local direct taxes were unknown. The circles and districts obtained all their tax revenues from local additions to state taxes and received substantial state aid in addition, mostly for schools. In the case of the circles, state aid supplied one-fourth (25.4 percent in 1905) of their income.[57] Communes received no state aid. Tax income was supplemented, however, by substantial surpluses earned by municipally owned industries and property.

In 1910 the local additions to state taxes were restricted to uniform percentages of state taxes. These restrictions were made even more stringent in 1918.[58] To what extent the extreme dependence of the local financial systems on that of the state resulted from the relatively unfavorable economic position of Bavaria, as compared with Prussia and Saxony, it is impossible to say; but the pressure on tax sources does not seem to have been great. The proportion of state and local expenditures going to debt service was higher in Bavaria than in the other two states in 1913-14, but not materially higher than in Prussia; and Bavaria's per capita taxes were lower than those of Saxony. Moreover, Bavaria was enjoying surpluses no less than the other states.[59] That Bavaria, starting with a kaleidoscopic tax system,

---

[57] J. Conrad, *Grundriss zum Studium der politischen Ökonomie*, Jena, 1909, II, 220-21.

[58] G. Schanz, "Der Finanzausgleich zwischen Reich und Ländern und der innerbayrische Finanzausgleich," *Finanz-Archiv*, XLIV, 692.—Laws of August 14, 1910 and August 11, 1918.

[59] Gerloff, *Finanz- und Zollpolitik, op. cit.*, p. 371, and *Einzelschrift* No. 10, *op. cit.*

should have developed a uniform and closely knit system in the course of the nineteenth century, while Saxony, with a less varied inheritance, should have fostered diversity, cannot be attributed solely to differences in wealth, although this was undoubtedly a contributing factor.

The complex origin of the Prussian state resulted, in its early history, in an aggregation of taxes which can hardly be dignified by the name system, a situation similar to that in Bavaria. At the opening of the nineteenth century even state taxes differed in cities and in rural areas. A series of excises on consumption and exchange were levied in the cities, and a crude land tax, *der Kontribution,* in rural regions. Local taxes were small, but varied. They were found for the most part in the larger towns and differed widely from province to province.[60]

In the three-quarters of a century from 1820 to 1893 Prussia developed from this heterogeneity of taxes a carefully planned and closely integrated system of state and local taxation. At the beginning of this period, as a result of von Stein's 1808 reforms, the towns had almost complete independence in matters of taxation. But this freedom was short-lived. Local tax powers had been severely limited during the eighteenth century, and a new series of restrictions was built up in the course of the nineteenth century. The right to levy local additions to state taxes was restricted in 1820,[61] and later legislation defined a narrow sphere within which local tax powers might be exercised. The state prescribed the form of the local additions to state taxes, and the taxes to which such surcharges might be added. Moreover, state consent was required for levies in excess of certain stated maxima and for the introduction of independent local taxes.[62] These restrictions were in the interest of a uniform and equitable tax system, however, rather than for the purpose of limiting local revenues, and local governments were not seriously handicapped

[60] For an account of the Prussian taxes of this early period see Wagner, *op. cit.,* IV, 14-36, 69-77.
[61] Law of May 30, 1820.   [62] Wagner, *op. cit.,* IV, 70.

by them. On the contrary, they benefited very definitely from lucrative taxes which would have been beyond their reach in the absence of state control. In the latter part of the nineteenth century approximately four-fifths of local revenues from taxes and fees came from additions to the state taxes on income, land, buildings, and trade. In fact, most of such revenues were from the income tax alone.[63]

In the hope of decreasing local dependence on the income tax a thoroughgoing reform of the tax system was made in 1893.[64] The state turned over the taxes on land, buildings, and trade to the localities, although the state continued to fix the bases of these taxes and to control the local rates. Local additions to the income tax were still permitted, but these were more narrowly limited, and it was required that they bear a definite relation to the amount of land, building, and trade taxes levied. Further, the municipalities were instructed to levy fees and special assessments as far as possible to meet expenditures which conferred special benefits; and while they were not definitely required to operate municipal industries at a profit, state officials were given the power to interfere when such industries were operated at a loss.

The effect of these changes was to decrease local additions to the income tax from 143 to 105 million marks between 1894 and 1895 and to increase land, building, and trade taxes from 28 to 82 million marks, thus increasing total local revenues from direct taxes. Local revenues from all taxes, fees, and assessments increased from 206 million marks in 1894 to 236 million marks in 1895.[65] Again local governments had been aided, rather than hampered, by new state regulations.

Taxpayer and government alike profited from a uniform and

[63] Wagner, op. cit., IV, 92-93.
[64] Law of July 14, 1893, effective 1895. Wagner, op. cit., IV, 78 et seq. Prior to this, in 1891, the state had revised its income and business taxes and introduced a collateral inheritance tax in place of the old probate duties (laws of June 19 and June 24, 1891). A new property tax for state purposes was introduced in 1893 (law of July 14, 1893).   [65] Wagner, op. cit., IV, 92-93.

well-balanced tax system which centered in a progressive income tax and kept consumption taxes at a minimum.[66] Taxes of all kinds were reasonable in amount. They were increasing, to be sure, but large surpluses from the Prussian railway and other state and municipal industries [67] kept the per capita burden lower than in other European countries.[68]

The state gave the local governments substantial grants-in-aid, in addition to providing uniform bases for their taxes.[69] These grants varied from fixed sums, *Dotationen,* for general purposes to subventions for specific purposes, the amount of which depended on some measure of need. Small amounts of state aid for schools were given before 1850, and by an act of 1850 the state took over the administration and expenses of the police in many of the larger cities. A distribution of state funds for general purposes was first made to the provinces in 1868, and by 1875 these *Dotationen* to provinces and rural circles had reached 15 million marks.[70] In addition to these sums for general use, nearly 19 million marks were given for roads, and smaller sums were distributed for other specific purposes. These supplied a substantial part of province and circle needs. Unlike school and police subventions, these sums were fixed in amount and remained unchanged until 1902,[71] when they were increased by 10 million marks: 7 million for poor relief and 3 million for highways.[72]

---

[66] All indirect taxes combined, excluding inheritance and increment taxes, amounted to 7.1 percent of state and local tax revenues in 1913-14. Consumption taxes, which were used exclusively by local governments, amounted to 3.5 percent of local tax revenues. *Einzelschrift* No. 10, *op. cit.* The income tax was not, of course, steeply progressive, as in later years.

[67] In 1913-14 nearly half the revenue for general state purposes in Prussia came from surpluses earned by the state railways, mines and forests, and other state property; and 14 percent of such revenue for local use came from municipal property and industries. *Einzelschrift* No. 10, *op. cit.*

[68] Wagner, *op. cit.,* IV, 790-91.

[69] A comprehensive account of these grants is to be found in J. Watson Grice, *National and Local Finance,* London, 1910, chs. xv-xvi. See also R. von Kaufmann, *Die Kommunalfinanzen,* Leipzig, 1906.

[70] Kaufmann, *op. cit.,* II, 429.   [71] Law of June 2, 1902.

[72] These *Dotationen* met more than half (58 percent) the provincial expendi-

State aid for education and police, partly in the form of subventions and partly in the form of direct state expenditures, increased very rapidly. By 1913 local governments were contributing to the support of state police, and the state government was
contributing to the support of local police. State contributions accounted for approximately half (49.5 percent) of the total net
cost [73] of police. There were between fifteen and twenty education
grants in 1913, meeting one-third (33.4 percent) of the net cost of
common schools, and a substantial share of the cost of higher
education.[74]

The origin and purpose of these state grants was widely varied.
Some were to meet the cost of new duties imposed by the state,
others to stimulate local initiative and improve the efficiency of
local administration, and still others to equalize the burden of
governmental costs in poor districts. The methods of distribution
were equally varied. Some were flat amounts, fixed originally
to equal the estimated cost of a required service. But flat sums
paid to a province were often redistributed to the circles within
the province on the basis of population, or, in so far as the money
was intended for highways, in proportion to area. Police subventions, beginning in 1908, were a fixed percentage of the cost;[75]
and school subventions were in part in proportion to school
children in average daily attendance, in part to meet the difference between the yield of a fixed tax and a fixed sum, and in
part according to other criteria. That part of the 10 million
mark *Dotation* of 1902 that was distributed by the provinces to
the circles was allocated, one-third in proportion to population,

---

tures in 1887-88 (Kaufmann, *op. cit.*, II, 430). In 1913 they were still important,
providing 36 percent of the tax income of the provinces. (B. Skrodzki, "Die Steuereinnahmen des Freistaates Preussens," *Zeitschrift des preussischen statistischen
Landesamts*, 68 Jahrg., Pts. 3-4, 1929, p. 331.) They were of less importance in circle
finance, meeting 18 percent of the expenditures of rural circles in 1877, and 7
percent in 1908. (W. Rath, *Stadt und Kreis*, 1928, pp. 82-83.)

[73] Net cost, *Zuschussbedarf*, is taken to be that part falling on the tax revenue.
Sonderbeilage zu *Wirtschaft und Statistik*, *op. cit.*, p. 10.   [74] *Idem.*

[75] The percentage of costs met from state funds was larger for state police than
for local police.

one-third in inverse proportion to the per capita state income
tax, and one-third in proportion to the ratio of the income tax
to local direct taxes.

Thus Prussia experimented with a wide variety of aids to local
governments. But the distribution of a fixed proportion of the
yield of a specific tax, the form of aid that has overshadowed all
others since the war, was unknown except for one brief experiment. Beginning in 1886 [76] the state distributed the excess over
15 million marks of its share of imperial customs duties from
cattle and agricultural products to the circles, one-third in proportion to population, and two-thirds in proportion to the proceeds of the land and building taxes. Most of the sums distributed
(42.5 out of 49.5 million marks between 1886 and 1889) went
to rural circles. The measure was designed as an aid to agriculture—compensation for the failure of the tariff to exclude completely foreign agricultural products. It was intended that circle
taxes should be reduced to correspond to the increase in revenues
from this new source. This was achieved only in moderate degree.
While the tax levies of the rural circles declined 18 percent between 1885 and 1889, the revenues from local taxes and customs
combined increased 68 percent. Thus any gains which may have
accrued to the owners of agricultural land came in the form of
increased governmental services, rather than in tax reductions.
The gains to the cities from this measure were negligible; and
it was in the cities that tax rates were highest. This single pre-war
attempt, in Germany, to distribute the varying yield of a specific
tax to local governments, can hardly be regarded as successful.
It was abandoned with the reforms of 1893.[77]

Altogether the state paid 318 million marks into local treasuries in 1913-14. This sum met 13 percent of local government
costs. The entire tax income of Prussia was only 537 million
marks in 1913-14. Thus three-fifths of the state taxes were returned to local governments. If one deducts, further, the 35 mil-

[76] Law of May 14, 1885.   [77] Kaufmann, *op. cit.*, II, 425; Rath, *op. cit.*, pp. 54-55.

lion marks paid to the Reich in *Matrikularbeiträge*, it is apparent that only about one-third of Prussia's tax revenue was used for the support of the state government.[78]

Comparing the tax systems of these three states, as they existed in 1913, Prussia left a larger share of the support of governmental functions to the local governments than did either Saxony or Bavaria. This is to be expected, in view of its greater size. To some extent it compensated the local governments for this by an extensive system of aids. But even with these a much larger proportion of costs was met from local resources than in the other two states. The Prussian communes had wider powers of taxation than had those of Bavaria. Not only were they less rigidly limited in the amount of local additions to state taxes which they could levy, but they could, with state consent, levy independent local taxes on income and property. They would seem not to have taken advantage of this latter provision, however. As far as can be ascertained practically all the direct taxes were levied on the state bases, and, as in Bavaria, nine-tenths of all local taxes came from local levies on state bases. The difference between the two states lies in the greater restrictions on the amount of local additions to state taxes in Bavaria, and the potential, if undeveloped, independent municipal taxes in Prussia. The Saxon communes, in sharp contrast to those of Prussia and Bavaria, probably obtained more than half their tax revenues from independent taxes.[79]

Dependence on the income tax is striking in all three states. In wealthy Saxony it produced more than three-fourths of state and local revenues. In Prussia, thanks to the 1893 reforms, it was reduced to a little less than half the local taxes, but continued to supply the state with approximately three-fourths of its income.

[78] Only 21 percent of state expenditures, including expenditures for industries, were covered by state taxes in 1913-14, owing to the large earnings of the Prussian railways and the public domain.

[79] The exact amount has not been found, but all direct taxes were independent in the five largest cities, in the majority of the smaller cities, and in a substantial number of rural communes.

Bavaria, as is to be expected in an agricultural state, leaned more heavily on real estate taxes, obtaining approximately one-fifth of its state and local revenue from this source. Also it obtained substantial revenues from the state beer tax, a source not available to Prussia and Saxony. Even so, 46 percent of state and local taxes came from the income tax in 1913-14.

The other German states showed no important variation from these types. All built the local tax system in some degree on state bases. Almost all gave local governments a large degree of independence in taxation. And all had established the income tax as the backbone of their systems, depending on it for from two-fifths to four-fifths of state and local tax revenue.[80] In the smaller states the state government tended to administer and support directly a larger proportion of governmental functions, and grants-in-aid were used correspondingly less. No state had developed grants to the extent that Prussia had. There is almost no trace in any of the state systems of a centrally administered tax having been distributed, as such, to underlying divisions.

Many of the essential characteristics of the pre-war state and local tax systems disappeared as a result of the provisions of the Weimar Constitution. State and local governments were deprived altogether of what had been the central tax of their systems, the income tax; and local governments, which in most states had had considerable independence in matters of taxation, were severely restricted in their taxing powers. The outstanding features of the post-war system, the central administration of most of the important taxes and the redistribution of fixed percentages of the yield to underlying jurisdictions, were practically unknown to the pre-war governments.

The relation of Reich to state taxes was little altered during the war. The Reich made no move to increase taxes until 1916, although tax yields had dropped below normal and the usual

[80] Income taxes provided 68 percent of all state tax revenue and 52 percent of all local tax revenue in 1913-14.

TABLE 4

STATE AND LOCAL TAXES IN SAXONY, BAVARIA,
AND PRUSSIA, 1913-14[a]

Tax	SAXONY			BAVARIA			PRUSSIA		
	Total	State	Local	Total	State	Local	Total	State	Local
	MILLION MARKS								
Income tax	160	72	88	130	57	72	818	340	478
All direct taxes	185	83	102	215	76	138	1,290	403	887
All taxes	207	95	112	284	128	156	1,452	467	984
	PERCENTAGE OF ALL TAXES								
Income tax	77	76	78	46	45	47	56	72	49
All direct taxes	89	88	91	76	59	89	89	86	90
All taxes	100	100	100	100	100	100	100	100	100

[a] Computed from data in *Einzelschrift zur Statistik des deutschen Reichs*, No. 6. To facilitate comparisons with post-war years these figures have been reduced to allow for losses in territory.

surpluses from imperial industries had given way to deficits. When taxes were finally imposed, beginning in 1916, they took the form of profits and turnover taxes, and new and increased consumption taxes, none of which interfered directly with state and local revenues.[81] But the failure to impose adequate taxes left the Reich in an embarrassed position and was an important cause of its complete absorption of the tax power in 1919.

[81] The state, however, was given a share in turnover taxes.

III

DIVISION OF TAXES BETWEEN THE REICH AND THE STATES UNDER THE WEIMAR CONSTITUTION

THE Weimar Constitution, adopted August 11, 1919, brought drastic changes in the distribution of tax powers among federal, state, and local governments. In fact, to such an extent were the powers of the Reich increased at the expense of the states, that it has been questioned whether Germany continued to be a federal state. The states retained a considerable sphere of independence, but at the pleasure of the Reich. It is significant that the *Staaten* of the Constitution of 1871 become *Länder* in the Constitution of 1919. The final reduction of the states to mere administrative districts in 1933 and 1934 would seem to be the logical outcome of the measures taken in 1919.

The Weimar Constitution gives the Reich jurisdiction over all taxes and income, in so far as it may claim them for its own use (Article 8). Further, the Reich may refuse the states the right to levy taxes on the same bases as Reich taxes or to levy taxes which might in any way impair the income of the Reich (Article 11). The Reich is given the right, also, to administer its own taxes (Article 11) and to control the financial administration of state and local governments, in so far as this is required for the uniform execution of national fiscal laws (Article 84).

The fiscal position of state and local governments is protected to the extent that the Reich must compensate these governments if it deprives them of former sources of revenue (Article 8), and it may not impose new duties on the underlying governments without at the same time providing them with new means of meeting the cost of such activities (Article 54). These provisions insure a limited income to state and local governments, but they offer no real guarantee of adequate income or any independence in adjusting income to needs. Moreover, any concessions the Reich may have made to state and local independence elsewhere in the Constitution, it recaptures in the emergency powers conferred by Article 48,[1] which makes possible the emergency decrees that in recent years have replaced normal legislative procedure.

This increased financial centralization was not achieved without opposition from the states; but the pressure for centralization was great. The financial situation was acute, and only through uniform and centrally administered taxes could the Reich hope to meet its heavy obligations from its depleted resources. Moreover, financial considerations were not the only factors in the larger problem of political unity. Erzberger, in his first speech as Minister of Finance, on July 8, 1919, warned of the danger of communism and concluded that the fiscal sovereignty of the Reich was the foundation for the rebuilding of the German nation. The new government stood in need of all the unifying forces it could muster. Financial centralization was an important step to this end.[2]

Thus the financial position of the Reich and the states was reversed. The states were now dependent on the Reich, where before the Reich had been dependent on the states. Bismarck's dream of a powerful central government had at last been realized—under a republic. That the jealously guarded local independence achieved under a monarchy should have been lost under a republic seems a strange twist of fate. But the importance of local independence was, perhaps, minimized by the increased popular control of the central government itself.

The constitutional provision that the Reich must compensate

---

[1] Article 48 provides, among other things, that if a state fails to carry out the duties imposed upon it by the national constitution or national laws, the President of the Reich may compel performance with the aid of armed force; and that if the public order and safety be seriously disturbed or threatened, the President of the Reich may take the necessary measures to restore it.

[2] For a comparison of the proportion of the tax revenues administered by the Reich and the state and local governments, respectively, see Appendix, Table 30, p. 349.

the states for any sources of revenue of which it might deprive them pointed to the return of taxes where they were collected, rather than to any redistribution of revenues to equalize burdens and resources. And this was the guiding principle in the redistribution of tax revenues that followed. Difficulties immediately presented themselves, however. Tax rates and tax bases had been radically changed during the war, and the Reich had no thought of serving merely as the administrative agent of the states; it planned to keep a substantial share of the necessary tax yield for its own needs. Thus the proportion of the tax revenues to be returned became, immediately, an important issue.

The revenue obtained by state and local governments from tax yields in the past offered the best measure of the amount which these governments were losing, but this had serious limitations as a standard for future tax distributions. The war years were clearly abnormal, and a pre-war standard would scarcely apply. Changes had been rapid. Population, wealth, and even territory, were no longer the same. Needs had accumulated during the lean years of the war. Further, the states and cities, with their financial independence, had exploited available resources very differently. Consequently, a fixed percentage of the Reich income tax would bear widely differing relations, in different communities, to the yield of the former state and local taxes and to current needs. As a result, the Reich, while basing its redistribution primarily on yield, was from the first involved in the problem of equalization.

The work of building up a new tax system was begun immediately upon the adoption of the Constitution and the basic features of the new system were established before the next fiscal year had begun. The administration of Reich taxes by Reich officials was provided by a law of September 10, 1919, and the State Tax Law of March 30, 1920, incorporated much of the preceding legislation and outlined the entire system of state and local taxation.[3] The wishes of the states were consulted in drafting these laws, but there seems to have been little agreement among them.[4]

Drastic changes in state and local tax systems followed. When Erzberger was asked what tax powers had been left to state and local governments, he is said to have replied, "The almost unlimited right to find new taxes." [5] Nevertheless, the resulting financial position of the state and local governments should not have been difficult. They were deprived of the income taxes, which had provided them with more than half their tax revenues in pre-war years, but two-thirds of the new income and corporation taxes, which, on the whole, were much higher than the old taxes, were to be returned to the state and local governments. Whether this change brought losses or gains in individual cases depended on the extent of their former taxes; but it is safe to say that any general loss lay in the inability of individual governments to adapt their income from this source to needs, rather than in a net loss of revenue for state and local governments as a whole.

The states were deprived, further, of the beer tax, which had been appropriated by the Reich in 1918. This meant a substantial loss of revenues to the southern states, for which they were probably not fully compensated by the special indemnities, based on pre-war production, which the Reich paid, beginning in 1919.[6] The local governments retained the right of levying retail taxes on beer and other beverages. The Reich took over the administra-

---

[3] See Appendix, Chart 4, pp. 324 et seq., of this and subsequent laws regarding the distribution of Reich-administered taxes to state and local governments.

[4] Markull, op. cit., pp. 18-20.

[5] W. Gerloff, "Schwebende Fragen des Finanzausgleichs," Schriftenreihe des deutschen Städtetages, Berlin, 1928, No. 5.

[6] The percentage of total collections allocated to Bavaria yielded less in 1924 than Bavaria's 1913 revenue from this source. The same percentage of the 1925 yield came to practically the same amount as Bavaria's 1913 beer tax, but in 1925 the Reich had reduced the maximum that Bavaria could receive to about half this amount.

tion of the inheritance tax and abolished the privilege of state surtaxes, but the states were to receive 20 percent of the yield of this tax as before and in addition were guaranteed at least the average yield of this tax for the years 1912 to 1916, inclusive. The new Reich land purchase tax (*Grunderwerbsteuer*) replaced similar state and local taxes, but the 50 percent that was returned, together with the privilege of levying a surtax, should have more than compensated the state and local governments for the loss.

Thus, for each tax that the Reich took over some compensation was offered. It was not until the introduction of the property tax (*Vermögensteuer*), in 1922, that the Reich appropriated a source of state and local revenue directly, without offering some indemnification. In addition the Reich distributed 10 percent of the turnover tax to the states and 5 percent to the communes. This was a new source of revenue and did not directly replace any state or local source of income.[7] Before the Reich took over the administration of this tax the sums paid over to state and local governments were regarded as compensation for administration. With Reich administration, in 1919, the 5 percent returned to the communes in proportion to collections might still be regarded as compensation for aid in collection,[8] but the 10 percent returned to the states in proportion to population is a clear, and somewhat unwilling, concession by the Reich to the power of the states.[9]

The states gained, further, from the discontinuance of the *Matrikularbeiträge*, and state and local governments were left in undisturbed possesssion of the land, building, and business taxes, which ranked second in importance to the income tax in pre-war state and local budgets. The Reich placed certain restrictions on the levy of these taxes, but the limitations were not rigid. Also, state and local governments had at their disposal an entertainment tax, which they were required to levy, the dog tax, and

[7] The first regular turnover tax was levied by law of July 26, 1918. Prior to that a turnover stamp tax had been levied by law of July 26, 1916.

[8] Schanz, *op. cit., Finanz-Archiv*, XLIV, 674.

[9] H. Delpech, *Les Aspects d'un fédéralisme financier; l'exemple Allemand*, Paris, 1933, p. 352.

various stamp and consumption taxes, in addition to the local retail tax on beverages. Further, communes were given the right to tax incomes not reached by the Reich tax, i.e., those under 700 marks, but this privilege was revoked after one year.[10]

Finally, the Reich provided special guarantees to prevent undue loss of revenue in individual states. In addition to the inheritance tax guarantee cited above, each state was guaranteed from the income tax a sum equal to the average state and local income tax levy in the years 1917 to 1919, or the 1919 levy plus 6 percent per annum in case this latter sum should be larger; and also a per capita distribution from the income and corporation taxes equal to 80 percent of the average per capita distribution. This latter guarantee, together with the per capita distribution of the turnover tax, marks the first attempt on the part of the Reich to equalize resources among the states, rather than merely to reimburse them for lost income. The amount and manner of the division of revenues between state and local governments was left to the discretion of the states, except for the distribution of the turnover tax and the indefinite provision that some of the income tax was to be given to local governments.

This tax system indicates that, in the first instance, state and local governments were fully compensated for lost revenue sources. The actual effects of the system cannot be measured, however, owing to the ensuing inflation, which makes statistics meaningless, even for 1920,[11] and which, in the end, completely nullified the earlier tax legislation. With inflation, state and local governments, unable to meet their obligations, began to issue their own currency; and the Reich, in a not-altogether-successful effort to prevent these issues of *Notgeld*, agreed to pay 75 percent of salary increases beginning January 1, 1921.[12] These salary payments soon overshadowed tax payments in importance.

Inflation for the time being reduced the state and local gov-

[10] Law of March 24, 1921.

[11] The fiscal year beginning April 1, 1920, was the first for which the new system was effective.

[12] Markull, *op. cit.*, p. 27.

TABLE 5

REICH AID TO STATE AND LOCAL GOVERNMENTS, 1920-21 TO 1922-23,
BUDGET ESTIMATES [a]

	1920-21	1921-22	1922-23
	BILLION MARKS		
Ordinary income of Reich.......	58.7	90.7	1,071.6
Total aid....................	9.8	20.5	1,281.6
Tax distributions............	9.6	18.9	264.7
Salary aid.................	0.2	1.6	1,016.9
	PERCENTAGES		
Ordinary income of Reich.......	100.0	100.0	100.0
Total aid....................	16.7	22.6	119.6
Tax distributions............	16.4	20.8	24.7
Salary aid.................	0.3	1.8	94.9
	AVERAGE MARKS PER DOLLAR		
	63	105	1,885

[a] Markull, *op. cit.*, p. 66. The fiscal year runs from April 1 to March 31.

ernments to beggars, and, though the actual duration of inflation
was comparatively short, its effects were far-reaching. The tangible, financial consequences were to free state and local governments, as well as the national government, from debt, and to leave
them with a greatly enhanced welfare burden. It seems highly
probable, also, that inflation accustomed state and local governments to the acceptance of national aid as no ordinary revision
of the tax system could have done, and perhaps encouraged them
to take unbalanced budgets lightly, and to borrow readily with
little thought of the morrow. And the Weimar Constitution,
whether through oversight or through the strength of the sup-
porters of states' rights, had failed to place any check on state
and local borrowing powers.

The Reich did not encourage any such attitude. Salary payments from the national government were reduced each month

in the early months of 1924 and ceased altogether with the beginning of the fiscal year on April 1; and the number of government employees was promptly and materially reduced.[13] At the same time, however, the Reich tax distributions to underlying governments were increased. Even before stabilization had been achieved, a new and comprehensive tax law governing state and local tax systems had been passed,[14] increasing the state and local participation in Reich taxes. The share of income and corporation taxes had been increased from 66.7 to 75 percent in 1921; the share of the turnover tax was now increased from 15 to 25 percent; the share of the land purchase tax was increased from 50 to 96 percent; and the share of the betting tax, first imposed in 1922, was increased from 50 to 96 percent. State governments were also receiving 50 percent of the motor vehicle tax under a 1922 law, or 96 percent if they imposed a tax on other vehicles. The old guarantees were continued and a new one, for the land purchase tax, was added.

State and local governments benefited again from further adjustments in the distribution of taxes as a result of the Emergency Tax Decree of February 14, 1924, effective February 1. This increased the state and local share of the income and corporation taxes from 75 to 90 percent; and while the percentage of the turnover tax distributed was cut from 25 to 20, the gains from the increased income tax distributions compensated several times over for the losses from the turnover tax. The rate of the turnover tax was reduced toward the end of 1924, but the reduction was accompanied by a guarantee that the monthly state and local revenues from the income, corporation, and turnover taxes combined, for the remainder of the fiscal year, should not fall below the average monthly revenues for August and September, preceding the reduction in rate.

The inheritance tax distribution was discontinued, beginning

[13] H. Herkner, "Steuernotwirtschaft; Steuerreform und Finanzausgleich, 1925." *Denkschrift des deutschen Städtetages*, Berlin, 1926, pp. 4-6.

[14] *Finanzausgleichsgesetz*, June 23, 1923, effective April 1, 1923.

February 19, 1924, but the guarantee was continued, and the states were offered, as additional compensation, the total yield of a stock exchange tax (*Börsenbesuchsteuer*) without deduction for cost of administration. This latter tax was abandoned before a year had elapsed, but the loss to the states was very small, being about two-tenths of one percent of the sums turned over by the Reich to state and local governments. Finally, 96 percent of the motor vehicle tax was turned over to the states without the condition that a tax on other vehicles must be imposed.

These generous increases would seem to be a tribute to the continued power of the states,[15] although it is quite possible that the Reich yielded willingly in view of the probability that reparation payments would devour any surplus revenues it might realize. It is true that the decree of February 14, 1924, turned over to state and local governments the support of police, welfare, and education, but these had been the responsibility of state and local governments when the first division of revenues was made in 1920. The new division of revenues was put into effect before the results of the earlier system could be measured. And while inflation had left the state and local authorities with heavy social obligations, which undoubtedly outweighed the gains from canceled debts, the Reich, too, was faced with new obligations in the form of large and growing reparation payments, which counterbalanced savings from debt cancellation. Moreover, state and local governments were provided with an entirely new tax on rentals, which proved extremely lucrative. This was imposed on rentals of all buildings constructed prior to July 1, 1918, and on rentals of newer buildings constructed with public aid.[16] It

---

[15] As late as 1924 Bavaria was demanding a revision of the Constitution and the restoration to the state of complete financial and administrative autonomy (*Denkschrift der bayrischen Regierung zu Revision der Weimarer Reichsverfassung*, January 8, 1924), and those favoring unity were conceding a decentralized, although unitary state.—Delpech, *op. cit.*, pp. 430-32. See also K. Krämer, "Die Finanzgebarung des Reichs und seiner Länder seit der Wahrungsstabilisierung." *Finanz-Archiv*, XLII, 407.

[16] A similar tax had been imposed before inflation.

had a twofold purpose: to force the owners of old buildings, who presumably had profited from the housing shortage, to help finance the government's housing program; and to reach the real estate owners who had profited from inflation, particularly those who had been able to pay off mortgages during the inflation period. The proceeds were devoted partly to housing, but the share for general purposes should have gone a long way toward meeting the new welfare burden.[17]

The Reich made an extraordinary effort to build up its own tax revenues and, favored by improving industrial conditions, closed the year 1924-25 with the astonishing surplus of nearly half a billion marks; this in spite of reparations and liberal concessions to the states.[18] State and local governments also fared well. The taxes distributed by the Reich in 1924 exceeded budget estimates by nearly 50 percent; and even in later years, with some experience to go on, these tax distributions regularly exceeded estimates by considerable sums.

The rapid expansion of expenditures in the next few years was inevitable. National, state, and local governments were stimulated by unaccustomed revenues, freedom from debt, the rationalization movement in industry, and the all-too-great eagerness of foreign capitalists to advance new loans. Social expenditures were greatly increased, in response to genuine need and to popular demand for an extension of social activities. The new Republic was, after all, a socialistic government.[19] An extensive and

[17] The total yield of this tax in 1925-26 was 57.4 percent of the net state and local expenditures for welfare and housing.

[18] The surplus was 496 million reichsmarks. F. K. Mann, *Deutsche Finanzwirtschaft*, Jena, 1929, p. 3.

[19] Governmental extravagance was fostered under the Republic both by the extension of the vote to a large group of persons paying no direct taxes and by the new system of revenue distributions that divorced revenues from expenditures. Not only were the Reich tax distributions to state and local governments wholly independent of state and local expenditures, but they regularly exceeded budget estimates in this early period. For the five years 1924-25 to 1928-29 the amount actually distributed exceeded the amount promised in the yearly budgets by more than 10 percent. This was reflected in state and local budgets by the fact that actual expenditures quite generally exceeded those provided for in the budget. While this is not

extravagant building program was undertaken in addition to the provision of essential housing. Less obvious, but of considerably more importance in the yearly budgets, were the increases in salary scales, made partly in order to compete with industry for able administrators, and partly, perhaps, for the purpose of obtaining leverage for future reductions to prove economy and great need when reparation payments should press.[20] The army of public officials likewise grew beyond the number necessary for efficient administration. The Social Democratic Party had to care for its own.[21]

This politics of waste and irresponsibility, more characteristic of American than German municipalities, was short-lived. The peak of Reich generosity had already been reached, and the Reich gave ear to the pleas of overburdened taxpayers more readily than to the representations of state officials in ensuing revisions of the tax program. The Weimar Constitution had done its work well. Compromise succeeded compromise in the years that followed; but in spite of occasional victories the states were steadily losing power to the Reich. Rising tax yields, resulting from favorable industrial conditions, brought state and local governments increasing revenues for several years, but drastic cuts in the Reich distributions reduced the state and local share in 1929, and when state and local taxes began to decline in 1931, revenues were seriously reduced.[22]

---

an unusual phenomenon in American states and cities, it has occasioned frequent comment among German officials and students of finance and is attributed largely to unexpected income. See, e.g., *Gutachten des Reichssparkommissars über die Verwaltung der Stadt Mannheim*, 1932, p. 28. When it is considered that the Reich tax distributions amounted to between two-fifths and one-half of all state and local tax revenues during this period, it is evident that these excess revenues are an important factor in the rapid growth of state and local expenditures.

[20] General increases in salaries were put into effect in 1925 and again in 1927. The fact that reparation payments were a factor has been suggested, in personal interviews, by more than one individual acquainted with financial developments during this period.

[21] J. Popitz, *Der künftige Finanzausgleich*, Berlin, 1932, p. 27, and C. Hoover, *The Third Reich*, New York, 1933, p. 38.

[22] See Appendix, Table 30, p. 349, for state and local share of Reich tax distributions.

The Reich began to reduce state and local tax claims to Reich income in 1925 in spite of the resolutions of the Dresden Conference of State Ministers of Finance, February 3, 1925, which demanded, among other things, a larger share of the turnover tax and at least 96 percent of the income and corporation taxes. The majority of state officials favored the complete restitution of these latter taxes to the states. The monthly guarantees for income, corporation, and turnover taxes introduced in the latter part of 1924 were extended until October 1, 1925, at which time the state and local governments' share in the turnover tax was advanced from 20 to 35 percent to compensate for the cut in the rate of the turnover tax.[23] At the same time, however, the share of the income and corporation taxes was cut to 75 percent. This was done in spite of state demands for an increase in the percentage and in the face of reduced tax rates, effective April 1. This cut was accompanied by further guarantees: that the state and local share of the three taxes should not fall below 2,100 million reichsmarks in the two succeeding years and that the turnover tax distribution alone should not fall below the state and local percentage (at that time 35 percent and in 1926, 30 percent) of 1,500 million reichsmarks. The first guarantee was not effective, since the state and local governments received more than the minimum guaranteed, but the turnover tax fell short of 1,500 million reichsmarks and, in consequence, this latter guarantee cost the Reich approximately 37 million reichsmarks in 1925-26 and 187 million reichsmarks in 1926-27.[24] This did not, of course, compensate for the reduction in income tax distributions. The revenue of the southern states was further impaired by the reduction of the maximum sums they might receive from the beer tax, although the percentages remained unchanged. Thus the total Reich tax distributions dropped nearly 5 percent in 1925-26 and were still below the 1924-25 level in 1926-27.

[23] This guarantee, like most of the others, was not effective, since the yield of the taxes exceeded the guarantee.

[24] *Einzelschrift* No. 16, p. 292.

State and local tax powers were restricted further under the law of August 10, 1925, by the prohibition of local guest taxes and of further increases in local beverage taxes. The law provided, also, that an increment tax must be imposed on the sale of real estate that had been acquired between January 1, 1919, and December 31, 1924, and this, in turn, limited the surtax on the land purchase tax to 2 percent, since the 4 percent was permitted only in case no increment tax was levied. While this latter provision was a further limitation on the taxing power of the underlying governments, the immediate effect was probably to increase their revenues a little. In this case, as in others, decreased tax power went hand in hand with increased revenue. In 1926 [25] the further restriction was added that new tax projects of state and local governments must be laid before the Reich minister of finance for approval.

The slight increase in Reich tax distributions in 1926-27 over 1925-26 was in spite of further cuts. The percentage of the turnover tax returned was reduced from 35 to 30, but the special turnover tax guarantee, which was effective throughout the year, kept the state and local share above that for 1925-26, in which year the higher rate and guarantee were effective for only six months. The income and corporation tax guarantee of a minimum at least equal to the 1919 yield plus 6 percent per annum was replaced with a guarantee of 125 percent of the 1919 yield. Since the old guarantee would have amounted to 142 percent in 1926-27, this limited the possibility of state participation.[26] The only changes in 1926 that favored the state and local governments were a substantial subsidy to the states for the police and the introduction of a merger tax (*Gesellschaftsteuer*), half of which was returned to the communes in compensation for losses from the closing of plants resulting from the rationalization of industry.

Meanwhile the Reich had reduced its own taxes as well as

[25] Law of April 27, 1926.   [26] Actually, these guarantees were never effective.

those of state and local governments. The reduction in income tax rates was more than compensated for by the increased percentage retained, but the brunt of the loss from turnover tax reductions fell on the Reich, and this tax was reduced by five successive steps, in the period from October 1, 1924, to April 1, 1926, from 2.5 percent to .75 percent. The turnover tax on luxuries was repealed. The capital transactions tax (*Kapitalverkehrsteuer*) was also reduced on April 1, 1926.

The Reich closed the 1925-26 fiscal year with a surplus of 180 million reichsmarks, but, with salary increases and tax reductions, the actual revenues for the year had fallen far below expenditures. It was only the large surplus of the preceding year which prevented a net deficit. The nominal surplus at the end of 1926-27 stood at 200 million reichsmarks, but the net expenditures for the year exceeded net revenues by more than 700 million reichsmarks. It was only through loans and the previous year's surplus that an apparent surplus was again realized.[27]

The yield of the income and corporation taxes and the consequent distributions to state and local governments were beyond expectation in 1926-27, and the yield of state and local taxes was likewise favorable. Nevertheless it was a year of unrestrained borrowing and unbalanced budgets on the part of state and municipal governments; and increased unemployment in the latter half of the year aggravated an already difficult situation.

The finance minister, Köhler, was a strong proponent of centralization, and the Reich was faced with growing reparation payments.[28] Consequently, the abolition of the guarantees to state and local governments was contemplated. But the smaller states, which could scarcely exist without the income these afforded, were supported by the larger states in their demands, and further compromises followed in the law of April 9, 1927. The Reich was unable to grant the local governments the privilege of

[27] Mann, *op. cit.*, p. 4.
[28] 100 million reichsmarks in 1926-27, 500 million in 1927-28, and 1,250 million in 1928-29.

levying surtaxes on the income tax, which two years earlier it had promised for 1927. It had been hoped that the income tax rates could be reduced to a point where this would be possible, but the reductions had not been realized. The coveted surtax privilege was deferred for two years, and in compensation the communes were permitted to continue the beverage taxes, which were to have been abandoned. Also, the maximum distributions to the southern states from the Reich beer tax were greatly increased.

The Reich gained a material victory in the reduction of the guarantees, although these were not abandoned. The 2,100 million reichsmark guarantee for the three taxes was replaced by a 2,600 million guarantee;[29] but since the distributions from the three taxes exceeded this sum without the guarantee, this was a concession on paper only; and the special turnover tax guarantee, which would have cost the Reich approximately 200 million reichsmarks, was abandoned. The poorer states were conciliated by the provision that the same sum as would have been obtained from the special turnover tax guarantee would be distributed on the turnover tax base, but the difference between 30 percent of the yield and 450 million reichsmarks came from the state and local governments' share of the income tax, not from the Reich's share. Another change, this one unfavorable to the poorer states, was the limitation placed on the 1920 per capita guarantee that it should not exceed one-third of the state's share on the collection base. This meant that a state could never receive more than it contributed, since without the guarantee the Reich's share was one-third of the state's share. The net saving to the Reich resulting from this limitation was less than two million reichsmarks in 1927-28, but it meant an appreciable loss of revenues to the four small states concerned.[30]

[29] The law provided that the difference between 2,400 and 2,600 million reichsmarks should be distributed in proportion to reductions in land, building, and business taxes, but owing to the wide variations in these taxes in the different states there was no basis for the distribution of these 200 million marks and this provision was practically inoperative.—A. Zarden, "Die Ziele der Finanzreform." *Vierteljahresschrift für Steuer- und Finanzrecht,* V (1931), 11.

[30] Waldeck, Lippe, and the two Mecklenburgs. The income and corporation tax

The picture of the financial relations of the national and state governments in 1927 would not be complete without some consideration of the distribution of the welfare burden.[31] The growth of unemployment had led to the introduction of emergency relief in 1926.[32] This increased welfare expenditures materially, but the Reich shouldered four-fifths of the cost of this relief and the communes, which contributed the remaining fifth, gained in an appreciable reduction of those welfare expenditures falling on local treasuries. In 1927, with improved industrial conditions, the total welfare burden was greatly reduced, even for the Reich, although it assumed an even larger share of the cost. The year 1927 should not have been difficult. Not only did the welfare expenditures decrease, but tax yields increased. In 1928 unemployment, and consequently welfare costs, rose again, but the increased tax income more than covered these increased costs, although the increases in tax income were not as marked as in the preceding year. State and local governments failed to live within their incomes. Increases in indebtedness, in 1928, amounted to more than one-third of tax income. But the difficulty would seem to have come from needlessly liberal expenditures rather than from rising welfare costs.

The revenues of the Reich, as well as those of state and local governments, improved during this period. Taxes yielded nearly ten percent more than had been anticipated in 1927-28, and the year closed with a surplus of nearly 400 million reichsmarks. This included, to be sure, the surplus of the previous year and nearly 200 million extraordinary revenues from reserves for the government's industries.[33] Nevertheless, in both 1927 and 1928 the tax revenues of the Reich, after deducting the rapidly increasing reparation payments, were substantially greater than in the

revenues of Waldeck were reduced by nearly one-third in consequence of this change. Hensel is of the opinion that only this guarantee made political existence possible for these four states.—*Vierteljahresschrift für Steuer- und Finanzrecht,* 1929, p. 31. Waldeck was taken over by Prussia in 1928 and the two Mecklenburgs were combined in 1933.

[31] For a more extended discussion of this see *infra,* pp. 114-28.

[32] *Krisenfürsorge,* Law of November 19, 1926.   [33] Mann, *op. cit.,* pp. 4-5.

year preceding. The fact that no important changes took place
in the division of revenues among the different governmental
jurisdictions between April 1, 1927, and April 1, 1929, is in
itself indicative that the financial position of all jurisdictions was
reasonably satisfactory. Also, further tax reductions were taking
place. The maximum for the motor vehicle surtax (under the law
of May 15, 1926) was reduced, beginning April 1, 1927, and a
further reduction in this tax was made, beginning April 1, 1929.
The income tax rates were reduced on January 1, 1928,[34] and
again on October 1, 1928.[35] The latter reduction was made without any preliminary hearings for the states, although they were
vitally concerned.[36] These reductions seem to have been justified,
in view of the extremely heavy tax burden that had been imposed
following stabilization, but the mild prosperity which the country
had been enjoying was over. Unemployment increased sharply
toward the end of the fiscal year 1928-29, and with a growing
welfare burden and rising reparation payments on one side,
and decreases in tax rates and shrinking tax bases on the other,
the financial situation once more became acute.

The Reich took steps to improve its own fiscal position but
made no attempt to aid state and local governments. The local
surtaxes on the income tax were again deferred, this time from
April 1, 1929, to April 1, 1930. For the fiscal year 1929-30 the
yield of the wage tax in excess of 1,300 million reichsmarks was
kept by the Reich to meet deficits in the pension and health-
insurance funds.[37] Also, the Reich was authorized to withhold
120 million reichsmarks out of any excess over 4,530 million
reichsmarks from distributions of the income, corporation, and
turnover taxes, but this provision was not effective since the yield
of these taxes failed to reach 4,530 million reichsmarks.

In 1930, with conditions getting steadily worse, the Reich

[34] Law of December 22, 1927.   [35] Law of July 23, 1928.
[36] O. Mulert, "Reichsaufbau und Selbstverwaltung." *Schriftenreihe des deutschen
Städtetages*, Berlin, 1928, No. 4, pp. 25-26.
[37] This excess amounted to approximately 96 million reichsmarks in 1929-30. 125
million was expected. *Einzelschrift* No. 19, pp. 21, 201.

again deferred the long-promised privilege of levying surtaxes
on the income tax, this time until April 1, 1932. Further, it imposed an additional tax on the incomes of single persons, and on
incomes in excess of 8,000 reichsmarks; and the proceeds of
these additional taxes, estimated at 145 million reichsmarks, were
not distributed. The excess over 1,300 million reichsmarks from
the wage tax was to have been withheld as before, as far as needed
for insurance funds, and the excess over 1,502 million reichsmarks, up to 30 million reichsmarks, was to have been withheld
for unemployment relief. Since, however, the yield of this tax
failed to reach 1,300 million reichsmarks, these provisions were
not effective. The maximum surtax permitted for the motor
vehicle tax was reduced once more, beginning April 1, 1930,[38]
and the land purchase tax, all but 4 percent of which was distributed to state and local governments, was reduced beginning
October 1, 1930. The municipal governments suffered slight
losses, also, from the discontinuance of the merger tax distributions beginning September 30, 1930, but these were important
only to a few communes.

The actual reductions made by the Reich in state and local
income in 1929-30 and 1930-31 were not large, but growing
obligations and diminishing resources left the communes in a
precarious financial position, and the Reich was forced to come
to their aid, first meeting deficits in local welfare budgets through
loans and eventually canceling the loans. Further aid was offered
in the form of a tax on mineral water, imposed April 1, 1930,
solely for state and local use.[39] The Reich retained only 4 percent
of this to cover the cost of administration. Also, beginning April
1, 1930, the Reich distributed one-sixth of the beer tax (after
deducting the special payments to the southern states) to all
states, the share of each being determined by collections. At the
same time the turnover tax rate was increased from .75 to .85
percent. This, of course, benefited the Reich more than the states,
but since the states were receiving 30 percent of this tax, they

[38] Law of April 15, 1930.   [39] Law of April 15, 1930.

were somewhat concerned. Increases in local beverage taxes were permitted by the decree of July 26, 1930, and further increases were permitted by the decree of December 1, 1930. Also, the July decree introduced an entirely new tax for local use, a citizen tax (*Bürgersteuer*), levied on all persons 20 years of age and over with an income in excess of 900 reichsmarks. This tax was graded according to income.

The December decree provided that the amount of Reich taxes distributed on the turnover tax base should be reduced from 450 million reichsmarks to 375 million. This did not decrease the total state and local share, but it worked to the disadvantage of the poorer states. Also, the amount that a state could benefit from the per capita guarantee was reduced from a maximum of one-third to a maximum of one-fifth, but this was made effective only with the fiscal year 1934.[40] Local tax power was even more narrowly circumscribed by the provision of the December decree that communes might not increase taxes on real estate and business until they levied both the beverage and citizen taxes.

Meanwhile the Reich was endeavoring to build up its own revenues. In the two years from January 1, 1929, to January 1, 1931, in addition to the increased rate of the general turnover tax noted above, increases were made in the customs duties and internal excises on a number of commodities, of which the most important were tobacco products, petroleum, beer, alcohol, and acetic acid. The property tax rate was increased for a single year, 1929-30, and with the discontinuance of reparation payments in 1931, the yield of the tax on industrial income (*Aufbringungsumlage*), reverted to the Reich treasury for general purposes. Finally, increases in the levies on wages for unemployment insurance benefited the Reich, since it was meeting the deficits in these funds.

The new taxes were not adequate to balance budgets in the face of industrial depression. In spite of increased tax rates, tax

[40] Later postponed until April 1, 1935.

yields fell and welfare burdens grew to unprecedented proportions. Moreover, it was apparent that the taxpayers' burden was becoming intolerable and that tax reductions, rather than tax increases, must follow. A decrease in the tax on bills of exchange (*Wechselsteuer*) had taken place as early as August, 1929, and in 1930, in addition to the reduction in the motor vehicle and land purchase taxes noted above, there were reductions in the merger tax and the tax on securities (*Wertpapiersteuer*). Only the strictest economy could meet the situation. The aim of the decree of December 1, 1930, was lower taxes and decreased expenditures. To this end it cut the distributions to state and local governments under the various guarantees, deducted 100 million reichsmarks from the distribution of the income, corporation, and turnover taxes to state and local governments, as the equivalent of estimated savings from salary cuts,[41] and permitted agricultural landowners to deduct from the land tax the income tax on the first 6,000 reichsmarks of income from agricultural property. The Reich reimbursed state and local governments for losses from this latter provision. This decree also provided that, beginning April 1, 1931, half the rent tax should go to the reduction of the land, building, and business taxes, 10 percent to be used for direct reduction, and 40 percent to be paid to an equalization fund for especially needy communes. An appreciable reduction in real estate and business taxes resulted, but the communes were unable to reduce their expenditures in proportion, and what they lost from these taxes they recovered from increased citizen and beverage taxes. The net result was a shifting, rather than a reduction, of the tax burden. No consistent reduction could be expected under the circumstances.

The decree of June 5, 1931, promulgated following the failure of the Credit-Anstalt, and just prior to the bank panic in Germany, introduced a surtax on wages and salaries for the benefit

---

[41] These salary cuts were recommended, but not required. With the reduction in Reich tax distributions, however, and declining revenues from other sources, legal compulsion was hardly needed.

of the Reich alone. And the decree of December 8, 1931, followed by a law of January 30, 1932, brought an increase in the
turnover tax rate from .85 to 2 percent. These increases were
accompanied by valiant efforts toward retrenchment. Both the
June and December decrees provided further salary cuts for
state and local governments; and this time the cuts were compulsory. At the same time the Reich came to the aid of the communes with direct welfare subventions, a small aid being granted
by the June decree and a very substantial one, 230 million
reichsmarks, by a decree of October 6, 1931. This policy of direct
Reich subventions to the communes for welfare expenditures
is still in force (July, 1936), although the amount given and the
conditions of payment have been changed and the amounts
greatly reduced.

With the end of 1931 tax reductions again appeared. The
mineral water tax was given up by the decree of December 8,
1931. The rates of both Reich and local beer taxes were reduced
shortly afterward, in March, 1932, and the privilege of local
surtaxes on the income tax, which was to have been granted
April 1, 1932, was indefinitely postponed. A 20 percent reduction of the rental tax was required beginning April 1, 1932, and
in May the valuation for the land purchase tax was cut 20 percent.
But local welfare expenditures could not be cut to fit these shrinking resources, and the Reich again came to the aid of local governments, and again with increased subventions rather than with
increased tax revenues. The decree of June 14, 1932, provided
increased welfare grants and protected the communes further by
providing that state laws might not be changed to the detriment
of the communes during the year. The Reich obtained the money
for these new grants by a new and higher surtax on wages
(replacing the 1931 surtax), by retaining the levy on industry
originally designed for reparation payments,[42] by reducing

---

[42] The rate of this levy was reduced, however, and 60 percent of the proceeds
were applied to agricultural aids in East Prussia and aids to small business concerns, rather than to welfare expenditures.

exemptions from the turnover tax, and by reintroducing the salt tax which had been abandoned in 1926.

No clear-cut policy is evident in these frantic attempts to balance budgets, nor can a logically developed plan be expected in such an emergency. Declining prosperity does not foster scientific financial programs. Taxes were neither increased consistently nor reduced consistently, nor is there any indication that tax burdens were being redistributed according to a carefully formulated plan. Revenue was sought where it could be found without drying up the source. But in the process the centralization of finances was materially increased. The Reich was beginning to deal directly with local governments, ignoring the states; and the local governments were aided through the assumption by the Reich of an increasing share of the welfare burden rather than through increased tax revenues.

The Reich had the upper hand—and the ultimate responsibility. It could place the burden of welfare expenditures on the municipalities if it chose, but when they staggered under the load it had no choice but to prop them up until they could support the burden placed upon them. In spite of every effort to economize, deficits grew. The Reich had not enjoyed even a nominal surplus since 1927-28, and the 1931-32 deficit was nearly 1,500 million reichsmarks.[43] State and local governments were likewise facing growing deficits, and with a formidable heritage of debts, left from the reckless financing of more prosperous years, credit was lacking. The new government which came into power in the spring of 1933 was confronted with an impossible financial situation. But whatever the shortcomings of the new administration, it was not lacking either in courage or in action.

It is not necessary to trace here the many changes in the tax laws during the three years that the National Socialists have been in control. Their avowed policy is the reduction of unemployment through tax reduction and through subsidies to a wide variety

[43] 1,474 million reichsmarks, or nearly one-fourth of its expenditures.

of projects for increasing employment. Actually a number of increases in taxes have taken place, as well as the more widely heralded decreases, but the trend has probably been downward. There has been a sufficient increase in taxable income, however, to offset any losses from tax reductions, and tax yields have increased. To this extent the financial situation has been ameliorated. What the government has gained, however, in reduced welfare burdens (and the reduction of the unemployed from six million to two and one-half million means very substantial reductions in welfare budgets), it has more than lost to date, in expenditures for the stimulation of employment, and the tax increases do not cover the difference. Thus the financial problem is still acute.

The distribution of resources and burdens among Reich, state, and local governments remains, meanwhile, in approximately its former state. A few changes should be noted, however. The meat tax (*Schlachtsteuer*), formerly a state tax levied in Bavaria, Saxony, and some of the smaller states, has been taken over by the Reich administration.[44] All but 4 percent of the yield is returned, however, for 1934—half in proportion to the yield of state taxes in 1933 and half in proportion to the yield of the new tax. Since the tax was not formerly levied in Prussia and a number of the smaller states, it offers substantial new revenue.

The Reich has adopted a uniform classification for highways throughout Germany, and a substantial proportion of these highways will be taken over and supported by the Reich.[45] Most of the remainder will be under the states or provinces. Hitherto the Reich has spent practically nothing for highways. Under the new regulations it will probably support more than 10 percent of the total highway mileage. The state and provincial highways will probably be increased from 30 percent to nearly 70 percent of the whole, and the local share will be cut from 70 to about 20

[44] Law of March 24, 1934, effective May 1, 1934.
[45] Law of March 26, 1934.

percent.[46] This is a very radical redistribution of burdens, and revenues have been adjusted accordingly. To meet the new burden the Reich is now withholding all but 90 million reichsmarks from the yield of the motor vehicle tax.[47] Exemption of new cars from the motor vehicle tax and the privilege of commuting the tax on old cars through a single payment was granted in 1933, with the result that the yield of this tax has been greatly reduced. This does not affect the state and local governments, however, in view of the 90 million reichsmark guarantee.

The state and local governments are more immediately concerned with the reduction of the tax on agricultural land by 100 million reichsmarks in 1933, which has practically wiped out the state tax on agricultural land, and with the contemplated reduction of the rental tax, beginning with 25 percent in 1935 and ending with the complete abolition of the tax in 1940.[48] This tax has come to be the largest single source of state and local revenues, and it is difficult to see how the gap that this will leave in state and local budgets is to be filled if it is finally repealed.

State and local governments are also concerned with the exemption of new buildings from the land and building taxes and with the abolition of the increment tax.[49] The latter is, of course, of little importance for the moment. The states still retain the varying state systems practically as they existed when the state legislative bodies were abolished, but the time is probably not far distant when a single, co-ordinated and highly centralized tax system will prevail throughout the Reich.

Through the years of industrial depression the immediate pressure of successive financial crises, international and domestic,

[46] *Der Gemeindetag,* September 15, 1934, p. 551.
[47] The guarantee for 1934 was 160 million reichsmarks per year, but this was decreased to 90 million for 1935, 1936, and 1937. Laws of April 11, 1933, May 31, 1933, March 28, 1934, February 28, 1935.
[48] This tax was not actually reduced 25 percent in 1935, but the state and local share was reduced 25 percent, the difference being applied to payment of local debts owed to the Reich.
[49] Laws of September 21, 1933, and October 16, 1934.

has shoved the "final" equalization of resources and burdens among the different governments into the indefinite future. But while it is recognized that delay is inevitable, careful plans for such equalization have been made. In fact, the decree of December 1, 1930, an emergency decree, outlined a complete system to be effective April 1, 1932. This could not, of course, be put into effect when 1932 came, but it is important as indicating what an acceptable distribution of resources in normal times might be, and much of it is still accepted as the ultimate goal.

The aims of this system are greater uniformity of taxes, combined with greater local freedom in levying taxes. These two seemingly incompatible ends are to be achieved by circumscribing still further the tax powers of the states. Uniformity is regarded as essential for fair competition in industry and to achieve a closely knit economy within the Reich. This is doubly desirable. Economically it is expected to improve industrial conditions and thus to increase the wealth of the country. Politically it strengthens the central government. Greater local independence likewise serves a double end. It gives the local authorities the freedom to adapt resources better to varying local needs and, in making the local governments more independent of the states, it weakens the power of the states.

To the end of uniformity, all important taxes, state and local as well as national, are to have a common base for the entire Reich. As early as 1925 the Reich had passed a law providing for uniform valuations for land, building, and business taxes.[50] This was to have been adopted as the basis of all state taxes, in so far as these were levied on capital values and not on yield. The law provided that it should be effective for agricultural land, beginning in 1927, and for improved property at such time as the Reich minister of finance should set. The valuations in question have been made and the Reich valuation is in use for Reich taxes and for some state taxes, but only in Saxony and Brunswick has

[50] *Reichsbewertungsgesetz*, August 10, 1925.

it come into general use for all the taxes to which it applies. The provisions of this law have been deferred, together with those of many another financial measure, indefinitely.[51] The difficulties of fixing values for any length of time in a period of rapidly declining real estate values have proved insuperable.

The provisions of the 1930 and the 1934 decrees go much farther than those of the 1925 law. The earlier law provided that the Reich valuation was to be used only if the taxes were levied on capital value. The later legislation provides for the same form of land, building, and business taxes in every state. These taxes are to be, presumably, the most important source of state income, since the rental tax is declining and the decree contemplates a decrease in income tax and corporation tax distributions. Communes, however, are granted three additional sources, the citizen tax, the beer tax, and the coveted local surtax on the Reich income tax.[52] The citizen tax and beer tax are to be uniform throughout the Reich, except as to rates. To make possible the local surtax on income, the rates of the Reich tax are to be reduced, and the Reich is to be compensated by the retention of a larger percentage of the Reich levy.

Greater local independence is achieved through the privilege of levying varying rates on the taxes at their disposal. This independence is distinctly limited, however. These taxes are to bear definite relations to one another, and one cannot be raised unduly without corresponding increases in the others. The final step of this plan is to abolish all the Reich guarantees, the special beer tax indemnity to the southern states and other special provisions of the present system.

Under such a system the taxes throughout the Reich would be uniform in everything except rates, and in the matter of rates all tax bases in the same community would be treated alike. But

---

[51] This law has been completely revised by law of October 16, 1934, but the date when it shall apply to land purchase, land, building, and business taxes has not yet been set.

[52] Later plans would eliminate the citizen tax.

the general level of taxes might differ widely from one community to the next. In this respect this plan varies widely from the trend of recent years. The possibilities for equalization would be much less. Not only would the Reich give up some of its present provisions for equalization, but the states, with more limited resources at their disposal, would have less opportunity for equalization among the communes within the states than they have at present. Each commune would stand on its own feet.

With improved industrial conditions such a system might be feasible, but under present conditions it is, at best, a remote possibility. There are many who maintain that, even in the indefinite future, such local independence is neither feasible nor desirable. Popitz, for instance, holds that the communes have no economic claim to taxes on income which arises from industrial relations covering a much wider economy, nor does he foresee the possibility of any reduction in income tax rates sufficient to make such local surtaxes possible. In his opinion greater equalization, not less, is essential for the ultimate tax system. And the opinion of Popitz carries great weight with the present government.

All signs point to greater uniformity. This is desired by the central government and private industry alike. Communes, being too small to administer independent taxes, are as content to levy on a Reich base as a state base, and the feeble voice of states' rights can no longer be heard. But the balance between equalization and local independence is yet to be achieved; and only the most courageous would guess which way the scales will tip when economic recovery releases them.

For the time being, with no surplus revenues for luxuries, it matters little what tax powers the communes have and what proportion of the tax revenues the Reich chooses to distribute. If it distributes less in tax revenues it inevitably assumes more of the welfare burden which was devouring nearly one-third of the resources of the combined governments in 1933-34 and was still a formidable sum in 1934-35. The manner of distribution is of genuine concern, however. Resources cannot be wasted, and a system of distribution which might send money where it is not urgently needed cannot be tolerated. Need has more and more been substituted for yield as a basis for allocating tax revenues, and to some extent grants for specific functions have been substituted for the distribution of specific taxes. This tendency, forced by depression, is in complete harmony with the centralization of power in the hands of the Reich and the subordination of the states. In a true federal state the redistribution of resources on a large scale is scarcely permissible, but, while the financial provisions of the Weimar Constitution pointed rather to the distribution of specific taxes in proportion to collections, the development of grants-in-aid is not opposed to the fundamental aims of this document.

Equalization has not been entirely a product of depression. From the first the turnover tax was distributed in largest part in proportion to population. The motor vehicle tax, introduced in 1922, was distributed largely on the basis of population and area. The merger tax, which was returned in part from 1926 to 1930, was returned in proportion to losses from the closing down of industrial plants. Two-thirds of the mineral water tax, beginning in 1930, was distributed on the population basis. The income tax, the most important of the taxes distributed, has from the first been returned where the income taxed arises, but also from the first the per capita guarantees have diverted small sums from the richer to the poorer states; and the standards used to measure the origin of income are inevitably only approximate measures and have been changed from time to time. It is not clear that any equalization has been achieved by the revision of these standards, but the income has probably not been assigned precisely as it would have been if the states had been levying independent taxes, although the original provisions of the 1920 law followed the earlier law for double taxation.[53]

Equalization is not limited to the redistribution of taxes. The

[53] Schanz, *op. cit., Finanz-Archiv*, XLIV, 675.

Reich had, even before the war, made small grants-in-aid for a number of purposes. Many of these have been continued. In addition many new aids have been granted. The police subvention was introduced in 1922, and it has reached more than 200 million reichsmarks a year. Special aids have been granted to needy border communities, both on the Rhine and in East Prussia, where changed boundaries have made the industrial situation especially bad, and where the national government has felt that it had a particular obligation. Also, subsidies for unemployment relief in recent years have been very large.[54] In addition to its own attempts at equalization the Reich instructed the states to equalize local burdens and authorized them to reduce individual commune shares in income tax and corporation tax distributions when communes increased their expenditures unreasonably.[55]

As a result of these various measures the percentage of Reich revenues distributed to state and local governments which was returned, at least approximately, to the state of origin, declined from 81.7 in 1925-26 to 46.5 in 1933-34.[56] The bulk of returned revenues is still in proportion to collections, however, and the states, rather than the Reich, are responsible for equalizing local revenues and expenditures.

Prussia, constituting three-fifths of the Reich and containing a wide diversity of industrial conditions, has been comparatively indifferent to Reich equalization. She stands to gain or lose little either way; and there is still ample opportunity for equalization among the communes after the Reich distribution has been made. But wealthy city-states, such as Hamburg and Bremen, and poor and tiny states, like Lippe and Schaumburg-Lippe, are vitally

[54] For the amount of revenue returned to state and local governments on some equalizing base, compared with the amount returned to the place of origin, see Appendix, Table 32, p. 352.

[55] Law of August 10, 1925.

[56] This includes police and welfare subventions. If only the distribution of specific taxes is considered, the percentage returned to the state of origin declined from 85 in 1925-26 to 76 in 1932-33. With the decline in welfare subventions, the percentage has risen again to 63.4 percent in 1934-35.

concerned with the first distribution. There is little opportunity for equalization within the state.

When uniform laws are ultimately established throughout the country, the final equalization among the communes will be determined by the Reich. It seems quite possible that this system of equalization will follow closely that now in effect in Prussia. At least this has the virtue of being already in effect in the largest part of the Reich, and it has proved itself adaptable to varying economic conditions. If the present centralizing tendency continues, however, the Reich may take over local burdens directly, as it has already done in the case of highways, rather than subsidize local governments to support these functions. The general expectation is that distributions of Reich taxes, as such, will play a decreasing rôle in local budgets in the future; and all recent legislation points that way. But whether the resulting readjustment will be achieved through more freedom of local taxation, through grants-in-aid, or through the assumption of more functions by the Reich itself, it is impossible to say.

IV

REDISTRIBUTION OF REVENUES WITHIN THE STATES

THE history of the German states during the fifteen years following the Weimar Constitution is one of continuous struggle with the central government for power; a struggle in which the states lost steadily to the Reich and were ultimately reduced to mere administrative units. Nevertheless, in the short time and with the limited powers allotted to them, some of the states, notably Prussia, constructed systems for the redistribution of tax revenues which are of more interest as experiments in equalization than the system of the Reich itself.

During the first five years, 1919 to 1924, the states retained a considerable degree of nominal financial independence, in spite of the centralization of important taxes in the hands of the Reich, but actually they became wholly dependent on the Reich, owing to inflation. During the second five years, 1924 to 1929, the Reich was drawing the net of financial control more closely around them, but rising tax yields left them with very genuine freedom in expenditures and in the utilization of those revenue sources still at their disposal. The taxes on land and buildings, business, and rentals were, after all, no mean sources of revenue in a period of comparative prosperity, and Reich tax distributions were unexpectedly large. The third period, however, 1929 to 1934, brought a rapid decline in the financial freedom of the states. The depression reduced the yield of available state sources on one hand, and stimulated the process of centralization on the other. Between the two, the states were rapidly reduced to subordinate administrative districts of the Reich, and the final *Gleichschaltung* of 1933 and 1934 was little more than formal recognition of an accomplished fact.

Before describing the fiscal systems of the German state and local governments it is important to consider the whole organization of local government and the distribution of functions between the states and the subordinate municipalities. The organization and the distribution of functions varies somewhat in the different states. Even within a state there are often variations from one section to another. The distribution of functions among the most important governmental units is given for Prussia in Chart 1. The units of government outlined here will be found to vary somewhat in the different provinces, but the variations are not important. The provinces of Prussia are divided into regions (*Regierungsbezirke*), not indicated in this chart, for certain administrative purposes, but these regions do not have independent financial power. The smaller states are not subdivided into provinces, and the local unit corresponding to the circle sometimes

CHART 1

ORGANIZATION OF PRUSSIAN STATE AND LOCAL GOVERNMENT [a]

State (*Land*)		
Principal functions: education, police, administration of justice		

Province (*Provinz*)		
Principal functions: welfare, highways, health		

Rural Circle (*Landkreis*)		City Circle (*Stadtkreis*)
Principal functions: welfare, highways, housing, health		Principal functions: welfare, education, highways, housing, health, police
City (*Stadtgemeinde*)	Rural Commune (*Landgemeinde*)	
Principal functions: education, welfare highways, police	Principal functions: education, welfare highways, police	

[a] Deviations from this organization are to be found in some of the provinces. Also, Berlin is directly under the state and is not subject to provincial control. In addition to the divisions given, special districts (*Zweckverbände*) are sometimes to be found.

TABLE 6

NUMBER, POPULATION, AND AVERAGE EXPENDITURES OF PRUSSIAN
LOCAL GOVERNMENT UNITS, 1931 [a]

Unit	Number	Average Population (In thousands)	Average Per Capita Expenditures (In reichsmarks) [d]
Province.........................	14	243.5	12
Rural circle......................	407	52.7	28
City circle [b].....................	115	110.4	166
Commune [c].......................	30,749	0.7	57

[a] Data from Statistisches Reichsamt, *Statistik des deutschen Reichs*, Vol. CDXL, Berlin, 1934.
[b] Excluding Berlin.   [c] City and rural.
[d] The per capita expenditures of the state were 56 reichsmarks for 1931.

appears under another name; but two or three layers of local government are to be found in every state.

The German local governments form a dual system, one being the agent of the state (now the Reich), and the other being a self-governing authority.[1] The tradition of self-government is strong, and the communes have had broad powers and important obligations in providing for the welfare of their inhabitants. In spite of this freedom, however, it is taken for granted that local authorities will discharge their duties without persuasion, and in consequence the stimulative grant-in-aid has never obtained any foothold in Germany. State aid has taken other forms, including direct state support of specific functions, equalizing grants, and, more recently, distributions of centrally administered taxes with no limitations on their use.

A detailed historical review of the frequent and often unimportant changes in revenue distributions in the seventeen different states, following the Weimar Constitution, would be both tedious and unprofitable. The changes in the distribution of Reich and state taxes to local districts in Prussia between 1924 and 1935 have been summarized in Chart 4.[2] For the rest, it is per-

[1] Popitz, *Der künftige Finanzausgleich, op. cit.*, p. 14.   [2] *Infra*, p. 318.

haps sufficient to say that Bavaria, suffering during the larger part of this period from agricultural depression, revised its provisions for equalization funds almost annually and ultimately developed a fairly flexible system, which left much of the final distribution to administrative discretion. Saxony, with more resources available, made few changes in her system after the first two or three years of experimentation and depended less on equalization funds than did Bavaria. Even so, she returned less than half of the tax distributions to the commune of origin. The smaller states developed a wide variety of systems of distribution, and the poorer ones tended to make frequent changes. All made some effort to equalize, but in most instances the small size of the state left little possibility of equalization on one hand and less need on the other. The communes might be in great need of aid, but if they were all poor, as was sometimes the case, it mattered little whether available resources were distributed in proportion to tax collections, population, or need. The various state systems of distribution, as of 1931,[3] are given in the Appendix, Chart 4, and the proportion of each tax redistributed is given in Table 7.

These systems can be evaluated only in the light of the entire state and local financial organization, since both the amount and the manner of distribution are influenced by the extent to which the state has assumed the support of government activities directly and the extent to which it has left these activities to local support. The proportion of net state and local expenditures borne by the state in 1931-32 varied from 31 percent in Prussia to 66 percent in Mecklenburg-Strelitz.[4] In general the smaller states

[3] 1931 has been chosen as the latest year for which detailed figures can be obtained, showing the effect of the different systems. Important changes since that year have been noted, however.

[4] See *infra*, Table 8. In estimating these percentages, state grants-in-aid are included under state expenditures, but not the Reich taxes redistributed to local governments, even when these are distributed for specific functions. The classification follows that of the *Statistik des deutschen Reichs*, Vol. CDXL, 1934. The Hanseatic cities are omitted since the predominance of the city itself in these city-states results in a quite different governmental structure.

REDISTRIBUTION OF REVENUES

TABLE 7

PERCENTAGE OF REICH AND STATE TAXES DISTRIBUTED BY STATE
TO LOCAL GOVERNMENTS, 1931-32 [a]

State	Income and Corporation	Turn-over	Land Pur-chase	Motor Vehicle	Mineral Water	Beer	Rentals
Prussia	52	55	100	100	100	50	57
Bavaria	39	50	50	45	100	...	18[b]
Saxony	53	55	100	50[m]	100	...	...[c]
Württemberg	33	60	50	...	100	60[d]	...[j]
Baden	35	35	50	...	100	...	64
Thuringia	45	60	50	...	100	...	50
Hesse	35	50	50	100	100	...	...[j]
Mecklenburg-Schwerin	20-40	17	50	...[e]	100	...	...[f]
Oldenburg	57	60	50	100[g]	100	...	...[c]
Brunswick	37	50	50	50	100	...	2½-7½[h]
Anhalt	40	50	50	100	67[k]	67	50
Lippe	40	50	50	40[l]	100	...	57
Mecklenburg-Strelitz	33	25	50	...	100	...	56
Schaumburg-Lippe	45	8	50	50	100	...	53[n]
Hamburg	50-75	50-75	50-75	...	100	...	...[i]
Bremen	50	50	50	...[e]	100	...	100
Lübeck	27	100	...	...	100	...	...[e]

[a] In the case of Reich taxes the percentage is that proportion of the sum received by the state from the Reich which is passed on to local governments.

[b] Approximately. This percentage varies slightly.

[c] Local governments have surtax privilege, however. State share for housing 100 percent to communes and districts.

[d] Not including special indemnity.   [e] No fixed percentage.

[f] Varies in different cities.

[g] In Lübeck and Birkenfeld districts. In Oldenburg district 50 percent.

[h] 7½ in cities, 2½ in rural communes.   [i] Varies with different taxes.

[j] Independent local tax.

[k] The state met the Reich requirement that the entire proceeds of the mineral water tax should go to local governments by pooling mineral water and beer tax yields and distributing two-thirds of the proceeds, this sum being greater than the entire yield of the mineral water tax.

[l] Reduced to 20 percent by law of March 31, 1935.

[m] Reduced to 20 percent by law of July 25, 1935.

[n] Reduced to 30 percent by law of June 7, 1935.

assume a larger proportion of the costs directly; but it should be noted that Bavaria, the second largest state, is among those states which have assumed the largest share of governmental expenditures, and Schaumburg-Lippe, the smallest state of all, has left a larger proportion of the costs to local governments than Bavaria, Saxony, or Württemberg.

TABLE 8

COMPARISON OF PROPORTION OF STATE AND LOCAL EXPENDITURES INCURRED BY STATE GOVERNMENTS WITH PROPORTION OF REICH TAXES RETAINED BY STATE GOVERNMENTS [a]

State	Percentage of Expenditures Incurred by State Governments	Percentage of Reich Taxes Retained by State Governments	Percentage of Reich and Rental Taxes Retained by State Governments
Prussia	30.9	46.2	48.1
Bavaria	51.1	71.6	74.9
Saxony	42.3	48.2	54.9
Württemberg	42.5	64.7	67.1
Baden	41.5	69.6	60.1
Thuringia	51.4	65.0	67.5
Hesse	42.6	61.1	61.3
Mecklenburg-Schwerin	54.3	75.6	65.1
Oldenburg	36.5	45.0	46.2
Brunswick	51.3	61.1	65.1
Anhalt	45.9	56.2	60.0
Lippe	53.8	59.6	65.0
Mecklenburg-Strelitz	65.8	76.1	67.5
Schaumburg-Lippe	42.0	72.4	70.8
Total	36.2	52.6	54.2

[a] *Statistik des deutschen Reichs*, Vol. CDXL, 1934. The expenditures for which these percentages have been computed are the *Zuschussbedarf*, that part of expenditures not covered by special income, such as grants-in-aid or fees.

When the percentage of expenditures assumed by the different states is compared with the percentage of Reich taxes which they retain for their own use, it is apparent that they have retained a disproportionate share for themselves. This is true of every state. All the states combined have retained more than one-half of the

Reich taxes, while assuming only a little more than one-third of the costs of government. When the rental tax, the one important state tax shared with local governments, is added to Reich taxes, the proportion retained by the state is even larger. This is not necessarily unreasonable. Local governments have sources not available to the states, in the form of the citizen tax and local taxes on amusements and retail drinks. There are no state taxes of corresponding importance which are not shared with local governments. Moreover, it is more appropriate for the states to take the larger share of the income tax and leave the real estate and business taxes in largest part to local governments, since local expenditures are apt to confer more direct benefits than state expenditures on real estate owners and business concerns. Nevertheless, it seems probable that the states have to some extent taken advantage of their authority and appropriated whatever has been necessary to balance state budgets, leaving the local governments to manage as best they can. The changes occurring between 1928-29, the year of greatest tax yields, and 1931-32, when the effects of the depression are evident, demonstrate this. In all but two of the fourteen states [5] the percentage of state and local expenditures met by the state government was less in 1931-32 than in 1928-29. This is, perhaps, to be expected, since the important increases in costs were for welfare, an essentially local function. Instead of helping local governments to meet this new burden, the majority of states, themselves in need of revenue, retained an even larger percentage of the declining Reich tax distributions for their own use. Only three states returned a larger proportion of these Reich taxes in 1931-32 than in 1928-29, and in none of these three was the increase in tax distributions in proportion to the increase in local expenditures. Only in Saxony and Mecklenburg-Strelitz, where the proportion of expenditures assumed by the state was greater in 1931-32 than in 1928-29, would the state government seem to have assumed its share of growing burdens. In nine states the local governments

[5] Excluding the city-states.

were left with a larger share of the burden and a smaller share of Reich tax revenues.

In Bavaria, where the discrepancy between the proportion of expenditures borne by the state and the proportion of Reich taxes retained has been very great, the local governments were not satisfied with their share in Reich and state taxes before the depression.[6] But where in 1928-29 the local governments met only 44 percent of costs, in 1931-32 they had to meet 49 percent. And where in 1928-29 they received 33 percent of Reich tax distributions, in 1931-32 they received only 28 percent of a smaller amount. This situation has since been alleviated by the greatly improved condition of industry in this state.

The greatest discrepancy is to be found in Schaumburg-Lippe, where the state retains nearly three-fourths of the Reich tax revenues and meets less than half the governmental costs. This has been possible because the state contains no large cities with heavy local expenditures, and it has suffered less from unemployment than most regions. Consequently, per capita governmental costs are exceptionally low. Only Lippe and Oldenburg have comparably low expenditures. Also, Schaumburg-Lippe has left the business tax almost entirely to local governments.

The proportion of each tax redistributed to local governments varies widely for most taxes, although municipalities always get a substantial slice of the three most important taxes: the income, corporation, and turnover taxes. The comparative uniformity in the proportions of land purchase and mineral water taxes distributed is the result of Reich requirements.

Turning to the bases on which Reich taxes are redistributed, two factors are recognized, the origin of the tax and the need of the community. But there are innumerable combinations and variations of these factors. These will be discussed in detail in a later chapter. It is sufficient to note here the extent to which different bases are used. Origin is used as the sole standard for the distribution of the land purchase tax in most states and as one

[6] Schanz, *Finanz-Archiv, op. cit.*, XLIV, 696.

of the more important standards for the distribution of income and corporation tax revenues in all states but one. The yield of a former local tax is also a common standard. This factor was introduced at first in order to guarantee to local governments their former income; but as late as 1931-32 it was still the basis for distributing at least a part of the income and corporation taxes in seven states, in spite of the fact that pre-war or pre-inflation income must have become a very inaccurate measure of current needs. This standard has also been used, in scattering instances, for other taxes.

The origin of some other centrally administered tax is occasionally the basis of distribution. Thus, in Saxony, both the corporation and turnover taxes are returned, in part, in proportion to the origin of the income tax, and other instances of this are to be found. The origin of the income tax has not proved such a satisfactory standard for the distribution of income tax money that its extension to other taxes would seem to be warranted. It should be noted, however, in the case of Saxony, that, while other taxes are distributed in part according to the origin of the income tax, the income tax itself is distributed in part on other bases. More common than the distribution of one tax according to the origin or yield of another, is the practice of pooling a part of the proceeds of one tax with those of another and distributing both according to some measure of need.

The most frequent standard for tax distributions is a simple per capita basis. This is found for at least a part of the turnover tax in eleven states, and instances of its use can be found for every other tax distributed to local governments. A few states, however, have not been satisfied with a simple per capita distribution and have weighted population according to the size of the commune, the proportion of school children, or both. Less frequent measures for tax distributions are highway mileage and area for the motor vehicle tax and the proportion of the population unemployed for other taxes. Occasionally the percentage of the tax to be returned to specific local units is fixed. The basis on which such percentages have been determined is not apparent.

The assignment of part of the proceeds of a tax to an equalization fund, to be administered at the discretion of state officials, is common practice. There is no state which does not have some such fund,[7] and there is no tax which has not been used, at least in part, for this purpose in some state. These funds are sometimes dedicated to a specific function, such as welfare, highways, or schools; sometimes they are for general use.

When the state is meeting a large part of the governmental costs through direct expenditures, the need for equalization is not so great as in the states leaving the larger part of the burden to local units. Mecklenburg-Strelitz, where the state had taken over about two-thirds of state and local costs, had no state equalization fund before it was merged with Mecklenburg-Schwerin in 1933,[8] and most of the small amount of Reich taxes which it redistributed to local governments was returned according to origin. In contrast, Oldenburg, where in 1931-32 the state was meeting only a little more than one-third of expenditures, and which in this same year redistributed a larger proportion of such taxes to local governments than any other state, returned less than half these taxes to the commune of origin and had a very substantial equalization fund. In the case of Oldenburg the widely scattered sections of the state have made central administration difficult, but the smaller states, which are more closely unified geographically, have depended less than the larger states on equalization through redistribution of Reich taxes according to need and more on direct support of education and other functions. There are, however, wide variations, and the extent to which the central government in Bavaria has assumed the direct cost of governmental functions suggests that only Prussia is too large for extensive centralization of administration. Certainly

[7] Bremen, however, depends on circle, rather than state, equalization.
[8] Law of December 15, 1933.

Prussia has not attempted to solve the problem by such central-ization, but has developed, instead, a complicated system for the transfer of Reich and state funds to local governments.

Prussia has the advantage of size and a wide variety of indus-tries which have made equalization at once possible and impor-tant. And Prussia has a heritage of administrative efficiency that has stood her in good stead. For these reasons, and because of the further fact that the future system of tax distribution will prob-ably be essentially the present Prussian system, however modi-fied, this system is of particular interest.

Prussia made many changes in the proportion of income and corporation taxes redistributed to local governments during in-flation, but no change was made in the proportion returned from 1924 until 1934, when the local share was reduced. No change has been made in the basis of distribution since inflation, except for increasing deductions from the local share returned accord-ing to origin. The sums deducted are used for special subven-tions and for equalization. At first by far the largest part of the local 50.5 percent was returned in fixed proportions to provinces, rural circles, and communes, respectively. The distribution among the local governments of each class was on the same basis as the Reich distribution, i.e., origin. Smaller sums were assigned to the school equalization fund and to the provinces and rural circles in compensation for the former *Dotationen*. Population, area, highway mileage, and former sums received from *Dota-tionen* determined the share of each local jurisdiction in these latter sums. The essential elements of this system of distribution have not been changed, but the introduction of numerous guar-antees and special subventions continually modifies its applica-tion and reduces the share available for the residual distribution. The first modification was to guarantee all communes at least 80 percent of their former revenue from income taxes, the difference being obtained from communes obtaining more than 200 percent of their former revenue. The year chosen for the standard was

1911-12, since that was the latest pre-war year for which adequate information was available. In 1925 this guarantee was increased, but made relative. The relative guarantee holds today. Those communes for which the estimated distribution of income and corporation taxes falls below the 1911-12 per capita income tax yield [9] have their bases weighted to equal 100 percent of the 1911-12 per capita yield. Thus, if a commune's estimated per capita share on an unweighted base were one-half of the 1911-12 per capita revenue, this base would be doubled. The result is to increase this commune's share at the expense of communes receiving more than their 1911-12 per capita income, since the total base is increased by this weighting and the share of those communes with unweighted bases is correspondingly diminished.[10] The communes with weighted bases do not necessarily, of course, receive 100 percent of their 1911-12 per capita income. In 1927-28, e.g., the estimated yield to which the commune bases

[9] Modifications were made in case the communes had evidence that the 1913-14 or 1914-15 yield was substantially greater than that for 1911-12 or in case population increases between 1910 and 1925 had been exceptional.

[10] To illustrate: Assume that in 1911-12 City A had a per capita income tax yield of 10 marks per capita and City B had a per capita income tax yield of 8 marks per capita. Assume further that, according to the Reich formula for determining origin, A is assigned 500,000 units (*Rechnungsanteile*) and B is assigned 900,000 in a given year. The unit for that year is assumed to be estimated at 10 pfennigs. The population of each city is assumed to be 10,000. Thus A is assigned 50,000 reichsmarks, or 5 reichsmarks per capita, and B is assigned 90,000 reichsmarks, or 9 reichsmarks per capita. Since A's 1911 per capita income was double this sum, A is assigned 1,000,000 units, or twice the amount assigned by the Reich formula. B's 900,000 units remain unchanged, since the 1911 per capita income is less than the present. If these two cities constituted the entire state and the sum available for distribution were that indicated by the above figures, 140,000 reichsmarks (1,400,000 units at 10 pfennigs per unit), then with the weighting resulting from the relative guarantee each city gets, not the 100,000 reichsmarks and 90,000 reichsmarks indicated by the number of units and the value of the unit, but 10/19 and 9/19, respectively, of the 140,000 reichsmarks available, or 73,684 reichsmarks and 66,316 reichsmarks, respectively. Thus, the city with the 1911 income of 10 marks per capita now receives 7.68 reichsmarks, and the city with the 1911 income of 8 marks per capita now receives 6.63 reichsmarks. Actually, the determination of shares for each commune is very much more complicated than this, since there are two taxes involved, income and corporation, each with its own system of allocation. These are combined according to proportions determined by administrative regulations. For a full and clear account of the way in which this guarantee is administered see F. K. Suren, *Preussischer Finanzausgleich*, Berlin, 1927, pp. 113 *et seq.*

were adjusted permitted a guarantee of 91 percent of pre-war per capita income. The actual yield permitted a guarantee of 95 percent.[11] The weighting is fixed in advance on the basis of estimated, not actual, income. It is apparent that the lower the estimated yield of the income and corporation taxes, the larger the number of communes falling below the pre-war average and the larger the proportion of the yield that will be diverted to such communes at the expense of others. Consequently, it is to the advantage of communes with current per capita yields in excess of pre-war yields to have the estimate placed above the actual yield, and it is to the interest of other communes to have the estimate placed below the actual yield. This offers opportunity for political pressure, and political pressure has been brought to bear.[12]

No figures are available to show the extent to which income and corporation taxes are diverted, as a result of this guarantee, in Prussia as a whole, but figures for individual cities indicate very substantial redistributions.[13] Popitz states that in consequence of this guarantee one can no longer speak of distribution of taxes in proportion to taxable capacity.[14] The practical effect is to favor East Prussia and the industrial section of the Rhine Province.[15] By happy accident these are sections in genuine need of aid. With the reduced yields of recent years the relative importance of this guarantee must have increased greatly. It is easy to understand, with the uncertainties that followed inflation, why the government should have reached back to a period of stable values for its standards. But the fact that the more or less chance conditions of a single pre-war year should have been allowed to continue to dominate the system of tax distribution after the administration had accumulated a new experience on which to build is only to be

[11] *Denkschrift des preussischen Landtags*, No. 2275, 1928-29, p. 4.

[12] Suren, *op. cit.*, pp. 127 *et seq.*

[13] Suren, *op. cit.*, pp. 126 *et seq.*, Popitz, *Der Künftige Finanzausgleich, op. cit.*, p. 121.

[14] Popitz, *Der Künftige Finanzausgleich, op. cit.*, p. 193.

[15] A. Hensel, "Der Landesausgleich," *Vierteljahresschrift für Steuer- und Finanzrecht*, 1929, III, 51.

explained on the ground that the government was awaiting more stable conditions and the revision of the Reich system before making any thoroughgoing changes. There would seem to be no justification for a system which takes from Berlin and gives to Frankfurt-am-Main when the per capita income tax yield in Frankfurt is 50 percent greater than the per capita income tax yield in Berlin.[16] Moreover, the system is so complex that Popitz rightly refers to it as a secret science of a small and consecrated circle.[17] Finally, it can be deliberately manipulated for political ends by underestimating or overestimating the amount of the tax available for distribution. There is, of course, no thought of extending this feature of the Prussian system to other states or of continuing it in Prussia indefinitely.

Other modifications of the basic distribution of income and corporation taxes followed the relative guarantee. Beginning in 1927, 10 million reichsmarks were deducted before the division between state and local governments for a special distribution to communes bordering on city-states. Beginning in 1929 a part of the corporation taxes allocated to communes was diverted to an equalization fund in those cases in which the commune's per capita share exceeded the average. Beginning in 1930 the estimated local cost of police was deducted from the local share of income and corporation taxes, and then distributed to the local governments on a different base from the residual income and corporation tax funds. Also, in 1930 it was provided that if the turnover tax fell below a fixed sum the difference should be taken from income and corporation taxes and distributed on the turnover tax base.

No exact estimate can be placed on the proportion of the local share which finally reaches the localities on the basis of origin, but it is certainly much less than half, if, indeed, any revenue can be said to be returned on the basis of origin under such a system.

[16] H. Bychelberg, "Der Finanzausgleich und seine Bedeutung," *Vierteljahresschrift für Steuer- und Finanzrecht*, 1931, p. 346.
[17] *Der künftige Finanzausgleich, op. cit.*, p. 193.

Mineral water and beer tax revenues have been added to the commune share of income and corporation taxes and are distributed in the same way.

The local share of the turnover tax is distributed to circles and communes on a weighted population base. The weighting has been changed several times, but at present the population is weighted for the size of the commune, the weight increasing to 2.25 for cities having more than 50,000 population. This weighted population is then weighted again for the proportion of school children in excess of the average for cities of that size. Thus a city of 100,000 population would be credited with 225,-000; and if the number of school children per 100 population exceeded the average for such cities by one percent (i.e., 11.8 instead of 10.8 children per hundred), the weighted population would be increased by one-tenth, or 22,500.[18] This city of 100,000 would finally be credited, under these conditions, with a population of 247,500.

The motor vehicle tax was at first distributed to provinces and circles in proportion to population and area. After many revisions a percentage of this tax, fixed by law, is now returned to each province, and the redistribution within the province is determined by a province committee. The basis for the percentages fixed by law is undoubtedly highway need, but the extent to which different tests of need may have determined them is not apparent, nor does this allow for changes in relative needs of the provinces, barring a revision of the law. The land purchase tax alone is distributed where collected.

This system is needlessly complex, and some of the provisions are admittedly emergency measures; but there has been a steady development toward a system of distribution which is measured by need rather than by tax yields. The relative guarantee would seem to have lost whatever value it may originally have possessed,

[18] The increase in weight is one percent for every one-tenth of one percent excess of the proportion of school children above the average.

and the police subvention system might well be simplified and still achieve the same results; but the base for the distribution of the turnover tax would seem to offer a reasonable measure of general financial need, and the increasing diversion of income and corporation taxes for specific functions reduces the importance of the relative guarantee. The bases on which the various sums deducted from the income and corporation taxes are distributed would seem to be suitable measures of need.

A similar trend toward equalization in the distribution of Reich taxes can be found in almost every state. In spite of the many variations in state provisions for this distribution, the movement away from the policy of returning Reich taxes to the place of origin stands out clearly. To cite some of the more important instances, Brunswick began to distribute part of its income and corporation taxes in proportion to population in 1927, and in the same year Anhalt began distributing part of its corporation tax in proportion to population. Württemberg began distributing part of these taxes in proportion to school children in 1930; and new and growing equalization funds have been built up, largely from the same taxes, in Bavaria, Württemberg, Hesse, Oldenburg, and Anhalt in recent years. In consequence, whereas in 1925-26 approximately two-thirds of the Reich taxes returned to local governments were returned to the community of origin, in 1931-32 this proportion had dropped to approximately two-fifths.[19] To what extent this trend is a normal development, resulting from experience with the new system, and to what extent it has been forced by depression, it is difficult to say; but the fact that the trend was apparent, even when economic conditions were comparatively good, suggests that central administration and uniform taxes must be followed by distribution of revenues to local districts in accordance with some measure of need. Local government needs bear no such uniform relation to local tax

[19] No exact figure can be arrived at, in view of the fact that where origin is one of several factors entering into a distribution formula it is impossible to earmark any specific sum as having been distributed according to origin.

sources that the return of fixed percentages of uniform taxes to the local districts in which they were collected can take place on any large scale. Equalization in one form or another is demanded.

The ultimate test of the adequacy of the present Reich and state systems of distribution would seem to be their adaptability to the needs of the bottom layer of government, the communes. The Reich itself has wide powers of adjustment, and thus far, although limiting their sources of income, the Reich has left the states almost complete freedom in deciding the manner and amount of sharing the available revenues with the local divisions. The intermediate provinces and circles, while endowed with few sources of income for their own exclusive use, have for the most part been granted adequate power to levy on communes for their needs. A brief description of the financial system of the Prussian provinces and circles should be sufficient to illustrate this, although the financing of these intermediate local governments, as well as the nature and functions of the governmental units themselves, vary widely from state to state.

In Prussia, the province has just two sources of revenue, distributions from Reich taxes and levies on the revenue of the circles. The latter is the only one which provincial officials can adjust to their needs, but such emphasis has been laid on the importance of keeping these levies constant from year to year that those provinces not fortunate enough to possess substantial reserves have met declining Reich tax distributions by cutting highway expenditures rather than by increasing their levies.[20] In fact, these provincial levies dropped 20 percent between 1928-29 and 1931-32.

The circles have a number of local taxes at their disposal, but they, too, depend for the bulk of their revenues on Reich tax distributions and levies on the income of the communes, the latter being the elastic element in their revenue system. Levies may be made both on the commune real estate and business taxes

[20] Statement of Prussian state official.

and on the communes' combined revenues from income, corpora-tion, and citizen taxes. The rate of the levy must ordinarily be the same for the taxes within each of these two groups, but the rates for the two groups may differ. In practice this means that, since the ratio of income, corporation, and citizen tax revenues to real estate and business tax revenues is higher in urban than in rural regions, the circle can favor rural regions by levying relatively more on the first group and can favor urban regions by levying relatively more on the second group. There are instances of circle levies on income, corporation, and citizen tax revenues in excess of 100 percent. It is apparent that the excess must come from real estate and business taxes, but it is paid in proportion to the receipts from the other taxes. Thus the rural taxpayers benefit at the expense of urban taxpayers, and urban and rural resources are equalized.

The revenues of the circles have, on the whole, increased more rapidly than those of other governmental units. In 1925-26 the per capita tax revenue for rural circles in Prussia was 181 per-cent greater than in 1913-14, whereas the per capita tax revenues of the cities had increased only 61 percent. The increase for all governments for the entire Reich during the same period was 141 percent.[21] In recent years, with the decline of other sources, the circles have tended to increase the levies on the communes. Be-tween 1928-29 and 1931-32 levies for rural circles in Prussia were increased 23 percent, and the proportion of circle revenues from this source grew, in consequence, from 27.6 to 39.1 percent. This can be explained in part by the transfer of functions from communes to circles. In welfare and highway administration, especially, there has been a marked tendency for the circles to take over burdens hitherto falling on the communes. Neverthe-less, the circles are in a stronger position financially than their subordinate communes and it seems probable that the circles, as well as the Reich and the states, have taken advantage of such

[21] Rath, *op. cit.*, p. 117.

power as they possess. Where in 1928-29 these levies took 17.6 percent of commune income in 1931-32 they took 29.2 percent.

Thus the communes are at the mercy of all the overlying governments. Not only can these decrease the communes' residual share in revenues at will, but also they can force the communes to shoulder an increasing share of the costs. As pointed out above, the local governments' share in tax distributions has decreased in recent years, while their share in expenditures has steadily increased.[22] To bridge the gap the communes increased their tax rates until they became intolerable and increased charges for local public utility services until revenue diminished because citizens could no longer afford to avail themselves of these services. Belated legal restrictions on such taxes and rates were scarcely needed. They had reached their economic limit. There was no elastic element left in the revenue system.[23]

Meanwhile commune expenditures were growing. Four-fifths of these were mandatory before depression, and while substantial economies were possible and have been effected, welfare costs have grown more than other costs could be cut. In this financial strait-jacket the communes have been practically helpless. All possibilities of adapting revenues to changing needs rest on the charity of superior governments.

The adaptability of this system to varying local needs can best be determined by considering individual cases. Even when local governments are grouped by size and form of government, averages eliminate just those local variations which it is important for the system to meet. Unfortunately, while data for groups of

[22] This includes circle revenues and expenditures.

[23] As early as 1924-25 the median business tax revenue in Prussian communes was 150 percent greater than in 1913-14, while the median income tax revenue was 25 percent lower than in 1913-14. The median real estate tax revenue was 30 percent higher than in 1913-14 (Rath, *op. cit.*, p. 112). At their peak, in 1930-31, business taxes yielded five times as much to the local governments as in 1913-14 (in local governments outside the Hanseatic cities), land and building taxes yielded between two and three times as much, and income and corporation taxes less than twice as much.

communes are quite complete, comparable data for individual communes are difficult to obtain. A limited study has been possible, however, of individual cases.

Twelve cities have been selected for this study, six comparatively well-to-do cities and six comparatively poor ones. The important data for these are given in the Appendix, Table 36. It is apparent that with such a small number of cases the medians given in the first two columns of the table are highly unstable figures. Examination of the data for the individual cities shows, however, that these medians represent very real differences in the two groups, although no importance can be attached to their exact values. The tests of ability and need applied in selecting the cities in the two groups were the per capita yield of the income and corporation taxes, the proportion of school children in the population, and the proportion of the inhabitants receiving public relief. Münster has been grouped with the well-to-do cities and Offenbach with the comparatively poor, although the per capita yield of the income and corporation taxes in Offenbach appears to be greater than that in Münster because of the exceedingly high proportion of the population of Offenbach and the comparatively small proportion of the population of Münster receiving public relief. Münster is the seat of provincial government for Westphalia. Also, there is a university in the city. Consequently a large proportion of its inhabitants belong to the professional classes. Münster is not wealthy, as are the other cities of the group; but with a comparatively small working population it has not suffered from depression to the same extent as the others, and its resources are more nearly in proportion to its needs than is the case in many wealthier cities. Offenbach, on the contrary, is an essentially industrial city which has suffered severely from unemployment. The figure of 171 per thousand inhabitants receiving public relief does not include the dependents of those receiving relief. If the average number of dependents in Offenbach corresponded to the average number for the Reich as a whole at this time, there were 346 persons per thousand—more than one-third of the inhabitants—receiving public support. The figures for income and corporation tax yields is, of course, based on 1929 income. If the actual yields were available for the later year for which the relief figures are given, the figure for tax yields, as well as the figure for those on relief, would doubtless place this city in the poorer group. In Duisburg-Hamborn, with a per capita income tax yield not far below that of Münster, 40 percent of the population were receiving public relief when unemployment was at its peak.[24]

All but two of the twelve cities given are in Prussia. Stuttgart is in Württemberg, and Offenbach is in Hesse. The latter is, however, so close to the Prussian Frankfurt-am-Main as to be almost a suburb of this wealthy city. Six of the cities, Cologne, Düsseldorf, Münster, Duisburg-Hamborn, Gelsenkirchen, and Herne are in two adjoining provinces, the Rhine Province and Westphalia, in a highly industrialized region. Two more, Breslau and Hindenburg, are in Silesia in the southeast part of Germany and have suffered seriously from the loss of territory on the eastern border.

A comparison of the two groups of cities for 1928-29 and 1932-33 shows that the wealthier cities were incurring much larger expenditures per capita in 1928-29 than were the poorer cities. In 1932-33, however, their positions are reversed, the per capita expenditures of the wealthier group having declined in every instance and the per capita expenditures of the poorer group having increased in five out of the six cities. The expenditures in question are net, after all special sources of income, including subventions, have been deducted; that is, they are the expenditures to be met from taxes and the surpluses from municipal industries. The reason for the changes in these per capita expenditures in the two groups of cities is, of course, that, with

[24] 180,000 out of 440,000.

shrinking resources, municipal salaries have been cut and all unnecessary expenditures eliminated. The wealthier cities were able to save more by such economies than they were forced to pay out in increased welfare burdens. The poorer group, however, having fewer luxury expenditures to be eliminated on one hand and much greater increases in welfare burdens on the other hand, found their total costs growing in spite of all economies. This is to be expected. When welfare expenditures are examined, however, it is apparent that, while the total welfare expenditures per capita are markedly higher in the poorer group of cities, the amount falling on local resources is distinctly less. Thus a smaller proportion of the net expenditures is going for welfare costs in the poorer group of cities than in the wealthier group of cities.

The difference between total welfare expenditures and welfare expenditures met from local resources comes largely from the substantial Reich subventions for unemployment relief. Through these the Reich would seem to have equalized most successfully, since that part of the welfare burden left to local resources is less in the group of cities with the more limited resources, although the total welfare burden in these cities is greater. Under these conditions, however, it is surprising to find that the total costs falling on local resources are greater in the poorer group of cities than in the wealthier group. Expenditures for other functions than welfare are much heavier in the poorer than in the wealthier cities. This can only be explained on the ground that the large number of unemployed have occasioned unusual city expenditures in other divisions of government. A public works program for the reduction of unemployment, for example, would not be charged to welfare as such. Reich subventions have been substantial, but there is nothing to indicate that they have been so generous that the cities receiving them have been tempted to indulge in unnecessary expenditures. A review of local tax rates is sufficient to make this clear. Two such rates have been given in

Table 36.[25] It is apparent from these figures that poor as well as wealthy cities have increased their local tax rates during the period in question, and the poor cities still have higher rates than the wealthy ones. The only exception to this is in the case of the business tax, which has been reduced in three of the poorer cities. In one of these, Duisburg, however, it is still as high as the highest of the rates in the wealthy cities. In the other two, Breslau and Hindenburg, the rates are lower than in the wealthy cities, owing to the special *Osthilfe* given by the Reich for the reduction of these taxes. Reich subsidies to the eastern sections of Germany have taken many forms in the past decade, and the equitableness of some of these has been challenged. But in this particular instance there would seem to be no question as to need. Hindenburg is especially poor; and the rate of the real estate tax in both Breslau and Hindenburg is still higher than in any of the other cities under consideration. In fact, only two of the 154 cities of Prussia had higher real estate tax rates in this year.

In this connection it should be noted that the low per capita relief expenditures in Hindenburg are due largely to the meager relief allowances. The allowance for a married couple without children is 40 marks per month in Hindenburg as compared with 67 marks per month in Stuttgart. Consequently, with approximately the same proportion of the inhabitants receiving public relief in the two cities, the total cost of relief is 40 marks per capita in Hindenburg and 71 marks per capita in Stuttgart. None of the other cities in question, and for that matter no other city of its size in Germany, has cut relief rates as low as Hindenburg.

The part played by specific Reich tax distributions in these

[25] The rates given are in percentages of the state base. The local taxes on real estate vary for improved and unimproved land and for agricultural land. Only the rate for improved land has been given in the table. This is, of course, by far the most important in cities of this size. For the business tax only the rate on yield has been given, since this is the only one these cities have in common. All the cities have, however, in addition to this, a business tax on wages or on capital. Tax rates are not given for the two cities outside Prussia since, with a different state base, rates would not be comparable.

cities remains to be considered. In 1928-29 these distributions were very substantial, covering from 20 to 40 percent of those expenditures to be met from taxes and the surpluses of municipal industries. Little equalization would seem to have been achieved, however, since the poorer cities received less per capita than the wealthy ones. A comparison of these tax distributions with welfare expenditures shows that the Reich distributions more than covered welfare expenditures in the wealthier group of cities and met 86 percent of such expenditures in the poorer group. In 1932-33, with greater welfare burdens and greatly curtailed tax distributions, only 15 percent of the welfare expenditures of the wealthier cities and only 14 percent of the welfare expenditures of the poorer cities were covered by Reich taxes. Even so, a greater measure of equalization would seem to have been achieved by these distributions. The poorer cities received both more per capita and more in proportion to their needs than did the wealthier ones. This offered slight compensation, however, for the fact that the per capita distributions of Reich taxes fell to one-third of their former size just when per capita costs were doubling. In time of stress the system of Reich tax distributions has failed miserably.

Turning to individual cities, the Reich taxes covered 6 percent of expenditures in Frankfurt-am-Main and 12 percent in Hindenburg in 1932-33. Frankfurt-am-Main is undoubtedly one of the richest cities in Germany, and Hindenburg one of the poorest. Measured in terms of an index which takes resources into account, as well as obligations, the cities rank as shown in Table 9.

The index as given is too crude for actual use in determining the variations in need of the different cities with exactness.[26] A detailed study of local budgets of the different cities might well reveal that the proportion of school children and the proportion of persons on public relief should not be given equal weight. Moreover, the figure for measuring local taxpaying ability is

[26] See Table 36, n. *h*, for explanation of index.

TABLE 9

COMPARISON OF TEN PRUSSIAN CITIES RANKED ACCORDING TO
INDEX OF NEED AND ACCORDING TO REICH TAX
DISTRIBUTIONS, 1932-33

City	Index of Need	Per Capita Reich Tax Distributions	Percentage of Net Expenditures Covered by Reich Tax Distributions
Hindenburg...............	1	5	1
Herne...................	2	4	4
Gelsenkirchen.............	3	1	2
Breslau.................	4	3	8
Duisburg-Hamborn........	5	2	7
Cologne.................	6	7	9
Münster.................	7	10	6
Frankfurt-am-Main........	8	8	10
Düsseldorf...............	9	6	3
Potsdam.................	10	9	5

undoubtedly faulty in that the figures are for an earlier year than
the other figures, and the relative ability of the cities in the later
year had doubtless changed materially. Even for the year in question income and corporation tax yields would reflect only dimly
the potential yield of local taxes. Nevertheless, the factors used in
constructing the index are believed to be important, and, in spite
of the limitation of available data, the index as given probably
offers some rough measure of the need of the different cities. If
this is true the Reich tax distributions, as modified by Prussia, did
achieve some small measure of equalization. At least the five poor
cities all received more per capita than the five wealthy ones. But
the extent of the equalization achieved by these distributions is obviously limited. Nor is this due solely to the greatly reduced sums
distributed in 1932-33. Reich taxes distributed to local governments as a whole exceeded Reich subventions to local governments for welfare in this year. Yet the subventions for welfare
achieved a very important degree of equalization. If the Reich tax
distributions had been allocated with equalization alone in view,

they could have been an important factor in equalizing burdens. With the systems of distribution in effect, however, only a minor degree of equalization was achieved.

To summarize, under present conditions the system of distributing tax revenues equalizes resources to a small degree. The same amount of money distributed on other bases could achieve a very substantial degree of equalization. When, however, more aid to the poorer communes became imperative, the Reich chose, rather than to make major revisions in its system of distribution, to divert new revenues from the system of tax distribution to a system of direct grants to the communes based on specific needs. Considering the state systems as a whole, it is apparent that, while moving steadily toward equalization of resources, the different parts of the financial structure have never been co-ordinated and are often working at odds. The greatest equalization has been achieved in school funds. Equalization for other specific functions lags far behind; and the distributions of tax revenues, as such, are in most instances on unsatisfactory bases. The *Reichssparkommissar* complains, in one memorandum after another, that state equalization has been inadequate.[27] This is generally recognized, and eventually a better co-ordinated system will doubtless be established; but tax reform must wait on the reallocation of governmental functions themselves, and the establishment of the new districts (*Gauer*). Meanwhile state administrators must be content to patch a little and to wait.

[27] See, e.g., *Gutachten über die Staatsverwaltung des Volksstaates Hessen*, 1929, p. 21; *Gutachten über die Landesverwaltung Lippes*, 1930, p. 29.

V

DISTRIBUTION OF SUPPORT OF SPECIFIC FUNCTIONS AMONG THE REICH, STATE, AND LOCAL GOVERNMENTS

CENTRALIZATION of administration of the various governmental functions has lagged behind centralization of financial administration. It is this fact that creates the problem of redistributing the centrally administered revenues among the underlying subdivisions in the first place; and the solution of the problems of redistribution may well come through the further centralization of functions. If the sums to be transferred play a minor part in local finances, most of the difficulties of distribution disappear. Under these conditions the division of support of the different governmental functions cannot be ignored.

Those functions absorbing the largest proportion of state and local tax revenues are education, highways, police, welfare, and housing. The five combined accounted for nearly two-thirds (65.5 percent) of net state and local expenditures [1] in 1913-14 and between three-fourths and four-fifths in recent years (78.6 percent in 1925-26 and 76.5 percent in 1931-32).[2] These same functions concerned the central government very little before the war. They accounted for only 4.9 percent of Reich expenditures in 1913-14. Since the war, however, the central government has assumed increasing responsibility for these activities, and Reich expenditures for the five together came to 17.9 percent of net

[1] Those expenditures not met from fees and other administrative revenue, designated in official reports as *Zuschussbedarf.*

[2] The classification commonly used in government statistics has been followed here. "Education" includes science, art, and the Church, as well as schools; "highways" include waterways; "police" includes fire protection and a considerable group of administrative functions not designated as police in the United States; "welfare" includes social insurance.

Reich expenditures in 1925-26 and 31.9 percent in 1931-32. Important changes in the support of these five functions are traced briefly below.

EDUCATION

Education has long been considered a function of the various states in Germany, but only since the war have the states assumed the major part of the cost. State support, as usual, has lagged behind control. Prussia gave small school aids to poor districts even before 1850, but as late as the eighteen-seventies the state was contributing less than 7 percent of school costs; and in spite of the fact that aid was quadrupled in the next decade it had reached only 12 percent of the total cost by the end of the nineteenth century.[3] Saxony, unifying the school system of the whole state as early as 1835, left the support entirely to local authorities until 1873, when state aid for poor districts was introduced.[4] Bavaria, on the contrary, began to contribute state funds for education as early as 1807, although the schools were left in the hands of the Church until 1883.[5]

All the states were making substantial contributions to the cost of schools by 1913, the proportion varying from 33 percent in Mecklenburg-Schwerin to 88 percent in Anhalt.[6] These contributions took many forms. All the states contributed to salaries, most of them paying a fixed percentage of the cost, or a fixed sum per teacher. Anhalt, at one extreme, paid all salaries for common-school teachers, and Oldenburg, at the other, contributed only in poor districts. All the states but Lippe contributed to building costs, although seven limited such aid to poor districts and five more included them in their contributions to school expenditures as a whole, rather than as specific building aids. In Hamburg and Lübeck the state met the entire building costs. Special aids to poor districts were given in the majority of states. The seven states

---

[3] Grice, *op. cit.*, pp. 270-71.
[5] *Idem.*
[4] *Einzelschrift*, No. 17, p. 21.
[6] *Einzelschrift*, No. 6, *passim.*

not making such contributions were all small, including the three Hanseatic cities, and, except Mecklenburg-Schwerin, were states which had shouldered more than the average proportion of school costs.

All the states contributed to the cost of higher education. Many of the special and higher schools were state institutions supported entirely by the state, and even when they were local institutions the state usually made generous contributions to their support. In consequence, the percentage of the cost of such schools met by the state was higher than the percentage of the cost of the common schools met by the state. Other educational expenditures, viz., the support of art, science, and the Church, were largely state expenditures. In 1913-14 all states combined met 32.7 percent of the cost of common schools, 35.8 percent of the cost of all schools, and 42.1 percent of all educational expenditures.

The diversity in state systems of school support before the war makes generalizations difficult. The systems were complex, as well as diverse. Prussia, for instance, included fifteen different school quotas in her 1902 budget.[7] Under these conditions a wide variation, both in the aims and in the form of support, is to be expected. Nevertheless, it can be said that education was accepted as a state function, even when the bulk of the support fell on the local district. State support was substantial in every case and the states were taking over an increasing share of the growing school burden. The increase in school costs was, of course, in large part a result of mandatory state legislation; and the states recognized this, to some extent, by meeting at least a part of the new costs imposed.

The purpose of state grants was rarely to stimulate local expenditures. When the state undertook to meet a fixed percentage of local school expenditures it did not leave any wide margin of discretion to local officials in determining the amount of such

[7] Grice, op. cit., p. 273.

expenditures. Instead of "buying" higher standards, as did the British government, with its earlier school grants, the German states required local authorities to maintain high standards and then recognized the obligation to meet at least a part of the cost thus mandated. Only in rare instances could a wealthy local government obtain more state aid by itself spending more. On the contrary there was a definite tendency to scale aid down as the wealth of the district increased; and a substantial part of state funds was reserved for especially poor districts. In the distribution of funds to these poor districts the tests of need varied. In Prussia small or rural districts were given more aid than large or urban districts on the assumption that they were poorer. But in most cases the grants were discretionary and the basis of distribution was proved need.

The tendencies apparent in the pre-war support of education have continued in the post-war period.[8] In accordance with the acceptance of education as a state function, the state has increased both its control of the common-school systems and its support, the proportion of common-school expenditures borne by the state having risen from less than one-third to more than one-half. No important change has been made in the support of other educational institutions and functions, and the state contributions to these form about the same percentage of the total as before.

Most of this increase in support of common schools has come through state contributions to salaries. Whereas in 1913 only one state was meeting all salary costs, in 1931 nine states were meeting all, or nearly all, such expenditures. Even where local districts contribute a part of the salary, the state in some instances pays the salary directly and withholds the local contribution from the districts' share in Reich taxes. Grants-in-aid have declined, since the substantial increases in direct state support make such aids less essential. The indefinite aids from state funds, based on

[8] See Appendix, Chart 5, p. 334, for a summary of state education grants.

TABLE 10

DISTRIBUTION OF SUPPORT OF EDUCATION AMONG REICH, STATE,
AND LOCAL GOVERNMENTS [a]

Unit of Government	MILLION REICHSMARKS			PERCENTAGE		
	1913-14	1925-26	1931-32	1913-14	1925-26	1931-32
Reich.........	3.9	26.2	26.9	.4	1.4	1.3
State.........	404.5	1,028.6	1,138.8	38.7	53.2	54.4
Local.........	599.5	806.4	850.4	57.3	41.7	40.6
City-State.....	38.3	71.4	77.0	3.6	3.7	3.7
	1,046.2	1,932.6	2,093.1	100.0	100.0	100.0

[a] From *Einzelschrift*, No. 6, and *Statistisches Jahrbuch für das deutsche Reich*. Local shares of Reich taxes which are earmarked by the state for school purposes have been included in local funds.

proved need, have likewise decreased. Where they have not been abolished altogether, their use has been greatly restricted. The largest part of the aids that remain are percentage grants.

Equalization of costs has not been abandoned, but achieved through the redistribution of local rather than state funds. The redistribution of part of the local share of the income tax, or other Reich tax distributions, is a new and growing form of aid to poorer districts. Prussia, for example, diverts $12\frac{1}{2}$ percent of the communes' share of income, corporation, beer, and mineral water taxes to a fund which is distributed to school districts in proportion to teaching positions; and part of the turnover tax in Prussia is distributed to districts with more than the average number of school children. Württemberg distributes 10 percent of the local share of income and corporation taxes, after deducting the amount of the equalization fund, to school districts in proportion to school children. Saxony, where the state pays the teachers' salaries directly, reimburses itself for one-third of the amount from the local shares of income and corporation taxes, thus redistributing the burden in proportion to taxes paid. Mecklenburg-Schwerin, Oldenburg, and Lippe also use part of the income and corporation taxes for school funds. The difference between these redistributions of the local share of Reich taxes and grants-in-aid from state revenues is a difference in name only. The same results would be achieved if each state were to retain a larger proportion of the Reich tax distributions and were to make provision for these equalization funds from its own revenues.

No important movement to enlarge school districts has taken place, in spite of the fact that these are extremely small. Saxony has established the *Bezirke* in place of the commune as the local school district since the war, and in Bremen the circle has largely replaced the commune, but otherwise the districts are much the same as before the war. In Prussia, in 1930, there were still 33,000 school districts, 14,000 of them one-school, one-teacher districts. The decline in grants to needy districts has been made possible, not by consolidation of districts, but by equalization from local funds and by increasing the proportion of expenditures assumed directly by the state.

To summarize, the important changes in the post-war support of education are the marked increases in direct state expenditures, especially for teachers' salaries in the common schools; the tendency to earmark fixed proportions of the local share in Reich tax distributions for education and to redistribute these in proportion to some measure of educational need; and the decreased use of the indefinite state aid given where need is proved to the satisfaction of state authorities.

Participation of the Reich has not been mentioned in the above discussion because it has played such a small part in education, in spite of the provision of the Weimar Constitution (Article 143) charging the Reich, as well as state and local governments, with the maintenance of education. The share of the Reich in the support of education before the war consisted of small contributions for art and science, going largely to specific museums and institutions and amounting to less than 2 percent of net expenditures for these purposes; and even smaller contributions to the higher schools, totaling less than one-half of one percent of the net cost of these institutions.

In 1925-26 Reich expenditures for higher schools had been cut to half their pre-war level and amounted to only one-tenth of one percent of the net cost of these schools. Contributions to art and science, on the contrary, had been substantially increased, meeting 7.6 percent of the expenditures for this purpose. In addition, the Reich was making small contributions to the churches (less than one percent of the governmental contributions) and small contributions (about three-tenths of one percent) to the common schools. These latter aids, which have been continued, are for teachers and for German schools in foreign lands. They are small in amount but perhaps significant in that they recognize Reich participation in what has hitherto been regarded as a strictly state affair. Indirectly the Reich has made important contributions to the schools through its tax distributions, but the actual earmarking of portions of these taxes for school purposes has been left to the states. The Reich has in no way controlled them.

The importance of education to the central government under the National-Socialist régime is very great. The new government has already taken over a large measure of control, and some measure of support will probably follow, although to date (July, 1936) no move has been made in this direction. For the moment the central government is harassed with too many other demands.

POLICE

The police of Germany have a wide range of activities, covering practically all governmental functions where compulsion is required. This leads to two classes of officials, the security police, primarily engaged in maintaining law and order, and the administrative police (sometimes subdivided into administrative and special) engaged in traffic control, fire protection, health protection, inspection of buildings and markets, and other regulative functions.[9]

[9] *Einzelschrift*, No. 17, p. 17.

State control of police for the purpose of strengthening central authority is not confined to the post-war period. But the limitations placed on armed forces by the Versailles treaty resulted both in the rapid growth of police forces and in increased centralization of control. The number of police has nearly doubled since 1913, and the proportion of state police has increased from less than two-fifths to more than four-fifths of the total.

There has been some tendency toward decentralization in the case of administrative police. The Württemberg *Gemeindeordnung* of 1906, for instance, expressly declared the administrative police to be a matter for local control, and this is repeated in the new *Gemeindeordnung* of March 19, 1930. In the majority of cases, however, no distinction is made between administrative and security police in the matter of control or of support.[10]

Police whose activities extend beyond the boundary of a single commune (*Landespolizei*) exist in every state, both for protection and for administration. These are supported primarily by the state, although the Reich has given substantial subventions for certain classes of officials. Police whose activities are confined to a single commune (*Ortspolizei*) are usually state police in the larger communes and local police in the smaller communes, although no clear line can be drawn. The support of these *Ortspolizei* is commonly shared by state and local governments, with the larger part of the support from the governmental division in immediate control.[11]

State police are not new in Germany. They existed in Prussia throughout the nineteenth century. The support was for a time left entirely to the localities (1808-20), for a time taken over by the state (1820-50), and for a time shared by the state and the locality. The sharing consisted first (1850-92) in the paying of salaries by the state and the supplying of the buildings by the local government; later (1892-1908) in the locality contributing to the cost of salaries at a fixed sum per capita, ranging from 70 pfennigs in the small cities to 2.5 marks in the large

[10] *Idem.*   [11] *Einzelschrift*, No. 6.

cities. Beginning in 1908 the state charged the local governments
with one-third of the cost of state police, and this division of the
costs continues to the present, although the basis of apportionment has changed.

State police were established at the discretion of the state, at
first only in the larger cities, but more recently in many smaller
communities. In 1930 some seventy cities and eighty rural communes had such police. In addition to this all rural communes
with a population of less than 2,000 are protected by the *Landespolizei* and have no local police force. Moreover, such local
police forces as remain are partially supported by the state.[12]

The present situation in Prussia is that all *Landespolizei* are
supported by the state, with aid from the Reich. *Ortspolizei* employed by the state are supported two-thirds by the state and one-
third by the communes. Communes do not, however, contribute
directly to the support of the police in their locality as formerly.
The local third of the cost is allocated to such communes, one-
half in proportion to population and one-half in proportion to
corporation and income tax collections, and this sum is deducted
from these taxes before distribution to the communes in question.
Ortspolizei employed by the communes are supported two-thirds
by the state and one-third by the communes. The state's actual
contribution is 3,000 marks per officer, the average salary per
officer being estimated at 4,500 marks. This money is distributed
to the communes in proportion to officers employed. The funds
for this grant are obtained by deducting the necessary sum from
the share of those communes with more than 2,000 population in
the income tax and corporation tax distributions.[13] The effect
is to spread the burden of the cost of local police over communes
with state police, as well as over those with local police. The
money does not come from state funds. If, however, the state had
chosen to reduce the total commune share in income and corporation taxes for the benefit of the state, and then to subsidize local

[12] *Einzelschrift*, No. 17, pp. 17-18.
[13] Law of August 2, 1929, effective April 1, 1930.

police from state funds, the effect would have been much the same, except that in the latter case communes under 2,000 would share in the burden as well as the larger communes. The net result of this new system of support is to spread two-thirds of the cost of both state and local police over all, or practically all, the communes in proportion to tax yields, and to charge the remaining third more directly to the communes concerned. Even for this third, however, only those communes with local police pay the cost in their own communes. The communes with state police meet one-third of the cost for the group as a whole, but this sum is apportioned among individual communes, half in proportion to population, and half in proportion to tax yields. Thus a considerable further equalization is achieved.

Other states have gone through much the same development as Prussia. All except some of the smaller states have both state and local *Ortspolizei*.[14] Outside Prussia the local police are supported entirely by the local government, except in Hesse, where in certain cities in the formerly occupied territory the state meets all of the cost of local police in excess of 1,200 marks per officer. State *Ortspolizei* receive from one-third to all their support from the state. The division of support for *Ortspolizei* is given in Table 40.[15]

All states have *Landespolizei* supported by the state with Reich subventions. Before the war the only Reich police aid was for the *Gendarmerie* on the Austrian and Russian borders, to prevent the smuggling of cattle. A similar subvention is now given to guard against murrain on the eastern border.[16] In 1921 the Reich took over the total cost of stream and waterway police. This was given up, however, in 1931. In 1922 the Reich provided a subvention for state security police (*Landesschutzpolizei*) equal to 80 percent of the cost.[17] This was to build up a police force which would

---

[14] Hamburg and Lübeck have only state *Ortspolizei*; Mecklenburg-Strelitz, before its consolidation with Mecklenburg-Schwerin, had only local. *Einzelschrift*, No. 6, pp. 392 *et seq.*

[15] See Appendix, p. 363.   [16] *Einzelschrift*, No. 6, p. 377.

[17] Laws of July 29, 1921, March 26, 1931, and July 21, 1922.

compensate in part for the reduction in the standing army. The Reich made certain conditions for the establishment of these police, designed to secure a nonpartisan force which would be responsible to the Reich. In 1930 this subvention was withheld from Thuringia because the Reich disapproved certain activities of the Thuringian minister of the interior. This subvention was distributed at first in proportion to area, population, and such special conditions as the existence of harbors, neutral zones, or highly industrialized areas. Beginning in 1927 the number of state police was substituted for area and population in determining the distribution of this money.[18]

The Reich attempted one further step in centralizing the police of the country, in 1922, by providing for a Reich criminal police to operate across state boundaries. The opposition of Bavaria prevented this law from being put into effect.[19] State criminal police have been established, however, in every state since the war. Only Saxony had such a police force before the war. These state criminal police have been taken over by the Reich secret police under the National-Socialist Government.[20]

The rapid growth of the police force has increased the cost of this function to local governments, but the larger part of the increase has fallen on the states and the Reich. The percentage of state and local costs borne by the state varies from 30 percent in Anhalt to 100 percent in Lübeck.[21]

HIGHWAYS

The national importance of highways was recognized in the constitution of 1871, Article 4 of which gave control of highways to the national government in so far as it should be in the interest

---

[18] *Einzelschrift*, No. 16, p. 158, and R. H. Wells, *German Cities*, Princeton, 1932, p. 166.

[19] *Einzelschrift*, No. 17, p. 17, and F. F. Blachly and M. E. Oatman, *Government and Administration of Germany*, Baltimore, 1928, p. 414.

[20] Law of April 26, 1933.   [21] See Appendix, Table 40, p. 363.

TABLE 11

DISTRIBUTION OF SUPPORT OF POLICE AMONG REICH, STATE, AND
LOCAL GOVERNMENTS [a]

Unit of Government	MILLION REICHSMARKS			PERCENTAGE		
	1913-14	1925-26	1931-32	1913-14	1925-26	1931-32
Reich.........	...	194.3	191.9	...	29.2	27.2
State..........	88.2	266.8	260.7	44.2	40.1	37.0 [b]
Local.........	97.0	176.5	223.4	48.6	26.6	31.7
City-State.....	14.4	27.5	28.6	7.2	4.1	4.1
Total.......	199.6	665.1	704.6	100.0	100.0	100.0

[a] *Einzelschrift*, No. 6, p. 368; *Statistik des deutschen Reichs*, Vol. CDXL.

[b] The decrease in the percentage met by the states is largely owing to the change in the Prussian system of support. If the income tax distribution for police support were credited to the state instead of to the local governments the proportions would be about the same as in 1925-26.

of national communications and defense. This right of the national government to control highways in the interest of defense and communications was continued by the constitution of 1919. The government did not make any important use of this right, however, under either constitution, until 1934. The Reich took over the control of waterways in 1921,[22] at the same time shouldering a large part of the burden of their support. But central control of highways was not attempted, nor did the central government undertake their construction, prior to the Hitler administration. Direct Reich expenditures for "highways" have been for waterways. The Reich has, however, distributed the proceeds of the motor vehicle tax to the states, to be used exclusively for the support of highways.

The national importance of highways was first recognized by the central government in 1934 [23] when a uniform classification was adopted for highways in all the states with the ultimate purpose of taking over the control and support of those regarded as

[22] Law of July 29, 1921.   [23] Law of March 26, 1934.

most essential for military or other national purposes. This was accompanied by a reduction in the share of motor vehicle revenues distributed to state and local governments. In spite of this change Reich highway expenditures were lower in 1934-35 than in the preceding year, although they were above those for earlier years.

Among the states there is little uniformity in the administration and support of highways. All states meet a part of the cost, and all leave the larger share of the burden to local governments;[24] but the classification of highways, the nature of state support, and the particular local units responsible for the different classes of highways has varied greatly from state to state.

The tendency for administration to be transferred from smaller to larger units of government is apparent in highway administration, although it is not as marked as in welfare administration. In Prussia, since 1925, the provinces have taken over a substantial part of the circle highways (about 4,000 kilometers), and in Hesse, in 1927, the provinces took over all the highways formerly belonging to the circles. In Mecklenburg-Schwerin those improved highways not in the hands of the state were transferred from the highway district to the larger *Amt* in 1926. In Anhalt such highways have been transferred from the commune to the circle. Nevertheless, important connecting highways are still in the hands of the communes in many states. In 1925-26 more than one-third of the highways outside of cities and villages were still maintained by the communes and less than one-tenth were maintained by the states.[25] The remainder were maintained by the intermediate provinces, circles, and districts.

State participation in highway control and support has not increased materially since the war. In fact, the percentage of the cost met by the states declined from seventeen in 1913-14 to ten in 1931-32. These figures, however, credit the expenditures from

[24] Except Mecklenburg-Strelitz before consolidation.
[25] *Einzelschrift*, No. 16, pp. 238-39.

motor vehicle taxes to local governments, where the state has distributed such revenues to local governments. The burden of support falling on local taxes has not increased materially, since the largest part of the post-war increase in expenditures has been met from motor vehicle taxes. As a matter of fact, expenditures for highways have increased less than those for education, police, or welfare. The increase in expenditures for highways between 1913-14 and 1930-31 (the peak year) was 126 percent, while the increase for educational expenditures for the same period was 133 percent, for police expenditures 291 percent, and for welfare 1003 percent. This is in marked contrast to the development in the United States, where expenditures for highways during this same period increased faster than expenditures for any of the three other functions listed. It is apparent that in the competition for limited public funds the development of highways has seemed less urgent than other governmental activities. This probably accounts for the failure of the states to make any important progress in centralization of highway systems and to lag in their own contributions. Such progress as has been made can be credited in large part to the motor vehicle tax distributions, which supplied the state and local governments, in 1930-31, with half the increase in expenditures over 1913-14.

Nevertheless, state governments have long recognized that highways are of more than local concern. In Prussia small grants (about 2 million marks) were made to the provinces as early as 1868 for various functions, including roads. The exact amount of these grants which was to be devoted to roads was left to the discretion of provincial authorities. In 1875 these provincial grants were extended to nearly 36 million marks,[26] of which the sum of approximately 19 million marks was granted specifically for main roads, and 15 million more was granted for general purposes, including roads. While the law left to the discretion of the provinces the portion of the latter sum to be used for high-

[26] Law of July 8, 1875.

ways, the major part of the money was distributed, half in proportion to population, and half in proportion to area—population presumably measuring need for poor relief, and area measuring need for roads.[27] These *Dotationen* remained practically unchanged until 1902, when 3 million more marks were added for highways.[28] The law itself specified the share of each province in the 3 million marks.

State aid for local highways was introduced during the latter half of the nineteenth century in Bavaria, Saxony, Württemberg, Baden, Oldenburg, Anhalt, the two Mecklenburgs, and Lübeck. In fact, the majority of states granted highway aids in some form. These aids were sometimes fixed sums, as in Prussia, sometimes mileage aids, as in the two Mecklenburgs, and sometimes discretionary aids, as in Baden.

Since the war some of these have given way to distributions of motor vehicle tax revenues, but in many states both are used. In general the states leaving the largest proportion of highway costs to local divisions have passed on to them the largest share of motor vehicle revenues. But the states as a whole have kept enough of the motor vehicle tax revenues to meet approximately half their direct highway expenditures, and have passed on to the local divisions only enough to meet one-fifth of local highway costs. Since in some cases the states are giving grants-in-aid for highways from motor vehicle revenues, although no motor vehicle tax money as such is distributed to local divisions, the best measure of the distribution of the highway burden is the percentage of highway expenditures from state and local sources, other than the motor vehicle tax, and from the motor vehicle tax. These percentages are given in Table 12.

The proportion of revenues from the different sources varies widely in the different states, but in no case does the state pay from state taxes as much as the local governments pay from local taxes; and in only four states do local governments meet less

[27] Grice, *op. cit.*, p. 238.   [28] *Finanz-Archiv*, 1903, XX, 367. Law of June 2, 1902.

TABLE 12

PERCENTAGE OF STATE AND LOCAL HIGHWAY EXPENDITURES FROM
MOTOR VEHICLE TAX, STATE TAXES, AND LOCAL TAXES,
RESPECTIVELY, 1928-29 [a]

State	Motor Vehicle Tax	Other State Taxes	Other Local Taxes
Mecklenburg-Strelitz...	59.3	15.7	25.0
Mecklenburg-Schwerin..	44.5	14.5	40.9
Oldenburg............	36.6	7.2	56.2
Thuringia............	32.9	2.1	65.0
Bavaria..............	31.5	5.3	63.2
Anhalt...............	26.3	3.1	70.6
Prussia..............	24.6	...	75.5
Hesse...............	21.5	7.2	71.3
Brunswick...........	19.2	17.7	63.1
Saxony..............	19.1	29.8	51.1
Baden...............	17.2	17.1	65.8
Lippe...............	15.7	36.1	48.2
Württemberg.........	14.9	19.8	65.3
Schaumburg-Lippe.....	14.8	37.3	47.9
Total..............	24.1	6.0	69.8

[a] Net expenditures for highways, excluding waterways. Figures for state and
local taxes from *Einzelschrift*, No. 17, pp. 218-19; for motor vehicle taxes from
Einzelschrift, No. 19, pp. 162-95.

than half the costs from their own taxes. In spite of grants-in-aid,
states are contributing comparatively little (6 percent) to the
support of highways beyond the motor vehicle tax revenues,
whereas local governments are bearing approximately seven-
tenths (69.8 percent) of the cost from ordinary local revenues.
The motor vehicle tax revenue amounts to approximately one-
fourth (24.1 percent) of the total.

Other tax revenues dedicated to highways are very limited.
The former tolls and levies on those making unusual use of the
highways may no longer be levied on automobiles, and the yield
of occasional draft animal taxes is negligible.

To summarize, the Reich has gone farther in its support of
highways than in its support of schools, but central support of
highways still lags behind central support of police in spite of the

1934 legislation looking toward extensive Reich control. At the other end, the relatively small state participation leaves two-thirds of the burden of highway support on local treasuries, as compared with two-fifths of the cost of education and one-third of the cost of police.[29]

TABLE 13

DISTRIBUTION OF SUPPORT OF HIGHWAYS AMONG REICH, STATE, AND LOCAL GOVERNMENTS [a]

Unit of Government	MILLION REICHSMARKS			PERCENTAGE		
	1913-14	1925-26	1931-32	1913-14	1925-26	1931-32
Reich.........	48.2	157.8	165.8	10.3	18.9	19.1
State.........	79.2	95.0	89.7	16.9	11.4	10.3
Local........	318.9	547.4	585.3	67.9	65.4	67.4
City-State.....	23.1	36.3	27.4	4.9	4.3	3.2
Total.......	469.5	836.6	868.1	100.0	100.0	100.0

[a] Data from *Einzelschrift*, No. 6, and *Statistik des deutschen Reichs*, Vol. CDXL.

PUBLIC WELFARE

Public welfare has been, and still is, regarded in Germany as an essentially local function. Increasing support from the Reich has been given grudgingly, and solely as an emergency measure; and state support meets a smaller proportion of the costs today than before the war. This is in marked contrast to the tendency toward centralization of support for education, police, and highways. For highway support the actual percentage of costs borne by local governments in 1931-32 was greater than for welfare, but the local unit for administration and support was in most instances larger for highways than for welfare.[30] Moreover, the new Reich highway legislation forecasts a centralization of high-

[29] It should be noted, however, that a large part of this local expenditure is that of the comparatively large Prussian province rather than of the smaller local jurisdictions.

[30] Thus in Prussia, in 1931-32, 77.5 percent of local welfare expenditures fell on the commune itself, compared with only 47.4 percent of local highway expenditures.

way expenditures at least equal to that now existing for police and education, whereas with improving industrial conditions the Reich is reducing its share of the welfare burden much more rapidly than the total burden is decreasing.

The division of support of welfare expenditures is considered here in more detail than the support of other functions because of the unusual difficulties arising from the financing of this function. Not only have welfare expenditures been larger than expenditures for other functions in recent years, but they inevitably vary in inverse proportion to resources. Consequently, requirements for welfare work have tended to dominate the whole system of distribution of taxes during the depression.

In 1913-14 welfare (including social insurance) accounted for only 7.7 percent of net governmental expenditures, national, state, and local. This was less than was spent on highways and only two-fifths as much as was devoted to education. In 1931-32, on the contrary, net welfare expenditures exceeded those for education, highways, and police combined, amounting to 27.5 percent of all net governmental expenditures.

This enormous expansion of welfare expenditures—an increase of more than 800 percent—could not be met from local resources, not only because local resources had been narrowly limited by the post-war financial system, but because welfare expenditures, by their very nature, are heaviest in the communities least able to bear them. The Reich alone could meet the situation; and the Reich has done so, but only as a temporary measure.

Before the war the Reich met the cost of social insurance in so far as it was not self-supporting.[31] In addition to this it met the small cost of supporting dependent persons with no established state residence. No grants-in-aid were made to state or local governments for any welfare expenditures.

[31] The administrative cost of health insurance, beginning in 1883, invalid and old age pensions, beginning in 1889, and widows' and orphans' pensions, beginning in 1911; and fixed contributions per person toward benefits other than health insurance.

The states spent even less for welfare purposes than the central government in 1913-14. Every state met the cost of dependents with no local residence, and the majority met the overhead costs of institutions for the care of insane, feeble-minded, epileptic, and crippled individuals. The care of inmates of these institutions was charged against the district in which the inmate had an established residence. Only in Saxony did the state contribute to such expenditures, meeting half the cost.

Seven states gave grants-in-aid to local districts for relief expenditures. In Prussia a fixed sum, 7 million marks annually, was distributed to the state poor administration districts (in some cases the province, in others the circle) for poor relief under the law of June 2, 1902. This was distributed, one-third in proportion to population, one-third in inverse proportion to state income tax collections, and one-third in proportion to the ratio of local direct tax collections to state income tax collections. The distribution was based on the population and taxes of 1900 and was not reapportioned from year to year. This was one of the few instances to be found in the pre-war financial system of an attempt to equalize the burden of governmental costs; but it is important only in so far as it indicates that Prussia was giving serious thought to the problem. The actual equalization achieved was small. The 7 million marks involved met only 3 percent of net state and local welfare expenditures in 1913-14. The central government of Prussia was contributing a smaller proportion of welfare costs than that of any other state, in spite of grants-in-aid. It was, in fact, generally true that the states giving subventions were those contributing the least to welfare expenditures. Subventions were less in use in the smaller states, but in these the administration of welfare was more highly centralized and the state was assuming directly from one-third to two-thirds of the total expenditure. From the point of view of equalizing burdens, this was, of course, more effective than any system of grants under a more decentralized administration. Only in Bavaria did the state fail either to provide grants-in-aid or to meet directly any important part of welfare costs. Nevertheless, the bulk of the burden of relief (in 1913-14 69 percent of net expenditures in all states) fell on local governments.

Owing to the small size of the local poor district, which was ordinarily the commune, a flexible system of support had been developed in most states, which made it possible for needy communes to receive aid from the circle or from some other larger administrative district. With this limited equalization it was possible, under ordinary conditions, to place the primary welfare burden on very small districts. But the small size of the circle itself prevented any extensive equalization, and such a system could not meet a major industrial depression.

The welfare burdens growing out of the war could only be met by national measures. Demobilization brought a new unemployment problem. The heavy war casualties left their quotas of disabled veterans, war widows, and orphans. And the loss of territory disrupted industry in border communities by cutting off the hinterland and resulted, further, in a large influx of refugees— German inhabitants of former German domains. The national government accepted this responsibility. Immediately following the Armistice the Reich assumed control of all public employment exchanges and established a system of out-of-work grants, planned originally for one year but actually continued in one form or another until 1924.[32]

Depression followed hard on the heels of demobilization, and inflation followed depression. Under these conditions little could be expected in the way of permanent and constructive policies. From 1918 to 1923 the Reich experimented with unemployment relief, work relief, subsidies to local governments, and loans to private employers.[33] In 1922 [34] the public employment exchanges

[32] B. Armstrong, *Insuring the Essentials*, New York, 1932, p. 521; and A. Epstein, *Insecurity, a Challenge to America*, New York, 1933, p. 371.

[33] Armstrong, *op. cit.*, p. 521.

[34] Law of July 22, 1922.

were converted into a federal system, and in 1923 [35] a system of contributory unemployment insurance was established. This was a relief measure rather than insurance, since, although contributions were levied against all employees subject to health insurance, benefits were reserved for the needy unemployed.[36]

By means of this act the central government established a uniform and compulsory system of unemployment relief throughout Germany, but it attempted to shift the burden of this relief to other shoulders. The Reich stood ready to contribute only in case expenditures should exceed the contributions provided for a period of two weeks, and even then half of any such deficit was to be charged against the state.

TABLE 14

DISTRIBUTION OF COST OF UNEMPLOYMENT INSURANCE, LAW OF FEBRUARY 16, 1924 [a]

Expenditures for	Reich	State	Circle	Employer[b]	Employee[b]
Insurance contributions...	½ of any deficit	½ of any deficit	1/9[c]	4/9	4/9
State officials...........	...	1/3	...	1/3	1/3
Labor exchanges.........	...	...	1/3	1/3	1/3

[a] Einzelschriften, No. 6, pp. 425, 431; No. 17, p. 15.
[b] Three percent was to be levied against payrolls, to be borne equally by employer and employee. Benefits were to be paid for 26 weeks.
[c] Originally one-fifth.

In 1924 a number of changes were made in welfare administration which affected the distribution of support. Among other things child welfare, which had been segregated from general welfare in 1922,[37] was made the obligation of the state instead of the local government,[38] to be delegated to the communes at the discretion of the state. This increasing interference on the part of the Reich may have brought desirable uniformity in welfare

[35] Law of October 15, 1923.
[36] Einzelschriften, No. 6, p. 422; No. 17, p. 15.
[37] Law of June 9, 1922.   [38] Law of February 14, 1924.

administration, but it was not followed up by increasing Reich support.[39] The central government's attempt to place the relief burden elsewhere was, however, doomed to failure. Launching a system of self-supporting unemployment insurance during a period of excessive unemployment was impossible, and the deficit met from Reich and state contributions in the first year of operation, 1924-25, amounted to more than one-third of the total expenditures.

The following year, 1925-26, with decreased unemployment, Reich contributions were negligible, but with rising unemployment in 1926 Reich and state governments were again called upon to meet a deficit. At the beginning of the year, February 1, 1926, the Reich had established an equalization fund to which one-third of the employers' and employees' contributions was to be paid.[40] Thus, if the districts where unemployment was relatively small received contributions in excess of expenditures, these surpluses could be applied in other districts where deficits appeared. This, in effect, pooled the funds of the entire country so that the government would not contribute to deficits in one district while surpluses were accumulating in another. But the total contributions were far too small, and the deficits met by the Reich and states exceeded two-fifths of the total cost in 1926-27.

Meanwhile the local welfare burden was becoming intolerable. Unemployment was long-continued, and unemployment benefits were given for only twenty-six weeks. At the end of that time the needy unemployed turned to the commune. To prevent the breakdown of the local relief system the Reich again came to the aid of the commune, this time with "emergency relief."

Beginning November 20, 1926,[41] the unemployed were to receive emergency benefits for a period of twenty-six weeks (thirty-nine weeks for those over forty years of age) after the lapse of unemployment benefits. Three-fourths of the amount of these

[39] *Einzelschriften*, No. 6, pp. 189, 424; No. 17, pp. 27-37.
[40] Law of January 18, 1926.   [41] Law of November 19, 1926.

benefits was contributed by the Reich and only one-fourth by the local divisions. This was continued with the introduction of the regular unemployment insurance in 1927, and the Reich increased its contribution to four-fifths of the total, beginning October 1, 1927.[42] Meanwhile, on April 1, 1927,[43] the Reich had taken over the state's share of the unemployment deficit, and the local ninth of the cost of unemployment insurance benefits.

A self-supporting system of unemployment insurance was introduced on October 1, 1927.[44] Contributions from employers and employees were the same as before, that is, 3 percent of the pay roll, and benefits of the same amount were paid for the same period. The new system differed from the former in receiving no regular contribution from any division of government, either for benefits or for the support of labor exchanges and labor officials, and in providing benefits for all contributors, whether needy or not. Thus the sources of income were decreased and the obligations increased. The Reich stood ready to loan money to the fund in case of deficit, but not to subsidize it. The new system inherited a balance of more than 100 million reichsmarks from the old system, and this, together with improving industrial conditions and the accompanying increase in employment, made it possible for the new system to pay for itself for more than a year and made possible the extension of benefits from twenty-six to thirty-nine weeks.[45]

Early in 1929 increasing unemployment brought deficits and government loans. During the next year the levy on wages was increased to $3\frac{1}{2}$ percent. In spite of this the deficit mounted until the debt to the Reich reached 623 million reichsmarks on April 1, 1930. Again the Reich's attempt to place the burden of unem-

[42] Law of September 28, 1927.
[43] Law of April 9, 1927.
[44] Law of July 16, 1927.
[45] For workers over forty, fifty-two weeks. Law of August 27, 1928. Epstein, *op. cit.*, pp. 375 *et seq.*, Metropolitan Life Insurance Co., *Unemployment Insurance*, 1932, p. 12, "Monograph No. 1."

ployment relief on other shoulders failed, and again the Reich assumed the burden. The 623 million mark loan was canceled, a direct subsidy of 184 million reichsmarks for the year 1930 was granted, and the Reich agreed to meet half of any deficit, the remaining half to be met from increased contributions.[46]

Every effort was made to make the system self-supporting. On one hand the levy on pay rolls was increased in successive steps until it reached 6½ percent on October 1, 1930; on the other hand the amount of the benefits was cut.[47] Government grants were discontinued by the decree of September 30, 1930, and no provision was made for either loans or further subsidies. In the three years of its existence the insurance fund had received 1,175 million reichsmarks from the Reich. Thenceforward it was self-supporting, but only with further reductions in the amount of benefits paid and reductions in the period for which the benefits were paid. Both the amount of the monthly payment and the number of weeks for which it ran were reduced in 1931 and again in 1932, so that by the middle of 1932 it was paid for only six weeks, unless need could be proved, in which case it was extended to twenty-six weeks. The benefits had decreased meanwhile to approximately two-thirds of the original sum.[48] In 1934 the period was reduced from twenty-six to twenty weeks. No further changes of importance have been made since, but the test of need has become increasingly severe.

These provisions achieved their end. The unemployment insurance funds have been more than adequate for this very limited insurance, and the surpluses have been used to subsidize other branches of unemployment relief. In the two years 1931-32 and 1932-33, 355 million reichsmarks were paid out of unemployment insurance funds for other unemployment relief. In 1933-34,

[46] Decree of July 26, 1930. *United States Labor Bulletin*, No. 544, July, 1931, p. 266.

[47] Zarden, *op. cit.*, pp. 4, 9; Armstrong, *op. cit.*, p. 530.

[48] *Der Städtetag*, July 7, 1932, p. 315.

778 million reichsmarks were available, enough to cover the entire cost of emergency relief.[49]

These surpluses were not, however, clear gain to public treasuries, for much of what the Reich gained by making the insurance system more than self-supporting, it lost again through the shortening of the period before the unemployed fell on the Reich-supported emergency relief. The period for which emergency benefits were paid was extended, October 23, 1931, to compensate for the decrease in the period for which insurance benefits were paid. The rates were scaled down, June 14, 1932, to the level of poor relief, and the need test was applied so that emergency relief differed from ordinary relief only in the fact of Reich support. But, as in the case of the reduction of insurance benefits, much of the apparent gain was really a transfer of the burden to another form of relief. The reduced emergency relief was so inadequate that communes had to supplement it through their child welfare agencies and in other ways. There is, after all, a minimum of subsistence; and in a period of increasing unemployment a reduction in the total welfare burden is impossible, however much the nonessentials may be cut.

The number receiving unemployment insurance reached its peak in 1930. Although the number of unemployed workers continued to grow, the rate of increase was not as rapid as in 1930, and the number exhausting their insurance benefits and falling on emergency relief was greater than the number of new insurance claimants. This process was, of course, greatly expedited by the shortening of the insurance period. The number receiving emergency relief increased until the spring of 1932 and then declined, although the total number of unemployed continued to increase for another year. Those falling entirely on local relief increased, in consequence, from 14 percent of the group receiving public support in December, 1929, to 58 percent in Decem-

[49] During the first six months of 1934-35 less than half this fund was applied to unemployment insurance and emergency relief.

ber, 1932. Where in 1929 the communes were supporting on ordinary poor relief some 333,000 unemployed in 1932 they were supporting not far from three million (2,887,000).[50]

Local resources were wholly unable to meet this demand, and again the Reich came to the rescue. By a decree of July 26, 1930, the communes had been given local beer and drink taxes to meet the welfare burden. Another decree, June 5, 1931, provided a subsidy of 60 million reichsmarks to be distributed among the communes for unemployment relief.[51] The Reich obtained the money for this from the emergency surtax on incomes. This was the beginning of a policy of direct subventions to the communes for poor relief which still continues. A second subsidy, this time 150 million reichsmarks, was authorized on October 6, 1931. It was supplemented by 80 million reichsmarks to be distributed to the local communes in greatest need. The emergency tax of 1931 was replaced by another emergency tax on all remuneration from labor, by law of June 14, 1932. This new tax was at higher rates and was to run until March 31, 1933. The proceeds, as in the case of the earlier tax, were to go to Reich funds for unemployment relief.

Later in the year the Reich went farther, providing a subsidy of 510 reichsmarks per person on local relief, with extra payments in case of sickness. This was supposed to meet from 80 to 85 percent of the local relief burden, although actually it

[50] This includes those not recognized as unemployed for purposes of Reich welfare grants.

[51] This subsidy was distributed first to the different groups of communes, classified according to size, in proportion to the total number of unemployed, as defined in the law, on local relief rolls. The money was subdivided within the group in proportion to the number of those unemployed in excess of 75 percent of the Reich average. This standard for distributing funds has been changed with almost every new subsidy. Since June, 1934, these subsidies have gone only to those districts in which the recognized unemployed exceed one percent of the population. The actual amount received is a fixed sum for each unemployed worker, the sum per individual varying with the size of the city and the percentage of unemployment. Under this ruling Württemberg, Mecklenburg, and the two Lippes received no further subsidies, and Brunswick, Oldenburg, and Anhalt had their subsidies cut off a few months later. *Der Gemeindetag*, June 15, 1934, pp. 364-65; July 15, 1935, p. 443.

amounted to considerably less, since the Reich failed to recognize some 400,000 unemployed that were wholly supported by communes, because they had no former employer who could be identified or for some other reason failed to meet Reich regulations.

On November 7, 1932, the emergency benefits had been extended, for persons already receiving them, until March 31, 1933, in order to prevent further increase in those falling on local support. This was again extended on March 15, 1933, for an indefinite period, and, beginning October 1, 1933,[52] the Reich relieved the communes of their contribution to this emergency relief. These two measures reduced the welfare burden of the communes very materially. In addition the Reich was subsidizing local poor relief. Beginning October 1, 1933, these subsidies were changed from a fixed sum each month to the cost of relief in excess of a fixed amount (26.7 million reichsmarks) each month. This brought a small reduction in the local burden at the time, and since unemployment increased during the winter it worked to the advantage of the communes. In 1933-34 the local share of the support of the unemployed dropped to 26 percent of the total compared with 58 percent in the preceding year.

These measures were accompanied by an active campaign against unemployment. Work relief had been a part of the Reich's program from the beginning, but the high cost of this form of relief had prevented it from becoming a major part of the program at any time. There was, however, a revival of this, through public works and through subsidies to a variety of private projects. These efforts, together with the general improvement in business conditions, brought the number of unemployed down from a high point of more than 6 million in January, 1933, to less than 4 million in the fall of 1933 and to less than 2 million in the fall of 1935.

But the cost of support remained a pressing problem. The sub-

[52] Law of September 22, 1933.

sidies to private work projects came almost entirely from public loans. A volunteer relief campaign was undertaken. Not only were people asked to give old clothes and to eat simple Sunday dinners, contributing the difference in cost to relief, but persons with bank or postal checking accounts and persons with salaries were requested to state the amount which might be deducted each month for the relief fund. This was not the first campaign for voluntary contributions, but it was pursued so actively, and the pressure of public opinion was so great, that the *Winterhilfe* of 1933-34 amounted to 358 million reichsmarks, about four times the sum given in the preceding year and 50 percent more than the money paid from local treasuries for unemployment relief during the same period. In 1934-35 the *Winterhilfe* reached 367 million reichsmarks, whereas public relief expenditures had been materially reduced.[53]

The reduction in public welfare expenditures resulting both from the reduction in unemployment and the increased private contributions—if the *Winterhilfe* may be regarded as private aid—is very material. The benefit has accrued to the Reich treasury, however, rather than to local governments, partly because the saving has come in largest part to the Reich-supported emergency relief, partly because the Reich has reduced its welfare aid to local authorities as much as local expenditures have been reduced. This is apparent from the figures given in Table 15.

On the assumption that relief is a local function, it is entirely reasonable that the reduction should go to the central government rather than to the local governments. The latter will at least benefit from increasing tax yields as business improves, and the same expenditure represents a smaller burden. It is not clear, however, to what extent the increased employment represents a genuine improvement in business and to what extent it is the result of artificial stimulation through government subsidies.

[53] *Wirtschaft und Statistik*, September, 1935, p. 697.

TABLE 15

LOCAL WELFARE EXPENDITURES AND REICH WELFARE AID,
1932-33 to 1934-35 [a]

Year	MILLION REICHSMARKS			PERCENTAGE		
	Total Expenditure	From Reich Aid	From Local Revenue	Total Expenditure	From Reich Aid	From Local Revenue
1932-33.	2,788	711	2,077	100.0	25.5	74.5
1933-34.	2,565	710	1,854	100.0	27.7	72.3
1934-35.	2,055	245	1,810	100.0	11.9	88.1

[a] *Wirtschaft und Statistik*, January, 1936, p. 86.

In so far as the increase in taxable income represents government subsidies, no real gain to government treasuries has been attained. The government cannot create surpluses by taxing its own expenditures. On the contrary, this is another, and costlier, form of relief. Much of this financing of work projects has been undertaken by local governments; and the fact that, for the moment, the financing has been achieved through bank loans, rather than taxes, makes the ultimate solution so much the more difficult. The complaints of the communes are, perhaps, not without foundation.[54]

One interesting feature of the development of the system of unemployment relief is the small and declining rôle played by the states. The specific obligations in the matter of relief expenditures which were imposed by the Reich on the states in the early years of the last decade disappeared with the 1927 system of unemployment insurance. State welfare expenditures dropped, in consequence, from 15.3 percent of the total in 1925-26 to 3.5 percent in 1931-32, and those for unemployment relief alone decreased from 35.9 percent of the total to practically nothing in the same period. Nevertheless many of the states have made a definite effort to relieve the local burden, and there is much less

[54] See, e.g., *Der Gemeindetag*, June 15, 1934, pp. 364-65; September 15, 1934, p. 559.

TABLE 16

DISTRIBUTION OF SUPPORT OF WELFARE AMONG REICH, STATE, AND LOCAL GOVERNMENTS [a]

Unit of Government	MILLION REICHSMARKS			PERCENTAGE		
	1913-14	1925-26	1931-32	1913-14	1925-26	1931-32
Reich.........	55.4	452.7	1,669.1	13.2	23.7	42.3
State..........	50.9	291.9	136.1	12.1	15.3	3.5
Local.........	289.9	1,089.7	2,006.1	68.9	56.9	50.9
City-State.....	24.3	78.8	131.0	5.8	4.1	3.3
Total.......	420.5	1,913.2	3,942.3	100.0	100.0	100.0

[a] Data from *Einzelschrift*, No. 6, and *Statistik des deutschen Reichs*, Vol. CDXL.

variation among the different states in the division of the welfare costs between state and local governments since the war than before.

Each of the six states which in 1913-14 was meeting less than 30 percent of state and local welfare expenditures increased its proportionate share in expenditures following the war, and each of the eight states which in 1913-14 was contributing more than 30 percent decreased its proportionate share. Since the six states which increased their share of expenditures include most of the larger states, notably Prussia and Bavaria, the actual percentage of welfare expenditures met by the state governments increased from 12 percent in 1913-14 to 15 percent in 1925-26. State expenditures have not kept pace, however, with growing demands, and in spite of occasional emergency measures to relieve and equalize local welfare burdens the state share in welfare expenditures has declined below the pre-war level. The recent action of the Prussian government in taking over 20 percent of all local welfare expenditures will increase this percentage again.[55] The basis of such welfare grants as the states provide is, in most cases, proved need.

[55] For summary of state grants-in-aid see Appendix, Chart 7, p. 340.

State intervention in welfare expenditures has taken the form of equalization of resources rather than direct state expenditures. The states, as well as the Reich, have accepted welfare as an essentially local function. There is a tendency to enlarge the local welfare unit. Whereas the pre-war district was usually the commune, the post-war district is more often the circle; but there is no further tendency to centralize welfare administration.

All authorities agree that local administration of relief is far more effective than central administration. Personal knowledge and personal contacts are important, and the rehabilitating agencies are mostly local. It would seem important, then, to leave administration in local hands, but to provide material support from central funds, even in normal times. While the emergency makes the problem more acute it does not change its essential nature. It merely throws into bold relief factors which are always an integral part of the problem. The poorest districts will invariably have the heaviest welfare costs. And districts with inadequate resources are to be found in the wealthiest countries in the most prosperous times. This would seem to make it imperative that a substantial part of welfare support should come from a wide area, however small the efficient administrative area is found to be. The Reich has not yet accepted this point of view, however.

HOUSING

The war left Germany with a serious housing shortage which private building, checked by exorbitant interest rates, was wholly unable to cope with. Consequently state and local governments, stimulated by the Reich, undertook to meet the need; and in the post-inflation years the net cost of housing met from public funds was approximately equal to highway costs. In 1926-27 and 1927-28 housing expenditures actually exceeded highway expenditures.

Governmental expenditures for housing before the war were

negligible. For most governmental units this was a new function; and a new source of income, the rental tax, was created to meet it. This tax was levied on pre-war rents, on the assumption that the owners of houses built before the war had profited, first from the housing shortage, and later from inflation, particularly in those cases where the houses had been heavily mortgaged and the mortgage had been paid off during inflation. The Reich law provided for differentiation between those houses which had been mortgaged and those which had not.[56]

In the period 1924 to 1931 approximately half the cost of housing was met from public funds. About three-fifths of the public funds came from loans from the proceeds of the rental tax,[57] and the remaining two-fifths came in about equal parts from state and local subsidies and from loans from other sources.[58]

In some instances local governments themselves engaged in building. This was true in Stuttgart, for instance. Occasionally they granted outright subsidies to private builders. In general, however, government aid took the form of loans at low rates of interest, usually 4 percent but occasionally as low as 1 percent.[59] In many instances the loans and subsidies were inadequately safeguarded, and the dwellings provided were often inappropriate and unduly expensive. With depression there was a general movement to smaller quarters to save rent, and many large apartments were left vacant. This concerns the present study, however, only in so far as it helps to explain the rapid rise of state and local expenditures following the war, and, perhaps, demonstrates once more the tendency to extravagance when unexpectedly large revenues come from sources for which local governments have little or no responsibility.

[56] *Einzelschrift*, No. 6, pp. 192 *et seq.*
[57] For the provisions of the various states for applying the proceeds of the rental tax to housing, see Appendix, Chart 4, p. 318.
[58] K. Wagner, "Dürfen wir noch bauen?" *Schriften des deutschen Vereins für Wohnungsreform e.V.*, No. 11, Berlin, 1933.
[59] *Bauhandbuch*, Berlin, 1930.

The provision of adequate housing has come to be accepted as an appropriate government function when the government can afford it. But this is an expenditure which can be cut in time of need, as police, school, and welfare expenditures cannot. Neither the increased need for small, low-rent dwellings, nor the need for work relief is sufficient stimulus when local budgets are seriously out of balance. Housing aids have declined more rapidly than building itself, and an increasing proportion of the rental tax has been diverted to general purposes. In 1927-28 and again in 1928-29 slightly more than half the rental tax was devoted to housing. Since that time the percentage has steadily decreased, being less than one-fourth in 1931-32 and probably not more than 5 percent in 1932-33.[60]

The rental tax has outlived its purpose. Any benefits the owners of pre-war buildings may have gained from war and inflation have admittedly long since been paid for. And while there is still a housing shortage it is no longer being met from this source. The proposed liquidation of this tax during the next four years will not affect the housing program. Nor can such a source of revenue be anticipated for future housing programs, barring another inflation.[61]

The present housing subsidies are part of the larger program of stimulating employment. And while the program has increased building from its low point in 1932, the financing has been achieved almost wholly through borrowed funds. Consequently, it plays no part in the current distribution of revenues among the different governmental divisions. Where the ultimate burden will rest it is difficult to say. If housing is to be a regularly accepted function of government, it will probably be assigned to local governments. Certainly local administration is ordinarily

[60] Figures are not available for all states, but for Prussia, which accounts for the largest part of this tax, the percentage had fallen to less than five in 1932-33.

[61] In so far as the proceeds of this tax have been loaned and the loans are repaid, there is, of course, a revolving fund available for future housing needs. Owing to financial difficulties, however, repayments have been much smaller than expected.

regarded as essential to its success.[62] If it is to be a luxury function, to be indulged in only when resources are adequate, the financing will doubtless be largely local. But if it is to be used as a relief measure, to stimulate employment on one hand and to provide housing for needy families on the other hand, support from the central government is as inevitable as it is in the case of welfare.

SUMMARY

No clear-cut policy is evident in the division of support of the various functions in the different states, but a marked increase in centralization of functions is apparent, not merely in the hands of the state, but in the hands of the Reich itself. Also, considerable equalization has been achieved, both through the increase in direct support from the central government and through grants-in-aid.

Just what constitutes centralization, in the process of transferring administration and support from the smaller to the larger unit, is a matter of definition. If the proportion of expenditures remaining with local authorities is the test, centralization has gone farther in education than in welfare. Yet there has been a definite movement to transfer welfare expenditures from the commune to the larger circle, whereas elementary education remains with the commune in so far as it is local at all. Moreover, the Reich has taken over a large part of the support of welfare and makes almost no contribution to education. The real status of the two is that the support of education is divided for the most part between the state and the commune, and welfare support is divided for the most part between the Reich and the circle. Both the local and the central authorities are smaller in the case of educational support. But the proportion of costs left to the

---

[62] Popitz, however, believes that this function must be centralized, since those communities with the greatest need for housing are the ones least able to meet the cost; and he is of the opinion that central financing and local administration would lead to the misuse of funds. See *Der künftige Finanzausgleich, op. cit.*, p. 147.

local unit is materially less in the case of education than in the case of welfare.

If the test of centralization is taken to be the proportion of costs borne by the Reich, then the highest degree of centralization is to be found in the case of welfare. But to take this, alone, as indicative of developments to be expected in the future would be misleading. The National-Socialist program demands a national police force and a national highway system; but it is not greatly concerned with a constructive public-welfare policy. Consequently, it may be expected that the centralization of police and highways will continue, whereas in marked contrast to recent English developments welfare administration and support will be relegated to local authorities and private agencies as rapidly and as fully as local and private resources permit. Only if certain economic forces prove stronger in the end than political policies can the reverse be expected.

Equalization has probably been carried farthest in school support. In fact, some critics believe that, in the effort to help the communes, centralization has been carried too far and local interest destroyed. Only Prussia and Württemberg would seem to have succeeded in equalizing school burdens without at the same time endangering local interest.[63] Equalization of police support is much more limited. The establishment of state police in certain cities has had quite another end in view, and those cities left with local police, usually the smaller ones, may have as great or greater need of aid than those with state police. In Prussia, alone, does the state contribute to local as well as to state police. The Hanseatic states and Lippe (beginning in 1934) have achieved the same end by establishing state police in all cities, but ten states are without police equalization. In highway support only Prussia and Bavaria have achieved substantial equalization; in housing support only Saxony.[64]

[63] H. Lichtenstein, *Die Finanzwirtschaft der deutschen Grossstädte von 1925 bis 1931*, Jena, 1933, p. 31. Popitz, *Der künftige Finanzausgleich, op. cit.*, p. 225.
[64] Lichtenstein, *op. cit.*, p. 15.

Equalization of welfare burdens has been achieved by the Reich rather than by the states, but as a temporary measure. The need of equalization is particularly great in this field, but it is not without its dangers. Even with existing aids the *Reichssparkommissar* reports that in Hesse administration has been so lax that many welfare recipients have been able to collect both unemployment relief and insurance.[65] This, however, would seem to be the result of duplication of administration in this field rather than of too liberal central support.

Eventually the division of administration and support among the different governmental jurisdictions will be uniform throughout the Reich. So much is fairly certain. But the nature of this division and the extent to which the specific costs of the separate functions will be equalized is still to be determined.

[65] *Gutachten über die Steuerverwaltung des Volksstaates Hessen*, 1929, p. 12.

VI

BASES FOR THE DISTRIBUTION OF SHARED TAXES

THE merits of the shared tax as compared with other fiscal devices for balancing revenues and expenditures among the different layers of government are discussed elsewhere. If the shared tax is selected, however, there is still the problem of finding a suitable basis of distribution. This has proved so difficult that it has seemed desirable to consider in some detail the wide variety of bases with which the German governments have experimented in recent years.

The base chosen for the distribution of a specific tax to local governments depends on the extent of equalization desired, on the one hand, and the extent to which the central government has monopolized resources on the other. If the central government were to take over all revenue sources it could achieve complete equalization by redistributing these entirely according to accepted standards of need, or it could achieve no equalization whatever by returning the revenues where they originated. Usually the government's goal is between these two extremes. But usually, also, the central government has no monopoly of resources; and if local governments are left with substantial independent incomes, central government revenues can be distributed solely on the basis of need without achieving complete equalization.

The return of taxes to the jurisdiction of origin is not as simple as it might at first appear, but distribution according to need is even more difficult. Expenditures themselves are not an acceptable measure because local governments may set quite different standards for themselves, or, with the same standards, spend different amounts because of differences in governmental efficiency. It is apparent that a satisfactory basis for the distribution of revenues according to need must be one that cannot be influenced by local officials, and one that will adjust itself to changes in need. It is apparent, also, that no one measure will be adequate. "Need" is the product of innumerable factors.

RETURN OF TAX REVENUES TO COMMUNITY OF ORIGIN

The centralization of tax administration which has necessitated the redistribution of taxes to underlying governmental jurisdictions was not originally for the purpose of equalizing resources. On the contrary, every effort was made to maintain the financial position of state and local governments as before, in so far as this was compatible with a system of uniform Reich taxes controlled entirely by the central government. To this end two factors were considered, the origin of the tax and the former state and local revenues from this source. The original Reich provisions for the return of income, corporation, turnover, land purchase, inheritance, and beer taxes were based, with two exceptions, on collections, modified in the case of income, corporation, and inheritance taxes by former revenues. The two exceptions were the special beer tax indemnity, based entirely on former yields, and the state share (but not the local share) of the turnover tax, returned in proportion to population. Even the latter exception would seem, in its intent, to have been an attempt to get the tax back where it "belongs," on the assumption that buyers, not sellers, ultimately bear the tax, rather than a deliberate attempt to equalize on the assumption that governmental needs are roughly in proportion to population.

Of those taxes included in Reich tax distributions in later years, only the stock exchange tax, for the few months of its existence, and the general beer tax distribution, have been returned entirely on the basis of collections. Collections are one factor, however, in the distribution of all these taxes, except the merger tax. In the case of the new meat tax the only considerations are present and past yields of the tax.

Nevertheless, so many modifications have been introduced that approximately one-fourth of the specific tax revenues returned were redistributed on other bases than tax yields in 1932-33; and if one adds Reich subventions, more than half (53.5 per cent) the money paid by the central government to underlying jurisdictions in 1932-33, compared with less than one-fifth (18.3 per cent) in 1925-26, was returned on other bases than tax yields. This latter comparison is the more significant since the Reich has not merely substituted other bases for yield in the return of specific taxes collected but has substituted grants for definite purposes for the distribution of fixed percentages of specific taxes. This process has been carried even farther by the states, in so far as these revenues have been redistributed to the communes. The complex nature of the bases on which distributions are made prohibits exact measurement, but it is safe to say that a very small share of the original tax yields is returned to the commune of origin as such and that this share is declining.

As a basis of distribution tax yields are open to two serious objections. The first objection is that the taxes centralized are usually those for which the tax base cannot be readily allocated to a smaller jurisdiction, and if the tax base cannot be successfully allocated for purposes of tax administration any allocation of yields is inevitably arbitrary. The corporation income tax is perhaps the best illustration of this. The income of a large corporation operating over a wide area "belongs" neither to the commune where the head office is located nor to the commune or communes where plants are situated. And the arbitrary allocation of its taxes to any or all of these communes results in such wide and meaningless variations in revenues that some of the states which have clung to origin as the basis for a substantial share of the personal income tax have modified it for the corporation income tax. Thus the industrial state of Saxony distributes only half the local share of the corporation tax to the communes of origin, and Prussia, Brunswick, and Anhalt make certain deductions from local shares when these exceed either personal income tax distributions or more than a given sum per capita. The small size of the communes has complicated the system of allocation unduly. Even comparatively small business concerns cross these local boundaries.

The second objection to tax yields as a basis of distribution is that such yields bear no necessary relation to needs. When the immediate jurisdiction controls the tax, rates can be increased or decreased as needs dictate. When the central government imposes a uniform rate this may easily produce more in a wealthy community than that community requires and at the same time be wholly inadequate in a poor community. To meet this difficulty the Reich and the states have diverted increasing shares of the taxes returned away from the place of origin. Only the land purchase tax is returned almost entirely on the basis of collections, but it is a comparatively small tax and readily allocated. Even this tax is redistributed on other bases in two states, Mecklenburg and Anhalt.

In the case of the income and corporation taxes origin is still the primary basis of distribution, and the Reich allocates the revenues not merely to the state but to the commune of origin,[1] the method of allocation following closely the former Prussian method. Further, the states are instructed to consider the Reich basis (origin) in redistributing the tax to the communes.

Careful examination of the system reveals, however, that the back flow is so blocked and diverted that only a small part trickles down to the commune of origin as such. In the first place, the various guarantees have diverted a substantial sum to other bases. In the second place, the emergency levies on income have not been distributed at all as income tax yields, although they are

---

[1] This is solely for the purpose of determining the state share and does not limit the state in redistributing revenues to local governments.

in fact distributed in large part to the communes in the form of welfare grants. Further, the commune share in that part of the Reich distribution which reaches the state in accordance with origin is usually redistributed, at least in part, on other bases. Thus in Prussia, after the deduction of various grants and equalization funds, a substantial share of the income and corporation taxes is returned to the communes on the basis of origin; but the basis is so distorted by the relative guarantee and the corporation tax limitations that the primary basis is hardly recognizable. The distribution of these taxes in Bavaria is dominated by prewar revenues. In Saxony population, as well as origin, is used as the residual base after school costs have been deducted. No state has accepted origin without modification as the basis of redistribution to local units, and in a number of states the amounts redistributed on other bases exceed the amounts returned according to origin.

The administrative problem of determining the claims, on the basis of origin, of each of the sixty thousand and more communes has been no simple one, and more or less arbitrary regulations have been applied for the assignment of the yield, taking into account the place where business is transacted, place of residence or head office, place where wages are paid, and place where property is located. These rules vary for private enterprises and for corporations, and for financial and other corporations. The regulations have also been changed from time to time. In the case of the wage tax, credit is given to the commune of residence, although the tax is actually collected from the employer. Between one-fifth and one-fourth of the workers taxed live in another commune from that in which they work.[2] This elaborate system of allocation would hardly be justified for the redistribution of a

[2] For a detailed account of the administration of the *Reichsverteilungsschlüssel* see F. Ungethum, "Die deutschen Städte im Überweisungssystem des Reichsfinanzausgleichs." *Schriftenreihe des deutschen Städtetages,* No. 17, 1932. According to Wilhelmi the Reich has had to depend on the states for the final determination of the commune quotas.—*Ruhr und Rhein*, X (November 1, 1929), 1446.

small and diminishing share of the yield of these taxes even if the results of the distribution were defensible. But the complaints against the present system are directed largely against the failure to equalize more. That is, in so far as the attempt to return money where it originated has succeeded, the system has been unsatisfactory.

Even if origin were a more acceptable basis for distributions, and the somewhat arbitrary regulations were to be regarded as substantially reasonable, it is apparent that the time and labor involved are in themselves serious drawbacks. Final allocation bases have not been fixed each year, and when eventually established they have been made retroactive. Thus the states not only cannot determine in advance what they will receive but after the distribution has been made they cannot be sure that it will be final.[3] The alternative is to base distributions on yields of earlier years. This alternative has, for the moment, been adopted, not because there has not been time to establish a more recent base, but deliberately, because the old base happens to be better adapted to current needs. Distributions are now being made on a standard fixed in 1931 on the basis of 1929 income. The latter year, one of comparative prosperity, favors the highly industrialized states such as Hamburg and Saxony, which have suffered most from depression and, consequently, have been in greatest need. Württemberg, which has suffered least from depression and which has everything to gain from a revised standard, has protested in vain. There can be no doubt as to the wisdom of this opportunist measure, but nothing could more clearly condemn the nominal basis of distribution.

In the case of the turnover tax little consideration is given to collections. In the beginning the Reich returned the local share, which was regarded as payment for aid in administration, on the

[3] The original intention was to revise the base once in two years. Actually, three final bases have been set since stabilization, the first in September, 1927, for 1926-27 and 1927-28; the second in May, 1929, for 1928-29, 1929-30, and 1930-31; and the third in November, 1931, for 1931-32 to the present.—Ungethum, *op. cit.*, p. 8.

basis of collections, and later, for the benefit of industrial cen-
ters, one-third was returned to the states where collected. But,
however much Saxony and Hamburg may have approved distribution on the basis of collections for the Reich standard, their
approval of this base has not extended to redistribution within the
state on this base. In no state is any part of the turnover tax returned to local units on the basis of collections; and collections as
a base would be hard to justify on any ground, in view of the
probability that a substantial share of the tax is shifted to
consumers.

Collections play a minor part in the distribution of the motor
vehicle tax by the Reich to the states, but, in so far as this is
passed on to local governments, collections play no part. This tax
is dedicated entirely to highway costs, and there are other and
better measures of highway need.

One-third of the short-lived mineral water tax was returned to
the states in proportion to collections. This was all passed on to
local governments, but in no case did the states use collections
as a base. The general beer tax distribution has gone to the states
entirely on the basis of collections. Most of this tax is retained by
the states, but in so far as it is passed on to local governments,
collections play no part in the redistribution. The new meat tax
also goes back to the states partly on the basis of collections, but
again collections are not the basis of redistribution to local divisions, and the Reich base is clearly a transition measure which
cannot long continue in its present form.

There would seem to be nothing in the German experience of
allocating centrally administered revenues to underlying jurisdictions which would support an argument in favor of distribution in accordance with yields. The political reasons for such
distribution are apparent. The wealthier district will inevitably
oppose the obvious subsidizing of poorer districts. In so far as
revenues are returned whence they came no one will lose; but
close examination of this principle shows that it has no sound eco-

nomic base. Where did the revenue arise? It is easy to demonstrate, even to the average citizen, that one cannot reasonably allocate the tax paid by a corporation doing a nationwide business to the narrow limits of a single commune; and if, as frequently happens, the workers in a factory live in another commune, has the commune in which they work no claim to the tax on their wages? If the right of any particular district to specific revenues cannot be demonstrated, the argument for distribution according to yield breaks down. Certainly the relation between taxable wealth and income and governmental needs is very remote. The reciprocal of the tax yield, which was one of the bases for the apportionment of the pre-war Prussian *Dotationen*, has not been incorporated in post-war systems, in spite of the many experiments in equalization.

FORMER REVENUES AS A BASIS OF TAX DISTRIBUTIONS

The frequency with which former revenues are considered in the distribution of current taxes is to be explained as a transition measure. It offers the governmental jurisdictions concerned some assurance that they will continue to receive an income comparable to that to which they are accustomed and that the usual functions of government can, therefore, be maintained. In the case of Germany, however, this continuity had been rudely broken by war and inflation before the new system was established, and for the most part the guarantees of former revenue represent an attempt to restore the comparatively satisfactory financial conditions which preceded the war. Too many changes had taken place in the intervening decade, however, to make the attempt successful.

The Reich at first guaranteed the states, from income and corporation taxes, their average revenue from income taxes in the period preceding the taking over of these taxes by the Reich, but this guarantee never proved effective, since the distribution on the regular base exceeded the guarantee, and it was later abandoned.

Prussia's relative guarantee has been described elsewhere [4] and need not be further described here. The base was nearly fifteen years old when it was first applied, and the lapse of ten more years since its first application has only made it more unsatisfactory. Through the chance of a comparatively low per capita income tax in 1911 Hanover had her share in the income and corporation taxes reduced from 24 to 19 marks per capita, in 1929, whereas Frankfurt-am-Main, with a relatively high 1911 income tax, had her share reduced from 38 to only 35 marks per capita in the same year.[5] Thus the wealthier city lost less than the poorer one. It is not, of course, the function of this guarantee to equalize, but whatever merit the 1911 base may have had when it was first adopted, as a fixed and known standard in a sea of uncertainties, has long since disappeared. If it operates to nullify the effect of sounder measures it is positively harmful.

In Bavaria each commune and circle receives that proportion of the state and local share of income and corporation taxes originating within its boundaries, as determined by the Reich standard, represented by the ratio of its income, property, and capital earnings taxes to all such state and local taxes levied within its boundaries during the period 1912 to 1919. This has the advantage over the Prussian system of being based on a longer and more recent period, but it brings its own difficulties. Some two hundred communes with valuable property had levied no such taxes during the specified period, and much of this property was lost during inflation.[6] These communes have no claim to income and corporation taxes under the formula adopted, although they have very genuine need. The state has attempted to correct this difficulty by establishing an equalization fund to be distributed at the discretion of state officials. But this puts these communes in the position of proving need, although they are perhaps contrib-

[4] See *supra*, p. 83.
[5] Popitz, *Der künftige Finanzausgleich, op. cit.*, pp. 121-22.
[6] Schanz, *Finanz-Archiv, op. cit.*, XLIV, 704.

uting as much, according to the Reich standard, as communes which receive their allotment as a matter of course.

Mecklenburg distributes the income and corporation taxes on a base similar to that used by Bavaria, but each commune is guaranteed at least 20 percent of the yield assigned by the Reich standard and may not receive more than 40 per cent. These limitations prevent the extremes from which Bavarian communes suffer, but the base would seem to have no particular virtue. Hesse and Baden distribute only a part of the tax on the basis of former yields, and Lippe guarantees the average income of 1912 to 1914.[7]

In the case of the other taxes, the amount of the special beer tax indemnity to the southern states, being compensation for lost revenue, was determined by the revenue displaced. The distribution by the Reich to the states of a share in the inheritance tax was accompanied by a guarantee of former income, a guarantee which continued for a time after the states' share in the tax itself had been abandoned. When the turnover tax was reduced, in 1924, the states were guaranteed their earlier revenue from this source for a few months. More recently, with the reduction in the motor vehicle tax, the states have been guaranteed a fixed sum from this source for three years; and with the transfer of the meat tax from the states to the Reich the states receive half of the proceeds for the first year on the basis of former state tax yields.

The only other instance in which former yield has been used as a basis for distribution of taxes is the motor vehicle tax in Saxony. A substantial share of this tax is distributed to local districts in proportion to the yield of the draft animal tax of 1925. This, too, might have been useful as a transition measure, but there seems to be no occasion for continuing it. Present highway needs, to which this tax is dedicated, probably bear little relation to the former tax.

[7] The former Mecklenburg-Strelitz guaranteed the 1913 yield.

As a transition measure there is much to be said for the use of former revenues as a basis for current tax distributions. The revenues of the immediate past are apt, under normal conditions at least, to be a fair measure of need; and the jurisdiction concerned has some assurance as to the amount of income it will receive. But it is only useful as a transition measure. It has no permanent place in the distribution system. The further the base year recedes into the past, the less significance it has in the determination of present needs. In view of all the changes of fortune which the various sections of Germany have experienced in the past twenty years, it is highly improbable that pre-war or pre-inflation tax revenues could bear any relation to present needs.

PER CAPITA DISTRIBUTION

If revenues are not to be returned to the community from which they came, the most obvious basis for distribution is population. This base has many advantages. It is easy to determine and not subject to manipulation; and it is probably the best single measure of need that can be found. Expenditures inevitably increase with increases in population. Moreover, it is understood and accepted as "fair" by the average citizen, a factor of no small importance.

In so far as revenues are not returned to the place where they are collected population is the most frequent base. Two-thirds of the Reich turnover tax is distributed to the states on a simple population base, and in Württemberg, Mecklenburg, Anhalt, Lübeck, and Bremen all the local share is distributed on this base. In several other states (Bavaria, Saxony, Baden, Oldenburg, Lippe, and Hamburg) population is an important factor in the distribution of the turnover tax to local governments. In still other states the population base for the distribution of the turnover tax has been weighted. These weighted bases will be discussed later. Population was also the most common factor for the distribution of the short-lived mineral water tax, being used for two-thirds of the Reich distribution and all or a substantial share of most state distributions.

In the case of income and corporation taxes origin is the more usual basis for distribution, but population is the basis for the most important Reich guarantee, and it is an important factor in the distributions of this tax to local governments in Saxony, Baden, Thuringia, and Brunswick and influences to a lesser degree the state distributions to local governments in Prussia and Anhalt. Population is found occasionally as a basis for the distribution of other taxes, entering into the Reich base for distributing the betting and motor vehicle taxes and into the state base for distributing the land purchase tax in Mecklenburg and Lippe, the motor vehicle tax in Lippe, and the beer tax in Württemberg.

Population as a standard for distributing taxes equalizes between rich and poor communities, but affords, at best, only a rough measure of needs. In sparsely settled territory the cost of government is apt to be high per capita, and per capita costs rise again in very densely populated communities. They are also influenced by the age distribution and economic status of the population, and by geographical factors. Some states have not been satisfied with the simple population base and have weighted population in an attempt to allow for other factors. The most frequent modification of the simple population base is weighting the population according to the size of the community. Thus for turnover tax distributions, Prussia, Thuringia, and Brunswick have weighted population according to the size of the commune, and Prussia has weighted it a second time for the proportion of school children. In other instances one factor in the population has been selected as the basis of tax distributions. Württemberg and Lippe both distribute a portion of the income and corporation taxes in proportion to school children, and Mecklenburg-Schwerin distributed the larger part of the mineral water tax in proportion to the number of unemployed supported by public funds. These differ from subventions in that the use of the money for schools or welfare is not definitely specified, and in that the total amount distributed varies with the yield of the tax, not with the base.

The usual reason for the selection of population as a basis of distribution is that this offers a rough measure of need. For the turnover tax and such special consumption taxes as the mineral water tax this reason is further strengthened by the fact that population is also a rough measure of the amount contributed by each community. When population is weighted, need alone is considered. The increase in weight with the increase in the size of the city corresponds roughly to the increases in per capita city expenditures which are normally found in the larger cities. In fact, the specific weighting used in the different states has been based on the actual differences found in the per capita expenditures of the different groups of communes. When population figures are weighted for the proportion of school children,[8] the proportion of the working population, or the percentage of unemployed, the costs of specific functions, such as education and welfare, are the influencing factors, although no limitation is placed on the commune's use of the money.

The frequency with which weighted population is urged for tax distributions in Germany makes it important to consider how such distributions would operate in specific cases. The use of such bases is so limited that no conclusions can be drawn from actual tax distributions, but it is possible to take the population structure and expenditures of different cities and determine the effect of such forms of distribution. The aim of this form of distribution is to adapt resources to needs, and the weighting in accordance with the size of the commune is based on the fact, noted above, that per capita expenditures increase with the size of the city. While this is true on the average, it is only necessary to call attention to the

---

[8] Weighting for the proportion of children is often urged, not merely because of increased school costs, but also because a high proportion of children indicates a large and relatively poor working population, and, in addition, owing to tax exemptions, reduces the income tax yield.

figures in Table 36 [9] to demonstrate that variations from the average may be important. Cologne, with a population of 750,-000, had a per capita expenditure of 134 marks in 1932-33, whereas Duisburg-Hamborn, with a population of 440,000, had a per capita expenditure of 151 marks, and Offenbach, with a population of 81,000, had a per capita expenditure of 170 marks. These were the expenditures remaining after the deduction of Reich welfare aid and all other special sources of revenue—the expenditures which must be covered from local resources and distributions of Reich taxes. Under these conditions to give Cologne more per capita than Duisburg-Hamborn or Offenbach is to make a bad situation worse. Under the Prussian system of weighting turnover tax distributions for the size of the city, Cologne should have received 2.20 marks per capita against 2.16 in Duisburg-Hamborn, and if this system had been extended to all Germany, Offenbach would have received 1.84 per capita. Turnover tax distributions in Prussia are weighted a second time, however, for the proportion of children of school age. And since Duisburg-Hamborn had a larger proportion of children of school age than Cologne, the discrepancy resulting from weighting in accordance with size was corrected, Cologne continuing to receive 2.20 marks per capita against 2.23 per capita in Duisburg-Hamborn. This second factor cannot be counted on, however, to correct the first, when the first is an inaccurate measure. If Offenbach had been under the Prussian system it would have continued to receive 1.84 per capita, since the number of school children in Offenbach did not exceed the average for cities of this size. If the population of the cities were weighted a third time, this time for the percentage of the population receiving public relief, a closer approximation to needs would be reached. This factor has not been used, however.

Popitz's plan for the distribution of Reich taxes, distributing half on a population base weighted for the size of the city, and

[9] See Appendix, p. 356.

half on a base weighted for the proportion of the working population, would materially benefit four of the poor cities given in
Table 36; but it would put Offenbach on a par with Düsseldorf
and Breslau on a par with Frankfurt-am-Main, Stuttgart, and
Münster. Popitz himself notes the discrepancy in the case of
Breslau and points out that special aids for exceptional cases
would still be needed.

The tendency for per capita local government expenditures to
increase as the size of the city increases has a twofold explanation.
The close proximity in which people live necessitates increasing
social control and increasing services for the common good. This
same population density tends to increase per capita real estate
values, however, and per capita business activity. Thus the base
of local taxes to some extent keeps pace with local needs. This has
not fully compensated, however, for the higher per capita costs in
the larger German cities in recent years.

A detailed analysis of revenues and expenditures of cities
grouped according to population classes reveals the fact that the
per capita costs of practically all important local functions
increase with the size of the city.[10] The most marked rates of increase, however, as the size of the city increases, are in expenditures for welfare, housing, and institutions. Other expenditures
are not out of proportion to increases in ability as tested by local
taxes. It is recognized that local tax yields are very imperfect
tests of ability, since local taxes are to some extent adjusted to
needs, but data on tax rates for real estate and business taxes in
individual cities, while showing great variation from one city to
another, reveal no tendency for rates to vary with the size of the
city. The median tax rates for both real estate and business taxes
were the same in 1932-33 for cities of more than 100,000 and
cities under 100,000 in Prussia. The available information is not
sufficiently complete to make it possible to speak with certainty,

[10] Comprehensive data covering the finances of cities grouped according to population are to be found in *Statistik des deutschen Reichs*, Vols. 387 and 440.

since tax rates for communes under 10,000 population are not available, but so far as data can be found they indicate that if welfare needs, and perhaps also housing needs, were used as bases for the distribution of Reich funds, they would offer a far more accurate measure of need than the size of the population. Welfare expenditures form an important part of local costs, even in normal times. On the average they increase rapidly with the size of the city; but they differ greatly in different cities in the same population group. A city which is the trading center of a large agricultural region will have very different welfare needs from a manufacturing city of the same size. Two cities depending on the same industries may have quite different burdens. Essen and Duisburg-Hamborn illustrate this. These two cities, lying side by side, each largely dependent not only on the steel industry but on the same corporation, had 44 and 73 persons per 1,000, respectively, on the relief rolls at the end of 1933. The Krupp Company had chosen to operate its Essen rather than its Duisburg plants. Welfare requirements would seem to offer the only index which will measure such differences in need, differences which arise from the increased burden on one hand, and the decreased ability to meet that burden on the other hand. Reich tax distributions conforming to these welfare needs will go much farther toward equalizing burdens from city to city than distributions on any weighted population base, and if welfare expenditures are deducted from total city expenditures, the remaining governmental costs and the local tax resources will increase with the size of the city at about the same rate.[11]

SPECIAL BASES FOR THE DISTRIBUTION OF HIGHWAY MONEY

Motor vehicle tax distributions, being dedicated to highway costs, are usually distributed according to some specific measure

[11] The ratio of expenditures to real estate and business tax yields for 1931-32 varies a little from one group of cities to the next but shows no tendency either to increase or decrease as the size of the cities increases.

of highway needs. The Reich distributes this money to the states, one-fourth in proportion to population, one-fourth in proportion to collections, and one-half in proportion to area. Since motor vehicle traffic is a function of population and area, and since collections for this tax are doubtless heaviest in areas of greatest traffic, these bases would seem to be reasonable. In 1931 this base was still further refined by weighting area in accordance with population density. This, in effect, increases the weight given to population and decreases the weight given to area.

Area has again been the basis for the state's distribution of motor vehicle taxes to local governments in Bremen, and one of three factors used to distribute that part of the income and corporation taxes in Prussia which replaces the former province and circle *Dotationen* for highways. A second factor in these latter distributions is population. For the most part, however, the states have substituted highway mileage for the Reich bases of distribution in redistributing motor vehicle revenues to local governments. This has been the sole basis of distribution in Mecklenburg, Oldenburg, and Brunswick and an important factor in the distributions in Hesse and Lippe. It is also used as the third factor in the Prussian *Dotationen*. For the rest, instances are to be found of tax collections and a former tax source as bases for a part of the redistribution of such revenues. Two states have set local shares at fixed percentages in the law, and five leave all or a part of the distribution of this tax to the discretion of state officials.

DISCRETIONARY DISTRIBUTION

Many instances are to be found in state distributions to local governments of distribution in accordance with need, as determined by some state official or body of officials. No state except Bremen is without some kind of state equalization fund distributed at the discretion of state officials,[12] and these funds are de-

---

[12] Bremen has substituted circle equalization funds for state funds.

rived primarily from Reich taxes. The advantages of such funds are clear. Need is the product of such a large number of variables that no formula can measure it with any degree of precision, and human judgment, if sufficiently detached and intelligent, has a flexibility which fixed standards lack. Opposed to this, however, is the danger of partiality, whether deliberate or unconscious. Moreover, the complexity of the problem is apt to stagger human judgment, and, in practice, those administering such funds honestly and intelligently almost inevitably resort to a formula. There is still the advantage, of course, that in the case of obvious misfits the formula can be disregarded.

Another factor arguing against the discretionary distributions is the effect on the community of having to prove need. The fact that more money is to be had for the asking, provided one makes a good case, often turns formerly independent and self-respecting communities into beggars. Nevertheless such equalization funds would seem to have a place in every system of distribution. It may be desirable to distribute the bulk of the available funds according to definite formulae, but there will always be exceptional cases of need which a rigid system of distribution will fail to reach. When funds are limited and needs are very great there is probably no substitute for these discretionary distributions. Under such conditions the probability of deliberate misuse is slight, and the formula, which inevitably allots some money to communities not in urgent need, is a luxury which the state can ill afford.

VII

FUNDAMENTAL CHANGES IN THE FINANCIAL SYSTEM UNDER THE WEIMAR CONSTITUTION

THE Weimar Constitution laid the foundation for a uniform and unified tax system, and the central government has worked steadily toward the construction of such a system, whether hampered or aided by the succession of financial emergencies which the country has faced since then. In consequence, there is no real duplication of taxes or tax administration, and the more important taxes are in the hands of the Reich. Real estate, business, and rentals taxes are still under the control of state and local governments and these vary in form from state to state. Also, the rates of these taxes, as well as the land purchase and citizen taxes, vary in the different local governments. But plans for uniform bases for these taxes have been made and partly executed, and it would seem to be only a matter of time until they will be in full effect. Germany has practically achieved the uniform tax system which has been the goal of many tax reforms in other countries in recent years.

The problem of local independence is not so easily solved as the problem of uniform taxation. Not only is it difficult to reconcile self-government with a uniform tax system, but disregarding the financial problem there is no agreement as to the extent of local self-government that is desirable in and of itself. Up to a certain point the ends of the present government are clear, as is the way to their achievement. Concentration of power in the hands of the Reich and the reduction of the states to mere administrative agencies has already been attained. Variations in state tax systems are only tolerated until economic conditions permit the adoption of the uniform tax system long since accepted and in considerable part incorporated in the law. More and more the Reich is dealing directly with the communes; and for the moment, at least, local authorities are the tools of the central government.

The final division of revenues between central and local governments, however, must await some decision as to the distribution of functions themselves among the various governmental jurisdictions. The ultimate division of functions between central and local government is indicated by recent legislation. Police, main highways, and education are increasingly controlled by the central government, and, except for education, the central government is providing material support. Whether the central government will take over the system of state school subsidies now in force or leave it to some intermediate layer of government with enough resources to provide for them is uncertain. Local roads, city streets, water, heat, light, and transportation systems, and such local institutions as markets and theatres are left, as formerly, to local control. Welfare, in spite of substantial aid from the central government in recent years, is still regarded as a local function, to be returned, so far as social insurance does not cover it, almost wholly to local control and local support when the emergency is over.

It is apparent that the government has gone much farther in reorganizing its tax system than in reorganizing governmental administration as a whole. Overlapping of administration is particularly serious in welfare. And it is far from clear whether local initiative is to be preserved in education, as Popitz urges,[1] or whether in the interests of equal opportunity or political unity a dead level of education is to be provided throughout the Reich. In fact, no comprehensive plan is yet to be found for the division of tasks between the Reich and its underlying jurisdictions.

Also, the manner in which these local functions are to be supported is still to be determined, although here there are many

---

[1] *Der künftige Finanzausgleich, op. cit.,* p. 225.

plans. The Reich's policy was dictated in the first instance by expediency, and it has continued to be dictated by expediency. The unequal size and resources of the different states, the large number of layers of government, and the exceptionally small size of the ultimate commune have complicated the problem. The original aim of the Reich was to compensate state and local governments for lost revenues. To this end it redistributed taxes largely where collected, or, if this led to obvious injustice, taxes were distributed according to the situs of certain properties or business. Attempts to equalize were limited, at first, to the use of population as the basis for distributing the turnover tax, and the adoption of minimum guarantees in case revenues fell below pre-war levels. But the return of Reich-administered revenues to the commune of origin in large sums is not feasible. So much has been demonstrated. Revenues and governmental requirements cannot be thus completely divorced. In spite of the extensive state controls exercised over local governments, the municipalities indulged in unprecedented extravagance in the years immediately following inflation, and the unexpectedly large distributions from Reich taxes contributed to this extravagance. With depression the system broke down completely, since it failed to send the dwindling tax yields to the areas with the most urgent needs.

Notwithstanding all the opportunist measures a certain piecemeal equalization has been achieved, as well as increasing centralization of the tax power. But the choice between varying local tax rates on real estate and business, and perhaps also on personal income, and the distribution, on some equalizing base, of revenues from taxes levied at uniform rates throughout the Reich, has yet to be made. The one leads to local self-government, with its local freedom, local responsibility, and individuality—all desirable ends. The other leads to uniform taxes and equal opportunity, likewise desirable ends. The question is how far inequalities are to be equalized.

Popitz's plan for the final division of revenues among the

different jurisdictions provides for specific subventions for police and schools and tax distributions on the basis of need to equal about one-third of local expenditures. This is including expenditures from subventions as local rather than state expenditures. The remaining two-thirds would come from local taxes and surpluses from local industries. Local surtaxes on income would not be permitted, however. Subventions and tax distributions would, on the basis of 1929 data, come to about equal amounts, but the total amount of the subventions would vary with need and the total amount of the tax distributions would vary with tax yields. In consequence, this proportion would change materially from year to year. No important redistribution of functions is contemplated in this plan. Equalization is to be achieved partly through subventions, partly through the tax distributions. The tax distribution has the advantage, compared with the ordinary subvention, of rising and falling with total tax income. In this way the local governments share with the central government the changing fortunes of the business cycle, and the central government is not forced to make all the adjustments. Much the same end could be achieved, of course, by changing the rate of contribution to teachers' salaries or reducing highway subventions, although such an adjustment would not be automatic. No important part of the taxes distributed would be returned where collected. Further, the local rural unit of government would be enlarged, even beyond the size of the present circle. This, too, would equalize resources. In view of the position of Popitz as Prussian minister of finance and his exhaustive studies of the problem, his plan has been widely accepted.

Another important plan, based on a detailed study of the effects of various systems of distribution in specific communes, is that published in a memorandum to the Prussian *Landtag* in 1929.[2] While designed for Prussia, it is equally applicable to the entire Reich. This, too, contemplates extensive equalization through

[2] *Denkschrift*, No. 2275, op. cit.

special police and school subventions, special equalization for poor districts, and per capita distributions of the residual revenues, population being weighted for the size of the commune, the proportion of school children in the population, and possibly the rate of growth of the commune. The possibility of local surtaxes on the income tax is not considered, since the plan is designed for the state, not for the Reich; but the absence of any provision for the return of revenues where collected, in spite of the fact that the amount of the contemplated tax redistributions is very large, suggests that equalization is regarded as the more essential, and perhaps the only, factor. Many other plans, however, urge the restoration of local surtaxes on the income tax, and the local governments themselves are eager for such a solution.

The final solution will doubtless offer some compromise between complete separation of central and local revenue sources and complete centralization of all sources. Genuine local self-government can be realized at neither extreme. Local self-support from independent tax levies leaves a large proportion of the communes much too poor to exercise local initiative, and complete dependence on the central government tends inevitably toward central control of all governmental functions.

Whether, in the ultimate adjustment, the government swings toward the greater equalization provided in the Popitz plan or the greater nominal local freedom of the local surtax on income is uncertain. But if welfare continues to be primarily a local function it is safe to guess that a very substantial degree of equalization will, perforce, take place. The attempt to restore to the communes the revenues collected within their jurisdiction from a uniform Reich tax is doomed to failure. No faction is urging it for any important tax distributions, and it has not even the virtue of simplicity to recommend it. In so far as local governments are permitted to reap the benefit of their own unusual tax resources, it will be on their own responsibility.

There is another possible solution which is receiving increasing attention, namely, the creation of a larger local governmental unit corresponding as far as possible to the local economic unit. The average German commune is, for rural government at least, needlessly and hopelessly small. Enlargement of the local governmental jurisdiction has frequently been suggested as a minor factor in the various plans for division of revenues, but it has rarely been advanced as the first requisite of a satisfactory division of governmental activities and revenues between central and local governments. Some consolidation of districts has taken place, notably the consolidation of the Ruhr into fourteen contiguous cities, but financial considerations have not always determined these consolidations, and where sparsely settled territory is taken into a city and the inhabitants supplied with the usual city services, they have proved costly.[3]

The proposed redistricting of the entire Reich into thirteen provinces of approximately equal size in place of the existing states is of interest in this connection, but the provinces in question are too large for truly local government. Moreover, the plan was so badly drawn that resources were most inequitably distributed among the provinces in question, and for this reason the redistricting has been indefinitely postponed.

The government has no comprehensive plan for the reconstruction of local districts on a self-supporting basis. Nevertheless, a number of those who have made a careful study of the problem, notably the *Reichssparkommissar,* are urging this as the only real solution.[4] The Oldenburg section of the state of Oldenburg has recently (1933) consolidated its local governments into six districts and five city circles. The local unit in question is still small enough to reap most of the benefits of local self-government, and at the same time the inequalities in wealth between one

[3] O. Bühler, *Die Finanzlage des Ruhrgebietsstädte,* Jena, 1932, II, 9. Reichssparkommissar, *Gutachten über die Verwaltung der Stadt Stuttgart,* p. 105.

[4] Reichssparkommissar, *Gutachten über die Landesverwaltung Württembergs,* 1930; *Gutachten über die Landesverwaltung Lippes,* 1930, and *Gutachten über die Verwaltung des Kreises Iserlohn.* Sonderheft der Monatszeitschrift, *Reich und Länder,* May, 1934.

local district and the next are not so great that any extensive equalization is required. Thus, with local resources equal to most local needs, some measure of local independence and local responsibility may be restored. This is a small beginning, but if it should prove successful it might well be extended. It should be noted, however, that Oldenburg, while comparatively poor, has a balance between agriculture and small industries not to be found in all sections of the Reich. Neither the Ruhr, at one extreme, nor East Prussia, at the other, could be divided into "natural" local economic units. The entire province of East Prussia would not make a self-supporting unit.

It is apparent that the possible compromises between a uniform tax system and local independence are many, and it seems probable that the happiest solution of the problem will not be attained by adhering to a single line of reform. The solution indicated is, rather, a complex one, involving a measure of redistricting, a measure of equalization, and, in all probability, limited variation in the tax system.

THE FISCAL SYSTEM OF
ENGLAND AND WALES

VIII

THE PLACE AND DEVELOPMENT OF GRANTS-IN-AID IN THE ENGLISH FISCAL SYSTEM BEFORE 1929

IN FEW, if any, countries do grants-in-aid play as important a part in the financial relations of national and local governments as in England.[1] Where other countries have provided local governments with a variety of local tax sources, as in pre-war Germany, or have taken over the administration as well as the support of functions commonly left to local authorities in less centralized governments, as in France, Great Britain has chosen to meet the increasing local government obligations through increasing grants from national revenues.

Only once in the past century has this development been checked. The local government reform of 1888 attempted to turn over to local authorities enough independent sources of revenue to meet their growing obligations without specific government aids. This reform failed to achieve its end. The 1929 reform, while making radical changes in the form of grants, would seem to have established the grant system more firmly than ever. Today the sums received by local governments from grants-in-aid are nearly as large as the revenues from local rates.

Before turning to the history of grants-in-aid it is important both to define the term and to place it in its proper setting in the national and local fiscal system. This in turn requires a brief account of the organization of local government, the functions for which each type of local unit is responsible, and the sources of revenue at its disposal.

[1] The ensuing discussion has been limited to England and Wales, although Scotland has practically the same system. Because of the great similarity in the two systems there seemed to be nothing to gain by including the Scotch system, and the necessity of pointing out frequent differences in detail, if the latter system were included, would only add to the length and complexity of the study.

Outside large cities there are three layers of local government. At the top is the administrative county, which has grown in power at the expense of the underlying units until it is responsible for the largest part of the administration of education, police, highways, and public assistance. The entire area of the administrative county is subdivided into municipal boroughs, urban districts, and rural districts. Municipal boroughs are usually small cities. Their governmental organization differs from that of urban and rural districts, and they have somewhat wider powers. Municipal boroughs may have their own police forces if they had a population in excess of 10,000 in 1881, and they may control their own schools if they had a population in excess of 10,000 in 1901. Urban districts, like municipal boroughs, tend to be thickly settled areas, but they may not have their own police forces, and they may control their schools only if their population exceeded 20,000 in 1901. Rural districts have no control over either police or education and they have less responsibility for roads than urban districts and municipal boroughs. In fact, since the Local Government Act of 1929 has been in force, they need have no responsibility for roads. Their main functions are health and housing. All these units of local government may operate such public utilities as seem desirable, but rural districts have, naturally, undertaken comparatively few of these services. The third layer of local government is the parish. Parishes cover the entire area of the country, but owing to their small size they have very few powers remaining. In urban areas they have no function whatever. In rural districts the parish council may protect and promote the interests of the narrower jurisdiction of the parish in the larger area of the district.

The county borough exists side by side with the county and is essentially a combined city and county government, having the powers of both the administrative county and the municipal borough. Most of the larger cities are county boroughs. The London government, however, is made up of a county and subsidiarv metropolitan boroughs. Here the county is responsible for education and welfare; the metropolitan boroughs for highways and health. Police are under the control of a special metropolitan police district which includes a wider area than the county. In the matter of public utilities the county operates the tramways, the boroughs are responsible for electricity, markets, and cemeteries, and the water supply is under a separate metropolitan board which, as in the case of the police district, covers an area larger than the county.

CHART 2

ORGANIZATION OF ENGLISH LOCAL GOVERNMENT

Administrative County Principal functions: education, police, highways, welfare, health			
			County Borough
Municipal Borough	Urban District	Rural District	Principal functions:
Principal functions: health, housing, minor roads, public utilities, often education, sometimes police	Principal functions: health, housing, minor roads, public utilities, sometimes education	Principal functions: health, housing, sometimes minor roads, sometimes public utilities	all county and borough functions

Parish

Nominal in urban areas.
Principal functions: protection of community interests.

The general plan of local government outside London is outlined in Chart 2. Size, as measured by area and population, and average expenditures are given in Table 17. It is important to note that there are great variations in the size of the different classes of units, whether measured in area or in population. In addition to the local units listed in the chart, special districts for water supply, sewers, drainage, or other special functions are found occasionally, but they are not important. The total net expenditures of all such districts have been a little more than one million pounds in recent years.

TABLE 17

NUMBER, SIZE, AND AVERAGE EXPENDITURES OF ENGLISH LOCAL
GOVERNMENT UNITS [a]

Unit	Number	AREA (IN SQUARE MILES)			POPULATION (IN THOUSANDS)			Average Per Capita Expenditure (In shillings)
		Highest	Average	Lowest	Highest	Average	Lowest	
County borough.......	83	80	14	4.0	1,003	160	24.0	133.0
Administrative county..	62	2,592	920	84.0	1,795	359	17.0	82.0
Municipal borough.....	263	37	6	0.1	134	21	1.0	71.0
Urban district.........	762	41	6	0.2	184	11	0.3	48.0
Rural district.........	630	385	80	2.0	88	12	1.0	17.0
Parish................	14,370	...	4	...	...	25	...	0.2

a Expenditure figures from *Annual Local Taxation Returns* for 1931-32.   Other figures from 1931 census.

The local governments have considerable freedom in administering the many important functions assigned to them. This is
especially true of the boroughs which as cities have a wider range
of activities than the urban and rural districts.[2] Many of these
boroughs also have special privileges granted by old and cher-
ished charters, but these charters rarely contribute powers of real
importance in dealing with modern municipal problems, whatever their historic interest and sentimental value. Local independence has been somewhat weakened, however, by the lack of
a powerful executive and the many requirements imposed by the
national government as conditions of receiving grants-in-aid.

It is true that local councils still exercise important powers, but
with the growing complexity of government the important but
onerous duties of office are more and more delegated to the paid,
full-time officials. The more important local offices have professional standing, and promotion may mean obtaining a position in
a larger city, instead of a better position in the same community.
This tends to give the incumbent a more-than-local point of view.
And with no strong executive to co-ordinate the different depart-

[2] Some urban districts are, of course, larger than some municipal boroughs, but
for the most part the boroughs are larger, and even where smaller they tend to
have greater concentration of population.

ments on one hand, and with the frequent contacts between national and local officials in the process of meeting national grant regulations on the other, central government standards, even when these are optional, are as apt to be observed as purely local interests.

As a result of the Local Government Act of 1929 (section 46), extensive alterations are being made in district boundaries by the county councils. The aim is to achieve a more effective and a more economical unit of government. The tendency is to consolidate districts where they are too small and poor to support a full-time official. The co-operation of the districts concerned is sought by county authorities, but this consent is not required and some consolidations are reported to have taken place with all the districts concerned protesting. In consequence of this redistricting the number of rural districts was reduced from 718 to 539 between 1928-29 and 1934-35, and the number of urban districts was reduced from 782 to 697 in the same period. Redistricting and consolidation meets with greater opposition in counties and boroughs than in districts. In the former, tradition is strong and special charter privileges, held for centuries, are treasured even though they are costly to the community. It remains to be seen whether the extensive reorganization proposed for distressed areas such as Tyneside and Merthyr Tydfil, involving extensive alterations of county and borough boundaries, can be achieved against local opposition.

The scope of local government, measured in terms of revenue and expenditure, is much more limited than that of the national government. Local governments spent only 35 percent of national and local tax revenues in 1931-32.[3] This is crediting local governments with the amount of grants-in-aid. The proportion of total tax revenues which was collected by local governments was only 18 percent in this same year. In the United States and Germany

[3] The fiscal year begins April 1, as in Germany.

local taxes have normally comprised a larger share of the total tax revenues than national and state taxes combined, although the balance in both of these countries has been shifting rapidly in recent years in favor of the central governments.

The local revenue system is simplicity itself. All these units of government have the right to levy rates; and the local rates comprise the one local tax source available, except for a few unimportant licenses administered by the counties and yielding only a little more than a million pounds a year, or about one-half of one percent of the yield of the rates. Thus local governments in England are even more restricted in their revenue sources than local governments in the United States. The rates are levied, much as the general property tax is levied in the United States, to cover the excess of estimated expenditures over other income. In contrast to the United States, few limitations have been placed on these rates.[4] National authorities have pursued the fairly consistent policy of encouraging local expenditures, rather than checking them; and when rates become too high the central government comes to the rescue with new or increased grants-in-aid.

The rates differ materially in their nature from the general property tax. In the first place they are levied on estimated net rental values instead of on capital values. In the second place they are limited to income from real estate. Personal property was definitely exempted as early as 1840.[5] In the third place they are levied on the occupier rather than on the owner. The owner pays on property which he himself occupies but unoccupied property is exempt.

Assessments are made locally, and prior to 1925 there was little uniformity. The valuation area since 1925 has been the borough or district. There are approximately 1,600 of these. To insure some degree of uniformity among valuation districts they

[4] Occasionally rates for specific purposes are limited, e.g., the library rate and special district rates for sewers and drainage, but no limitations are placed on general rates.

[5] Royal Commission on Local Taxation, *Final Report, 1901*, Cd. 638, p. 33.

are grouped into about 350 assessment areas.[6] An assessment committee is responsible for equalizing valuations within the assessment area, but, while the committee has power to order changes in valuations, its function is to act on complaints brought to it rather than to take the initiative in finding inequalities in valuation. To insure uniformity within the county there is a county committee. The majority of counties have appointed full-time county valuation officers or retained professional valuers as advisers, but a substantial minority have had little or no technical assistance.[7] There is also a central valuation committee, in consequence of recent legislation, but this acts in a purely advisory capacity and there are two intervening committees between this central committee and the officials making the actual valuations.

This hierarchy of committees has an important function to perform. Uniform valuations, not merely within the county but within the whole of England and Wales, are essential to the equitable operation of the new financial system; and it is decidedly in the interest of each valuation district to keep its own valuations relatively low. The central government has not contented itself, however, with setting up committees. Uniform rules of valuation have been prepared, a revaluation once in five years has been provided for, and, since 1930, railroad property, formerly left to the mercy of local officials, has been valued as a unit by a national Railway Assessment Authority. Thus the essential machinery for securing uniform valuations would seem to have been provided, although direct county valuation has much to recommend it in view of the fact that the county rate normally exceeds the rates of the underlying districts. Each local unit determines the amount of its own rates, but all the rates in a given area are levied on the ratepayer, annually or semiannually, as one consolidated rate.[8] Collections are also combined. The administration is largely in the hands of boroughs and districts.

[6] *Rating and Valuation Acts, 1925 to 1932, Report of the Central Valuation Committee,* 1934, p. 115.   [7] *Ibid.,* p. 91.

[8] Occasionally special rates are levied independently, but the exceptions are rare.

A second source of local revenue is the earnings of municipal industries. "Trading services" are important local functions and account for approximately one-fourth of all local expenditures. In some instances these services yield surplus revenues which are applied to the reduction of rates. More often they incur deficits which must be met from the rates. Sometimes local authorities have been deterred from using these trading undertakings as a source of net income by the fact that any such income is subject to the income tax. Since the local rates are levied on the occupiers rather than on the owners of real estate, rates and water or electricity charges are for the most part paid from the same pockets. Moreover, it is common practice to levy the cost of water supply against users in proportion to their valuations for rates, instead of in proportion to water consumed. Only in the case of industrial concerns is a metered service usual. For the ordinary householder this amounts to meeting the cost of water supply from the rates. Consequently, if water charges are increased in order to relieve rates, the result for most ratepayers is merely to transfer the cost from rate bills to water bills. And if, in the process, an income tax is levied, there is net loss to the community. Also, it is widely accepted that these trading services should not be exploited for the benefit of other governmental activities. The usual policy of local authorities is, in consequence, to operate trading services at cost.

Where deficits occur from a trading service it is usually because capital charges are exceptionally high, either because of unfavorable geographical conditions, or because the undertaking was developed immediately after the war when construction costs were abnormal. In one instance a large deficit was explained by the fact that the water and sewer systems were constructed for five times the existing population.[9] They were undertaken in part as a scheme for the relief of unemployment. Unfortunately, the excessive unemployment which instigated this activity is resulting

[9] Interview with the rural district accountant.

in a decline in the population of the district, and the high rates, to which the deficits from these undertakings are contributing, are a further stimulus to emigration.

Water supply, cemeteries, and transportation systems occasioned the greatest deficits in 1932-33, in the order named. Markets, electricity, and gas, on the contrary, produced substantial surpluses in the same year. The deficits of all such trading services for all local units in 1932-33 amounted to 2.7 million pounds and the surpluses to 1.4 million pounds. This leaves a net deficit of 1.3 million pounds for the entire country. These figures are very small in budgets totaling some 440 million pounds. It is apparent that trading services have not been used as a source of net income, as in Germany, nor are they a serious drain on tax resources, as in the United States.

The third important source of local income is the grant-in-aid. Grants bring local governments more revenue than trading services, but less than the rates.[10] Before describing the development of these grants it may be useful to state exactly what has been included under this term, since there is no complete agreement as to its meaning.[11] In the *Report on Local Taxation* by H. H. Fowler [12] the term "grants-in-aid" is limited to payments by the central government to recognized local authorities for functions administered by these local authorities, and this usage has been adopted in the following discussion as far as practicable.[13] Payments to private organizations, or to individuals performing functions generally regarded as a local responsibility, are sometimes regarded as grants-in-aid. The early school grant to voluntary

[10] Rates yielded 145 million pounds in 1932-33. Grants-in-aid yielded 127 million pounds and trading services 114 million pounds in this same year. The income from trading services is gross.

[11] For a general definition of the term see *supra*, pp. 9-10.

[12] H.C. 168, 1893.

[13] This conforms to Sidney Webb's definition, "By a 'Grant in Aid' the English administrator understands a subvention payable from the Exchequer of the United Kingdom to a Local Governing Authority, in order to assist that Authority in execution of some or all of its statutory duties."—Sidney Webb, *Grants in Aid*, London, 1920, p. 7.

educational organizations is an illustration of this. In 1891-92, twenty years after local authorities were charged with the responsibility for education, the amount of the school grant going to voluntary schools was still greater than the amount going to local authorities. Indemnities to private individuals and local governments for losses incurred through national action are frequently called grants-in-aid. These have been included in grants-in-aid here in so far as they go to local authorities, since there would seem to be little choice between the indemnity for the loss of rates on government property and that part of the block grant which is compensation for losses from derating. The 1893 *Report on Local Taxation* [14] includes the money paid to local authorities for loss of rates on government property, together with payments to private individuals for such activities as voluntary schools, under the heading "Other local charges transferred to or borne by annual vote of Parliament." This group also includes payments for functions which were formerly performed by local authorities, but which have been taken over entirely by the central government. An illustration of this is the payment for district auditors' salaries. These officials have been subject to appointment by the central government since 1879, and their salaries were made payable directly by the central government at that time, although the local districts have since been charged for audits and so have contributed something to the cost.[15] Before 1879 these auditors were locally elected officials and the central government contributed part, and for a short period all, of their salaries. These salary payments would thus seem to have been grants-in-aid prior to 1879 and direct national expenditures after that date, and they have been so classified here; but the point where a function becomes national rather than local is not always so clear.

Another instance where classification is difficult is the payment

---

[14] H.C. 168, *op. cit.*   [15] H.C. 168, *op. cit.*, p. 80.

for a function which is regarded as a national obligation, but which can be more conveniently performed by local officials. Such a payment is direct compensation for services rendered rather than a grant. Thus the national government pays specific sums to the Metropolitan police authorities for definite services rendered the government. These payments are frequently excluded from the list of grants, but the national interest is important in many locally administered functions, and it is not always possible to draw the line between the two. In the ensuing discussion the term grants-in-aid has been used in its narrower sense, but these other payments have been noted when they seem to form an integral part of the national and local financial system, or to throw some light on the national government's policy.

Grants-in-aid would seem to have originated in 1831 with a special grant of 90 pounds per year to Berwick Corporation for the repair of Berwick bridge, an expenditure formerly met from the Civil List, and dating back to Charles II.[16] It continues today, although the bridge in question has been superseded, for purposes of traffic, by a modern structure. This very modest forerunner of the grant system was followed shortly by a grant for school buildings, beginning in 1833. This went to two volunteer societies, however, and not to local authorities. Education did not become a function of local government until 1870. In 1833, also, a grant was first made for the Metropolitan police force, which had been established in 1829. In 1835 the first grant for an entire class of local authorities was introduced, with the reimbursement of the counties by the central government for half the costs of criminal prosecutions at Assizes and Quarter Sessions and for a part of the cost of removing prisoners to the place of trial. This

[16] *Government Grants to Local Authorities*, Cmd. 3157, 1928, p. 11. The following account of grants-in-aid has been taken largely from the reports of the various government commissions on local government and taxation, especially H.C. 168, *op. cit.*; Royal Commission on Local Government, *Evidence*, C. 9528, 1899; Departmental Committee on Local Taxation, *Final Report*, Cd. 7315, and *Appendix*, Cd. 7316, 1914.

came as the result of the recommendations of a Parliamentary Committee appointed to investigate the rating system.[17] The committee justified such a grant on the ground that the function thus subsidized was of national importance, and this justification has been regularly used by the long succession of committees and commissions which have since investigated the problem of local finances when recommending further grants for an ever-widening range of functions, until most important local activities have come to be regarded as "national" or "seminational" in character. The actual relief to rates resulting from these first grants was not great. They amounted to only 2.7 percent of local revenues from rates and grants in 1842-43. But central government aids did not stop with these comparatively unimportant beginnings. On the contrary, the movement gathered momentum in succeeding years.

The local rates, like any tax on real estate, bore heavily on the agricultural interests, and the national government sought to compensate the farmers for the repeal of the Corn Laws by further grants for the relief of rates.[18] Beginning in 1845 the national government assumed the entire cost of criminal prosecutions and voted further sums for the maintenance of prisoners in local jails. In the same year, for the benefit of the poor-law unions, it assumed half the salaries of their medical officers, all the salaries of teachers and industrial trainers in workhouses, and the fees of poor-law auditors. In consequence of these changes the proportion of local rate and grant revenue coming from grants increased from 2.7 percent in 1842-43 to 5.4 percent in 1852-53.

In 1853 the voluntary school societies in agricultural districts benefited from a capitation grant, the first school grant for maintenance. In 1852 and 1854 local governments received new grants for the administration of justice, and in 1856 they received a

[17] *Report on County Rates*, H.C. 542, 1834, pp. iii-iv.   [18] C. 9528, *op. cit.*, p. 12.

grant for police. Since the police grant was accompanied by the requirement that counties and county boroughs establish police forces and the grant reimbursed them only to the extent of one-fourth of the pay and clothing costs of approved police forces, this measure was not primarily one for the relief of rates. Police grants constituted approximately half the total grants for some years after their introduction. The only new grants in the next decade were comparatively unimportant ones for Metropolitan fire brigades, introduced in 1865, and for public vaccinators, introduced in 1867.

The Education Act of 1870, which made elementary education a local government obligation, introduced substantial education grants. The main grant was originally distributed according to examination results but the number of children in average daily attendance was made the basis for distribution shortly afterward. A second grant was provided in 1870 to equalize the burden in poor districts. This met the deficiency in districts where a three-penny rate produced either less than 20 pounds, or less than 7 shillings, 6 pence, per child. The actual sums distributed under this latter grant were quite small. In 1891-92 the scholar grant amounted to 1.5 million pounds and the equalizing grant to only 8 thousand pounds; but later revisions of the equalizing grant increased its importance until in 1911-12 it accounted for nearly one-fourth (24.3 percent) of the elementary school grants.[19]

Other new grants followed the 1870 school grants in rapid succession. In 1872, when local authorities were required to appoint medical officers of health and inspectors of nuisances, a grant equal to half their salaries was introduced. In 1874 the county and county borough police grant was increased from one-fourth to one-half the pay and clothing cost and a new grant of 4 shillings per week for pauper lunatics was instituted. Also in 1874 the national government made substantial increases in its

[19] Cd. 7315, *op. cit.*, p. 24.

payments to local authorities to compensate for the loss of rates through the exemption of government property. All these grants in 1874 were primarily for the relief of rates.

In 1875 the government began to make payments toward local expenditures for the registration of births and deaths, registration having been made compulsory by law of 1874. In 1876 it increased its grants for the maintenance of children in industrial schools and introduced a special school grant for sparsely populated areas. In 1877 it took over the entire cost of prisoners. In 1882 the first general highway grant was given, 250 thousand pounds, to meet one-fourth of the cost of main roads. This was doubled in 1887. Thus in 1887-88 grants-in-aid exceeded 4 million pounds and amounted to 13.6 percent of local revenues from rates and grants. Moreover, the national government had taken over the administration and support of some functions entirely, thereby relieving local authorities of further burdens. Expenditures thus transferred were estimated at 2.7 million pounds in 1887-88.[20]

The obverse of this was, of course, that local expenditures were increasing much faster than the national government was assuming them, and the national government was itself responsible for much of the increase. The larger part of the grants had come with the imposition of new duties, the government assuming, at best, half the cost of these new obligations. Relief of local rates, combined perhaps with a desire for further central control, was the motive for the aids for administration of justice in 1835, the several aids of 1846 and 1874, the grant for necessitous schools in 1876, and the doubling of the highway grant in 1887. For the rest, school, police, highway, and health grants accompanied new duties, the cost of which to local authorities far exceeded the amount of the central government's contribution. Local rates increased threefold during this early period of grant development. Fortunately rateable values were likewise increasing rapidly so

[20] H.C. 168, *op. cit.*, pp. 90-91.

that the increased burden for the country as a whole was not great,[21] although agricultural districts undoubtedly suffered.

All the grants in 1887 were for specific functions. Most of them were apportioned on the basis of actual expenditures or some simple measure of need, such as the number of school children and the number of pauper lunatics. Only the small school "aid" grant and that for sparsely populated areas took into account local ability to pay. Little thought was given to equalization. These grants were for the general relief of rates, or, more frequently, for the purpose of buying local government consent to new duties. In both cases the aim was to achieve higher standards of local administration by making available more money than the local authorities could or would supply and by stimulating local authorities to greater effort. The percentage grants tended to increase local expenditures, since in many instances every pound spent by the local authority was matched by a pound from the Exchequer. Furthermore, they were usually conditioned on a given standard of efficiency and the local governments had to measure up to this standard to obtain them at all. Effective central supervision probably prevented any serious extravagance, but such a system favored the wealthier communities, since these alone could take full advantage of the central government's offers.

The local government reform of 1888 (largely the work of the Chancellor of the Exchequer, Viscount Goschen) aimed to separate central and local finances. To this end an independent fund was established, known as the Local Taxation Account. This was made up of 40 percent of the yield of probate duties and all the proceeds of certain licenses. The latter were distributed to the counties in proportion to collections, the former in proportion to discontinued grants. The only important specific grants continued were those for elementary education, but, except for roads, the

---

[21] Local rates amounted to approximately 14 percent of rateable values in 1842-43 and 18 percent in 1885-86.

counties were required to assign the revenue from the probate duties to the cost of specific services in the same manner as the old grants, so that the subordinate local authorities were in much the same position as before.[22] Only the road grant disappeared, as such. Road expenditures were supposed to be met from the "free balance."

The counties stood to gain or lose with the varying yield of the new sources. Actually, the new revenue was more than sufficient to compensate for the old grants, and further new income from surtaxes on beer and spirits was assigned to the local authorities in 1890. This was primarily for the purpose of meeting police pensions, but the excess, which proved to be substantial, could be used to reduce rates or to aid technical education.

Goschen's desire to separate state and local finances was not realized. Separate accounts were kept for the assigned revenues, but they were actually administered by the national government, and the education grant, together with some minor grants, continued to come from national revenues. Grants for specific purposes from the general tax revenues of the national government dropped from 13.1 percent of the local income from rates and grants in 1887-88 to 6.2 percent in 1891-92, the first year that the new system was in full effect; but in the years that followed new grants were introduced and old ones increased, while the revenue from the new local sources remained almost stationary. In 1928-29, just before the Local Taxation Account was abandoned, the grants from the general tax revenues of the national government had increased until they accounted for 32.1 percent of all local income from rates and grants, whereas the taxes provided by the 1888 reform amounted to 3.8 percent.

The 1888 reform was scarcely in effect when new grants began to appear. In 1890 the national government undertook to meet part of the indemnity to owners of diseased cattle slaughtered by

[22] Some of these grants were stereotyped at the 1887-88 amount. Others varied as before.

government order, the remainder coming from the Local Taxation Account. Previously the whole sum had come from local funds. The school grants were extended in 1891, and again in 1897. In 1896 rates on agricultural land were cut by one-half and the central government made good the loss by a grant from general revenues equal to one-half the 1895-96 rates. In 1898 the national government instituted grants for homes for inebriates. Only a few of these homes belonged to municipal authorities, however. In 1899 the national government undertook to meet half the rates for clerical tithes. In 1902, when counties and county boroughs were established as education authorities in place of the former districts, school grants were revised and again materially increased. In 1905 the Unemployed Workmen Act introduced a new local activity that shortly called for substantial government aid. In 1906 another education grant for overburdened districts was added. And in 1908 and 1909 provision was made for discretionary grants for roads, small holdings and allotments, and drainage projects.

Meanwhile no new sources of assigned revenue were added, although in 1908 a number of the licenses were turned over to the administration of county councils and the levies were made optional. A grant of 40,000 pounds was made to cover the cost of administration. In 1909, 1910, and 1911, liquor licenses, the beer and spirits duties, and the motor vehicle tax—that is, all the important assigned revenues except the estate duty—were standardized at the 1908-9 yield. In the case of the beer and spirits duties the change protected local interests, since the revenue from this source was declining,[23] owing to increased national taxes. But the local governments made a bad bargain. The changes were instigated by a Liberal government in need of money for its own social reforms. Anything the Exchequer lost from stereotyping the beer and spirits duties it more than made up from stereotyping the liquor and motor vehicle licenses. In a few years the surplus

[23] From 1.3 million pounds in 1900-1 to 1.1 million pounds in 1908-9.

from the latter, alone, exceeded the entire local beer and spirits revenue. Local governments were promised half the yield of the land value tax imposed in 1910, but the failure of this tax meant that the promise was never realized.

In the long run, however, the local governments probably did not lose; for what the central government took away with one hand it gave back with the other. The motor vehicle revenues went to the road fund from which the Road Board voted local authorities substantial grants. And the Liberal government's reforms included old age pensions, established in 1908, and health and unemployment insurance, established in 1911—measures which reduced the burden of the poor rates substantially.[24] Moreover, there was no cessation of new grants. Scarcely a year passed without at least one new grant. Percentage grants were introduced for local expenditures for treatment of all disease (1911), maternity and child welfare (1915), venereal disease (1916), care of the mentally deficient (1916), registration of electors (1918), county agricultural committees (1919), provincial museums (1919), care of the blind (1920), port sanitary authorities (1920), care of the tubercular (1921), and probation of offenders (1925). School grants were again revised and enlarged (1918), police grants were increased (1918), and highway grants grew steadily. A series of housing acts, beginning in 1919, provided substantial housing subsidies; further derating of agricultural land, in 1923, brought a new grant in compensation; and, largely as a part of the public-works program for reducing unemployment, substantial subsidies were granted for land drainage, sewer systems, and parks and open spaces (1920). Thus the amount of grants increased fourfold between 1913-14 and 1928-29, the year preceding the general revision of the system. Meanwhile local rates only a little more than doubled. Consequently, the proportion of local rate and grant revenue that was

[24] The average rate in the pound for poor rates did not rise above the high point of 1s. 1¾d., which it reached in 1905-6, until 1915-16.

supplied by grants increased from 24.5 percent to 35.9 percent.[25] Nevertheless, the burden on the rates was felt to have become unbearable, and the demand for derating was the driving force in the 1929 reform.

It is apparent that England experimented with a variety of grants in this long period of grant development. Most of the aids to local governments were for specific functions. Compensation for derating agricultural land is the only important exception to this. But the functions aided cover all important local government activities, and the methods of distribution were as numerous as the grants themselves. Before discussing these, however, it is important to classify and define the different forms of grants. The terms used in the discussion below follow English usage fairly closely,[26] but since there is no complete agreement as to their use, it has seemed necessary to define them here.

According to the restrictions on their use, grants may be classified as block or allocated grants. A block grant is one not specifically earmarked for the maintenance of a particular service.[27] Thus the new grant under the Local Government Act of 1929 is clearly a block grant, and a grant for health expenditures might be considered a block grant if no particular health service were specified. The grant for salaries of medical officers of health, on the contrary, is an allocated grant.

Block and allocated grants may in turn be classified, according to the amount paid out by the government making the grant, as fixed and variable grants. The new block grant is also a fixed grant, whereas percentage grants are inevitably variable. Both block and allocated grants may be further classified according to the basis of distribution as percentage, unit, formula, and discretionary grants. The percentage grant varies with the amount

[25] See Appendix, Table 42, p. 365.

[26] See, e.g., Cd. 7315, *op. cit.*, *passim*, and H. Finer, *English Local Government*, London, 1933, pp. 446-50.

[27] W. E. Hart and W. O. Hart, *Introduction to the Law of Municipal Administration*, 1934, p. 156.

of local expenditures for specific functions. The unit grant varies with some objective measure, such as the number of school children, or the miles of highway. The formula grant is based on a number of measures. It may, like the former elementary education grant, combine the unit and percentage grant, or it may, like the 1929 block grant, combine a series of units. The discretionary grant leaves the distribution to the judgment of the administrative officials.

Grants may be classified, further, according to their purpose. The purposes most widely recognized are improvement of local government services, compensation for lost revenue sources or for new burdens imposed, general relief of local taxes, and equalization of local resources. It is apparent that the purpose of the grant will influence the basis of distribution. Percentage grants are useful for stimulating local governments to higher standards but cannot equalize resources; whereas the 1929 block grant, distributed according to a formula designed to equalize, offers no incentive to more or better local services.

Reviewing the history of grants in England prior to 1929 one finds that the purpose of most grants was the improvement of local government services. This favors the allocated grant rather than the block grant, and block grants are found only as compensation for lost revenue sources, as in the case of the grants provided by the Agricultural Rates Acts of 1896 and 1923. This also favors variable rather than fixed grants, and again fixed grants are found only as compensation. The grant under the 1896 Agricultural Rates Act was the only large fixed grant prior to 1929. Finally, it favors percentage grants, although unit and even formula and discretionary grants can be designed for this end. The only formula grant prior to 1929 was that for elementary education. Unit grants appear more frequently, but the percentage grant is characteristic of the English system. Practically all the later grants were in this form. Even the education grants, with their varied bases, set 50 percent of approved expenditures as a minimum, and this was frequently the determining factor in the amount received. And most of the discretionary grants were standardized by administrative regulations at fixed percentages of the cost. This was true of the highway grants, the unemployment grants, and the agricultural education grants.

There can be no question but that the guiding motive in the development of the grant system before 1929 was the desire to bring local administration up to national standards of efficiency and to maintain it there. This motive was accompanied, perhaps, by a sense of obligation to assist with the burdens imposed. Equalization of resources was a factor only in the school grants, and there it was one of the less important factors. Such a situation was only possible because, on one hand the national government had shouldered such a large proportion of the total burden, and on the other hand the local unit for administration for most functions was fairly large. Eighty-two percent of national and local net expenditures fell on national tax sources and only 18 percent on local rates during the decade 1921-31.[28] Even before the war national taxes provided more than two-thirds of the total tax income. In Germany, where equalization has been a far more important factor in tax distributions and grants, a much larger share of the burden has fallen on local resources. There has been a steady tendency to increase the size of the local district in England. This was apparent long before the 1929 reform. The welfare district was changed from the parish to the poor-law union in 1835; the school district was changed from a group of parishes to the county or county borough in 1902; and the road district was enlarged in 1864, and an increasing proportion of the cost of roads has been charged to the still larger county since that date. Maintenance of police has from the beginning been a function of county and county borough authorities. Enlarging the area of charge for these important functions has reduced the need for equalization.

[28] Computed from data in J. Sykes, *British Public Expenditure*, London, 1934, p. xii.

Another factor which has made equalization less imperative is the nature of the expenditures which have been centralized. The national government has not only met a large proportion of the costs, but, with unemployment insurance and old age pensions, it has met a substantial part of the welfare burden,[29] the burden that, above all others, makes equalization necessary. In spite of these ameliorating factors, inequalities in local rates, rather than the total rate burden, were responsible for the demand for derating which resulted in the 1929 changes.

[29] Approximately three-fourths in 1928-29.

IX

THE LOCAL GOVERNMENT ACT OF 1929[1]

THE system of grants-in-aid in effect in 1928 had grown over a period of one hundred years, one grant at a time as specific needs were recognized. At no time was the entire system overhauled or co-ordinated. Even the 1888 reform made no important revisions in the underlying system. Poor unions, urban and rural districts, and municipal boroughs received the same grants on the same bases. Only the counties stood to gain or lose by the change. Grants which may have been reasonable at first outlived their usefulness. Certainly the fixed grant paid as compensation for the derating of agricultural land in 1896 bore little relation to local losses from that derating thirty years later; and the license revenues fixed at the 1908-9 level were equally meaningless. Percentage grants grew in favor rather than unit grants, but both existed side by side, and the varying percentages of expenditure met by the national government seem to be historical accident rather than a measure of the degree of national interest in the functions in question. Education grants were thoroughly revised and integrated in 1918, but health and welfare grants became increasingly varied and were never co-ordinated. Reform was due for the whole system.

The depressed state of industry was, of course, the fundamental reason for the 1929 changes, and the Local Government Act was an essential feature of the government's recovery program. Prolonged unemployment had greatly increased the expenditures of local authorities. The rates for poor relief tripled between 1919 and 1927. With declining income the burden of the rates would have become greater even though the amount had

[1] 19 Geo. V., ch. xvii.

remained stationary. To have the amount increase seemed intolerable. Moreover, the increases were greatest just in those localities least able to pay. The absence of any important equalizing factor in the grant system was more than ever apparent. The average rate in the pound was nearly 13 shillings in 1927-28. This was high, being more than 60 percent of annual rental value. But in a number of districts, especially in the coal mining counties, rates exceeded 20 shillings,[2] the full annual rental value. In a few cases rates exceeded 30 shillings, or 150 percent.

The reform was designed to aid industry in three ways: directly, through derating; and indirectly, through reducing the cost of local government and through equalizing the burden. The cost of government was to be decreased through economies effected by the reorganization of local districts and the transfer of certain functions to larger local units. Equalization was to be achieved partly through the larger unit of administration and partly through the formula for the distribution of grants.

Specifically, the 1929 Act provided for the complete exemption of agricultural land and buildings from local rates (section 67). Such real estate had already been derated under earlier acts to the extent of 75 percent for the poor rates,[3] which constituted the larger part of the rates, and to a lesser extent for other rates. It provided, further, for the valuation of "industrial hereditaments and freight-transport hereditaments" at 25 percent of net annual rental value for purposes of rating (section 68).[4] This applies only to the property actually used in the business of mining, manufacture, or transport. The resulting losses to local au-

---

[2] There were 95 such districts in 1927-28. *Report of the Ministry of Health*, 1933-34, p. 207.

[3] Poor rates were those levied by the union authorities. They were not limited to the expenditures of poor-law authorities or to expenditures for poor relief, and they constituted about 70 percent of all rates. H. Finer, *op. cit.*, p. 423.

[4] Under earlier legislation railway property was valued at 25 percent of rental value for the levy of certain district rates on the assumption that these rates were expended for purposes which did not materially benefit the railways. Under the new law railways are valued at 25 percent of this reduced valuation for such rates, or one-sixteenth of estimated rental value.

thorities are estimated on the basis of 1928-29 rates, and the authorities are reimbursed in full by the new grants (section 86).

The second feature of the 1929 Act which concerns local financial problems is the transfer of functions to larger areas. All functions of the poor-law authorities are transferred to the counties and county boroughs (section 1), and the former unions are abolished. This has reduced the number of authorities administering poor relief from 631 to 145, so that the average size of the new unit of administration is more than four times the size of the old. This alone has been a material factor in equalizing resources. Further, all highway functions of rural districts have been transferred to the counties (section 30). Since the rural districts were some 640 in number and the counties 62 this means that the rural highway district is, on the average, ten times its former size. Important economies and equalization of resources should result. There has been, further, a partial transfer of highways from urban districts to counties, but the administration and support of residence streets and, in exceptional cases, through highways, is left to urban authorities (sections 31 and 32).

The third important feature of the 1929 Act from the point of view of local finances is the substitution of a block grant for a large number of the former allocated grants. All the old grants have been discontinued except those for schools, police, and housing, and part of the road grants (section 85).[5] This is not as radical a change as might appear at first. The larger number of grants was swept away, but the grants remaining accounted for between 80 and 90 percent of the revenue distributed by the central government in 1928-29. The many criticisms directed against percentage grants by proponents of the new bill when it was under consideration would seem to apply equally to school, police, and road grants, although the school grants do contain certain equalizing factors; but the abolition of the least defensible grants, such

[5] Part of the grants for maternity and child welfare are continued under certain conditions (section 62).

as the fixed compensation for derating agricultural land and the stereotyped license revenues, and other small and scattered grants which scarcely justified the administrative labor involved, was clear gain. The locally administered dog, game, and other licenses remain.

The amount of the new grants is more than sufficient to compensate for the discontinued grants and derating, as estimated on the basis of 1928-29 rates and grants. The annual sum for England and Wales for the first grant period is:

Purpose of Grant	Million Pounds
To cover losses on account of derating............	22.3
To cover losses on account of discontinued grants...	16.3
Additional amount	5.0
Total.................................	43.6 (section 86)

The 5 million pounds commonly referred to as "new money" is not all net gain to the local authorities. The government draws upon the road fund for the general exchequer contribution to the extent of the discontinued road grants in the standard year plus 2.6 million pounds (section 87).[6] Since the road fund is intended for road grants alone and the discontinued road grants are fully covered by the first provision, it would seem that the discretionary road grants received by the local authorities from the road fund must be curtailed by the 2.6 million pounds applied to the general exchequer contribution. In consequence, only about half this 5 million pounds can be counted strictly as "new money."[7] No official explanation seems to have been offered for

[6] The share of England and Wales, i.e., 80/91 of 3 million pounds.

[7] It should be noted, however, that the road grants have regularly been appreciably less than the revenue of the road fund. In consequence the balance in the fund was close to 20 million pounds at the end of the year 1924-25. In the two succeeding years the Chancellor of the Exchequer "raided" the fund in order to balance the national budget, and 19.2 million pounds were diverted to general purposes. In 1926 it was provided, further, that the Exchequer should regularly retain one-third of the tax on pleasure cars and motorcycles as a luxury tax. This amounts to approximately 5 million pounds a year. In addition, the road fund surplus was again diverted to general national expenditures in the 1935-36 budget, to

this extra sum. It was suggested in debate in the House of Commons that it was given because the formula "did not fit" and the additional sum was to prevent it from "hitting anybody too severely." [8] In any event, it undoubtedly oiled the legislative machinery when the bill was passed; to have fixed grants at the old level for three years to come would have aroused a storm of protest. And there can be no reasonable doubt that the local authorities have put it to good use.

Ultimately this block grant is to be distributed entirely according to the formula discussed below, but to prevent injury from rapid change a sum equal to 75 percent of the losses from rates and grants is distributed to the counties and county boroughs in proportion to such losses for the first and second grant periods, that is, through 1936-37 (sections 88 and 134). This amount is reduced to 50 percent of losses for the third grant period of five years, to 25 percent for the fourth grant period, and disappears entirely in 1947-48. The remaining sum is distributed in proportion to the weighted population formula (section 88). If, however, the total received by any county or county borough under this distribution falls short of a sum equal to the losses from rates and grants in the standard year plus one shilling per capita for the population of the standard year, the local district in question receives an additional exchequer grant to cover the deficit (section 90). After the first grant period this additional grant is equal to the deficiency as calculated above, or (in case it is larger) to the deficiency calculated by taking the difference between the actual grant and the losses in the standard year increased by "a sum equivalent to one-third of the excess of the county apportionment for the period in question over what would have been the county apportionment for the period in question had the General Exchequer Contribution for that period been

---

the extent of 4.5 million pounds. Thus there is no guarantee that local authorities will receive the entire income of this fund.

[8] Lawrence in *Parliamentary Debates*, CCXXIII, 294-95.

the same as the General Exchequer Contribution for the first fixed grant period" (section 90). Thus far this alternative provision has been of no significance, since the increase in the General Exchequer Contribution in the second grant period over the first is very small. These grants are in addition to the sum of 43.6 million pounds.

Turning to the relation of the county to the underlying subdivisions, the county distributes to municipal boroughs and urban districts a per capita sum equal to half the county apportionment divided by the total population of all the counties. Rural districts receive one-fifth of this sum per capita, that is, one-tenth of the average per capita distribution for counties as a whole (section 91). The smaller share of the rural districts is justified by the transfer of functions to the county.

These capitation grants are increased for "losing" areas and decreased for "gaining" areas (section 94). Losses and gains are determined by estimating the rate in the pound which would have been required in the standard year to meet uncovered expenditures and the rate which would have been required if the provisions for derating, grants, and transfer of functions had been in effect. The estimated yield of the difference between these two rates is the estimated loss or gain of the district.[9] Losing districts are reimbursed by the full amount of their estimated losses for the first five years of the new system, after which this supplementary grant is reduced by one-fifteenth each year, disappearing with the beginning of the fifth grant period. Half of this supplementary grant is provided from national revenues and is in addition to the General Exchequer Contribution. The other half is derived from deductions from the capitation grants of gaining districts in the county in proportion to gains. In cases where half the amount of losses of losing districts in the county exceeds the amount of gains in gaining districts in the county, the excess is

[9] These estimates are made by central government officials and local officials do not know the exact basis on which their gains or losses are calculated.

provided from further exchequer revenues. The levy on gaining districts declines and disappears as the reimbursement to losing districts is cut and ultimately abolished.

Further compensation is given to districts within the county for losses from special and parish rates (section 92). That part of the grant to the county, based on 75 percent of losses from rates and grants, that covers losses from special and parish rates is passed on to the subdivisions that formerly levied these rates, and the county must make good, further, the other 25 percent of the loss for the first and second grant periods. In the third and fourth grant periods the share in the grant passed on to special districts for special rates is reduced to 50 and 25 percent, respectively, as that part of the general grant distributed in proportion to losses is reduced to 50 and 25 percent of these losses in succeeding grant periods. Moreover, reimbursement by the county for any part of the loss not so covered is optional after the second grant period.

Finally, if the sum of the General Exchequer Contribution and the additional and supplementary grants is not sufficient, in the case of an individual county, to cover the amount due to the subdivisions of the county, the national government meets the deficiency through a special grant (section 89). Such grants were made to Surrey in the second grant period and to Middlesex in both the first and second grant periods. In these cases the counties, as such, received nothing whatever from the new grant.

It remains to consider the weighted population on which the total grant will ultimately be distributed if the new system survives twenty years without amendment. Each county and county borough share of the residual grant at present and of the total block grant finally is determined by its proportion of the weighted population of England and Wales. The weighted population is determined as follows:

The estimated population of the county or county borough is increased (1) if the number of children under five years of age exceeds 50 per thousand, by the percentage by which the number of children exceeds 50; and (2) if the per capita rateable value is less than 10 pounds, by the percentage by which the rateable value falls short of 10 pounds.

The population so increased is further weighted (3) if the number of unemployed insured men plus one-tenth of the unemployed insured women exceeds 1.5 percent of the population, by a percentage equal to ten times the excess over 1.5 percent; and (4) (a) if the population is less than 100 per mile of road, by the percentage by which the population falls short of 200 per mile; or (b) if the population is 100 or more per mile of road, by the percentage which 50 bears to the population per mile (Schedule 4, Part 3).

Applying this formula to a hypothetical case, assume that the population of a county is 1,000,000, the number of children under five per 1,000 population is 55, the rateable value per capita is 8 pounds, the percentage of unemployed in the population, as measured by the formula, is 3, and the population per mile of road is 200. The population of 1,000,000 is increased (1) by 100,000 (10 percent of 1,000,000) for children under five, and (2) by 200,000 (20 percent of 1,000,000) for low rateable value. The resulting weighted population of 1,300,-000 is then further increased (3) by 195,000 (15 percent of 1,300,000) for excess unemployed, and (4) by 325,000 (25 percent of 1,300,000) for population per mile of road. The total weighted population comes to 1,820,000. If this county had had a population of 50 per mile of road, the weight added for sparse population would have been 975,000 (75 percent of 1,300,000), bringing the total to 2,470,000.

The number of children under five years of age was chosen as a factor for weighting on the assumption that the proportion of children under five is high in the working population. It is, in other words, a measure of poverty.[10] The particular standard of

[10] Chamberlain in *Parliamentary Debates*, CCXXIII, 97.

50 was selected because it represents a minimum.[11] In the first grant period only the City of London received no weighting for this factor. In the second grant period one county borough and four Metropolitan boroughs in addition to the City of London received no weighting for this factor.

The rateable value per capita was selected as a measure of local taxpaying ability. It was estimated that very few districts would have more than 10 pounds per capita after the derating. Thus this figure was chosen as a maximum. Actually, seven county boroughs, the City of London, and some of the Metropolitan boroughs have received no weighting for this factor in the first and second grant periods.

The proportion of unemployed is both a measure of need and of inability to support local government. The 1.5 percent is not a minimum, but it was far below the average of 2.2 percent at the time that the formula was introduced. Fifty-six counties and county boroughs in the first grant period and 15 in the second, received no weighting for this factor. It has been proposed that the weight given this factor should be reduced in the succeeding grant periods as the proportion of the block grant distributed on the basis of the formula increases.[12]

The loading for sparsity of population is, of course, some measure of highway burden. No explanation is offered for the selection of the specific standard. All counties receive some weighting for this, and the actual weight added varied from 7 to 101 percent in the first grant period. This factor is not applied to county boroughs. The specific bases chosen in each case are such that the population of practically every county [13] receives some weight for each factor excepting unemployment, and the majority have their populations weighted for this, too. The reason for applying the last two factors to the population after it has been

---

[11] Ministry of Health, *Proposals for Reform in Local Government*, Cmd. 3134, p. 16.

[12] Cmd. 3134, *op. cit.*, p. 16.

[13] And county borough, for the three factors applied to county boroughs.

weighted by the first two factors is not clear. The effect is, of course, to increase further the weighting for those counties with relatively high weights for factors in both the first and second groups. This should result in greater equalization, if the factors chosen in the first place are equalizing factors. If, however, it is desirable to emphasize the cumulative effect of the different factors it might have been still better to have applied each factor to the population as weighted by all the preceding factors.[14]

TABLE 18

RELATIVE WEIGHTS ASSIGNED TO FACTORS IN THE BLOCK-GRANT FORMULA

Factor	ESTIMATED[a]	ACTUAL[b]	
	1928	First Fixed-Grant Period	Second Fixed-Grant Period
(1) Actual population.........	37.4	39.0	37.0
(2) Children under five.......	28.4	24.0	17.7
(3) Low rateable value.......	16.6	15.0	13.8
(4) Unemployment..........	2.8	8.5	19.8
(5) Low population density...	14.8	13.6	11.7
Total..................	100.0	100.0	100.0

[a] Association of Municipal Corporations, *Reform in Local Government and in the Financial Relations between the Exchequer and Local Authorities,* 1928, p. 9.
[b] Computed from data in *Annual Report of the Ministry of Health,* 1933-34, p. 423.

The actual proportion of the grant distributed on the basis of weighted population that is assigned to the different factors, with the existing distribution and composition of the population in England and Wales, is given in Table 18.

It is apparent that, for the country as a whole, the relative importance of the different weights is far from equal. The unem-

[14] The formula is, of course, empirical. No scientific claims are made for it. One of the officials who assisted in the investigations preliminary to the recommendation of the formula explained to the writer that cumulative weighting was carried this far and no farther because they knew what results they wanted and this gave just those results.

ployment factor has increased markedly at the expense of the other factors, rising from the least important factor to the most important with the exception of the actual population. The decline in importance of children under five years of age is partly owing to the increasing importance of unemployment, but also, partly, to the decline in the birth rate. The number added to the actual population for this factor dropped from 24 million in the first grant period to 19 million in the second. In the case of other factors there were slight declines in the absolute as well as in the relative weights, except for actual population which increased a little more than one-half million between the first and second grant periods. Certain modifications were made in this system for London. Poor relief was transferred to the county, as elsewhere (section 18), but highways were left in the hands of the Metropolitan boroughs. The classification grants for highways, which were retained in other counties, were abolished in London, and a corresponding sum was added to the County's share of block grants (Schedule 2 and Schedule 4, article 2). The former equalization fund for London was abolished (section 98).[15]

[15] This equalization fund was established in 1894. Each parish paid into the fund the equivalent of a penny rate and this was redistributed among the Metropolitan boroughs and the City of London, in proportion to population, for health expenditures. There also existed in London a Metropolitan Common Poor Fund, established in 1867. This was derived from a uniform rate levied throughout the Metropolis and distributed among the unions in proportion to persons in receipt of indoor relief and in proportion to certain other relief expenditures. (Royal Commission on London Government, *Report*, Cmd. 1830, 1923, pp. 84-86.) In spite of these equalization measures, rates in the Borough of Poplar were more than double rates in the City of London in 1928-29 (23 shillings, 4 pence, compared with 9 shillings, 2 pence). Rateable values per capita in 1928-29 in the City of London were more than one hundred times as great as rateable values per capita in Poplar. In 1931-32 they were nearly two hundred times as great, since derating diminished the base in Poplar substantially, whereas values in the City of London increased. This is a striking instance, however, of the failure of population to measure need. The residents of the City of London number only 11,000, but the day population is enormous. This day population contributes nothing to the cost of schools, welfare, and housing, but it is obviously an important factor in police, highway, and sanitation costs. It is apparent, however, from the fact that rates in Poplar were more than double the rates in the City of London, although schools were supported by the county as a whole, and there was substantial equalization for both health and welfare, that a day population of this type contributes more to taxable values than it does to costs.

The amount of the County's block grant is determined in the same manner as that for county boroughs. The redistribution to Metropolitan boroughs is as follows: each borough receives a sum equal to 75 percent of its losses from derating and the discontinued grants, plus one-third of the grant distributed according to formula, except that in apportioning this among the different boroughs the weighting for unemployment is not applied (section 98). In calculating losses from rates and grants, rates formerly levied for the equalization fund are not included and the boroughs are credited with the highway and health grants which elsewhere are credited to the counties (Schedule 4, article 2). "Additional" and "supplementary" grants are made here as in other counties.

With regard to the future development of the system, the amount of each local unit's share in the block grant is fixed for a period of five years, except for the first two "fixed-grant periods" which are three and four years, respectively (section 86). The shorter period at first was partly to enable fairly quick adjustment should experience prove this advisable, partly to make it possible to utilize the 1931 census returns at the earliest possible date. It was expected that a census would be taken in the future once in five years so that the revision would be based on accurate and recent data, but this plan has been dropped for the time being.[16]

Local authorities are promised that exchequer grants will be increased with each new grant period if rates have increased, so that the proportion of grants to rates will be maintained at the level of the first year for the country as a whole (section 86). Individual shares will be readjusted according to changes in the amount and composition of the population. That is, weighted population will be recalculated. The guarantees described above continue with the modifications noted.

[16] No census has been taken in 1936.

TABLE 19

TOTAL GRANTS PAYABLE UNDER PART VI OF THE LOCAL GOVERN-
MENT ACT OF 1929: ENGLAND AND WALES[a]

IN MILLIONS OF POUNDS

Grant	First Year of First Fixed-Grant Period	First Year of Second Fixed-Grant Period
75 percent of losses on account of rates and grants (section 88)..	28.9	28.9
Amount apportioned on weighted population base (section 88)..	14.6	15.0
Additional exchequer grants (section 90)..........	0.4	0.2
Deficiency grant in administrative counties (sec. 89)	0.1	0.2
Supplementary grants (section 94)..............	1.0	1.0
Total...................................	45.1	45.4

[a] Ministry of Health, *Annual Report*, 1933-34, p. 321.

The cost of the Local Government Act of 1929 to the national
government is largely the reimbursement for derating, 22.3 million pounds. There is, of course, in addition to this, the 5 million
pounds of "new money," but in view of the diversion of a substantial sum from the road fund to the general exchequer grant
and the fact that the new grant is fixed for several years, whereas
the old grants tended to rise each year, the additional burden on
national revenues is only a fraction of the latter sum. Finally,
the 1.5 million pounds of "additional" and "supplementary"
grants are a new charge on the national exchequer. The bulk of
the new burden was to have been met from a tax on imported
light oils. Also, a part of the lost rates are recaptured in the income tax, since this permits the deduction of such rates in arriv-
ing at taxable income. Yields from these sources have not measured up to expectations. The depression was not anticipated at
the time that the act was passed. But the larger part of the new
grants has been covered by these sources.

In the seven years since the Local Government Act of 1929 has been in operation no important changes have been made in its provisions, but several revisions have taken place in the financial relations of national and local governments outside of the scope of this act. The national government had hoped to regain a substantial part of the cost of compensation for derating from increases in taxable income (Schedule A) arising from higher rental values when the quinquennial revision of these valuations was made. Unfortunately the revision came in the midst of depression, and this hope was not realized. With increased obligations and shrinking income, the national government sought to cut expenditure through the National Economy Act of 1931, which made it possible to revise the police, education, and other grants not included in the 1929 act. In consequence of this 1931 act education grants were revised and the guarantee of a grant equal to at least 50 percent of approved expenditures was abolished. Owing to this change the proportion of education costs met from grants fell from 53.8 percent in 1929-30 to 48.2 percent in 1932-33.

Not all the changes since 1929 have been at the expense of local governments. On the contrary, new housing subsidies were introduced in 1930 and 1931. Also, the national government has continued to extend transitional benefits for unemployed workers so that they have not fallen on local poor relief; and it has taken over the entire administration of able-bodied poor relief beginning October 1, 1935, levying on the counties and county boroughs to the extent of 60 percent of their 1932-33 expenditures for this purpose.

Grants for employment schemes have continued and increased, and a new "distressed areas grant" was introduced in 1933.[17]

[17] In 1905-6, before the introduction of social insurance, 82.3 percent of the cost of poor relief fell on the rates. With the introduction of health insurance, old age pensions, and unemployment insurance, the burden of poor relief diminished and that part of the insurance cost falling on public funds was met from national taxes. In 1913-14, 41.0 percent of the cost of poor relief and social insurance was met from

This is distributed to those counties and county boroughs, mostly in the coal-mining regions, where the expenditures for relief exceed a rate of two shillings in the pound. The fixed sum of 440 thousand pounds is distributed in proportion to such excess expenditures. Thus further equalization is achieved.

In 1933 the government attempted to transfer the responsibility for new housing from the local authorities to private enterprise by putting a stop to further commitments under the 1924 Housing Act, and in place of increased subsidies to these, the national government offered to meet half the losses of local authorities, under the 1925 act, on guarantees to private building associations. This applies only to guarantees after the act was passed and subject to the approval of the Minister of Health. This left the local authorities without government assistance for new housing programs except for slum clearance. The result was almost complete cessation of building by local authorities, except for replacement of houses condemned and torn down as slums. The 1935 Housing Act, however, again opens the way for local government building, with subsidies varying with the cost of the site on which houses are built. The minimum subsidy is 6 pounds per flat per year. This new housing is limited to relief of overcrowding as defined in the act. The Local Government Act of 1933 consolidated the laws relating to all governmental organization and functions but did not change the financial provisions.

---

local rates. In 1929-30, just before the introduction of the new system, only 26.8 percent of these costs were met from local rates. In 1932-33, in spite of the abolition of the welfare grants, the proportion of such expenditures met by local authorities had declined to 22.4 percent. This did not fall exclusively on the rates, but on rates plus block grants. If one applies to welfare the same percentage that block grants bear to the sum of rates and block grants, only 17 or 18 percent of welfare costs were met from local rates. Grants for unemployment schemes and necessitous areas have been excluded from these estimates since it is impossible to distinguish between relief expenditures as such and public works. It should be noted, however, that special grants for unemployment were 2.5 million pounds in 1929-30 and 4.4 million pounds in 1933-34.

X

THE REVISED SYSTEM IN OPERATION

IT IS too early to measure the full effects of the Local Government Act of 1929. Only in 1947, should the provisions of this act continue, will the temporary guarantees against loss be withdrawn and the weighted-population formula be in full force. Meanwhile, however, some of the effects are apparent, and some estimate of the financial position of local governments under the existing grant system can be made.

The derating provisions of the act have been more frequently criticized than any other feature. To judge the merits of derating it is important to consider the incidence of the rates and the extent of the burden they impose on ratepayers in general, as well as the specific claims of the derated industries to such relief. Rates are paid by occupiers rather than owners. There are exceptions to this in practice, but the exceptions are not important. Where the occupiers are tenants, and not owners, it is probable that a certain amount of the burden of the rates is shifted to the owner. Certainly rents plus rates determine what the tenant can afford, and if high rates drive tenants away, lowered rents may lure them back. It is, however, difficult to determine the extent to which rates are shifted and difficult, in consequence, to measure burdens. Rates increased considerably following the war. The average rate per pound of rateable value nearly doubled between 1918-19 and 1921-22, rising from 7 shillings, $8\frac{1}{2}$ pence, to 14 shillings, $7\frac{1}{2}$ pence.[1] This was the peak, however, and in 1928-29 the average rate was only 12 shillings, $5\frac{1}{2}$ pence. This would seem to mean that the average tenant was paying in local taxes about 60 percent of what he was paying in rent—a substantial

[1] Ministry of Health, *Annual Reports.*

contribution from the average individual's income. Actually, the burden was probably appreciably less than this. No comprehensive data on valuations can be found, but there is general agreement that undervaluation prevailed.

Prior to the introduction of quinquennial valuations, the first of which was effective April 1, 1929, local valuation officers commonly failed to revise valuations with changing rentals, and with the rapid changes arising from the war, valuations tended to lag far behind.[2] Moreover, the rent restriction act, which limited rentals to 140 percent of pre-war amounts, brought wide variations in rents. With a change in tenants the controlled rent no longer applies, but as long as an old tenant remains his rent may not be increased above this point. Decontrolled rents are frequently 40 to 50 percent above controlled rents but the valuation officer is not apt to use the decontrolled rent where the two exist side by side; and before 1929 pre-war buildings were often valued on the basis of pre-war rents, so that even controlled rents were above the valuation. Where pre-war valuations obtained they were, perhaps, not more than half as much as the rents actually paid by the tenant. In these cases the tenants' contributions to local taxes would be approximately half the nominal rate in the pound, and a rate of 12 shillings would amount to 30 percent, rather than 60 percent, of the actual rentals paid.

Rates in a number of districts exceeded 20 shillings prior to 1929. If the valuation were equal to actual rents, this would mean that the tenant paid more in local taxes than he paid in rent. In a few districts rates exceeded 30 shillings. Even allowing for undervaluation and perhaps some shifting to the landlord through lower rents, this would seem to be a heavy burden. The cause for complaint lay in the inequalities, however, rather than in the general level of the rates. In urban districts, where the greatest inequalities obtained, rates varied from 8 to 34 shillings in the

[2] Even before the war there were many and serious discrepancies. See, e.g., J. Stamp, "Land Valuation and Rating Reform," *Economic Journal*, 1911.

pound in 1928-29. Differences in valuations in different districts doubtless accounted for some of this, but the largest part of it must have represented genuine differences in burden.

The derating provisions of the 1929 act were not directed at inequalities in the rates, however, nor did they offer relief to the ordinary householder. Relief was granted to those engaged in specified industrial activities, all participating equally, regardless of burdens and ability to pay. What, in fact, the government chose to do was to subsidize farmers, mine owners, manufacturers, and shippers at the expense of the users of light oil. In support of this derating it is frequently contended that industry should not bear burdens equal to those placed on residents, since local government services benefit residents rather than industrial concerns. Education, health, housing, and welfare costs are incurred for individual human beings, not for business; and highway costs and police and fire protection, which may benefit business equally with private individuals, account for the smaller part of local government expenditures.[3]

Disregarding for the moment the fact that rates are commonly justified on the theory of ability to pay rather than benefit, it is not clear that industrial establishments are in no way responsible for local government costs for education, housing, health, and relief. It is true that the immediate benefit accrues to the employees, not the industrial establishment. But it is also true that these costs are heaviest in the industrial cities. In residential cities there is no occasion for subsidized houses; a large part of the children are educated in privately supported schools; free medical services are not widely used; and the relief burden is at a minimum. The eleven cities with the highest rates in 1929-30, the last year of the old system, are mostly manufacturing cities, including Sheffield, Stoke-on-Trent, Merthyr Tydfil, and West Ham. The eleven cities with the lowest rates for the same year are resi-

---

[3] Such expenditures accounted for about one-third of the rate burden in county boroughs in 1929-30.

dential cities, mainly seaside resorts, including Bournemouth, Blackpool, Brighton, and Southend-on-Sea. It is not, however, necessary to name the cities to prove this point. The heavy losses in rateable values in one group and the small losses in the other, as given in Table 20, are sufficient evidence.

TABLE 20

COMPARISON OF TAX BURDENS AND LOSSES FROM DERATING IN THE COUNTY BOROUGHS WITH THE HIGHEST AND THE LOWEST RATES BEFORE DERATING

Rates	RATE IN 1928-29		PER CAPITA NET EXPENDITURE 1928-29 [a]		Percentage of 1928-29 Rateable Value Lost From Derating
	Shillings	Pence	Pounds	Shillings	
Eleven county boroughs with highest rates					
High............	29	0	6	18	20.1
Median..........	20	1	6	6	13.4
Low.............	17	8	5	3	9.7
Eleven county boroughs with lowest rates					
High............	12	0	6	8	5.9
Median..........	9	5	5	12	2.7
Low.............	7	1	5	0	0.9

[a] From rates and grants.

It is apparent from the data given in Table 20 for these two groups of cities that the rates per pound of rateable value in manufacturing cities were about double the rates in residential cities. These higher rates were not merely the result of lower rateable values. The median per capita net expenditure was 14 shillings higher in the manufacturing cities than in the residence cities. This is a substantial difference. Thus, before industry was derated, the burden falling on the local ratepayers was greater, however measured, in industrial than in residential cities. If the local rate burden was higher in industrial cities than elsewhere while industry was still bearing its proportionate share of that burden, it would seem that the ordinary ratepayer was subsidizing industry, rather than industry subsidizing the ordinary ratepayer.[4] Had the industries in question paid adequate wages, there would have been little need for subsidized houses, public baths, free medical service, and public assistance. If benefit is to be the standard for local rates, valuations of industrial properties must be increased, not reduced. Nor can the complete derating of agricultural property be justified on this basis. It is surely not merely as residents that the farmers profit from local government services. Highways, at least, are essential to the farm. Yet farm real estate is contributing nothing at all.

The Conservative Government made no attempt, however, to justify derating on this ground. Derating was purely and frankly a recovery measure. If industry were to be unburdened to this extent it would be encouraged to expand. Employment would increase, and with increased employment would come the usual train of events leading to prosperity. Chamberlain, in his speech in the House of Commons when the bill was under discussion, protested that "critics overlook the fact that you cannot benefit industry without increasing employment," [5] and in the book published by the Conservatives in defense of the bill one finds the statement that if all productive industries, efficient and inefficient, are aided equally, efficiency is encouraged and benefits will "filter down from the producer." [6] The Conservatives would not seem to be conversant with recent economic thinking. Are merchants to be regarded as unproductive? And will the benefits "filter down"? [7] Sidney Webb pointed out that since rates are a fixed charge a business running part time will hardly be influenced by

---

[4] Unless, of course, it could be demonstrated that the inhabitants of industrial cities enjoyed more and better services at municipal expense than the inhabitants of the residential cities.

[5] *Parliamentary Debates*, CCXXIII, 86.

[6] D. W. Gunston and G. Peto, editors, *Rating Relief*, London, 1929, p. 8.

[7] It should be noted in fairness to the Conservatives that in the case of the freight transport they did not trust to the filtering process but provided that the derating should be accompanied by a corresponding decrease in freight rates.

the derating in making a new contract, since rates are not a factor in the cost of the additional business.[8] Rates are, of course, a consideration in building a new factory or in reopening one which has not been occupied recently, but most of the derating undoubtedly went to the benefit of manufacturers already in business.

One cannot consider the possible effects of derating without making some allowance for the condition of manufacture in Great Britain in recent years. The depression has been most serious in coalmining, shipbuilding, the iron and steel industries, and the cotton-textile industry; whereas some types of manufacture, such as automobile, artificial silk, and tobacco manufacture, and breweries, have been comparatively prosperous.

The depressed industries have for the most part been concentrated in a few areas, notably Durham, Cumberland, and South Wales. With the financial system in force prior to the Local Government Act of 1929, closing a colliery, shipbuilding yard, or steel mill reduced local rateable values materially since these are not rateable when not in use and increased local government costs because of the added relief problem. Thus, larger sums had to be obtained from a smaller base, and the rate in the pound levied increased materially. This tended to drive out such surviving industries as could move and practically prohibited new industries from coming into the area. High rates in depressed areas have, consequently, aggravated an already bad situation. Some localities have been practically reduced to taxing the unemployed for their own relief, the residents being almost entirely former employees of idle industrial plants, while the nonresident property owners, with whatever taxpaying ability they may possess, have escaped entirely.[9]

[8] *Parliamentary Debates*, CCXXIII, 447.
[9] Note, e.g., Brynmawr in the South Wales coal district, with 74 percent of its workers unemployed in May, 1934. This is the percentage of insured male workers, but it is apparent from the fact that the number of such unemployed accounted for one in four of the entire population in this year, as well as the fact that coal mining is Brynmawr's only industry, that practically all the workers must have been of this

The marked movement of industry to the south of England in recent years [10] has many causes, but it is most often attributed to the high local rates in the industrial areas of the north, which are largely occasioned by the relief problem.[11] In consequence the derating of factories can to some extent be justified as an aid to distressed areas. Whether in fact the remission of three-quarters of the rate burden has served to check the movement of industry from depressed to prosperous areas has not been ascertained. But, while rates do not bulk as large in factory costs as before, the fact that prosperous areas benefited along with depressed areas means that the differential advantage remains. If the government's primary objective had been to encourage the development of industry in depressed areas it could have been achieved more directly and effectively in other ways. Moreover, in so far as the apparent movement southward is the development of one type of industry, which is more suitably located near large markets and which has never had a real foothold in the north, and the decline of another type of industry peculiar to the north, rates can at best have minor importance in determining location.

In some few instances the derating may have operated as a check on the growth of factories in certain prosperous areas. Here local authorities have not always been eager for additional factories, bringing with them, as they do, increased exemptions from the rates and increased population, which has to be housed

---

class. Ministry of Labour, *Reports of Investigations into the Industrial Conditions in Certain Depressed Areas*, Cmd. 4728, 1934, p. 145.

[10] It is, perhaps, not quite accurate to speak of industry as moving south. What has actually happened is that the shipbuilding, coal, iron, and steel industries, and cotton textiles, located mostly in the north, have suffered from long-continued depression. The prosperous industries have been automobiles and light industry, located in the Midlands and London area near the largest market. Thus the industries in the south have grown while the northern industries have declined. For a full discussion of this see A. Thatcher, *Some Financial Problems Arising out of the Drift of Industry and Population*, Institute of Municipal Treasurers and Accountants, May, 1932.

[11] See, e.g., Cmd. 4728, *op. cit.*, p. 83.

and educated at local expense. The local district is reimbursed for derating only on the basis of 1928-29 losses, and only temporarily for that. Property which is turned over to industrial uses after that date is derated, but the local district receives no compensation from the national government for the loss. While local authorities cannot prohibit factories, they can increase their costs by higher rates for water and power, and in other ways put obstacles in their path. There is no reason to believe, however, that this discouragement of industry has been widespread.[12]

The derating of prosperous industries equally with the depressed industries aroused much criticism in the House of Commons at the time that the bill was under discussion, and it would seem a little difficult to justify even as a recovery measure. The consensus of opinion is that it has not achieved its purpose. Recovery there is, in a measure, but it does not seem probable that derating has played any important part in it. In the case of agriculture further subsidies may be needed; but it does not seem at all certain that the tenant farmers, constituting two-thirds of the total, will not find their rents rising in consequence; and in many regions, such as Sussex and Salop, the farmers are comparatively well-to-do.

In any case, the ends in view are national and the subsidies should probably be national. It is true that local authorities as a whole are compensated for losses as a whole from national funds; but individual authorities are compensated for individual losses only temporarily and partially. The loss of approximately 12 percent of the only local tax base seriously restricts the possibilities of governmental expansion on local initiative. And the average does not tell the whole story. Losses in individual rural districts varied from 3 to 57 percent.[13] When distributions of grants in proportion to losses cease, it seems quite probable that some

---

[12] No actual instances of this have been found, although the statement that this has occurred has occasionally been made by officials interviewed.

[13] Cmd. 3134, *op. cit.*, p. 5.

districts will have difficulty in supporting the functions left to their control. Only on the asssumption that the presence of manufacturing, mining, transport, or agricultural property in a district contributes little or nothing to the costs of local government will the ultimate adjustment prove reasonably equitable. Nevertheless, it is extremely difficult to revoke such privileges, once given, and no effort is being made to restore derated property to the tax base. The gradual change from the old system to the new gives opportunity for serious maladjustments to be corrected, but the correction will probably come from further grants from the national government. The local governments' tax base has been permanently impaired.

The fundamental questions would seem to be, not whether local governments will be cramped by inadequate revenue, but whether the government is justified in shifting this burden from agricultural and industrial ratepayers to national taxpayers, and whether the inevitable loss of local freedom which comes with increased central government support is justified by the gains to these particular ratepayers. The answer to both of these questions would seem to be in the negative. The derating which was the principal reason for the Local Government Act of 1929 would seem to be its least defensible achievement.

The economies effected by the revision of district boundaries and the transfer of highway and welfare support to larger governmental units cannot be readily ascertained. The general trend of expenditures is meaningless, in view of the fact that depression followed on the heels of local government reform and inevitably increased the welfare burden. Highway expenditures were likewise influenced by depression, since they could to some extent be deferred as an economy measure, or they could be expanded as a work-relief measure. Consequently, the influence of the 1929 reform on expenditures for these specific functions, and on all expenditures has been obscured by other and more potent factors.

The amount of rates and grants reached the high point of 289 million pounds in 1930-31, 11 percent above the 1928-29 level, and have since declined; but even with the decreases in 1931-32 and 1932-33 rates plus grants were above the 1928-29 level in these years. Rates did not go down by the amount paid by the national government in lieu of rates on agricultural and industrial property. This amounted to 22 million pounds. The reduction in rates in 1932-33 as compared with 1928-29 was a little less than 20 million pounds. In 1933-34 rates increased again slightly.

TABLE 21

LOCAL RATES AND GRANTS BEFORE AND AFTER THE LOCAL GOVERNMENT ACT OF 1929 [a]

Fiscal Year Beginning April 1	MILLION POUNDS			PERCENTAGE		
	Rates	Grants	Total	Rates	Grants	Total
1928.........	166.0	93.8	259.8	63.9	36.1	100.0
1929.........	156.3	114.3	270.6	57.7	42.3	100.0
1930.........	149.9	138.7	288.6	51.9	48.1	100.0
1931.........	148.3	135.5	283.8	52.1	47.9	100.0
1932.........	146.3	126.6	272.9	53.6	46.4	100.0
1933.........	147.7	131.8	279.5	52.8	47.2	100.0

[a] Figures include all rates and all grants, whether for capital or revenue account, and whether for specific or general purposes.

The revision of district boundaries and the consolidation of districts achieved so far is considerable. Some counties have already effected a thoroughgoing redistricting of the entire county, in some instances reducing the number of urban and rural districts to approximately half the former number. The total number of boroughs and districts has been reduced by about 200 in seven years.[14] County and county borough boundaries are also being revised. In so far as this contributes to the efficiency of local government it should reduce the cost. Of more importance, perhaps, from the financial point of view, is the equalization

[14] From about 1,800 to about 1,600.

achieved by the wider area of support. Some comparatively wealthy residential areas have been combined with poorer industrial areas. Such consolidations have not always had the approval of the wealthier districts concerned, but they have been accomplished none the less.

The transfer of poor relief to the county was made with surprisingly little protest when one considers the importance of the change. The fact that all officers employed prior to November 12, 1928, were transferred, and that the local boards of guardians were quite generally retained as subcommittees of the county public-assistance committee, and continued to carry out much the same duties as before with a minimum of supervision from the county, doubtless contributed to the general acceptance of the change. What was, in fact, achieved was a larger area for support, except in the case of the county borough, combined with a decentralized, and therefore individualized, administration.

The complete transfer of the relief of the able-bodied poor to the national government under the Public Assistance Act of 1934 is a more important step toward the centralization of this function. This means that the largest part of outdoor relief has become a national function and that the counties are mainly concerned with institutional relief. Unlike the 1929 changes, which increased the area of support and retained, for the most part, the decentralized administration, the 1934 act goes farther in centralizing administration than in centralizing support. Local advisory committees are retained, but the Unemployment Assistance Board has wide powers, and relief rates have been standardized. These relief rates take into account rents paid, and any sources of income individuals receiving relief may possess, but they fail to take into account differences (other than rents) in the cost of living in different areas, with the result that in some districts the sums are generous and in others, apparently, inadequate. Sixty percent of the sums paid by the counties for the relief of the able-bodied in the year 1932-33 are to be contributed by the counties toward the cost of the new system. This is, for the time being, a substantial further relief to county treasuries, but in view of the fact that 1932-33 was a year of extensive unemployment and high relief costs, it is conceivable that, with improved conditions, some counties may find their contributions exceeding costs. Nor is it certain that the high degree of centralization of administration is going to be satisfactory.

This transfer of the relief administration was considered at the time that the Local Government Act of 1929 was under discussion and discarded in favor of the block grant, because it was felt that centralized administration of public assistance would not be successful.[15] Later increases in public-assistance payments for political ends in cities which could not afford the additional burden, notably West Ham, are generally cited as causing the change in point of view and the resulting transfer of administration to the central government. It is difficult to determine to what extent the demonstration in the House of Commons, which led to the postponement of the full operation of the act until October 1, 1935, was purely political, to what extent it was caused by cutting over-generous relief rates in a few districts, and to what extent it was occasioned by genuine grievances. Even if the protests were fully justified, however, the trouble would seem to have arisen from transition problems, not from difficulties inherent in the centralization of administration, as some critics have claimed. There can be no doubt that the centralization of relief administration offers genuine, perhaps insuperable, difficulties; but in view of the necessity for central support and the consequent necessity for some substantial measure of central control, it is to be hoped that this experiment in thoroughgoing centralization of relief administration will be given every opportunity to demonstrate its possibilities and shortcomings. If it should prove successful, it

[15] E. Lund, *Proposals for the Relief or Readjustment of Local Rates*, Institute of Municipal Treasurers and Accountants, 1928-29 session, No. 16, p. 7.

may be that the central government will assume full support, also, leaving local resources for those functions for which local authorities still have a wide margin of freedom and responsibility.

The transfer of road administration to the counties has not been as acceptable a change as the transfer of poor relief. Fear has been expressed that the county will neglect the subsidiary rural roads in order to have the best possible main highways. And at the other extreme the danger has been pointed out that the county may improve subsidiary roads unduly, with resulting heavy and needless expenditure. Both dangers doubtless exist. There is a very real conflict here among the different sections of the county served by different roads. The time has long since passed when main roads can be regarded as a local matter, but many subsidiary rural roads are of as purely local concern as the residence streets of a city. Yet there are very real advantages in the wider area of support, and the larger administrative unit offers possibilities of economy that cannot be overlooked. Moreover, there is not the need for local and individualized administration in this impersonal service that there is in welfare work; and there is the safeguard that any local districts desirous of retaining jurisdiction over unclassified roads and urban districts wishing to maintain county roads may do so if they measure up to county standards of efficiency (sections 32-35).

Some of the protest against the transfer of highways has come from local officials who are less concerned with the efficient performance of this particular task than with the fact that one by one their duties and powers are slipping from them, endangering, perhaps, the offices themselves. Some protest has come from disinterested individuals who are genuinely concerned lest, with the diminishing importance of district councils, the abler citizens will no longer be attracted to their service. Nevertheless, while many counties have delegated highway maintenance to the underlying districts, an increasing number are taking over all highway work directly, with apparent satisfaction to themselves and the under-lying districts. Twenty-two counties in 1931-32, and 30 counties in 1933-34, had taken over all rural highways.

The redistribution of the financial burden among the different classes of local authorities, resulting from the transfer of these functions to county authorities, has met with some criticism. Municipal boroughs are subject to the county rate for highways and in consequence are contributing to the support of rural roads. County boroughs make no contribution to roads outside their boundaries except in accordance with the individual financial adjustments made at the time that the county borough was first constituted. The consequence is a much higher rate for highways in municipal boroughs than in county boroughs, although it would seem that county boroughs have the same obligation to contribute to rural highways as municipal boroughs.[16] The injustice of this has been emphasized by the treasurer of one municipal borough in a thorough discussion of the problem.[17] When, however, total rates are examined, it is found that the average county-borough rate is higher than that levied in municipal boroughs. Nor is this to be accounted for wholly by the additional amenities offered in the larger cities. A further analysis of the rates shows that the median public-assistance rate is nearly one shilling higher in county boroughs than in municipal boroughs. If the county boroughs make no contribution to rural roads, neither do they receive any contribution from the rural districts toward their public-assistance expenditures; whereas the municipal borough aids the rural districts in supporting highways and is aided by them, in turn, in supporting the poor. In other words, the wider area of charge under which the municipal borough is functioning pro-vides a give and take which is, perhaps, not inequitable in the end.

[16] For 1934 the median highway rate for county boroughs was 2 shillings, and for municipal boroughs, 3 shillings, 4 pence. Computed from data in *Preston Rate Returns* for 1934-35.

[17] A. E. Dean, *Government Grants to Local Authorities*, Institute of Municipal Treasurers and Accountants, May, 1932, pp. 6 *et seq.*

Turning to the question of substituting a single block grant distributed according to an equalizing formula for a variety of grants, mostly for specific purposes and distributed in proportion to expenditures, the first problem concerns the relative merits of the new block grant and the discontinued grants. The abandonment of the fixed sums paid both for the agricultural derating since 1896 and in lieu of the actual yield of certain revenue sources since 1908 needs no defense. They had been continued only because it was difficult to take away from the local units money to which they had become accustomed. The sums paid bore no relation to need, losses, or local tax payments. The percentage grants, on the contrary, were fundamental to the former system. Whenever the national interest seemed to call for higher standards in local government service, the percentage grant, accompanied, of course, by central supervision, was introduced. The fact that the local authorities had to meet only one-half, or perhaps only one-fourth, of the cost of the service stimulated them to continually greater effort. The close and effective supervision on the part of central authorities prevented the extravagance which these percentage grants might otherwise have encouraged, but the fact remained that the wealthy districts could often avail themselves of the national government's offer, when the poor districts, being unable to meet even half of the costs, could not.

The achievements of this system have been notable. To quote Sidney Webb, "The National Government, in the course of three-quarters of a century from 1832 successively 'bought' the rights of inspections, audit, supervision, initiative, criticism, and control, in respect of one local service after another," and thanks to these grants-in-aid England achieved a system of local government which combined the efficiency of the bureaucratic systems of France and Germany with the freedom of the "American Anarchy of Local Autonomy." [18]

[18] *Grants in Aid, op. cit.,* p. 6.

Nevertheless, the system has its limitations, and reaction followed its extreme development in the war and early post-war period. In addition to the criticism that it benefited wealthy districts most, it was pointed out that it forced endless central supervision and interference which was often annoying and even oppressive. Instances were cited of local authorities who had gladly bought back the freedom they had sold by meeting the full cost of a project themselves in order to avoid the delay and red tape incident to government aid. Chamberlain, defending the Local Government Bill in the House of Commons, pointed out that the Bill would eliminate the examination of many small details of local government which was irritating to the local authorities and costly to the national government.[19]

Whether, in fact, local authorities have achieved any material freedom from central supervision is not clear. With the abolition of a number of minor grants a certain amount of detailed supervision in relatively small matters, which probably never really justified itself, has been discontinued. This is a genuine gain. There would seem to have been no slackening in control of essentials, however, and consequently no appreciable increase in local independence. The percentage grants remaining are far more extensive than those abandoned, and the Minister of Health has the power to withhold any part of the block grants if he has evidence of inefficiency (section 104).

The percentage grants may, of course, be still further reduced in the future. The reduction of these grants was first recommended by the Commission on National Expenditure in 1922,[20] and a greater reduction than was achieved in 1929 was recommended by the Committee on Local Expenditures in 1932.[21] The abandonment in 1931 of the guarantee of 50 percent of expendi-

---

[19] *Parliamentary Debates*, CCXXIII, 105.

[20] *First Report of the Commission on National Expenditure*, 1922, Cmd. 1581, p. 105.

[21] *Report of the Committee on Local Expenditure for England and Wales*, 1932, Cmd. 4200, p. 17.

tures for elementary education as a minimum grant is a further step in this direction. It may well be that the percentage grant is a luxury which England can no longer afford. For the moment, however, there seems to be no disposition to abandon those remaining.[22]

From the local point of view, the block grant has the advantage over the percentage grant of giving local authorities more freedom in applying their resources to those services that seem to them most urgent. If their judgment is not always sound, at least they are in a better position to judge of the relative importance of these services to their community than any central authority. Further, it opens the way to equalization of resources, which the percentage grant cannot do. This is of increasing importance as governmental costs rise.

The particular formula selected for the distribution of the new block grants is designed to equalize. All five factors point to that end. Certainly no area in great need could fail to benefit from its provisions. But whether the factors selected are the "best," and whether each receives the weight due it, are matters for debate. None of the factors is an accurate measure of need, and there is no guarantee that combining them gives an accurate measure.

Considering the individual factors, the most weight, 37 percent, is given to the actual population. In addition, the actual population serves as a multiple for all the other factors entering into the final weighted population which determines each local share in the block grant. This is not difficult to justify. In the long run the cost of government is influenced more by the number of people governed than by any other single factor. This is so generally accepted that when comparisons in governmental costs are to be made, the data are regularly presented as per capita costs. More-

[22] On the contrary, there have been some increases. The new grant for rural water supply is discretionary, but in practice it is distributed in proportion to expenditures, and the percentage grant for school buildings has been increased (January, 1936) from 20 to 50 percent.

over, population is a simple base to determine and a "fair" measure from the popular point of view.

A per capita distribution of central-government funds will always result in an appreciable amount of equalization as long as there are great variations in per capita wealth and income. Under a per capita distribution poor districts will get more, and wealthy districts less, than they contribute to the fund so distributed. It cannot achieve complete equalization, however, since per capita distributions are necessarily the same and per capita needs are greater in the poorer areas. Poverty increases health, school, and housing needs, as well as direct welfare costs. If the poorer city is found to be spending less than its richer neighbor, resources, not needs, are dictating its policy. The simple per capita distribution fails, also, to make allowance for the greater per capita needs of the more densely populated areas. In view, however, of the tendency for per capita wealth to increase with per capita expenditures, as the size of the city increases, the weighting of population for the size of the community, so frequently found in German distribution formulae, offers no certain corrective for the latter shortcoming of the simple per capita distribution. The weighting factors selected for the English formula offer a better opportunity for equalization of both resources and needs.

One shortcoming of the use of population as a measure of need has become apparent with the recent shifts in population from northern England and South Wales to the south of England. A declining population brings with it no corresponding decline in governmental costs. Some savings there will be, of course, in time, but half-empty schools cost nearly as much to run as schools fully utilized. Debt service cannot be reduced at all; and the remaining population is apt to contain more than the usual proportion of aged and dependent persons in need of public assistance. Consequently, the depressed areas can ill afford to lose that portion of the government grants which is remorselessly cut off with each decline in population. Increased weighting for unemployment was insufficient to prevent Glamorgan and Monmouth from receiving less in the second grant period than in the first, although their financial condition had grown increasingly precarious, and county rates had to be increased.[23]

The weighting for children under five years of age determines the distribution of 17.7 percent of the block grant. This factor in the formula has been criticized more than any other since, at best, it is an indirect measure of poverty. One opponent of the formula contends that suburban residential districts tend to have a large proportion of children under five years of age and to suffer the least from derating.[24] Further, it is pointed out, the children themselves do not increase governmental costs greatly. The heavy costs are for schools, police, and roads, and small children can hardly add appreciably to costs for these. Young children, of course, affect the cost of welfare, housing, and health.[25]

In defense of children under five years of age as a measure it should be noted that all the three first-named functions are still supported by special grants, whereas among the three latter functions only housing receives special grants. Consequently, some two-fifths of the expenditures met from local rates and block grants in 1932-33 were for health, housing, and welfare. Furthermore, the figures do not seem to bear out the contention that the proportion of children in some wealthy districts, especially in seaside resorts, is high.[26] The figures published in the Ministry of Health's *Proposals for Reform in Local Government*[27] show that the four county boroughs with the smallest proportion of

[23] Rates in Glamorgan were 13 shillings, 2 pence in the first year of the first grant period and 14 shillings, 10 pence, in the first year of the second grant period. Rates in Monmouth were 11 shillings, 10 pence, and 12 shillings, 5 pence, respectively, in these two years.

[24] Beckett in *Parliamentary Debates*, CCXXIII, 335.

[25] Health includes in the English government classification such services as parks and all sanitation.

[26] See, e.g., *The Economist*, December 8, 1928, p. 1042; Association of Municipal Corporations, *Report, op. cit.*, p. 10.

[27] Cmd. 3134, *op. cit.*, pp. 26 *et seq.*

children under five years of age are wealthy seaside resorts and that none of the ten county boroughs with the highest proportion of small children falls within this group.

Those who prefer rateable value per head as a measure of need will be somewhat reassured to find that none of the ten county boroughs with the largest proportion of children has a rateable value in excess of five shillings per capita. This after allowance has been made for derating. Five out of the ten boroughs with the highest proportion of children are among the ten with the lowest rateable value per capita, and seven out of the ten with the fewest children are included in the ten county boroughs with the highest rateable value per capita. In fact, the four boroughs with the fewest children are identical with the four with the highest rateable values.

Those who prefer unemployment as a measure of need will also be somewhat reassured by the fact that six of the ten county boroughs with the highest proportion of children are also among the ten county boroughs with the highest proportion of unemployed; and eight of the county boroughs with the lowest proportion of children are among those that received no weighting at all for unemployment in the preliminary schedules. It does not, of course, follow that this is a better measure of poverty than the more direct measures such as unemployment and rateable values. It is, however, a more stable value than unemployment and less subject to manipulation than rateable values. And it should be remembered that grants are fixed for a period of five years. Moreover, the children under five years of age will become school children in the course of the grant period and a very direct factor in governmental costs.

It is impossible to say how much weight should be given to a factor of this kind. All the evidence indicates that in England at the present time and for the purpose in hand it is a reasonable factor to be included in the formula until such time as really accurate measures of need and ability have been determined. But it is at best an empirical measure. There is no certainty that in other places and at other times it would measure poverty as satisfactorily as it does in England today. In fact there is already evidence that it is becoming a less satisfactory index of poverty in England and Wales than it was when the formula was devised. During the first grant period weighting for children under five years of age increased the actual population by 62 percent. In the second grant period, owing to the decline in the birth rate it increased the actual population by only 48 percent. This decreases the relative importance of children under five years of age as a factor in weighting. Of more significance, however, is the fact that the decline is greatest in the poorest regions. The actual population of Surrey, the wealthiest county in England and Wales, barring London, was increased for children under five years of age by the same percentage in the second grant period as in the first. Whereas the counties of Durham, Glamorgan, and Monmouth, the counties which have suffered most from unemployment, received much less weight for children under five years of age in the second grant period than in the first.[28] This decline would seem to be the direct result of prolonged unemployment. It is probably caused largely by the migration of the younger workers to areas where opportunities for employment are greater, leaving a larger proportion of older people in the remaining population. While the weighting for children under five years of age is still materially greater for the poor counties than it is for the wealthy counties and substantial equalization results from its use, it is apparent from the marked changes in the short space of four years that it is not as stable a measure as might be expected and cannot be trusted as a measure of poverty. It is conceivable that in time those areas in which industry is expanding will receive more weight for this factor than the areas where industry

---

[28] The percentage weighting added to population for children under five years of age declined between the first and second grant periods from 88 to 68 in Monmouth, 90 to 62 in Glamorgan, 106 to 86 in Durham, and remained constant at 32 in Surrey.

is declining. Again the formula fails, as it did in the case of population itself, to measure the changing needs which come with rapid shifts in industry and population.

The weight allotted to low rateable values in the second grant period was 13.8 percent, a little less than the weight in the first grant period. Many, including the members of the Association of Municipal Corporations, urged that too little weight was given in the formula to this factor even in the first grant period. Most of those arguing for the assignment of greater weight to rateable values would, as a matter of fact, prefer to see the local authorities fully and directly compensated for losses from derating. Such compensation would absorb about half the total block grant. The use of rateable values in the formula repairs in some measure the damage inflicted by derating; but inequalities in rateable value per capita are not, primarily, the result of derating. In the absence of derating there would still be a place for such an equalizing factor; probably as important a place as it has in the existing formula. It is, perhaps, the closest approximation that can be achieved to the ability of local government to support itself, since rateable values are the base of the local authorities' only tax income. But this is only half the problem; it gives no clue whatever to what per capita local governmental costs should be.

At this point some consideration of local valuation machinery is pertinent. Uniform valuations for the levy of rates are essential to the successful operation of the local government financial system. The premium placed on undervaluation is very great. Municipal boroughs and urban districts administering elementary education may find their own rates higher than the county rate, but for the most part the county rate exceeds that of the subsidiary jurisdictions. County rates amounted to nearly two-thirds (64.4 percent) of all rates levied in administrative counties in 1931-32.[29] Thus the rate relief which one district could achieve at the expense of other districts in the county, by under-

[29] This is excluding London and the county boroughs.

valuing property within the district as compared with valuations elsewhere, is substantial. This predominance of the county rate makes uniformity within the county imperative.

Uniform valuations among counties are also important as a result of the new distribution formula for the block grant, and the importance of uniformity will grow as a larger proportion of the grant is distributed on the basis of the formula. That county whose valuation falls farthest below the 10 pounds per capita set as a standard will have its population weighted most for the low valuation factor. At present about 2 million pounds is distributed on the valuation base. When all the grant is distributed on the basis of the formula it will amount to 6 million pounds, assuming no change in the total block grant or in the proportion distributed on the valuation base. Finally, every education authority, whether county, county borough, municipal borough, or urban district, will gain from undervaluation under the present education grant regardless of the valuations of other authorities.[30] The withdrawal by the national government of the guarantee of at least 50 percent of local expenditures for elementary education has increased the importance of the deduction of a sum equal to the yield of a seven-penny rate from the amounts calculated on the basis of teachers' salaries, children in average daily attendance, and other factors. Poor districts could always increase their school grants by undervaluation, but wealthy districts had nothing to gain as long as the 50 percent minimum obtained. Today London is receiving from grants only about one-third of the elementary education expenditures falling on rates and grants, and the wealthy municipal borough of Richmond, Surrey, obtained only one-fourth of such expenditures from grants in 1933-34. Such cities would not have found their education grant reduced

[30] Another factor favoring low valuations, although not affecting the local rate burden, is the fact that valuations of local authorities are apparently used in large measure by the national government in assessing income taxes under Schedule A. This concerns private property owners only, and would influence local valuers only to the extent that they yielded to pressure from private individuals.

by increases in valuations under the old 50 percent minimum, but now every pound added to the valuations reduces their grant by seven pence.

Under these conditions it is pertinent to inquire how far uniform and full valuations have been achieved. The present law provides for valuation on the basis of "the rent which might reasonably be expected." This should be more equitable than the actual rents formerly prescribed, in view of the large number of subsidized houses belonging to local authorities and the controlled rents, which are still an important factor. The rent restriction act limits rentals which can be charged to a sum equal to 140 percent of the pre-war rental. This continues until a change in tenancy, when the landlord is no longer bound by the restriction. Unrestricted rents are in most instances substantially greater than restricted rents. In some instances they are double and more, although these cases seem to be exceptional.

There can be no doubt that valuations have been greatly improved since 1925. The valuation of April 1, 1929, the first quinquennial valuation under the new system, was materially above the preceding valuation for the country as a whole, and it is the consensus of opinion that the second valuation, April 1, 1934, is much better than the first. Most of the local valuation officials with whom the writer has talked agree that methods of valuation are much the same throughout the country, in so far as they are acquainted with the valuations elsewhere, that the county valuation officer is very active in checking up the work of the district valuation officials in most counties, and that the district officials themselves have a sufficient interest in valuations in other districts in the county to keep a watchful eye on them. They do not, of course, claim perfection, and discrepancies in valuation methods and results were occasionally pointed out. To determine the rent which a tenant might reasonably be expected to pay is no simple task, and there are honest differences of opinion as to how it should be determined.

Methods of valuation cannot be described here in detail, but a few points affecting uniformity of valuation may be briefly noted. Valuation officials quite generally begin with actual rentals. With these as a guide they zone the area to be valued. Then, in the case of ordinary dwellings, the average rental per square foot is ascertained within a given zone and this is applied throughout the zone in question, with modifications, of course, for special conditions. In the case of shops, frontage is often taken into account as well as square feet. For types of property which are not actually rented with sufficient frequency other methods must be adopted. Often professional valuers are employed for public utility properties, or the county valuation officer undertakes to value such properties.[31] Differences appear, however, in the selection of the actual rentals used in determining average rents. Some officials average rents as they find them, restricted and unrestricted, together with the subsidized rentals of council houses. Others take only the unrestricted rents on the assumption that they represent the rent that a tenant might reasonably be expected to pay. Still others take only restricted rents in zones in which these predominate and unrestricted rents in zones in which unrestricted rents predominate. Since the difference between controlled and uncontrolled rents is usually very great, the results of such valuations must be far from uniform. How far such differences in practice are to be found within a county has not been ascertained, since the valuation officials interviewed were in most instances in different counties. Most of the officials believed that differences within a county were not great, although some cited important variations. In one case, when two officials in the same county were interviewed, it was found that they had used different methods. These same officials reported that in their county the county valuation official paid little attention to local valuations. In one county it was reported that a certain degree of equalization not contem-

[31] For a brief description of valuation methods see W. H. Routly, "An Introduction to Rating and Valuation." *Institute of Municipal Treasurers and Accountants, 1934-35 session, Lecture No. 1.*

plated by law was achieved through undervaluation in the poorer districts. This was done with the knowledge and tacit consent of the county valuation committee and apparently, also, with the consent of the wealthier districts. Elsewhere the opinion was occasionally expressed that valuations in the richer areas tended to approach full rental value more nearly than valuations in poorer areas.

It seems probable that in the majority of counties in which the county valuation officer is active important differences in method do not occur. There would seem to be no adequate check, however, on differences from county to county. One valuation official claimed that his county had set 60 percent of net rentals as a standard for all districts within the county. While uniformity within the county might be achieved on such a basis, it is clearly not conducive to uniformity among different counties. The Central Valuation Committee is purely advisory. It suggests methods for valuation, but it has no power to require uniform valuations and apparently does not even point out discrepancies in individual cases. If increasing emphasis is to be placed on valuations, it would seem to be important for this central body to have more power than at present.

In spite of the exceptions noted it is apparent that England has come much nearer to achieving uniform valuations than the United States. The provisions of the 1925 Rating and Valuation Act and subsequent legislation would seem to have set up adequate standards and machinery for obtaining uniformity, and it is generally agreed that existing inequalities are rapidly disappearing. Perfection is not expected. There are many difficulties inherent in the task; but it seems highly improbable that any serious discrepancies resulting from competitive undervaluation will be permitted to continue long, and there is good reason to believe that sufficient uniformity will be achieved to prevent undue hardship arising from defective valuation, in spite of the importance which such valuations play in the new system. If it should seem desirable to increase the weighting for the valuation factor in the formula, the difficulties of valuation will hardly prove deterrents.

Unemployment is probably a better test of need for governmental expenditure on one hand and inability to meet governmental costs on the other than any other single factor. Its value is impaired, however, for the purpose in hand by the fact that it fluctuates rapidly, and for a grant fixed five years in advance its use may well be questioned. A grant fixed in a period of depression might still be operating in a period of prosperity; and the industrial community with the greatest unemployment in the first period may be the most prosperous area in the second. This would seem to be a good reason for not giving too much weight to unemployment. In view of the further fact that the national government had already taken over the bulk of the direct costs of unemployment relief before the Local Government Act of 1929 was passed and has since taken over a substantial part of the remaining cost of the support of the able-bodied unemployed, the inclusion of the proportion of unemployed in the formula can only be justified as a measure of poverty and because certain sections of England, particularly the mining and textile regions, are faced with such a protracted unemployment problem that it may be regarded as almost permanent.

As in the case of the other factors it is impossible to say how much weight should be given to such a test of need. When the formula was devised, in a period of comparative prosperity, the estimated weight of this factor was very small. In the first fixed-grant period it had the least weight of any factor in the formula. In the second grant period, however, it has outstripped in importance all the other factors except actual population. When it is considered, further, that a number of counties receive no weight whatever for unemployment, it is apparent that unemployment has more importance as an equalizing factor than the weight given to it would indicate. In Durham, Glamorgan, and Monmouth this factor alone is responsible for more than one-third of the grant distributed according to the formula. In so far as the unemployment in certain areas in England at present appears to be permanent, this factor would seem to be essential to any equalizing grant. But the use of such a factor for a fixed grant of five years under other conditions, where the number of unemployed rises and falls rapidly, would be less suitable.

The final factor in the formula, weighting for population sparsity per mile of highway, is definitely to meet highway needs. There is also, perhaps, some thought of compensating rural areas more or less permanently for losses from the complete derating of agricultural land. This factor accounts for 12 percent of the weighted population in the second grant period. For administrative counties, which alone profit from this factor, the weighting for sparse population amounts to 19 percent in the second grant period. A few agricultural counties are receiving between 40 and 50 percent of their share in the block grant as a consequence of the weighting for sparsity of population. Since per capita highway costs increase with sparse population this would seem to be an appropriate measure of needs. Highway expenditures absorbed about 30 percent of the income of administrative counties from rates and grants in 1932-33. On the assumption that all functions have equal claims to the block-grant revenue, 19 percent of the block grant distributed on the basis of highway needs would seem to be not unduly large. Most of these counties are spending at least as much for highways as their share of the block grant resulting from this factor in the weighting. A few Welsh counties are receiving more on this basis than the proportion of their expenditures going to highways would seem to justify.[32] Whether under these conditions the weight given to this factor is excessive is also a matter of opinion.

[32] Radnor, Montgomery, and Merioneth receive 47, 46, and 40 percent, respectively, of their block grants as the result of weighting for sparsity of population. Their expenditures for highways account for 39, 40, and 26 percent, respectively, of costs met from rates and block grants in 1932-33.

No official explanation is offered for the application of the first two factors in the formula to actual population and the last two factors to population weighted by the first two. The effect, of course, is to increase the weight for unemployment and sparsity of population in those areas which have a large proportion of small children or low valuations. In so far as the various factors are measures of need a good argument might be advanced for applying each factor in turn to the population weighted by all preceding factors. Inquiry as to why some factors were applied to simple population and others to weighted population brought the reply that this procedure gave the desired results.[33] All stress the fact that the formula is empirical; no one suggests that it has any scientific value. The only claim made for it is that it "works." Being empirical, it is fully recognized that it may not continue to be equitable. It is expected that revision may come soon and frequently. Meanwhile there is very general satisfaction. It seems probable, however, that this satisfaction comes as much from the fact that every district was guaranteed against losses from the new system, at least at first, and that most made substantial gains, as from the equity of the distribution formula.

One final point remains to be considered in connection with the block grant: the fixed period for which it is given. The principal reason for not revising the grants annually is the difficulty of obtaining reliable data for the distribution formula. With the quinquennial census which was anticipated when the act was passed, accurate data for revision would be available once in five years. An additional advantage of the fixed-grant period is the certainty of such a grant. Both the national and local governments know for some time in advance just what can be counted on. This raises the question as to whether the factors in the formula are themselves sufficiently stable so that no injustice is apt to occur from using them for a five-year period. The actual variation in the ratio of the population weighting in the second grant period to

[33] See *supra*, p. 192, n.

the population weighting in the first grant period for each factor in the formula was: population, 101.5; children under five years of age, 79.3; low rateable values, 98.5; unemployment, 254.2; and sparsity of population, 93.7. In individual counties and county boroughs the variation was far greater. It would appear that at least unemployment and children under five years of age have been highly unstable factors. The factor of children could be materially stablized by extending the age limit of the group included. As it stands, none of those included in one grant period is included in the next. If the entire group under ten were included, for example, this factor would be far more stable. The unemployment factor could be stabilized by the use of a moving average. Such procedure would, of course, only be justified on the assumption that the poverty indicated by the larger proportion of small children in the earlier period continues after the children have gone and that unemployment leaves an aftermath of burdens which impairs the financial position of the local unit for some years after the actual unemployment has declined. If this is not the case the question is not the stabilization of the measures but rather the more frequent readjustment of the grant to changing conditions.

Local authorities, accustomed to fairly regular annual increases in grants, have been very much disturbed by a fixed grant. To maintain that the five-year period means stagnation [34] is, however, an overstatement of the case. For the first grant period local authorities received more in total grants than in the last year of the old system, and the amount of the grant is to be readjusted with each new grant period so that the ratio of grants to rates will be what it was in the first year of the new system. It is, of course, true that expansion during the grant period must come from rates—with the not unimportant exceptions of education, police, housing, and highways. But if, in consequence, rates have increased 10 percent, for example, during the five years in

[34] Greenwood in *Parliamentary Debates*, CCXXIII, 116.

question, the amount of the block grant will be increased 10 percent for the new period. If the ratio of grants to rates had not
been increased for the first year of the new system there might
be cause for complaint. Actually, however, the percentage of local
rate and grant revenue coming from grants was raised from 36
in 1928-29 to 48 in 1930-31. It would take a considerable increase in rates in any five-year period to bring this back to the
old ratio.

With the exception of the block grants, the largest single grant
received by local authorities is that for elementary education.
This grant is likewise distributed on the basis of a formula which
takes into account both needs and ability. Need is measured by
the number of school children and actual expenditures, and ability by the product of a seven-penny rate. Prior to 1931, however,
only a limited equalization was achieved. Poor counties and
county boroughs, it is true, benefited from the formula, receiving
in some cases as much as two-thirds of the elementary school costs
from the national government. But wealthy districts benefited
from the guarantee of 50 percent of approved expenditures, so
that the proportion of expenditures met by the central government
did not vary greatly from one district to the next.

The increase in the scholar grant in 1931 together with the cut
in the percentage of teachers' salaries paid and the abolition of
the minimum guarantee have resulted in much wider variations
in this grant. Grants in 1932-33 covered less than one-fifth of the
elementary education costs in the wealthy residential city of
Bournemouth and two-thirds of such costs in Merthyr Tydfil, a
depressed coal-mining area. In municipal boroughs similar variations can be found. Jarrow, which is exceptionally poor, was
receiving a little better than three-fourths of its income from this
source in 1933-34, and Richmond, which is wealthy, was receiving just one-fourth. The factors in the education grant are much
the same as those which have found wide acceptance in other

countries, and there seems to be no dissatisfaction with them here. Why they have not been extended to higher education, in place of the percentage grant, is not clear.[35] The problems seem to be much the same.

When the elementary education grant in approximately its present form was first proposed by the 1901 Commission, the 36 shillings per child suggested represented nearly half of the costs. Today the cost per child is between two and three hundred shillings, and the 45 shillings per child paid is less than one-fifth of the actual cost. It has been suggested that if the grant per child were raised to one approaching half of the present cost and the deduction for equalization were increased over a seven-penny rate, equalization more nearly approaching what was intended when the original recommendations were made could be achieved without increasing the total grant. One estimate indicates that a grant of 92 shillings per child, equalized through the deduction of the product of an eighteen-penny rate, would cost the government approximately the same as the grant of 45 shillings with the deduction of a seven-penny rate.[36] Shrewsbury, a moderately well-to-do municipal borough which received approximately half its expenditures for elementary schools from the government grant in 1933-34, would find its grant slightly reduced by such a change; Jarrow, with more than half its workers unemployed, would receive more than nine-tenths of its elementary school costs from such a government grant; and Richmond, a wealthy Surrey borough, would get nothing at all. It is doubtful if equalization would, or should, be carried to this extreme. It is difficult to reconcile either national or local administration with a financial plan which throws practically all the support on the local authorities in some instances, and on the national government in others.

Highway grants rank second to education grants in amount

[35] This change has been recommended. See, e.g., the Board of Education, *Memorandum on the Grant System*, 1926, Cmd. 2571, p. 11.

[36] Dean, *op. cit.*, p. 17.

among the grants for specific functions, in spite of the reductions made in these by the 1929 act. The national government still contributes to the counties 60 percent of approved expenditures for the maintenance of Class I roads, and 50 percent of approved expenditures for the maintenance of Class II roads. Contributions are also made to construction expenditures, the percentage of costs varying with different projects at the discretion of the Ministry of Transport. The amount of the discontinued road grants is allowed for in the amount of the block grant distributed, and the sparsity of population factor in the distribution formula is intended as a measure of highway needs.

The specific road grants equalled 27.8 percent of the highway costs of local authorities falling on rates and grants in 1932-33. In addition to this the sum of 3.5 million pounds was transferred from the road fund to the block grant to meet the cost of discontinued road grants. England and Wales received 3.1 million pounds of this sum. If this is added to the specific grants, 34 percent of the highway costs falling on rates and grants were met from the road fund in 1932-33. The remainder came from local rates and, through the block grant, from general exchequer revenues. Compared with American standards this is a small proportion of highway costs to be met from motor vehicle taxes. This is not because motor vehicle taxes are low, but because they are not earmarked for highways to the extent that they are in America. The gasoline tax, an import duty, never reaches the road fund at all, but is paid into general exchequer funds. In the case of the motor vehicle license tax, one-third of the proceeds of licenses for pleasure cars and motorcycles has been deducted by the national government, since 1926, as a luxury tax, before the money reaches the road fund. This amounts to approximately 5 million pounds a year. And with the 1929 act 3 million pounds is diverted from this tax after it is paid into the road fund, as a general contribution to the block grant. This is in addition to the sum contributed to the block grant to cover specific losses from discontinued highway grants. As long as highway expenditures more than equal the proceeds of motor vehicle taxes, it is perhaps not important to earmark the proceeds of these taxes for this function. Moreover, as long as the government justifies the taxes at least in part as luxury taxes rather than benefit taxes there is no occasion to demonstrate that, directly or indirectly, the motorist is receiving full value for his tax.

The specific highway grants remaining are percentage grants and as such make no contribution to the problem of equalization, although the grants for construction may be used to some extent to equalize, since the percentage met from the road fund is left to the discretion of the Ministry of Transport. Material equalization of the highway burden has been achieved by the 1929 act, but it has come through the transfer of rural highway costs to the county rather than through the grants.

The police grants were not changed by the 1929 act. They continue to meet 50 percent of approved expenditures as before. Since police costs and taxable values tend to vary directly with density of population, there is no special need for equalizing the burden of this particular expenditure. The present division of police costs is on the assumption that this is a seminational service in which the national government and local authorities are equal partners. Unless percentage grants are to be abandoned entirely and equalization carried to an extreme hardly contemplated at present, this would seem to be a reasonable position. There is still ample room for further equalization of burdens in connection with functions where the cost tends to rise as ability declines.

The amount of grants for housing exceeds the amount of grants for police and nearly equals that for highways. Housing has become an important factor in many borough budgets, and it is the most important function of a large number of urban and rural districts. It is not exceptional for these districts to devote half of their rate and grant funds to housing. The urban district of Tilbury, in Essex, allocated 63 percent of its rate and grant revenues to housing in 1928-29 and 58 percent in 1932-33. In 1932-33 the rural district of Whitchurch, in Salop, spent 76.5 percent of its rate and grant funds for housing. Housing is not a new local function. Local authorities have had the power to provide housing since 1851. But it became important only with post-war legislation providing generous national subsidies.

Housing is the one local function toward which the national government contributes more than half the net cost. Grants were between four and five times as large as rates for housing in 1932-33. The basis of these grants varies under the different acts. The Housing Act of 1919 provided a grant equal to any deficit incurred by local authorities for their housing schemes over and above the product of a one-penny rate levied by the local authority. Under this act the grant is about six times as large as the rate contribution. Local authorities were encouraged to build at any cost, and few restrictions were placed on them. Building costs were exorbitant, and local authorities were not greatly concerned with economies, since their contribution bore no relation to costs. It is generally admitted that the act was ill-considered and justified only as a measure "to avert revolution."

Later housing acts were more carefully drafted and placed greater responsibilities on local authorities. The subsidies have taken the form of fixed contributions per house, thus putting the burden of extravagance on local authorities and giving them the benefit of any economies they may effect. Even so, the national contribution is generous, amounting to nearly four times the local contribution in 1932-33. In addition to this the various housing acts have made provision for subsidizing private housing schemes, both directly and through local authorities.

The government's housing policy was changed with the Housing Act of 1933. This was an attempt to turn housing back to private enterprise. Subsidies on new council housing projects were discontinued, except for slum-clearance projects. The subsidies on houses already constructed continued, of course, as before. In place of new subsidies for council houses the government agreed to meet half the loss incurred by local authorities on guarantees for loans for private housing projects. These projects must, of course, be approved by the Ministry of Health. Losses on loans have been very small thus far, in spite of the fact that these loans equal 90 percent of the cost of the property. After two years, however, the government reverted to the former policy of subsidizing houses built directly by the local authorities. Under the Housing Act of 1935 local authorities receive grants of fixed amounts for new houses, the amount of the subsidy varying with the cost of the site. The purpose of this act is to relieve overcrowding, and subsidies are given only where overcrowding, as defined in the act, occurs.

The amount of building which has taken place since the war is very great. It is estimated that 2,328,385 houses were built between the signing of the Armistice and May 31, 1934. Half (50.6 percent) were subsidized. One-third (32.5 percent) were built directly by local authorities.[37] The increase in population in the decade between 1921 and 1931 was only two million. Clearly much has been done to relieve the overcrowding caused by cessation of building during the war. In the four years 1931 to 1934 building was at the rate of 231,000 houses per year.[38] The estimated increase in population for these years is approximately the same as the increase in the number of houses. England expects a stationary, or even a declining, population. Many districts in which population is already declining have continued to build houses. It is apparent, under these conditions, that even though there is still sufficient need for new houses to justify the 1935 Housing Act, this need cannot continue long. Consequently, no

[37] Ministry of Health, *Annual Report*, 1933-34, pp. 153, 302.

[38] *The Times*, April 9, 1935, p. 9. In the year 1934-35, 285,000 houses were built by private enterprise alone. The number of council houses built in this year was greatly diminished, however, by the laws then in effect. *A Century of Municipal Progress, 1835-1935*, London, 1936, pp. 211-12.

material increase in housing subsidies can be expected. Housing is a popular government undertaking. Moreover, in many rural and urban districts it is one of the few functions left to district officials. It is not at all certain in some instances that the expansion of housing has not been dictated by the council members' interest in votes and the administrative officials' interest in creating full-time positions for themselves rather than by genuine need. The fact that the government's generous subsidies leave only a minimum burden to be borne by local rates is apt to encourage such expansion. Some local authorities have actually been able to make a profit on their houses.[39]

The fact that subsidized houses are designed for that portion of the working population unable to pay ordinary rents means that the housing burden is usually heaviest in the poorest districts. The government is paying the same amount per house to rich and poor districts alike; but in so far as this expenditure is greatest in the poorest districts the substantial grant allowed acts to some extent as an equalizer, not of housing costs, but of all governmental costs.

The remaining grants for specific purposes are comparatively small, the largest being a little more than one million pounds in 1932-33 for sewers and sewage disposal. The only other function accounting for more than 250 thousand pounds in 1932-33 was "small holdings." In spite of the government's effort to do away with the small grants for specific purposes, which involved more administrative detail than was justified by the amount of money, the *Annual Local Taxation Returns for 1932-33* reports specific grants for 34 of the 46 functions appearing in its classification. Twelve of the 34 functions receiving specific grants receive two separate grants, one for current expense and one for capital expense. There is still opportunity for simplification. The

[39] One urban district, e.g., reports that it has been able to sell a substantial number of its houses at a figure covering cost of construction. It continues to receive a subsidy from the national government for these houses which it no longer owns.

grants involved are in some cases percentage grants, in some cases unit grants, and in some cases discretionary. Their importance in the general financial scheme is too small, however, to justify detailed consideration of them here.

XI

THE FISCAL POSITION OF THE VARIOUS TYPES OF LOCAL GOVERNMENTS UNDER THE PRESENT SYSTEM AS ILLUSTRATED BY SPECIFIC CASES

THE real test of the existing system is not so much the isolated consequences of specific provisions as the cumulative effect of all the provisions combined in individual areas. The increase in the total amount of grants brought gains to local governments as a whole, and the numerous guarantees prevented losses, at least for the time being, to individual local authorities. Each county borough and the composite of local units forming each administrative county are guaranteed against loss (as compared with 1928-29) for all time, except as more property may be derated for agricultural or industrial purposes. The guarantees for the subdivisions of the county are temporary, however, and in the end many of these jurisdictions will lose to other authorities within the county or to the county itself.

The increase in local government expenditures was not large between 1928-29, the last year in which the old system was in full effect, and 1932-33, the latest year under the new system for which complete data are available. The sum of rates and grants increased about four percent in these four years. This small change is not surprising in view of the depression. With pressure for increased expenditure on one side and pressure for greater economy on the other, there is a tendency to maintain the status quo. Examination of detailed figures reveals a decrease in welfare expenditures, no change in police expenditures, and increases in expenditures for other functions, particularly housing. The apparent decrease in welfare expenditures is the result of a revised classification under the 1929 act (section 5), placing assistance in certain cases under various health acts instead of under the poor law. Expenditures for those services formerly included under poor relief have, in fact, increased somewhat, as would be expected in a period of increasing unemployment. Nevertheless, the expenditure per case handled has decreased for both indoor and outdoor relief, and credit for this should go at least in part to the consolidation of institutions and to other economies effected by the larger administrative unit. The increases in housing expenditures are most marked in county boroughs and rural districts. The provision for slum clearance under the 1930 Housing Act is probably largely responsible for the former, and the rural housing subsidies under the 1931 Housing Act are probably largely responsible for the latter. The 1924 Housing Act was still in force during this period, however.

Changes in the distribution of expenditures among the different classes of local governmental units are more marked than changes in expenditures for different functions. The transfer of highway and welfare support to the county unit has resulted in important increases in county and county borough expenditures and corresponding decreases in the expenditures of rural districts and the former poor-law unions; and this in turn has redistributed the tax burden among individual taxpayers. This redistribution has affected county-borough taxpayers less than taxpayers in the administrative county, since the county borough was the unit for highway administration before the 1929 act was passed. The former poor-law union was often larger than the county borough, but even here the readjustment has not been great in most cases, since the largest part of both rateable values and expenditures was usually within the borough boundaries.[1]

---

[1] The only important exception to this seems to have been West Ham. Here the county borough comprises less than half the rateable value of the former union, whereas the largest part of the poor-relief burden was within the borough boundaries. In consequence, it is estimated that the rate for poor relief would have been 12.5 shillings in 1926-27, if the borough had had to support its own poor, instead of the union rate of 8.7 shillings. Cmd. 3134, *op. cit.*, p. 24.

The welfare burden is normally concentrated in urban communities, and the highway burden in rural communities. Consequently, in administrative counties the increased burden of highway costs now imposed on urban communities is to some extent offset by the decreased burden of welfare costs. Rural communities, too, tend to gain from one and lose from the other; but it is hardly to be expected that gains will regularly offset losses in individual cases. Some wealthy urban residential communities find both their highway and welfare rates, now included in the county rate, increased, and some poor rural areas profit from the wider area of charge for both functions.

To cite specific cases, in 1933-34 the urban district of Weston-super-Mare, a comparatively prosperous seaside resort in Somerset, paid to the county approximately 90,000 pounds for support of county roads and received back in grants from the county for expenditures incurred on county roads within the district only 9,000 pounds. This district had, of course, been subject to a county highway levy before the 1929 act, but the county rate levied in 1933-34 was between two and three times the county rate levied under the old system in 1929-30. The district probably has not lost as much from the transfer of poor relief to the county; but even this rate would have been a little higher in 1929-30, had it been a general county levy, and the increase in the public-assistance burden since that date seems to have been greater in other parts of the county than in this district.

In contrast the rural district of Llantrisant and Llantwit Fardre, in Glamorgan, gains from the wider area of charge for both highways and poor relief. In fact, the gains as estimated by the Ministry of Health are so large as to practically cancel the capitation grant. This district, as a "gaining area," had 3,020 pounds deducted from its capitation grant of 3,150 pounds in 1934-35, whereas as a "losing area," Weston-super-Mare, received a supplementary grant larger than its capitation grant.

In the absence of these temporary guarantees against loss Weston-super-Mare, losing from the wider area of charge for both highways and poor relief, would have been subject to a total rate of 10.7 shillings instead of the actual rate of 9.3 shillings in 1933-34. Conversely, Llantrisant's rate would have been reduced from 22.6 shillings to 21.8 shillings. This moderate degree of equalization should have caused Weston-super-Mare no hardship, and it seems probable that most districts losing from both changes were sufficiently wealthy to have met the added burden without difficulty. Under the circumstances the value of the transition guarantees, except, of course, as a political expedient, may well be questioned. Weston-super-Mare has been able to reduce its already low rates in consequence of these provisions, whereas Llantrisant, with excessive rates prior to the change, has been forced to increase them.

The outstanding change in the financial position of local governments as a whole for this period has come, not from wider areas of charge for highways and poor relief, but from the large increase in the amount of grants. Grants increased from 35 percent of rate and grant income in 1928-29 to 47 percent in 1933-34. This is almost wholly the result of the new block grant—grants for all specific functions except housing having declined.

The cities have gained the least from the change. In London the proportion of rate and grant income received from grants increased between 1928-29 and 1932-33 from 27 to 31 percent, and in the county boroughs it increased from 31 to 40 percent. In the administrative counties this proportion increased from 40 to 54 percent for the combined governments of the county and its subdivisions. For the county government itself the proportion of income from grants has declined; but what the ratepayer loses here in higher county rates he more than makes up in the reduction of borough or district rates. In the underlying divisions the gain is least in municipal boroughs and greatest in rural districts.

The rural areas have been distinctly favored by the change, and their gains will increase somewhat as the temporary provisions of the act lapse.

Comparing the first and second grant periods, London has lost, owing to decreased population and even more to a decrease in the proportion of children under five years of age. The increased unemployment was not sufficient to offset these factors. The county boroughs gained what London lost, in consequence of rising population and growing unemployment, which more than offset decreases in the weighting for children under five years of age and for low rateable values. The administrative counties remained in much the same position as in the first grant period. Whether or not these trends will continue in the third grant period depends on many uncertain factors. If, however, the present movement of population from large cities to small communities continues and if industrial conditions improve, the administrative counties may gain at the expense of both London and the county boroughs. In any case the distribution formula insures that in the great majority of cases the most money will go where the population is both numerous and poor.

Turning to individual local units, the proportion of rate and grant revenue contributed by grants varies widely. In the case of county boroughs the extremes are 21 percent in Eastbourne [2] and 60 percent in South Shields. This is a somewhat wider variation than was to be found in 1928-29, when the major part of the grants was distributed on a percentage basis.

Analysis of county borough grants by functions shows that no appreciable change has taken place in police grants, which continue on a percentage basis, and the range in percentage for these is very small. The range in the percentage of education expendi-

[2] Bournemouth received an even lower proportion, 14 percent, of its rate and grant revenues from grants, but in this city the police force is consolidated with that of the administrative county and the police grant is credited to the county. Consequently this percentage does not reflect the actual gains of this city from grants.

TABLE 22

HIGH, LOW, AND MEDIAN PERCENTAGES OF RATE AND GRANT
REVENUES RECEIVED FROM GRANTS IN COUNTY BOROUGHS,
1928-29 AND 1932-33 [a]

	High	Median	Low
Total[b]			
1928-29.............	55.0	36.3	24.7
1932-33.............	60.0	40.8	21.2
Police[b]			
1928-29.............	53.4	50.0	46.9
1932-33.............	52.5	49.5	45.6
Education			
1928-29.............	67.6	52.7	46.8
1932-33.............	64.0	50.9	27.7
Housing			
1928-29.............	89.5	70.3	12.8
1932-33.............	100.0	76.3	26.9
Highways			
1928-29.............	38.5	12.5	2.5
1932-33.............	21.1	5.1	...

[a] Computed from data in *Annual Local Taxation Returns.*
[b] Excluding those cities for which the police grant is credited to the administrative county.

tures met from grants, on the contrary, is wide and increasing, largely in consequence of abandoning the 50 percent minimum. The range in the proportion of housing costs met from grants is wide in each year. This is likewise true of highway grants. The latter have been substantially reduced, however, whereas the housing grants have been increased.

The proportions of net expenditures met from grants in the cities receiving the largest and the smallest percentages of net expenditures from grants in 1932-33 are given in Table 23.

Eastbourne, which receives the smallest proportion of grants, can well afford to meet its own expenditures. This is a wealthy seaside resort. Rateable values per capita are higher than in any other city, and rates in the pound are moderate in spite of the comparatively small income from grants. Only two cities had

TABLE 23

COMPARISON OF PROPORTIONS OF RATE AND GRANT REVENUES
RECEIVED FROM GRANTS IN COUNTY BOROUGHS WITH
THE HIGHEST AND LOWEST PERCENTAGES

	1928-29		1932-33	
	Eastbourne	South Shields	Eastbourne	South Shields
Percentage				
Total...................	23.7	32.8	21.2	60.0
Police..................	48.7	50.0	49.2	50.2
Education...............	48.9	61.0	34.1	64.0
Housing................	52.6	83.7	59.1	74.2
Highways...............	7.5	24.5	...	21.1
Shillings				
Rateable value per capita...	202.0	100.0	287.0	82.0
Rate in the pound.........	9.4	18.0	7.8	10.5

lower rates in this year. These cities, Blackpool and Bournemouth, were the only ones receiving a smaller percentage of their
education expenditures from grants than did Eastbourne in
1932-33. These, too, are wealthy seaside resorts, with high rateable values per capita. It is apparent that the deduction of the
proceeds of a seven-penny rate from the education grant, as
otherwise calculated, is an important factor in equalizing. Housing grants were below the average in Eastbourne in 1932-33, and
the city received no grants whatever for highways. Only one other
city received no highway grant.

Eastbourne also lost from the application of the weighted
population formula. It was one of six cities, all seaside resorts,
the population of which received no weight for either low rateable
values or unemployment in the first grant period. The only factor
for which the Eastbourne population was weighted was children
under five years of age, and the weighting for this was small. Only
Bournemouth and Blackpool had their population weighted as
little as Eastbourne. In the second grant period, beginning in
1933, Eastbourne was the only city the population of which re-

ceived no weight for unemployment. All the tests of ability used point to Eastbourne as the city best able to support itself, and the equalizing factors in the present system are sufficiently effective to place it at the bottom of the list of cities in the total proportion of aid received.

South Shields, which is at the top of the list, has many claims to aid. It is in the depressed area of Tyneside. Thirty-one percent of its insured population was unemployed in June, 1934. This is about twice the average for Great Britain at that time.[3] Rateable values per capita are very low. Only seven county boroughs had lower per capita values in 1932-33. Considering specific grants, South Shields received from grants a larger percentage of its net expenditures for education and highways than any other city in 1932-33. The proportion of housing expenditures from grants was, however, a little below the average. In the distribution of block grants, South Shields benefited from the weighting for children under five years of age. The actual population was nearly doubled by this factor. Only eight other cities received equal or better weighting for children in the first grant period. It profited also, although somewhat less, by the factor of low rateable values, and again from the unemployment factor. This last was the most important factor in the weighting in both grant periods, and in the second grant period it added more than twice the actual population to the weighted population. Only the neighboring cities of Gateshead and Sunderland and the city of Merthyr Tydfil in South Wales obtained as much weighting for unemployment in the first grant period. In the second grant period the weighting for unemployment was equaled only in Sunderland, West Hartlepool, and Merthyr Tydfil.

The cumulative effect of all these factors was to weight the population of South Shields nearly four times in the first grant period and about four and one-half times in the second grant period. Only Gateshead, Sunderland, and Merthyr Tydfil were

[3] Cmd. 4728, op. cit., p. 117.

equally favored. The total grants for South Shields were larger in proportion to rate income than those for other cities with equivalent population weighting, largely because of a more extensive housing program, which was heavily subsidized by the central government.[4] The net result was to bring this city's rates down from 18 shillings in the pound in 1928-29 to 10.5 shillings in 1932-33. Eastbourne, at the other extreme, was also able to reduce its rates, but only from 9.4 shillings to 7.8 shillings. Gateshead, Sunderland, and Merthyr Tydfil have also been able to reduce their rates, but not to the same extent as South Shields, although they are probably poorer. The rate in South Shields rose again, in 1934-35, reaching 12 shillings. Gateshead had a rate of 15 shillings in this year, Sunderland 16 shillings, and Merthyr Tydfil 27.5 shillings. All these cities had higher rates in 1928-29. Material relief has been received, but there would seem to be need for even greater equalization.

The administrative counties had their burdens increased by the 1929 reform, and the government has not reimbursed them for even as large a proportion of their expenditures as before. Consequently, county rates have been greatly increased. But what the counties have lost, their subdivisions have more than gained; and even the counties as such have profited a little by equalization of resources.[5]

The proportions of net expenditures met from grants in the counties receiving the largest and the smallest percentages of net expenditures from grants in 1932-33 are given in Table 25.

The county receiving the largest proportion of its rate and grant revenues from grants is Huntingdon, an agricultural county which lost heavily from the derating; and it is the derating which accounts for the exceptional grants in this county, totaling more

---

[4] The proportion of housing expenditures met from grants was, however, a little below the average.

[5] The median percentage of rate and grant income from grants increased slightly between 1928-29 and 1932-33, but the arithmetic mean dropped from 55.3 percent in 1928-29 to 53.3 percent in 1932-33.

TABLE 24

HIGH, LOW, AND MEDIAN PERCENTAGES OF RATE AND GRANT
REVENUES RECEIVED FROM GRANTS IN ADMINISTRATIVE
COUNTIES, 1928-29 AND 1932-33 [a]

	High	Median	Low
Total			
1928-29.............	66.7	58.7	36.7
1932-33.............	75.9	60.3	22.4
Police			
1928-29.............	69.0	49.0	40.0
1932-33.............	57.2	46.4	37.7 [b]
Education			
1928-29.............	67.6	58.4	47.3
1932-33.............	63.9	54.4	39.8
Highways			
1928-29.............	54.4	40.8	19.1
1932-33.............	51.4	31.2	14.8

[a] Computed from data in *Annual Local Taxation Returns.*
[b] Excluding Middlesex, which is in the Metropolitan Police District.

TABLE 25

COMPARISON OF PROPORTIONS OF RATE AND GRANT REVENUES
RECEIVED FROM GRANTS IN ADMINISTRATIVE COUNTIES
WITH THE HIGHEST AND LOWEST PERCENTAGES [a]

	1928-29		1932-33	
	Huntingdon	Middlesex	Huntingdon	Middlesex
Percentage				
Total..................	57.6	36.7	75.9	22.4
Police.................	45.8	6.5	46.1	7.3
Education..............	61.2	47.3	57.7	44.1
Highways..............	20.8	19.1	18.9	22.5
Shillings				
Rateable value per capita...	107.0	142.0	65.0	166.0
Rate in the pound........	7.2	4.3	8.0	6.1

[a] Computed from data in *Annual Local Taxation Returns.*

than three-fourths of the rate and grant revenues. Grants for special functions are not unusually large. The education grant is a little above the average, the police grant is a little below the average, and the highway grant is considerably below. Nor is the weighting of population under the formula exceptionally heavy, although the weighting for low rateable values and population sparsity is substantial. A large part of the block grant (43 percent in the first grant period) distributed to Huntingdon is compensation for losses on account of rates. Only five counties receive a larger part of their block grants on this base. Also because of exceptional losses, this is one of the few counties to profit by the guarantee of a sum equal to losses plus one shilling per capita. Since the districts within the county are reimbursed from supplementary grants, not from the general grant, for losses other than the small losses on account of special rates, and since the general grant per capita is unusually large, the share of the block grant retained for county use is large.

The transfer of poor-relief and highway expenditures to the county has not increased county burdens in Huntingdon as it has elsewhere. The welfare burden is exceptionally light, and while the highway burden is heavy, this county was one of the few that had taken over the support of rural roads before the 1929 act was passed, so that no further adjustment was called for. In consequence of this and the large grants, the county has experienced only a small increase in the county rate; and while this rate was above the average in 1928-29 it was below the average in 1932-33.

Apparently the compensation for losses has been generous, and Huntingdon has been placed in a relatively favorable position. As the share of the general exchequer grant distributed in proportion to losses declines, Huntingdon's share in this will be greatly diminished. But what it loses from the general grant it will regain from the additional grant. If in the future demands on the county treasury in Huntingdon increase more rapidly than

demands on other local treasuries, Huntingdon may lose from the
new system. If, however, it experiences only a normal increase in
expenditures, the county ratepayer will continue to profit. Huntingdon's problem seems to be not whether adequate revenues can
be obtained with reasonable rate levies but whether adequate
responsibility can be obtained on the part of local authorities
when three-fourths of the county's costs are being met from national funds.

There is no indication that the large grants have encouraged
needless expansion of government activities. The comparatively
high per capita costs incurred by the county are to be accounted
for by the large highway mileage in proportion to population.
Expenditures per mile of highway are not excessive. The average
of all local rates in the county has dropped from 11.7 shillings
in 1929-30 to 10 shillings in 1933-34. The county's own rate has
increased slightly, but it is materially less than the former county
and poor-law rates combined. It is apparent that thus far the
county's gains have been applied to rate reductions rather than
to expansion of government costs.

The county which received the smallest proportion of its rate
and grant revenue from grants in 1932-33 is Middlesex, which
obtained only 22.4 percent of its revenue from this source. This
is partly because a large part of the county is covered by the
Metropolitan Police District, and in consequence the largest part
of the police grant is not credited to the county. After allowing for
this, however, the Middlesex grants are still relatively lower than
those of other counties.

Middlesex is primarily an urban area covered by the suburbs
of London. It includes large industrial districts, and the losses
from derating were heavy. In fact it ranked next to Huntingdon
in the proportion of the block grant received as compensation for
rate losses. Huntingdon received 43 percent of the block grant
on this base in the first grant period, and Middlesex received 40
percent. But, whereas Huntingdon had its population more than

tripled under the weighted population formula, Middlesex did not even have its population doubled. Only Surrey had its population weighted less, relatively, than Middlesex. The result of this is that the capitation grant paid to the underlying local authorities has exceeded the county's share of the block grant, and while the national government makes good the deficit there is nothing left for county use. Surrey is the only other county in which the county government receives no share in the block-grant distribution. Middlesex also receives a comparatively small percentage of its education expenditures from grants. Surrey, alone, receives less. This is the result of the deduction of the yield of a seven-penny rate. Surrey had the highest per capita rateable value of any county in 1932-33, and Middlesex stood third.

As the grant distributions in proportion to losses diminish, Middlesex probably will not receive less in grants, in spite of the heavy losses from derating and the relatively small weighting of the population. This is because the losses from discontinued grants are very small and the actual population large. This county's share of the grant distribution on the basis of the formula is very substantial, not because of heavy weighting, but because of the sheer size of the population itself.

The equalizing influence of the new system of distribution is apparent in the figures for the two counties given in Table 25. Huntingdon is not one of the depressed areas, and it has no serious unemployment problem to deal with; but its tax base is small in consequence of the complete derating of agricultural property. Middlesex, on the contrary, is one of the wealthiest counties, and in spite of heavy losses from derating, the rateable values per capita are exceeded only in Surrey and East Sussex. The 1929 reform materially increased the proportion of Huntingdon's revenues from grants and reduced the proportion of revenues from grants in Middlesex. Both counties have increased their rates in consequence of new obligations, but the increase in

Middlesex is greater than the increase in Huntingdon, and the difference between the rates of the two counties has been materially reduced. The test of equalization does not rest with the county rates alone, however. To measure the full effect of the change in the counties it is necessary to review also the changes in municipal boroughs and urban and rural districts.

A complete study of the rates and grants in municipal boroughs, urban districts, and rural districts has not been made, but forty of each of these three types of local units have been selected for detailed study. The units selected represent extreme rather than typical cases. They include the local authorities with the highest and the lowest rateable values per capita and the highest and lowest rates in the pound. They also include those in which rates changed most as a result of the new system and those losing the most from rateable values.[6]

Municipal boroughs and urban districts are treated alike under the new system, but their financial position is very different from that of the larger cities organized as county boroughs. Where the Local Government Act of 1929 cut the one remaining link [7] which bound county borough finances to those of the surrounding area through limiting the poor-law rate to the area of the county borough, it tied the municipal borough and urban district finances more closely than ever to those of the county. This was achieved both by extending the area of charge for highways and public assistance to the entire county and by taking conditions in the county as a whole to measure need in apportioning the grant and then reapportioning it within the county on a simple per capita basis. The first provision has tended to militate against the urban

---

[6] The data for these 120 districts are not published and the figures were supplied through the courtesy of officials in the Ministry of Health.

[7] There are frequent exceptions to this in the financial adjustments resulting from redistricting. New county boroughs have frequently bought their freedom by agreeing to pay fixed annual sums to adjacent districts, usually for highway support, and usually for a limited period of time. These are fixed sums, however, which are not changed by changing conditions in the surrounding districts.

communities, and while these have been guaranteed against loss for the time being, the fact that these guarantees are temporary, whereas the county borough guarantees are permanent, has only added another grievance in the opinion of a number of local authorities. The apportionment of county borough grants on the basis of weighted population, and the apportionment of municipal borough and urban district grants on the basis of simple population, gives poor county boroughs an advantage over poor municipal boroughs.

One municipal borough treasurer has protested against requiring municipal boroughs to contribute to rural highways while county boroughs are exempted from this obligation, although the latter are partly responsible for the wear and tear on highways in neighboring districts.[8] He points out further that those county boroughs which have lost because of the transfer of public assistance have been reimbursed for such losses although "they were simply asked to meet *the cost of their own poor.*" This is, however, only one side of the picture. County boroughs do contribute to some extent to highway costs in surrounding districts through special financial adjustments; it cannot be taken for granted that the surrounding communities have no responsibility for the cities' poor; and if the municipal boroughs lose from spreading the highway costs they usually gain from spreading the public-assistance costs, a responsibility which, according to Mr. Dean's argument, they might reasonably be asked to assume. Urban areas have not fared as well as rural communities, but this is not necessarily unjust, and, if rates are any test, municipal boroughs and urban districts have fared better than county boroughs under the new system. A comparison of rates in 1928-29 and 1932-33 shows that rates, including county levies, are lower in the latter year in municipal boroughs and urban districts than in county boroughs and that they dropped more during this four-year period. Municipal boroughs and urban districts have an

[8] Dean, *op. cit.*, p. 31.

advantage over county boroughs in the wider area of charge for the public-assistance rate, and it is the public-assistance burden which has kept county borough rates above those of the other urban communities. The differential in favor of the latter will, of course, decline as their guarantees are withdrawn.

The apportionment of the grant to municipal boroughs and urban and rural districts on a flat per capita basis, to which Mr. Dean also objects,[9] is not so readily justified. It has the advantage of administrative simplicity, but the industrial community which has lost heavily from derating and whose residents are largely unemployed workers receives no more than the residential community of the same size with no losses from derating and no unemployment problem. It is true that some equalization is achieved by the per capita distribution; and the burden of public assistance, which is in inverse proportion to ability, does not fall directly on these local authorities. But it is not clear why the equalizing process introduced by the weighted population formula should stop with the county government. The real question is, however, whether the degree of equalization achieved in this way is adequate; and this can best be answered by considering individual cases. The effect of the 1929 act in certain exceptionally poor and exceptionally wealthy boroughs and districts is described below.

Jarrow, in Durham, is a part of the industrial area of Tyneside, lying between Gateshead and South Shields. It is in the midst of a densely populated urban area and borough boundaries form extremely arbitrary demarcations. The borough is so completely built up that it has been necessary to obtain land outside the borough boundaries for new housing schemes. Jarrow has been suffering from as serious an unemployment problem as any municipal borough in England. It is essentially a one-industry town, and the shipbuilding yards on which it depends have been closed for some years. It is inhabited almost entirely by workers,

[9] *Ibid.*, p. 33.

and the percentage of the insured population that were unemployed in June, 1934, was fifty-seven.[10] A local official estimated the unemployed in March, 1935, at 70 percent of the workers. The population, which is somewhat more than 30,000, is declining.

This borough's losses from the 1929 derating were about 13 percent of its total valuation. These losses were not especially heavy because the value of the shipyards, which have been in financial difficulties for some years, had been written down to a small figure before derating was introduced. In 1928-29 Jarrow was obtaining nearly half (48 percent) of its rate and grant expenditure from grants. The education grant accounted for 70 percent of all grant money, and the housing grant accounted for more than half the remainder. There was also a substantial highway grant. In 1932-33 grant revenues were meeting more than two-thirds (69 percent) of the total rate and grant expenditures. Again, the larger part of this was the education grant. This grant had increased substantially, owing to the changes in the distribution formula, although the total net expenditure for education had remained practically the same. Housing and highway grants had also grown. The latter were largely for purposes of work relief. Most of the remaining grant money (14 percent of rate and grant expenditure) was from the block grant. In 1933-34 the situation was much the same. Since Jarrow is a "gaining area" the block grant will increase in the future as deductions for such areas diminish.[11]

In spite of the large proportion of income from grants, rates are high. They fell from 21.3 shillings per pound in 1928-29 to 19.7 shillings in 1932-33. In 1933-34 they were down to 17.8, but they rose again in 1934-35 to 18.3 shillings. The high county rate is partly responsible for this; but no other urban area in

[10] Cmd. 4728, *op. cit.*, p. 117.

[11] For comparative financial data for this and the other local governments described below see Appendix, Table 46, p. 369.

Durham had as high a rate as Jarrow in 1932-33, nor did any municipal borough in England or Wales have as high a rate in this year. The same is true in 1933-34 and 1934-35 for the 128 municipal boroughs recorded in the *Preston Rate Returns*.[12]

This is, however, only a part of the story. The cost of unemployment is estimated at 355 thousand pounds for Jarrow in 1933-34.[13] If this had fallen entirely on borough rates these rates would have been 64 shillings per pound for relief alone. Actually a little less than one-fifth of this was met by local authorities, the remainder coming from unemployment benefits and transitional payments to which the local governments make no contribution. Even that part falling on local authorities was spread over the entire county, to the benefit of Jarrow. Had Jarrow had to meet its own share of the public-assistance costs falling on the county, the rate for this purpose would have been in excess of 12 shillings, whereas the cost of public assistance falling on county rate and grant money was equivalent to about 8 shillings in this year. On the assumption that the county's share of the block grant is apportioned to all county functions in proportion to expenditures, that part of the public-assistance cost actually falling on county rates would have amounted to about 4 shillings in the pound. If this is a reasonable assumption, Jarrow contributed to the county about one-third of what it cost the county for public assistance.[14] On the same assumption, Jarrow's contribution to the total cost of unemployment in Jarrow amounted to about one-sixteenth of all expenditures and about one-fifteenth of the cost falling on national and local treasuries.

Even this is not the whole story. The largest part of the rates is levied on ordinary householders, and the majority of the house-

---

[12] *Rates Levied in Various Towns*, 1934-35.   [13] Cmd. 4728, *op. cit.*, p. 119.

[14] It is impossible to say what proportion of the county rate should be assigned to public assistance. Rates for specific functions are figured on the basis of the cost to be met from rates and block grants. The actual county levy falling on Jarrow in this year was 8.4 shillings. This includes public assistance, police, highway, health, higher education, and other county services.

holders of Jarrow are on public relief. Being on the relief rolls does not excuse occupiers from the rates. It is common practice for the landlord to pay the rates when rents are small, but if this is done the rents must be high enough to cover the additional cost. Consequently, directly or indirectly, a large part of the local rates is met from relief payments. It would seem, then, that the national government is contributing indirectly, through its transitional payments and unemployment benefits, a substantial part of the local rates. All these factors considered, it is probable that not even one-fifteenth of Jarrow's unemployment costs are coming from local resources. This is inevitable. There are no important local resources in Jarrow. It is impossible to tax the unemployed for their own support.

Jarrow is, of course, exceptional, but the difference is only one of degree. Hartlepool, described below, is in much the same position, and similar conditions can be found in South Wales and Cumberland. Places of this kind should probably be treated, as in fact they are being treated, as special cases.[15]

The national government's obligation is clear. Jarrow's fate is the result of international forces, and Jarrow cannot be asked to solve it. Shipbuilding, iron and steel, and the coal industries are essential industries and are affected by national policies. The falling off of foreign trade is largely responsible for their present acute distress. In one way or another the communities suffering from these depressed industries must be provided for from national resources. Just how provision should be made is not so clear; and the right to independent government may well be challenged when two-thirds of the money expended by local authorities comes directly from the national government. The new public-assistance regulations afford appreciable further relief to such

[15] Investigations of these depressed areas have been made from time to time by the government, and special "unemployment" and "distressed-area" grants have been made to move the unemployed workers to areas where employment is available and to bring new industries into the area, but to date these projects have been on too limited a scale to solve the problem.

areas; but local authorities lose all control and continue to contribute 60 percent of the former cost. In districts such as Jarrow, where by far the largest part of the burden falls on the national government in the end, it would seem more reasonable for the national government to meet the entire cost of the functions it administers and leave a larger share of the cost of locally administered functions to local support.

Hartlepool, also in Durham, is a borough in genuine need of aid. With a population in excess of 20,000, it had a lower rateable value per capita in 1932-33 than Jarrow. The borough is almost wholly dependent on coal mining, and population is declining, owing to industrial conditions. The percentage of insured workers that were unemployed in June, 1934, was 45, and the unemployment was of long standing.[16]

Hartlepool supports its own police and schools. This accounts for the large proportion of its revenues received from grants in 1928-29. The school grant amounted to 70 percent of the grant money in this year. Most of the rest was for police and housing. Under the present system the proportion of education costs met from grants has increased although the cost of schools has decreased. Also, the police and housing grants have grown, and there is a small highway grant. These account for two-thirds of the grant revenues in 1932-33. The remaining third is largely from the block-grant distribution.

The percentage of all rate and grant expenditure from grants increased from 44 to 81 between 1928-29 and 1932-33. Rates have been reduced from 20 shillings in 1928-29 to 16 shillings in 1932-33. But 16 shillings is still a high rate. Only one municipal borough in twenty had rates as high as this in 1932-33. This rate had been reduced in 1934-35 to 14.7 shillings. Even this is high. Nearly one-third of that part of the expenditures of local government (including Hartlepool's share of county government) falling on rates and block grants was for public assistance in

[16] Cmd. 4728, op. cit., p. 116.

1934-35. This was exceptional. The average public-assistance cost in municipal boroughs, measured in relation to rateable values, was less than one-third as much as that in Hartlepool.

Hartlepool has benefited materially from the new system. The block grant nearly equaled the rates in 1934-35,[17] and rates are appreciably lower than in Jarrow. Nevertheless, the borough is still in a very difficult financial position.

Whitehaven, Cumberland, is another borough situated in a depressed area. Its population of a little more than 20,000 is estimated to have increased slightly between 1928 and 1932 in spite of increasing unemployment which reached its peak in 1932. This, too, is a one-industry town, depending almost entirely on coal mining. The employment situation has improved since 1932, but 32 percent of the insured workers were still unemployed in April, 1934,[18] and there is no assurance that the improvement, such as it is, is permanent. Some of the mines are under the sea and the expense of operation is becoming prohibitive.

Whitehaven was the only one of the forty municipal boroughs studied which obtained more than half its rate and grant income from grants before the 1929 reform. The proportion has been increased somewhat by the change—from 55 to 66 percent. Whitehaven's high percentage of grants in 1928-29 is largely to be explained by the heavy housing expenditure. The largest grants, however, were for education. In 1932-33 grants and rates had both increased, but grants had increased more than rates. Part of this increase was the result of increased education and housing grants, but the major part of the increase came from the block grant, which supplied 11 percent of Whitehaven's rate and grant revenue in 1932-33. Since, like most districts where welfare expenditures were heavy before derating, Whitehaven has had a large share of its per capita grant deducted as a "gaining area,"

[17] This includes Hartlepool's share of county rates and grants, apportioned according to rateable values. *Rates Levied in Various Towns, 1934-35.*

[18] Cmd. 4728, *op. cit.,* p. 10.

its block grant will increase rapidly in the next few years as this deduction diminishes.

The rates levied in Whitehaven were reduced from the comparatively high level of 17.3 shillings in 1928-29 to 12.7 shillings in 1932-33. This is a moderate rate. The decrease came from a reduction in the combined county and poor-union rates. The borough rate increased. In 1934-35 the rate levied in Whitehaven was only 11.2 shillings. This was a little below the average for the 128 municipal boroughs recorded in the *Preston Rate Returns* for that year.

Whitehaven is in a more favorable position than Jarrow and Hartlepool. Per capita rateable values are higher than in either; per capita borough expenditures are lower than in Jarrow and about the same as in Hartlepool; and county rates are lower than in either. If the rate in the pound levied is an adequate test of burdens, the national government's contributions under the present system are sufficient to meet Whitehaven's needs. This has been achieved, however, only by contributing in grants from national funds nearly two-thirds of the borough's rate and grant expenditures, by transferring the welfare burden to the larger area of the county and then contributing to the county some three-quarters of the county's rate and grant expenditures, and finally by placing the whole public burden of unemployment insurance benefits and transitional payments on the national government. Local resources are totally inadequate to cope with the situation.

Port Talbot, in Glamorgan, is another coal-mining town situated in a depressed area. Mining is supplemented, however, by iron and steel and tinplate mills. The percentage of insured men unemployed in June, 1934, was thirty-four.[19] The population of a little more than 40,000 is declining.

Port Talbot had the highest rate in the pound of any municipal borough in 1928-29, and while this rate has been reduced under

[19] Cmd. 4728, *op. cit.*, p. 146.

the new system, it was still the highest municipal borough rate in 1932-33 except that for Jarrow. This remained true in 1934-35, according to the *Preston Rate Returns*, in spite of further reductions.

Per capita rateable values were a little higher than those in Jarrow and a little lower than those in Whitehaven in 1928, and again in 1932 and 1933. The losses from derating were much the same, relatively, as in these other two boroughs. Per capita expenditures in 1932-33 were a little smaller than in Whitehaven, and the proportion of expenditure from grants was likewise less. Rates, however, were much higher in Port Talbot, largely because of the higher county rate. With lower per capita costs than Jarrow, and higher per capita values, it has been possible to keep the rate in Port Talbot a little below that in Jarrow, but it is still excessive. Both Port Talbot and the county in which it lies are receiving more than three-fifths of their net income from the national government, but this is not enough. Again, this is a case for special treatment.

Godmanchester would seem to have been amply compensated grants in 1932-33 to more than cover its rate and grant expenditures. It is a small town of about two thousand inhabitants in an agricultural area. The population is declining. Rateable values per capita were low in 1928-29, as is to be expected in such a small town, and they have been greatly reduced by derating. The town lost about one-third of its rateable values in consequence of the derating. Net expenditures per capita are also low, however, having been about 19 shillings per capita in 1932-33. This is less than one-third of the expenditures per capita in any of the boroughs discussed above. The town does not support police or education, and highway costs are small. More than half the grants received in 1932-33 were for housing, an activity which yielded the town a net profit in this year. Most of the remaining grant is the borough's share of the block grant.

Godmanchester would seem to have been amply compensated

for its heavy losses from derating. The rate in the pound levied in the borough for all local governmental units, including the county, dropped from 12.8 shillings in 1928-29 to 9.3 shillings in 1932-33. This was well below the average rate for municipal boroughs in this year, and the borough rate itself was very small. The town will not lose its favorable position when compensation for losses is withdrawn. A capitation grant of 12 shillings, the rate now paid to municipal boroughs and urban districts without adjustment for gains or losses,[20] would have been sufficient to cover all the costs of this borough falling on rates and the block grant in 1932-33.

Okehampton, in Devon, is another borough whose grants were sufficient to cover all rate and grant expenditure in 1932-33. It is a town of between three and four thousand inhabitants. The population is increasing slightly. Rateable values are also increasing. The town suffered little from derating, and per capita valuations rose 56 percent between 1928-29 and 1932-33. Valuations per capita are not high, since the town is small, but for the same reason per capita expenditures are low. The town does not support police or education. Okehampton would seem to be in an even stronger financial position than Godmanchester, with higher per capita valuations and lower per capita expenditures, and Godmanchester's position is incomparably better than that of the boroughs in depressed areas.

About two-fifths of Okehampton's grant revenues are for housing. Most of the rest of the grant money comes from the per capita distribution of the block grant. This town was getting almost no grants in 1928-29. Today, with much the same functions to perform, and higher rateable values, it is getting enough income from grants to meet all of its rate and grant expenditure. Rates in the pound have dropped from 11.3 shillings in 1928-29 to 7.2 shillings in 1932-33, and most of this is for county purposes. Only one other municipal borough in England and Wales had a

[20] The provisional capitation grant for the second grant period is 12 s. 1 d.

lower rate in 1932-33. This seems to be an instance in which the block grant fails to measure need and overgenerous aid is granted to a community with small requirements.

It is a well-known fact that local governmental costs per capita tend to increase with the size of the community, but the capitation grant treats all communities alike. The experience of Okehampton and Godmanchester suggests that the amount of expenditure falling on rates and the block grant in small towns will ordinarily be covered in largest part by the capitation grant. In the case of Godmanchester the heavy losses from derating may justify a large grant, but this is chance compensation. In the case of Okehampton, where no such losses were experienced, it has made possible a very substantial reduction in already moderate rates.

The situation in one other small municipal borough is deserving of comment. Montgomery, in Montgomery County, is the smallest metropolitan borough in England and Wales with less than one thousand inhabitants. It is located in an agricultural region and seems to have lost relatively more from the derating than any other borough, the rateable values per capita in 1932 having been less than two-thirds their 1928 level. Population decreased 8 percent between 1928 and 1932. The borough is not responsible for police or education, and it has no housing program. Nevertheless, per capita expenditures are larger than in Godmanchester and Okehampton. Grants for specific purposes are practically nonexistent. Montgomery's capitation grant, even without the temporary compensation for losses, would be sufficient to cover losses from derating at the old scale of rates. The rate levied in the borough has increased from 12.5 shillings in 1928-29 to 16.3 shillings in 1932-33. This is high, but the county rate is responsible for the major part of it.

Analysis of county finances in Montgomery shows that the public-assistance rate is high, but not exceptional. The heaviest county expenditure is for highways. This accounts for nearly half the whole cost. Montgomery is a sparsely populated county with a relatively large highway mileage. The block-grant formula makes allowance for this factor in costs in its weighting for sparse population. No other county received as much weight, relatively, for this factor. Nevertheless the weight given is inadequate if the heavy road expenditures and the high rates can be taken to measure need and ability.

Thus the borough of Montgomery is suffering under the double load of high county and (for its size) high borough expenditures. Had it not chanced to be organized as a borough instead of a rural district—and the population density is no greater than in the average rural district—its position would have been much worse. Its capitation grant as a rural district would be one-fifth as much as its grant on a borough basis, and while it would be relieved of the support of minor roads, the borough expenditure for these in 1932-33 was only a fraction as much as it would have lost from the grant had it been a rural district.

Montgomery's difficult financial position cannot be attributed to any specific shortcoming of the existing system. One may criticize the capitation grant on the ground that it does not take the size of the community into account, but if allowance were made for size Montgomery would get less, not more. One may also point out that there is no justification for borough government in this case, but if Montgomery were not a borough it would in the long run lose more from the reduced grant than it would gain from shifting the entire highway burden to the county, although temporarily compensation for losses might hold its grant at the present level. This is one of those exceptional cases which cannot be fitted with a formula.

Richmond, Surrey, a residential suburb of London, is one of the wealthiest municipal boroughs in England. Losses from derating were very small, and increases in rateable value per capita have been large since 1928, owing to growing population and the general prosperity of the region. In spite of its wealth Richmond has gained from the 1929 changes. The percentage of rate and grant income derived from grants increased from 16 percent in 1928-29 to 28 percent in 1932-33. This increase, together with increased rateable values, made it possible to reduce rates from 11 shillings in 1928-29 to 8.6 shillings in 1932-33. Rates have remained constant at 8.6 shillings for several years.

Richmond has lost from the withdrawal of the 50 percent minimum guarantee for the education grant. Whereas in 1928-29 the borough received 50 percent of its elementary education income from grants, in 1932-33 it received only 25 percent from this source. But Richmond's share in the block grant is substantial, offsetting losses from other grants and constituting more than half its grant income. Part of this is temporary, since Richmond is a "losing area," but the major part of it is Richmond's normal capitation share. This block grant amounted to 19 percent of the borough's rate and grant expenditure in 1932-33.

The proportion of rate and grant expenditure coming from grants was smaller in Richmond in 1932-33 than in any other borough in England and Wales. Even this relatively small percentage was more than Richmond needed. Very few boroughs have lower rates. Wealthy boroughs such as this do not stand in need of aid, and the appropriateness of even a small grant for the "relief of rates" in such cases may well be questioned.

Wimbledon, the municipal borough which with the exception of Richmond received the smallest proportion of its rate and grant expenditure from grants in 1932-33, differs from Richmond only in degree and need not be discussed here. It clearly does not need a capitation grant in relief of rates.

Hove and Bexhill, in East Sussex, present a more extreme situation than Richmond and Wimbledon. These seaside resorts were the wealthiest municipal boroughs in England in 1932-33, in terms of per capita rateable values, and they obtained somewhat more of their income from grants than did the Surrey boroughs described above. In 1928-29 Bexhill received most of its comparatively small grant income for education and the remainder for housing. Hove, with its own police force, received a police grant, and also a small highway grant, in addition to education and housing grants. In 1932-33 the education grants had shrunk to a fraction of their earlier size in both boroughs, owing to the withdrawal of the 50 percent minimum. This was to be expected in view of the high rateable values in these boroughs. There were no other important changes in grants for specific purposes. The block grant was substantial in both places, accounting for more than three-fourths of Hove's grant money in 1932-33 and more than four-fifths of Bexhill's. Grants as a whole are not large, but they have increased substantially, those in Hove having doubled and those in Bexhill having tripled between 1928-29 and 1932-33. Hove has a growing population and therefore growing needs, but Bexhill's population is estimated to have declined slightly between 1928 and 1932, and it is Bexhill's grants that have tripled.

Hove was able to reduce its rates materially in consequence of the larger grants. Only five boroughs in England and Wales had lower rates in 1932-33. Bexhill's borough rate decreased, but not enough to offset the growing county rate, so that the total levy in the borough increased somewhat. Neither Hove nor Bexhill would seem to need the new capitation grants which are meeting approximately 40 percent of their rate and grant expenditures. It is even clearer here than in the cases of Richmond and Wimbledon that the new system is bringing certain wealthy areas unnecessary aid.

Urban districts present much the same problems as do municipal boroughs. The poorest urban district in England and Wales in 1932 in terms of rateable value per capita was Mallwyd, in Merioneth. Its financial position parallels that of Montgomery, described above, in many respects. It is situated in a poor agricultural area, and with a population of less than seven hundred scattered over an area of more than 14,000 acres it is clearly urban only in name. Such a small district is not, of course, responsible for education, and it has not engaged in any housing program. Consequently grants for specific purposes are small, although it did receive a highway grant in 1928-29. It meets about the same proportion of its expenditures from grants as does Montgomery (48 as compared with 51 percent), and expenditures have grown rapidly since the introduction of the new system. In fact, per capita expenditures were four times as high in 1932-33 as they had been in 1928-29. In spite of this, rates as a whole were reduced to a moderate level. The increased expenditure went largely to capital outlay.[21] This district was deurbanized and incorporated in an adjacent rural district in 1934, with a resulting decrease in its per capita grant to one-fifth of its former amount. The loss is equivalent to the yield of a 6 or 7 shilling rate in the former district and far exceeds the saving in highway expenditures. The county, which was instrumental in the change, has profited correspondingly. The change seems to be amply justified, however. The character of the region does not seem to warrant urban organization, nor has the essential cost of government required the more generous urban capitation grant.

The urban districts of Abertillery and Bedwellty, in Monmouth, had the highest rates of any urban districts in England and Wales in 1932-33. These districts are in the coal-mining region and have suffered from protracted unemployment. The percentage of insured workers unemployed in June, 1934, in Abertillery was fifty-five.[22] This is comparable to the situation in Jarrow.

Rates have not decreased in these districts in consequence of the 1929 reform, yet grants have materially increased. The ordinary grants for specific functions in both districts have remained almost unchanged, but per capita distributions from the block grant in 1932-33 contributed nearly one-quarter of the grant income of Abertillery where the education grant contributed most

[21] Letter from former District Clerk.   [22] Cmd. 4728, *op. cit.*, p. 145.

of the remainder and contributed 60 percent of the grant income of Bedwellty, where education is not a district function.

Both county and district expenditures have increased in these two districts. Public-assistance rates are high, owing to extensive and protracted unemployment, and also, perhaps, to a relatively high scale of public-assistance payments which the workers, accustomed to high wages, have demanded. County and districts alike are burdened, further, with heavy interest charges on loans for housing and public-works projects. Here, again, unemployment is the fundamental cause.

Comparing Abertillery with Jarrow it is apparent that the higher rates and the relatively small proportion of grants are primarily the result of higher per capita costs, although slightly smaller grants and somewhat lower rateable values per capita in Abertillery have contributed to this end. If, however, expenditures could be reduced to the scale found in Jarrow, the financial position of this district would still be intolerable. Abertillery and Bedwellty are not classified as "derelict" communities. That term is reserved for districts where the unemployed form an even larger proportion of the workers and where the prospect of recovery is even less bright.[23] Nevertheless, they can hardly expect to regain their former prosperity.

No simple financial reform can meet situations like these. The financial policy of such communities may not be above criticism, but the fundamental fact is that they have become parasitic communities through no fault of their own, and nothing short of a redistribution of population or industries will change the situation. Until the situation is changed special national aids must be provided. The block grant was not designed to meet such extreme cases; nor should it be used for such areas. If adequate income for extreme cases were to be provided by the automatic working of a formula, submarginal communities such as these might be

[23] Cmd. 4728, *op. cit.*, p. 130.

perpetuated indefinitely, depleting national resources without any enduring benefit to themselves.

Gellygaer, in Glamorgan, is in much the same position as the two Monmouth districts described above. It is another coal-mining district with extensive and protracted unemployment. It had the highest rate of any urban district before the 1929 reform (34.9 shillings in 1928-29), and while the rate has been materially reduced it was still extremely high (23.8 shillings) in 1932-33.

Gellygaer's expenditures per capita are not excessive, but it is saddled with heavy loan charges for water and sewer systems built when costs were high and for other public works undertaken primarily for the relief of unemployment. County rates are high, owing to public-assistance costs, and with low rateable values the total rate is extremely high. This is again a case where financial problems cannot be solved by revision of the financial system. The whole economic structure is due for reform.

Wantage, in Berks, is an urban district receiving more income from grants than it needs for its entire rate and grant expenditure. Expenditures are moderate. More than half its grant revenue came from housing grants in 1932-33, but the per capita distribution from the block grant was large. The only rate levied was, in consequence, for county purposes, and the county rate was low. Wantage seems to have profited unduly from the capitation grant.

Newburn in the depressed area of Tyneside, Northumberland, is another urban district receiving overgenerous grants. As in the case of Wantage, most of the grant revenue is for housing, but the capitation grant is nearly 30 percent of all grant money. All grants combined were sufficient to cover 92 percent of the district's rate and grant expenditures in 1932-33, in spite of the fact that per capita expenditures were nearly double those in Wantage in that year. The largest part of expenditures is for housing, and the housing program is operated at a profit. A small district rate is levied, but county and district rates combined are below the average.

Tilbury, in Essex, has not been so fortunate. Per capita expenditures in this district were very high in 1928-29, and they have risen still higher. In fact they were nearly three times as high as Newburn's in 1932-33 and nearly five times as high as Wantage's. Rateable values have declined, as in the case of Newburn, although they are somewhat higher per capita than Newburn's. Where rates in the other two districts were moderate in 1932-33 and below their earlier level, rates in Tilbury, which were high before the 1929 reform, have increased. County rates are responsible only to a minor extent for this high level. Unlike Wantage and Newburn, where county rates account for all or most of the levy, in Tilbury county rates are only about half the total. Public works which the district can scarcely afford seem to be largely responsible for Tilbury's high rates. This, too, is a case for special treatment. No formula can meet the needs of a district whose rates are excessive after the national government has met two-thirds of its net expenditures.

Frinton-on-Sea, in the same county as Tilbury, offers a marked contrast. This district had the highest rateable values per capita of any urban district in 1932-33.[24] It is a small residential district with about two thousand inhabitants. Rates were moderate in 1932-33 and had been reduced from the 1928-29 level. Rateable values had increased. Expenditures per capita were high, partly on account of substantial highway expenditures. Housing is of minor importance.

Grants as a whole are not abnormally high and meet a smaller percentage of rate and grant expenditure in Frinton than in Tilbury, because of the very small housing expenditures in the former district. But grants have increased much more, in consequence of the new system, in Frinton than in Tilbury, and Frinton

[24] The area of Frinton has been radically altered by a redistricting order, effective 1934.

is meeting half (49 percent) its rate and grant expenditure from grants. Frinton's share in the block grant is more than four times as great per capita as Tilbury's share; yet rateable values in Tilbury are less than one-quarter of those in Frinton. This is the result of temporary provisions. Frinton is a losing area, and Tilbury a gaining area. Consequently, substantial reductions are made from Tilbury's per capita distribution and substantial additions are made to Frinton's. Some equalization between these two districts has been achieved, and greater equalization will be attained as the temporary provisions of the act are withdrawn. It may well be questioned, however, whether so gradual a transition was needed and whether in the end Frinton's per capita share should equal Tilbury's.

The four Surrey districts of Esher and the Dittons, Coulsdon and Purley, Weybridge, and Sutton and Cheam illustrate the effect of the new system in comparatively wealthy residential districts. These districts are essentially London suburbs. They were getting relatively little income from grants in 1928-29, and most of what they did receive was for housing. In 1932-33, however, the major part of their grant income was from the capitation grant, and the proportion of their total income from grants had increased. Grants contributed relatively less, however, to the net expenditures of these districts than to those of the average urban district. In fact, Sutton received a smaller percentage from this source than did any other district in 1932-33.

Population has been increasing rapidly in all these districts, and rateable values per capita have increased, in spite of derating, in all but Sutton. This (together with the larger grants) has made it possible to reduce rates to a very low figure. Weybridge's rate was the lowest of any urban district in 1932-33. Sutton, with a small decrease in rateable values and a very large increase in per capita expenditures, has suffered a slight increase in rates, but rates are still low. These are losing districts, and in consequence their share in the block grants will decline in the next few years, but the final adjustment should still leave them with ample resources. Again, as in the case of Frinton, it may be questioned whether the slow transition was necessary.

Roxby-cum-Risby, in Lincoln, a rural community in spite of its urban organization, lost more than half its rateable value in consequence of derating. But the compensating grants have been so generous in this case that the district levied the lowest rate of any urban district in 1931-32—just enough to meet county requirements—and levied no rate whatever in 1932-33, meeting the county levy out of its own balance. The district's share in the block grant exceeded district rate and grant expenditure by 62 percent in this year. In 1933-34 a levy of 5 shillings was imposed, but this was less than the county rate. This is a comparatively poor district, in terms of rateable values per capita, with low per capita expenditures. Compensation for losses in rateable values was needed, but the compensation received would seem to have overreached the mark. This is, of course, a temporary situation. The actual capitation grant is only about one-third as much as the present exchequer grant, and as the supplementary grant is withdrawn local ratepayers will again be called on, in all probability, for reasonable contributions.

Billingham, Durham, is another urban district which has lost heavily from the derating and has been amply compensated. The presence of a large new chemical plant is primarily responsible for the heavy derating losses, but the per capita values remaining are still large. Billingham has escaped the serious unemployment that has impoverished most of the county of Durham, but with poor relief transferred to the county it no longer escapes contributing to the support of the unemployed. Billingham's contribution to public assistance in other parts of the county nearly counterbalances its gains from the block-grant distribution, and with increased expenditures in the district itself rates are higher than before the change. Nearly four-fifths of this district's share in the exchequer grant in 1932-33 came from the supplementary grant. When this is withdrawn and the district receives only the capitation grant, its position will be far less favorable.

Another district which should be noted is Rishworth, in York, West Riding, a small and essentially rural area. Rishworth received no grants whatever in 1928-29. In 1932-33 four-fifths of its rate and grant expenditure came from the exchequer grant. Yet the rates levied had increased owing to increases in the county levy. The district rate was very small. In this case the gains to the district from the exchequer grant have been offset by the losses resulting from spreading the relief and highway costs over the entire county.

The most striking change in the finances of rural districts is the decline in expenditures resulting from the transfer of highway costs to the county. Highway expenditures accounted for more than half the rural government costs under the old system. With this exception expenditures of rural districts as a whole are approximately the same as before the 1929 act. Expenditures for individual functions show no marked increases or decreases, and the total expenditures, barring highway expenditures, increased only 5 percent between 1929-30 and 1932-33. Individual districts, however, have deviated materially from their former financial status, although none has been found in which expenditures increased.

In Llanwrthwl, Brecknock, per capita expenditures had decreased in 1932-33 to less than one-third of their 1928-29 level. This is a sparsely populated district with about one person to 60 acres, and consequently rateable values per capita were higher in 1932-33 than in any other rural district in England and Wales. There is no occasion in such a district for a municipal housing program or for the trading services which are often required in more thickly settled rural areas. As a result per capita expenditures were exceptionally low in 1928-29. Sixty percent of these expenditures were incurred for highways. With the transfer of highways, the principal district expenditure disappeared. Between 1928-29 and 1932-33 rate and grant expenditures declined from 302 pounds to 95 pounds. In the same period grants increased from 56 pounds to 1,338 pounds. The latter sum was sufficient to meet the rate and grant expenditures of that year fourteen times over. Under these conditions it is not surprising to find that the rate levied in the district in recent years has regularly been lower than the county levy. The district is paying county levies partly out of grant revenues. This would seem to be another case in which compensation for losses had overreached the mark. This district has recently been abolished, however, by a redistricting order.

Another interesting case is Hastings, in East Sussex. This district had comparatively high road expenditures in 1928-29. With their disappearance, housing, the cost of which is largely covered by grants, was the most important expenditure. The per capita share of the block grant was not large, but in 1932-33 grants, supplemented by surplus revenues in the district treasury, were sufficient to more than cover the district's expenditures. In fact such expenditures would have been covered without the block-grant distribution. The rate actually levied was less than the amount required by the county. In consequence, this comparatively wealthy district had the lowest rate of any rural district in England in this year. The gain came from the transfer of highway costs, however, rather than from the block-grant distribution. The latter was quite small.

In 1928-29 Sibsey, Lincoln, had even higher per capita net expenditures than Hastings and has reduced them nearly as much. The transfer of highway expenditures to the county is the principal reason for the decrease, but there have been other reductions in expenditures. Most of Sibsey's grants are for housing. Ignoring both housing and highway expenditures the district met less than one-fourth of its rate and grant expenditure from grants in 1932-33, whereas in 1928-29 it had met three-fourths of such expenditures from this source. Rateable values have been more than cut in half by derating, and in terms of per capita valuations the district is one of the poorest in England. Yet Sibsey's very modest per capita share in the block grant seems to be ample compensation. The rate in the pound has been more than cut in half. In fact it has regularly been lower than the county rate alone in recent years. Balances from preceding years have made this possible. But with the highway burden removed, this district's rates would be low even at the old level of expenditures.

A quite different situation is represented by Llantrisant, in Glamorgan. This district had the highest rates of any rural district in both 1928-29 and 1932-33. The rates were higher in the latter year than in the former. The high county rate in Glamorgan accounts for a little more than one-half this rate, but the district rate is likewise excessive. Yet district expenditures have dropped in Llantrisant, and the proportion of costs met from grants has increased from 35 to 53 percent. Llantrisant is in a distressed area with serious unemployment. Housing is a heavy expenditure, but this is met largely from grants for the purpose. The district is, however, seriously burdened with the debt charges on water and sewer systems built after the war, when costs were at their peak, and designed for a population five times as large as that residing in the district. In this instance a public works program, undertaken partly as a relief measure, acted as a boomerang. Unemployment of such long standing cannot be aided by mortgaging the future. There has been a steady migration from this area to regions where conditions are more favorable; and the debt burden is falling with increasing severity on the diminishing and impoverished population remaining.

Auckland, in Durham, also has high rates, although not so high as Llantrisant's and somewhat lower than under the earlier system. Rateable values have declined in Auckland, but so, also, have per capita expenditures, with the transfer of highways to the county. This district is receiving a smaller percentage of its rate and grant expenditures from grants than is any other rural district, largely because of the relatively small housing grant, although the block-grant share is also small. As a gaining district Auckland has had its capitation grant materially reduced. The high rates in Auckland are caused largely by the high county rate in Durham, but the district rate has contributed its share. Even with the lapse of the supplementary grant deductions the district rate will be high if other factors remain unchanged. The fundamental difficulty in such districts as Llantrisant and Auckland is the low rateable value per capita. With inadequate local resources rural district authorities cannot meet even the small obligations left to them without either extreme dependence on the central government or exorbitant levies.

Sunderland, in Durham, has a lower rate than Auckland, although it is situated in a depressed area and per capita district expenditures are more than double those in Auckland. Rateable values in Sunderland are a little higher than in Auckland, but the fact that Sunderland is meeting 59 percent of its rate and grant expenditure from grants, whereas Auckland meets only 30 percent from this source, is the principal factor benefiting Sunderland. These higher grants are partly for housing. Not only are Sunderland's housing expenditures larger than Auckland's, but they are more than covered by grants, whereas Auckland is contributing more than one-third of the cost from rates. Sunderland is also favored, however, by the block-grant distribution, which is larger per capita than Auckland's. Sunderland's deductions, as a gaining district, have been much smaller than Auckland's. Sunderland's rates are high, but the district is responsible for only a very small part of them.

Stockton, another district in Durham, is in a very different position from either of the two preceding districts. The district was wealthy in 1928-29 in terms of rateable values. The derating cut these values in half, but it is still well-to-do in comparison with other districts, especially in Durham, and the actual rates levied in Stockton are below the average in spite of the high county rate.

The district had moderate rates in 1928-29, and more than three-fourths of its expenditures were for highways. With the disappearance of highway costs the remaining expenditures are more than covered by exchequer grants. In fact these grants were nearly three times as much as the rate and grant expenditures in 1932-33. Consequently this is another district meeting part of the county rate levy from its share in the exchequer grant.

Codnor Park and Shipley, in Derby, is another district in which grants more than cover the rate and grant expenditure. Like Stockton it lost heavily from derating, and the compensation, for the time being, at least, is more than ample. It is using excess grant income to meet part of the county levy, and the resulting rates are lower than any of the other districts under consideration, excepting Hastings.

Two districts in Cardigan—Tregaron and Cardigan—offer interesting illustrations of the working of the new system in very poor districts. Tregaron has the lowest rateable value per capita of any rural district in England and Wales. Both districts lost from derating, but their losses were not exceptional. Both have very low per capita expenditures. Rates are high, but not excessive, and they have been substantially reduced below their former level. In both districts contributions from the rates for highways alone in 1928-29 exceeded contributions from rates for all purposes in 1932-33. In both cases the grants, largely from the block-grant distribution, seem to be adequate. Very little of the comparatively high rates levied is for district purposes.

This review of individual cases taken by itself would give a distorted picture of the effects of the Local Government Act of 1929. Extreme cases have been sought and found, but they do not represent any considerable number of communities. The misfits are surprisingly few. A system which meets half the local government costs from central funds might be expected to encourage irresponsible local expenditures. Only in a handful of instances, however, is there any indication that this has occurred, and even in these cases the evidence is not conclusive. The central control which accompanies the grants together with the high type of local officials appointed have prevented this abuse. Even in well-to-do districts the increased grant money has been used to a large extent for the relief of ratepayers.

The equalizing measures in the 1929 reform have served their purpose well. Poor districts have invariably profited by the system and profited more than their wealthier neighbors. The formula attempts to measure both need and ability, and it has been surprisingly successful in view of the fact that it is frankly empirical. In a number of instances in which the formula has failed, the remedy of redistricting has been successfully applied. There are still many poor areas whose needs are not adequately met by the change, but no simple fiscal measure could hope to deal with the extremes of wealth and poverty to be found in England today. Nothing short of revision of the entire industrial structure can cope with this situation.

The flat per capita grant to the subdivisions of the county seems to be a provision of more doubtful value. The number of a community's inhabitants may bear a fairly close relation to the costs of local government as long as local governments are not responsible for welfare burdens, but it bears little relation to local resources, particularly in view of the eccentricities of derating. The temporary guarantees against loss to some extent obscure the effects of this capitation grant, but it is clear from the individual instances cited above that it is erratic in its working. The fact that grants as a whole have been materially increased has, however, prevented genuine hardship.

The selection of a single year as a basis for measuring losses has resulted in chance variations in estimated losses which bear little relation to actual losses. In the rural district of Hemsworth, in York, West Riding, for example, no compensation is received for an important coal mine which was constructed, but not in operation, in 1928-29. Moreover, some of the parishes in this district, because of financial pressure, failed to levy rates in 1928-29 to meet heavy loan charges for a sewage system, although the obligation had already been incurred and the charges must ultimately be met from such rates.[25] Had such rates been levied in 1928-29 these parishes would have been duly compensated. The fact that this district's finances have improved under the new system, in spite of these uncompensated losses, suggests that no widespread hardship has resulted from the chance working of the system, but rather that the compensation as a whole has been overgenerous.

The guarantees against loss may have been inevitable as political measures, but it would be hard to justify them on any other ground. It is particularly difficult to understand why the county and county borough guarantees should be permanent, while those for the subdivisions of the county are temporary. The county borough which suffers from derating will be compensated by the low rateable value factor in the distribution formula; and, whether suffering from derating or not, grants on the basis of the formula will vary with need. The municipal borough, on the contrary, has no such assurance that grants will vary with need. Some communities, poor to start with, have had rateable values cut in half by the derating. These may find their financial position more difficult than before the change when direct compensation for losses ceases, in spite of certain mitigating factors.

It is the derating itself, however, which is the most questionable feature of the new system. The losses from this have tended to be heaviest in the poorest districts. Employees are more likely to live in the vicinity of a mine or factory than is the employer; and wealthy residential communities have suffered little or not at all from this change. The inequalities thus created have been offset in counties and county boroughs by the equalizing provisions of the act; but without derating even greater equalization would have been achieved. More serious than this is the reduction

[25] Interview with District Accountant.

in the already narrow local tax base. Other local sources of income are not easy to find, and some communities have been left with such restricted resources that no important degree of local independence can be maintained.

The primary aim of the 1929 act was relief to ratepayers, and the final test of its success lies with the reduction of rates. Rates decreased from 167 million pounds in 1928-29 to 145 million pounds in 1932-33. To this extent ratepayers have gained. But the gain goes to the owner of derated real estate rather than to the ordinary ratepayer. Accepting the estimate of 22.3 million pounds for losses from derating, the amount of the rates falling on property subject to rates was 144.7 million pounds in 1928-29 compared with 145.4 million pounds in 1932-33. The valuations, of course, increased so that the average rate in the pound fell from 12.4 shillings to 10.8 shillings in those four years. In so far as the increased valuations represent increases in the actual rental values the ordinary ratepayer's burden has decreased. To some extent, however, this increased valuation is the result of improved methods of assessment and represents a closer approximation to actual rentals rather than an increase in the rentals themselves.

Considering the different types of district Table 26 shows that rates have declined in both county boroughs and administrative counties but that where county borough ratepayers enjoy a reduction of only two pence, on the average, ratepayers elsewhere have profited by an average decrease of more than one shilling. The advance in the county rate as such has been more than compensated for by the reductions in the rates of the underlying areas. It is apparent that the new system has reduced the burden of the rates somewhat in all types of local governmental units, but the greatest gains have gone to rural areas.

The aim of the 1929 reform was not merely to reduce rates, but also to equalize them. To determine the extent to which this aim has been realized it is necessary to turn to rates in individual local districts. Here one finds that the highest rates have been

TABLE 26

AVERAGE RATES LEVIED IN THE POUND ᵃ

Unit of Government	1929-30 ᵇ (In Shillings)	1932-33 (In Shillings)
London ᶜ.	10.8	10.2
County borough, all rates.	13.3	13.1
County borough, borough rates.	10.2	13.1
Administrative county, all rates ᵈ.	11.6	10.5
Administrative county, county rate ᵈ.	4.5	6.6
Municipal borough, borough rate.	7.2	5.5
Urban district, district rate.	5.6	3.6
Rural district, district rate.	4.1	1.3
Poor-law union, union rate ᵈ.	2.2	. . .

ᵃ Computed from data in *Local Taxation Returns.*
ᵇ The 1929-30 rates have been estimated on the basis of the old system. That is, the derating of agricultural property and the compensation from the government for this derating has been ignored. The rates on property, other than that derated, were not affected by this derating during the last six months of the fiscal year.
ᶜ Includes all rates levied within the administrative county, excluding London.
ᵈ Excluding the County of London.

reduced. In 1927-28 there were 95 local authorities with rates in excess of 20 shillings. In 1932-33 there were only 18 such authorities.[26] Three factors have been operating to reduce the number of these excessive rates. In the first place valuations have been improved. This means that they approach full rental value more nearly and also that there are fewer discrepancies from district to district. The effect of this is both to reduce and to equalize the nominal rates in the pound without affecting the total burden. In the second place the total amount of the rates has been reduced. If this reduction were spread equally over all districts there would be fewer districts with rates in excess of 20 shillings. Finally, some equalization of burdens was anticipated, both as a result of the wider area of charge for public assistance and rural highways and as a result of the application of the distribution formula. With all these factors influencing rates the marked decrease in the number of authorities levying rates in

[26] Ministry of Health, *Annual Report,* 1932-33, p. 161.

excess of 20 shillings is not, alone, adequate proof of equalization. As a further test the standard deviations for rates in the different districts have been computed for 1928-29 and 1932-33. These are given in Table 27.

TABLE 27

VARIATION IN THE AMOUNT OF THE RATES IN THE POUND LEVIED
IN DIFFERENT TYPES OF LOCAL UNITS, 1928-29 AND 1932-33 [a]

Unit of Government	AVERAGE		STANDARD DEVIATION	
	1928-29	1932-33	1928-29	1932-33
County boroughs..........	14.64	13.10	3.71	3.15
Municipal boroughs........	14.17	11.77	2.75	2.34
Urban districts............	14.22	11.88	3.65	2.90
Rural districts............	11.72	9.27	2.71	2.27
All local governments......	13.25	10.97	3.43	2.95

[a] Compiled from *Rates and Rateable Values, England and Wales*. Rates are the total levied in each district for all local governmental units. The figures are in shillings and fractions of shillings.

It is apparent from these figures that some equalization has taken place, in the nominal rates at least, although the results would be disappointing to any believer in thoroughgoing equalization. The achievement in 1932-33 is no test, however, of the final achievement of the new system since the larger part of the block grant is still being returned on a basis proportioned to losses. An attempt to obtain some measure of the final effect of the formula has been made by computing the rates that would have been necessary in county boroughs in 1933-34 if the entire grant had been distributed on the basis of the formula and there had been no compensation for losses. County boroughs were chosen for these computations because they receive the grant directly from the national government, in proportion to losses and weighted population, and they retain the entire sum. This simplifies the problem of measurement. The results are given in Table 28.

TABLE 28

VARIATION IN THE AMOUNT OF THE RATES IN THE POUND THAT
WOULD HAVE BEEN LEVIED ON COUNTY BOROUGHS IN 1933-34
UNDER VARIOUS CONDITIONS [a]

Rates	Average	Standard Deviation
1. Actual rates levied, 1928-29...................	14.64	3.71
2. Rates which would have been required in 1933-34 if the old system had continued [b]...............	13.63	3.49
3. Actual rates levied, 1933-34...................	13.11	3.25
4. Rates which would have been required in 1933-34 if the entire block grant had been distributed on the basis of the formula [c].....................	12.28	3.12
5. Rates which would have been required in 1933-34 if the entire block grant had been distributed on the basis of the formula, and if no provision had been made for derating [d].....................	11.02	2.52

[a] Computed from data in the *Preston Rate Returns*, 1934-35, and the Ministry of Health, *Annual Report*, 1933-34. Figures in shillings and fractions of shillings.

[b] This has been computed by adding to rates in 1933-34 the difference between the block grant and the discontinued grants. In so far as the amount of discontinued grants might have changed during this interval these estimates are open to error.

[c] Additional and supplementary grants have been ignored in making these calculations.

[d] This has been computed by adding to rateable values as of 1933-34 the amount of the estimated losses in valuation through derating as of 1928-29. In so far as the value of the derated property may have changed during this interval, this is open to error. Actually, it is probable that these values have increased somewhat, as have the valuations of property still subject to the rates, so that the actual rates would be somewhat lower than those estimated.

According to these estimates, if the former system had been continued the average rates would have been less in 1933-34 than they were in 1928-29. Also, the variation would have been less. Valuations increased more rapidly than governmental costs during that period. The economies effected have in large part offset the growing burdens arising from depression. This would hardly have been possible if the national government had not assumed such a large proportion of the welfare burden. Even so, it is surprising to find that without the 1929 change the variation in rates would have been diminished. The inequalities in wealth in the different areas of England seem to have been accentuated, if anything, during this period. There was a marked increase in unemployment in some regions, notably in South Wales, Cumberland, Durham, and Tyneside; whereas some of the cities in the Midlands and large areas in the south of England were enjoying genuine prosperity in the latter year. A factor which may have contributed to the apparent decrease in rate inequalities is the tendency of valuations to lag behind actual values in periods of rapid change. Valuations in the depressed areas probably have not been reduced in proportion to declining values. Thus any savings in governmental costs arising from declining population might result in nominally lower tax rates, although in fact expenditures had not declined as rapidly as actual rental values. In the same way prosperous communities would find governmental costs rising more rapidly than valuations although perhaps not more rapidly than actual values. Since the low rates are in prosperous areas and the high rates in depressed areas, the apparent variation in rates would decline as a result of this lag, although the variation in actual burdens might be increasing. Another factor which has probably played an important part in reducing the variation in rates is the abolition of the 50 percent minimum in the education grant. This has made the large education grant more of an equalizing factor.

Whether these factors are, in fact, the explanations of the smaller standard deviation found it is impossible to say. Too much emphasis should not be placed on the figures, since they afford at best a rough measure of what would have taken place in the absence of the 1929 reform. Actually, of course, the discontinued grants would not have remained static at the 1928-29 level; nor would the local authorities have spent exactly what they did in 1933-34 in the absence of the new aids. The point is emphasized because it has occasionally been claimed that, with the economic developments which have occurred since 1929, rate inequalities would have increased in the absence of the equalizing effects of the block-grant distribution; and that the new system might be regarded as having achieved an important degree of equalization even though the actual variation in rates were found to be as great now as formerly. If, however, the figures can be taken as indicative of what would have taken place under the old system, these claims would seem not to have been justified.

The actual rates levied in 1933-34 are lower, on the average, than either the actual rates levied in 1928-29 or those which might have been levied in 1933-34 in the absence of the 1929 reform. Also the variation is smaller. But the reduction in variations is less than might be expected, if the economic developments of the period in question had not operated to offset the equalizing effects of the change. There can be no reasonable doubt that the weighted population formula itself should be an effective equalizing force.

Only about one-third of the block grant was distributed on the basis of the formula, however, in 1933-34. The remainder was distributed in proportion to losses from the change. In so far as the money was distributed in proportion to losses, the old conditions were maintained. To measure the influence of the equalizing formula itself, estimates have been made of what each county borough would have received in 1933-34 if the entire block grant had been distributed on the basis of the formula. It is apparent, from the lower average rate required, that the county boroughs as a whole would have gained by this. The gain would be largely at the expense of London, which loses heavily from the use of the formula as a basis of grant distribution. Moreover, there would be a further reduction in the variation in rates. This is to be expected, and as the compensation for losses declines, greater equality can be anticipated.

One further test has been applied to these county borough rate figures to measure the effect of derating. Adding the 1928-29 valuations of derated property to the 1933-34 valuations, rates have been computed for the different county boroughs. If the 1928-29 valuations of the derated property are a fair measure of the 1933-34 value of this property,[27] it is apparent that the derating provisions of the 1929 act have offset in large measure the equalizing features. This bears out the contention made above [28] that the presence of industrial enterprises in a community increases the cost of government out of proportion to the increases it brings in rateable values. It is true that the equalizing features of the 1929 act are sufficient to more than offset this, but a large part of the equalization which the formula might have achieved has been nullified by derating.

The county borough figures do not give any measure of the equalization achieved through the transfer of functions to a larger area of charge, since county boroughs were scarcely affected by these provisions. The municipal boroughs and urban and rural districts would benefit directly from this, and only indirectly from the equalizing formula, since their share of the block grant is redistributed by the county on an unweighted population basis. Variation in rates in these underlying local units have been reduced under the new system, as indicated in Table 27, but it is impossible to say to what extent the wider area of charge has contributed to this.

Throughout this part of the discussion the "rate in the pound" has been taken as a test of equalization. It is perhaps pertinent at this point to inquire how far this can be accepted as a fair measure. The possible inequalities in valuations themselves have already been noted. Unfortunately there is no record of these. The highest rates in the pound are to be found in South Wales. Per capita valuations are also lowest in this section, and there is a widespread belief among financial officials elsewhere that while actual rentals are lower in South Wales than in other parts of the

[27] Actually, the value of derated property is probably somewhat greater, as the valuation of other property has increased somewhat; but the difference should not be so great as to invalidate the comparison.

[28] See *supra*, pp. 200 *et seq.*

country undervalution also is greater here than elsewhere and is contributing substantially to the low per capita values and the high rates in the pound. Such slender evidence as the writer has obtained from valuation officials in South Wales confirms this belief. The poverty of South Wales cannot be questioned, and the real burden of the rates is doubtless higher than in most other areas, but the differences in rates in the pound are not accurate measures of the actual differences in the ratio of rates to rents.

These differences in valuation are not the only factors impairing the value of the rate in the pound as a test of equalization. Rates are widely accepted as an approximate measure of taxpaying ability on the assumption that the rents individuals pay will increase with income. This is in general a reasonable assumption. But there is some evidence that rentals take a larger proportion of the average citizen's income in some parts of England than in others. If a workingman in London, say, receives the same wages as a workingman in Lancashire, but pays 16 shillings a week in rent while the Lancashire worker obtains an equally good house for 12 shillings a week, and if rates are 10 shillings in the pound in London and 20 shillings in the pound in Lancashire, then the London and the Lancashire workingmen will pay equal amounts of their equal incomes in rents and rates combined. Each will pay 24 shillings a week. If these rates were completely equalized and the rate in the pound in both communities were fixed at 15 shillings, then the Lancashire worker would pay 9 shillings on his 12 shilling rent, or 21 shillings in all, and the London worker would pay 12 shillings on his 16 shilling rent, or 28 shillings in all. In other words, complete equalization of rates under these conditions would upset the genuine equality of rents and rates combined in proportion to income which had previously existed.

Actually, of course, wage levels and rent levels are not strictly independent variables. Where one is high the other, likewise, tends to be high. Consequently, the rate in the pound is some test of the relative burden of rates. But the meager data available suggest that the relationship is not sufficiently close to justify the belief that complete equality in burdens can be attained by complete equality in rates. Rates tend to be high where rents are low, and there are some indications that, while wages in these areas are also low, the differential is greater in the case of rents, so that of two individuals with equal income, the one in the low-rent area is better able to bear a higher rate.[29]

Another factor which impairs the value of rates in the pound as a measure of inequalities is the unequal services provided by the different local authorities. The community with high rates may be providing many services the cost of which is met from the rates, whereas the community with low rates may be leaving such services to private enterprise. Consequently, the citizen in the low-rate community may be paying as much in rates and charges for these services as the citizen in the high-rate community who meets all these costs through his rates.

Under these circumstances complete equalization of burdens cannot be attained by complete equalization of rates. These considerations do not seem to be of sufficient weight to invalidate the comparison of rates as approximate measures of equality or to deter the actual process of equalization on the moderate scale on which it is contemplated.

[29] There are, of course, other considerations. In the area where wages and rents are lower, individuals will be in a position to pay the same proportion of their incomes in rents and rates only if all of the costs of living are lower in proportion to the lower wages.

XII

NATIONAL SUPPORT AND LOCAL SELF-GOVERNMENT

A UNIFIED tax system is easily attained in a unitary state, and England achieved it many years ago. Local rates may vary in amount, but the form and base of this single local tax is the same throughout England and Wales, and all other taxes are national. The reconciliation of local self-government with a substantial degree of equalization of tax resources is not so readily accomplished, however, and England is still faced with this problem.

The need for equalization seems scarcely to have been felt in the prosperous pre-war period. It is true that the Royal Commission on Local Taxation recommended in 1901 that a poor-law grant be distributed in inverse proportion to rateable values,[1] and the Departmental Committee on Local Taxation recommended, in 1914, that the education grant be determined by the difference between a standard expenditure and the yield of a standard rate;[2] but these recommendations are exceptional, and only in the case of the education grant was such an equalizing measure adopted. The grant system was developed to stimulate local authorities to more and wiser expenditures. This was possible, partly because the country was comparatively wealthy and partly because the national government had assumed directly such a large share of governmental costs, including the costs which bear most heavily on poor communities, that the burden on local rates was not heavy.

The decline in prosperity and the greater inequalities in the geographical distribution of wealth which have developed with the decline of some of the basic industries since the war have

[1] *Final Report*, Cd. 638, p. 28.   [2] *Final Report*, Cd. 7315, p. 78.

made the need of equalization more acute. The national government has attempted to meet this need partly by assuming the support of the unemployed through transitional payments, partly by the equalizing factors in the education grant and the block grant, partly by widening the area of charge, and partly by making special grants to depressed areas.

There can be no reasonable doubt that these measures have been beneficial. The assumption by the national government of the bulk of the cost of unemployment has done more to equalize resources than the equalizing grants, however. The amount contributed by the national government to unemployment costs exceeds the amount contributed to equalizing grants, and unemployment costs are probably a more accurate measure of need than the grant-distribution formula. If it is desirable to extend national aid beyond the present amount, this can easily be achieved through the assumption of the entire costs of public assistance. If the national government is successful in administering this function, the levy on local governments of 60 percent of their 1932-33 contributions should probably be abandoned. Even though there is no need for further national support, England, like other countries, is faced with the problem of contributing enough to the support of local governments to make local initiative a reality and not just a form without at the same time contributing so much that local responsibility is weakened or destroyed. The diversion of any part of local resources to the support of functions over which local authorities have no control while the national government is forced to contribute half or more of the support of locally administered functions is a contradiction. The national government might better reduce the amount of its grants-in-aid and let the local authorities apply their limited resources entirely to functions for which they are responsible.

Some degree of equalization has been achieved by the Local

Government Act of 1929 and subsequent revisions of the financial relations of national and local governments. This is demonstrated by the fact that the variation in rates levied has been reduced, and the further fact that in most instances the governmental units with the lowest rateable values per capita are receiving the most, relatively, in grants-in-aid.

Further equalization could be achieved without increasing the total of the national government's contributions. The education grant might readily be used to attain greater equality by increasing both the number of shillings per child and the amount of the penny rate deducted in the present formula. The block grant, too, could be adjusted to reduce the emphasis placed on actual population and to increase the emphasis on other factors in the weighting; and this or some other measure of need might be applied to the redistribution among the subdivisions of the county as is done now for the Metropolitan Boroughs of London. Where grants are used to direct local activities into desirable channels or are conditioned on maintaining specific standards for specific functions there is no particular reason for distinguishing between rich and poor communities. But grants designed to reduce the burden of local taxes must conform to a different pattern. Why, after meeting nearly one-third of their highway costs, more than one-third of their education costs, half their police costs, and most of their housing and public-assistance costs the central government should distribute to the wealthy counties of Surrey and Middlesex 12 shillings per capita, for relief of ratepayers or expansion of government activities at the option of local authorities, is not clear. Any abstract right of these communities to a share in the national tax revenues seems to be overbalanced by the resulting loss in local responsibility.

Inequalities in resources among the different local units are still great, and in many instances the districts with the highest rates are now receiving more than half their tax income in grants. It is apparent that if the high-rate districts were to receive enough aid from the national government to bring local rates down to the average, the national government would be contributing two-thirds, three-fourths, and even nine-tenths of local income in a substantial number of cases. This is not compatible with local initiative. The control cannot safely be turned over to the junior partner.

The national government has been able to carry its grant system as far as it has only because of thoroughgoing central supervision and control of local authorities. But the danger is not merely that of irresponsibility. There are considerable areas in England and Wales that are no longer self-supporting. The fact that local rates are excessive, even after the national government has contributed most of local government costs, is evidence of this. This is not a temporary depression phenomenon. Adequate equalizing grants in such communities result in maintaining the status quo with no permanent benefit to the community in question and a serious drain on national resources. The solution for such areas is not preservation of local government but complete national control, at least for the time being, and perhaps ultimate liquidation of the community in extreme cases. The English government is endeavoring to solve the problem of depressed areas through migration and other industrial adjustments. This is not essentially a financial problem. It is important, however, that such adjustments should not be retarded through overgenerous equalization of resources.

In communities quite capable of supporting themselves the new system removes the incentive to local effort which is the outstanding merit of the percentage grant. Some critics regard this as the principal shortcoming of the block grant. This factor is not readily measured, but if local initiative is seriously impaired by the withdrawal of the stimulus of the percentage grant it is an indictment of the local self-government which the new system was designed, in part, to foster.

Greater freedom in local administration is one of the merits claimed for the new system, and in fact many detailed specifications and restrictions have been withdrawn along with the minor grants which they accompanied. But the important controls remain. This is essential in view of the large amount of central government aid. Moreover, the transfer of highways to the county and the transfer of public assistance first to the county and finally to the national government have deprived the smaller jurisdictions of some of their most important functions. The rural districts, especially, have been left with so few obligations and powers that they are in danger of overdeveloping the housing activities and public utilities left to their care merely for the sake of something to do. Finally, the derating has robbed all the local authorities of a substantial part of their tax base and has curtailed their independence correspondingly. Grants for general purposes, designed to cover the resulting losses, cannot be increased or decreased at will by local authorities. Thus it seems that while the Local Government Act of 1929 may have added something to the form it has seriously undermined the substance of local self-government.

CONCLUSIONS

XIII

THE PROBLEM OF CENTRAL-LOCAL FISCAL
RELATIONS IN THE LIGHT OF GERMAN
AND ENGLISH EXPERIENCE

INCREASING fiscal centralization in the post-war period is the product of much the same forces in Germany and England. Perhaps the fundamental cause is the increasing facility of communication and transportation, which makes the whole nation a closely knit social and economic unit. This, in turn, necessitates a unified tax system, and it demands uniform governmental services for an increasing number of functions and a governmental authority which is not restricted to narrow local boundaries. Another force which has at least accelerated the centralizing process in recent years is the increasing weight of the tax burden resulting from post-war and depression conditions and perhaps from a growing sense of social obligations. Slender resources must be husbanded if in the end budgets are to be balanced; and only by pooling the resources of the entire nation can the expanding list of essential public services be provided.

Germany stood in greater need of centralization than England after the war because the centralizing process had not progressed as far as in England,[1] and because the political and financial situation made central control more urgent. Consequently revision of central and local fiscal relations came earlier in Germany, and the revision was more thoroughgoing.

In both countries the revision of the tax system narrowed the

[1] Germany was a decentralized federal state, with widely varying state and local tax systems, and only 40 percent of all government expenditures incurred by the central government and 40 percent of all taxes collected by the central government (1913-14). England was a unitary state, with a uniform tax system, and with 54 percent of all government expenditures incurred by the central government and 70 percent of all taxes collected by the central government (1913-14).

local tax base; and in both, the central government chose to reimburse local authorities from national revenues rather than to relieve them of obligations, although some transfer of functions from local to central hands has taken place. There were, however, important differences in the immediate motive for reducing local tax sources in the two countries, and the manner of reimbursement differed accordingly. The Reich, appropriating former state and local taxes, offered the logical compensation of a substantial share of the revenues taken over to the jurisdictions within whose boundaries they were collected. Only as financial pressure increased was the Reich forced, reluctantly, to redistribute a substantial share of such revenues in accordance with financial need rather than origin.

In England the exemption of a substantial part of the local tax base from taxation offered the national government no new sources of revenue from which local compensation might be drawn. England, too, recognized local losses as the immediate consideration in distributing the new grant. But the money came from general revenues, not from specific sources, and local need rather than local losses was accepted as the ultimate basis of distribution. Whether this choice was made because of superior wisdom, because the central government was more certain of its power in England than in Germany, or because this form of distribution was more economical and the central government with no new tax powers at its disposal was less inclined to be generous would be difficult to say. All these factors doubtless played their part in the choice.

England's problem was much simpler than Germany's, since England was a unitary state and had established a uniform tax system long before the war. Now that Germany, likewise, has achieved a unitary state and has very nearly attained a uniform tax system, it may be that she, too, will develop a system of distribution resembling more closely the English pattern. Tradition is strong, however, and local authorities in Germany will not relinquish easily their demands for the re-establishment of some measure of their former financial independence.

The German system of shared taxes and the English system of grants-in-aid are equally favorable to unified tax systems; and neither method is incompatible with a substantial measure of local independence, although the grant system lends itself more readily to central control than the system of shared taxes. The fact is, however, that Germany has not depended on financial aids to any important degree for control of local government. The states and the Reich have exercised more rigid control over local governments than has the central government of England. It is true that local governments have had a wide variety of functions to perform—and important ones—and they have had some freedom in performing them. But the central government has set rigid standards for many of these functions and has required the maintenance of these standards instead of offering the persuasive percentage grant. It is not merely financial necessity, therefore, that is responsible for the increasing limitations on local freedom.

The local sphere of activity is becoming more narrowly circumscribed in England, also. The substitution of the block grant for some of the former percentage grants removed a certain number of central government restrictions, but the transfer of functions from smaller to larger jurisdictions (accompanied by the restriction in the local tax base) has materially diminished the sphere of activity at least for the smaller divisions of government. The transfer of functions was made in part, but not entirely, for financial reasons.

The difference between local independence in England and in Germany seems to be one of form rather than degree. The local authorities in England have a narrower range of functions than do local authorities in Germany, but they have greater freedom in the manner in which these functions are performed. In both countries financial limitations are probably the most important factors in restricting local activity, but the increasing social and economic unity of the entire country is the fundamental reason for the centralization of both finances and the governmental functions they support.

No attempt has been made in this study to answer the question what functions, if any, are more effectively administered by local than by central authorities. It should be noted, however, that the persistence of local administration over a wide field of activities, even when the major part of the support falls on the central government, suggests a very general belief in the efficacy of local control. Certainly it is more adaptable to varying local needs than control by the more remote central agency. The actual policy of different countries throws some light on this problem, and a comparison of existing practice in England and Wales and in Germany is given in Table 29.

The functions selected are those which play the most important part in local government. The importance of these functions in combined central and local budgets is indicated by the percentage of total central and local expenditures incurred for different functions, in the first section of the table. The smaller proportion of all expenditures going to the functions specified in England and Wales is primarily because of the heavy expenditures for war debts, accounting for nearly one-third of all national and local expenditures. Allowing for this, it is apparent that the functions under consideration have much the same relative importance in England and Germany.

In the distribution of expenditures and taxes between central and local governments wide variations are apparent. England shows the greater centralization. Not only does the national government spend directly a larger share of the tax income than does the national government of Germany, but it supplies the local governments with a larger proportion of their income. This would still be true if state taxes and expenditures had been classified as central rather than local. Considering specific functions, it is apparent that administration, if not support, is still largely in local hands except for the function of welfare. This situation has, of course, changed somewhat since the year for which the comparison is made.

TABLE 29

DISTRIBUTION OF SUPPORT OF SELECTED FUNCTIONS BETWEEN CENTRAL AND LOCAL GOVERNMENTS IN GERMANY AND IN ENGLAND AND WALES, 1931-32 [a]

| Function | PERCENTAGE OF TOTAL CENTRAL AND LOCAL EXPENDITURE | | | | | | PERCENTAGE OF LOCAL EXPEN- DITURE MET FROM CENTRAL GOVERN- MENT REVENUES | |
| | INCURRED FOR DIFFERENT FUNCTIONS | | INCURRED BY LOCAL GOVERNMENT | | MET FROM LOCAL TAXES | | | |
	Germany	England	Germany	England	Germany	England	Germany	England
All................	100.0	100.0	58.9	32.4	55.0	16.8	28.5	46.4
Police.............	4.9	2.5	99.9	100.0	72.8	50.5	27.1	50.5
Education.........	14.6	10.3	98.7	93.1	98.7	45.9	1.3	50.7
Welfare [b].........	27.5	14.3	64.1	22.9	57.7	22.8	9.3	0.1
Housing..........	2.5	1.8	97.7	100.0	97.7	19.5	...	80.5
Highway [c]........	6.0	6.6	100.0	100.0	68.1	66.8	31.2	33.2

[a] Data for fiscal year ending March 31, 1932. Data for England and Wales are from *Financial Accounts of the United Kingdom* and *Local Taxation Returns for England and Wales.* Data for Germany are from *Statistik des deutschen Reichs,* Vol. CDXL. The expenditures included are those falling on tax revenues. In the case of total expenditures the tax revenues themselves have been used. In the case of expenditures for specific functions all administrative income, including the proceeds of loans as far as these could be allocated, has been deducted from actual disbursements. Expenditures from grants have been assigned to the government which finally spends them, not to the government making the grant. The proportion of total direct national expenditures assigned to England and Wales is the proportion that local taxes bear to all local taxes in the United Kingdom. If the proportions were to be determined by actual collections of national taxes, a larger part of national taxes would be assigned, and if they were determined by population, a smaller part of national taxes would be assigned. In determining the national expenditures for the specific functions given it was possible to get the amount actually spent by the national government in the area in question. State expenditures have been classified as local in Germany.

[b] Including social insurance, but not public works expenditures for unemployment relief.

[c] Motor vehicle and gasoline taxes dedicated to highways are included in these figures.

As long as administration remains under local control there is every advantage in making the local spending authorities responsible for the revenues passing through their hands. This means developing local taxes as far as is compatible with the need for uniform taxes. There is very little defense for a local income tax even in the form of local additions to a centrally administered tax. On one hand the source of income is as wide as the economic organization which produces it; on the other hand any important variations in local rates result in the growth of tax oases. Even without the stimulus of a variable income tax there is a tendency for wealthy residential districts to grow up apart from industrial and working-class districts. Under these conditions a local income tax makes the income created by owner, worker, and industrial equipment together available only to the district in which the owner resides, whereas the costs of the industry to local government fall largely on the districts where the factory is located and where the workers live. This segregation of costs and resources would be stimulated further by a variable local income tax. It seems doubtful whether Germany will return to this particular pre-war arrangement even though something akin to "normal" times should again be experienced in that country; modern industrial organization is making it increasingly unsuitable for local use.

Taxes on real estate, whether on rentals or on capital values, and whether charged to owner or occupier, are more appropriate sources of local income. Since real estate is at once tangible and immovable and since it has a definite local situs there is less chance for evasion or double taxation of this source than of personal income. Moreover, while the difference is admittedly one of degree, the owners and occupiers of real estate, as such, benefit from local expenditure more directly and more substantially than receivers of income, as such. This is no mean source of revenue, as the proceeds of the different taxes now in use in different countries show, even after making full allowance for the fact that it has doubtless been unduly exploited in the past. A substantial amount of local government can be supported from this source alone in most communities, unless the English policy is to be extended and local taxes are to be limited to residential real estate.

Other local sources of revenue seem to be taxes on local business, especially retail trade, amusements, and hotels, and a certain number of nonbusiness licenses, such as the dog tax. These rarely yield important revenues, and they tend to become nuisance taxes. Nevertheless, they should probably not be overlooked. To some extent they may spread the burden without hardship, and there may be cases in which the development of such sources will contribute enough to local independence to more than justify their use.

Earnings of local industries are also potential sources of net income and have been so used in Germany. While profits on these industries tend to reach the same group of individuals reached by real estate taxes, the incidence is somewhat different, and there may be cases in which the spreading of the burden in this fashion is desirable.

How far available income can be made to go in any given community toward the support of those functions for which local administration is preferable will depend on the wealth of the community in question. In so far as the actual national aid given in the past can be taken as a guide, it is apparent that there is a substantial and increasing margin between local expenditures and local income. The time has passed when separation of sources and complete independence of national and local finance is possible, unless local functions are to be transferred to the central government on a larger scale than present practice indicates.

Such a transfer is, however, one solution of the problem. Quite aside from financial considerations, local services affect an ever widening area, and more and more they are coming to be of national concern. Education, main roads, police, and public welfare are to an increasing degree accepted as national responsibilities. But this is not sufficient to justify the transfer. The greater efficiency of the central government is apt to be impaired by the rigidity of bureaucracy, and the relative effectiveness of national and local administration, regardless of responsibility, must be weighed in the balance. If, however, England should demonstrate that national administration of public welfare is feasible, local funds might be released for other and more constructive uses, to the advantage of all.

Even with some transfer of administrative responsibility there has been, and doubtless will continue to be, some lag of local revenues behind costs. This will fall on central-government treasuries. The central government's contribution to local costs can be met, as in Germany, by sharing specific percentages of specific national taxes, the money being returned to the place where it was collected or on some equalizing base; or it can be met, as in England, by grants-in-aid, the amount being determined by some standard of need.

Almost any degree of equalization of resources is readily justified on the ground that the nation as a whole is an economic unit, the parts of which are so interdependent that any allocation of wealth or income to the district in which it happens to be taxed is clearly arbitrary. Taxation in accordance with ability and expenditure in accordance with need have long been accepted principles of government finance. It is the "good of the whole" which is considered. But individual taxpayers are more readily reconciled to this philosophy if the jurisdiction within which it is applied is rather narrow. The desire for personal benefit from personal contributions lingers, and the chance of this diminishes as the area of support is widened. Thus wealthy communities oppose the growth of national rather than local support of governmental functions, especially through grants-in-aid or the redistribution of national taxes, since the transfer of wealth is more obvious here than in the case of direct national expenditure.

Benefit cannot be ignored. Even today there are revenue sources which are inherently local. The English rates are essentially local in character. There are also governmental services the value of which accrues largely to the immediate community. Fire protection and the maintenance of residence streets probably belong in this category. To tax local householders for such services appeals to our sense of justice and has the very practical advantage of placing the burden so directly on the beneficiaries that there is little danger of irresponsible expenditure. When, however, the local householders are largely the underpaid employees of a nonresident manufacturer, the taxation of local householders for strictly local purposes is neither feasible nor tenable. A living wage may be more satisfactory than subsidized houses; but in the absence of a living wage subsidized houses offer partial compensation. The tax system cannot remove the original fault, but it can assuage the resulting ills. What the employer fails to contribute in wages he may be forced to contribute in income taxes. Under these conditions national support of any and all functions can be justified, however local the benefits accruing, as long as the functions are essential.

Few would sanction national support of local functions which offers some communities more than others. Equal, not unequal, educational opportunity is the avowed aim of the ordinary school grant. In actual practice the percentage grant, giving the most to those that spend the most, results in giving the most aid to the community with the most elaborate service. This is justified on the theory that local expenditure is voluntary, and that the community which fails to maintain a high enough standard and adequate expenditures to obtain the maximum from the central government's offer is wilfully neglecting its own best good. But if the failure of local governments to meet the national government's requirements is due to extreme poverty the justification of the percentage grant breaks down. If one takes the extreme position that claims on national resources are in proportion to needs there would seem to be no limit to national support except that it should in fact be in proportion to needs and that in so far as one community is to enjoy better services than its neighbor these must be supplied at local expense.

The effective check on national support of local functions comes not so much from any doubt as to the claims of local functions to a wider area of support than the immediate jurisdiction administering the function as from the difficulty of obtaining responsible administration when the bulk of the support comes from elsewhere. If half or more than half of all or any of a local government's expenditures are to come from the central government, local responsibility will be seriously weakened. Even though local tax rates are high, the local taxpayer is inclined to assent without criticism if he believes that the community will obtain in benefits double, or more than double, what it is called on to pay for; and if local rates are not high, extravagant and reckless expenditures will be tolerated.

Complete equalization of resources would demand contributions from the central government equal to 90 percent and more of local government expenditures in some communities, with only nominal contributions in other communities. Inequalities in wealth are as great as this. It is unthinkable that a government which is reimbursed for 90 percent of its expenditures by outside authorities should be free to spend at will. The degree of control which is essential to insure responsible expenditure is so great under these circumstances that local initiative or independence is at best nominal. But when a community is as poor as this, local initiative would be meaningless if both central control and central support were removed. It is probable that in such cases even the semblance of local government must be abandoned and that temporarily at least the essential governmental functions must be administered directly by the authorities paying the bills.

It does not follow, however, that local self-government must be generally abandoned. The average community is quite capable of a large measure of self-support, and in so far as local independence is both desirable and possible in a given community there would seem to be no reason why it should not continue, even though other communities have their freedom restricted. There would seem to be no more cause for granting equal independence to all communities than there is in the case of individuals. An individual who is unable to support himself and falls on public relief loses a large measure of freedom. He may be deprived of the privilege of choosing his place of residence. He may not be allowed to reject an uncongenial job. In the same way a community which is no longer self-supporting must submit to outside controls.

There may be little choice between the English and German systems from the point of view of obtaining a unified tax system and a reasonable degree of local independence, but there are important differences between the two systems from the point of view of economy. Economical administration of resources cannot be attained by returning a fixed share of a specific tax to the jurisdiction where it arises. The wide variations in local tax rates which have made independent local taxes intolerable are ample proof of the fact that local resources do not match local needs; and the levy of a uniform rate on a uniform base does not correct the difficulty.

With local independence in taxation some flexibility is possible in adapting revenues to needs. The residents of poor districts may pay higher taxes and enjoy poorer governmental services than the residents of wealthy districts, but the balance between taxes and services is within their control. With a uniform tax returned to the districts from which it comes, the inequalities remain, and the adjustment must be made entirely through the quality and quantity of governmental services. Moreover, the inequalities in resources are so great that a rate which will support the minimum of governmental services in the poorest areas will permit luxurious and wasteful standards in the wealthiest ones. Germany has found the system of returning large amounts of shared taxes to the district of origin quite unworkable, and, while still adhering to this system of distribution in principle, she has so modified it in practice that the ultimate distribution of shared taxes is influenced only to a minor degree by the origin of the tax revenues in question. This objection to the German system of distributing shared taxes does not extend, of course, to the sharing of taxes on some equalizing base.

The advantage of the shared tax is, of course, that central and local governments share alike the changing fortunes of prosperity and depression. This is reasonable as long as central and local governments have equal powers of adjustment to these changing fortunes. But when the power of adjustment through new taxes, higher tax rates, or increased borrowing is largely in the hands of the central government, the local authorities can no longer be asked to share the losses of depression equally with the central government. The central government is apt to find its own needs more urgent than those of local governments, and the local governments, lacking the guarantee of either the fixed grant or the grant which varies with need, will probably be called upon to bear more than their share of the losses. The central government cannot, of course, be expected to provide local authorities with as generous grants in times of depression as in times of prosperity. But if the adjustment is made through scaling down a unit grant, or even a fixed grant, it is apt to come more slowly, and to take local needs more fully into account.

Neither Germany nor England has adhered strictly to the system first adopted. As tax yields, and consequently local shares, declined in Germany, the Reich was forced to come to the rescue of local governments with increased unemployment relief subsidies. In England, where the block grant had been guaranteed for several years in advance, the national government was unable to balance its own budget when revenues shrank, and while the new block grant was left intact, the education grants were reduced so that the local governments bore their share in the reverses of fortune through a different channel.

Certainty is an attractive quality in a revenue system, but as long as certainty cannot be achieved for the system as a whole, there seems to be no reason for placing all the risk on the national government. At the same time the major risk surely belongs to the government which has the control. If tax yields rise, it may be desirable to cut tax rates rather than to increase the amounts distributed to local governments; and if the yields fall, new sources and higher rates can sometimes be made to fill the gap. These are matters which the central government decides. Thus the fixed sum is preferable to the fixed percentage of a specified tax; but it is clear that a fixed sum cannot be maintained in emergencies.

Having accepted grants-in-aid as preferable to distributions of specific taxes, there is still the question of the relative merits of block grants and grants for specific functions, of fixed grants and variable grants, and likewise the problem of measuring need. When the purpose of the grant is to stimulate local governments to higher standards of education or better health services, it must, of course, be for a specific function. But when the grant is to eke out inadequate local incomes, the block grant is perhaps a little more flexible and a little simpler. Actually the greater flexibility and simplicity are more apparent than real, and there is little choice between the two. Grants made for specific functions rarely cover the necessary cost of these functions, and if local governments are not forced to match central government aids, aids for schools or highways make it possible for local authorities to divert more of their own tax revenues to other functions or to reduce local taxes just as effectively as though no strings had been tied to the grants. As for simplicity, one grant is simpler than many; but one grant distributed on the basis of a complex formula has little advantage over several grants distributed on the basis of simpler formulae. A single grant of any size distributed on the basis of a simple formula is out of the question, for need is determined by many factors and cannot be simply measured. The English block grant has brought substantial relief to all the admittedly poor local governments, but whereas one county has had its share determined largely by the weighting for unemployment another has benefited only because of the weighting for sparse population. To have used either of these factors alone or any one of the other factors entering into the formula would have led to unjustifiable inequalities. In spite of the intricacies of the formula some advantage seems to lie with the block grant. It is more obviously for the relief of local tax burdens than is the specific grant, the effect on local finances is a little easier to trace, and it is probably a little simpler to administer than a number of specific grants.

The basis of distribution of any grant depends first on the purpose of the grant. When the aim is to stimulate local governments to higher standards, the base chosen will attempt to measure the expenditure necessary to achieve that standard. When the aim is to relieve the local taxpayer, the base will attempt to measure needs in excess of the amount which local resources can reasonably supply. In either case the determining factors are so complex that no simple measure is adequate. England has found the percentage grant satisfactory in encouraging local governments to expand and improve their standard of services; but these have been satisfactory only because of the constant and thorough supervision of the central government. Other countries with less control could not hope to meet with the same success. Even in England it fails as a measure of need, since expenditures are influenced by resources as well as needs.

The primary factor in determining a community's need is the size of its population. Consequently population is usually selected as the basic factor. But since per capita needs and resources vary widely, population is usually weighted to allow for other factors. The selection of these other factors will vary with time and place. They are at best indirect and empirical tests of the need in question and depend in consequence on changing conditions. Under these circumstances it is pertinent to inquire whether the best results cannot be achieved by discretionary grants, each case being decided on its own merits. There is much to be said for discretionary grants. As long as no formula is perfect some communities will receive more than they need. The discretionary grant is, or can be, more economical, and it has been resorted to in Germany where need is greatest. Unless poverty is extreme, however, the disadvantages probably more than offset the gains. The administering authorities themselves regularly resort to formulae to aid them. It is not possible to consider all the merits of a thousand cases. There is still the advantage of being able to disregard the formula when it obviously does not fit, but against this there is the chance of favoritism and greater uncertainty. Any moderately well-to-do country will probably prefer such waste as will arise from the imperfections of a rigid formula. Nevertheless, there is a place for the discretionary grant in dealing with extremely poor areas. These probably cannot and certainly should not receive adequate income as the result of the operation of an equalizing formula since they would receive most of their income from the central government without any corresponding control. Only the discretionary grant, coupled with special controls, can meet these exceptional cases.

It is apparent that there is no ideal solution of the problem of reconciling a uniform tax system with local self-government. The two are inherently opposed. A uniform tax system must be a centralized tax system, and local self-government is meaningless unless adequate revenues are available to make nominal powers effective. To some extent revenues can be transferred from central to local governments, but there are serious drawbacks to a system where the spending agency is not responsible for the largest part of the revenue at its disposal. Adequate central control can, of course, be maintained under such conditions, but as controls increase the flexibility, which is the principal merit of local administration, diminishes; and an extensive system of controls may prove far more clumsy than direct central administration.

The only possible solution is a compromise. Uniform taxes may be in themselves desirable; but it may sometimes be necessary to sacrifice a uniform tax system, at least to the extent of permitting variations in local rates, for the sake of adaptable and responsible local administration, since this, too, is desirable. And, in turn, a measure of local self-government must be sacrificed to the need for a better tax system. In the end local government may give way to centralizing forces which extend beyond the fiscal system. But for the time, at least, a substantial sphere of local activity can undoubtedly be retained, even under relatively unfavorable conditions. To retain it, however, demands not merely a carefully planned financial system but a thoroughgoing reorganization of local government itself.

APPENDIX

APPENDIX

CHART 3

PROVISIONS FOR DISTRIBUTION OF REICH TAXES TO STATE AND LOCAL GOVERNMENTS, 1920-35 *

Tax	1920	1923
Income and corporation taxes	66 2/3% returned to state where income taxed arises;[a] state must distribute some to local governments.[b]	75% returned to place where income taxed arises.[g] In determining origin at least 1/10 must be assigned to commune of head office and 1/4 to commune of residence. Local share to be returned at least in part on same basis as Reich distribution.[h]
Turnover tax	10% to states in proportion to population; 5% to communes where collected.[c]	State same. Local 15% to communes where collected; situs of industry to be considered in determining commune of origin.[h]
Land purchase tax	50% (for entailed lands 25%) to states where land has situs.[d]	96% returned as before; state must distribute at least half to communes on same basis.[h]
Inheritance and merger taxes	Inheritance: 20% to state of situs of real estate and residence of owner of personalty.[e]	Same.
Beer tax	Percentage of collections: Bavaria 13.55 (max. 78 mil. RM); Württemberg 2.5 (max. 15 mil. RM); Baden 1.6 (max. 10 mil. RM).[f]	Same.
Motor vehicle tax	. . .	50% (with imposition of tax on other vehicles 96%), 1/2 distributed in proportion to population; 1/2, to area.[i]
Betting tax	. . .	96% distributed, 1/2 to state where business is, 1/2 in proportion to population; 1/3 for breeding.[hj]

* For notes to Chart 3 see page 316.

CHART 3: PROVISIONS FOR DISTRIBUTION OF REICH TAXES TO STATE
AND LOCAL GOVERNMENTS, 1920-35 *—Continued

Tax	1920	1923
Stock exchange, mineral water, and meat taxes	. . .	. . .
Guarantees and special provisions	Income tax distribution must at least equal average amount levied, 1917-19, for state and local purposes, or 1919 yield plus 6% per annum. This may be decreased only if Reich assumes state and local functions.*e* Each state guaranteed 80% of average per capita distribution of income and corporation taxes, the difference to be paid from the Reich share. States guaranteed average yield of inheritance tax for 1912-16.*b*	State may obtain 100% of land purchase tax if it elects to administer the tax itself. Communes guaranteed average yield of any comparable tax levied prior to January 1, 1918. Income and inheritance tax guarantees continue.*h*

Tax	1924	1925
Income and corporation taxes	90% returned as before.*k*	75% returned as before.*m*
Turnover tax	20% returned to states in proportion to population; distribution to communes optional.*k*	35% distributed 2/3 in proportion to population and 1/3 in proportion to yield.*m*
Land purchase tax	Same.	Same.
Inheritance and merger taxes	Distribution discontinued beginning February 19, 1924.*k*	. . .
Beer tax	Same.	Percentage of collections same, but maxima reduced to: Bavaria 17.2 mil. RM; Württemberg 3.2 mil.; Baden 2.2 mil.*m*
Motor vehicle tax	96% without requiring imposition of vehicle tax; distributed as before; half must be used for highways.*k*	Same.

* For notes to Chart 3 see page 316.

CHART 3: PROVISIONS FOR DISTRIBUTION OF REICH TAXES TO STATE AND LOCAL GOVERNMENTS, 1920-35 *—Continued

Tax	1924	1925
Betting tax	Same.	Same.
Stock exchange, mineral water, and meat taxes	Stock exchange: 100% where collected; [k] distribution discontinued January 1, 1925.	. . .
Guarantees and special provisions	Monthly guarantee for December 1, 1924, to March 31, 1925, of average yield of income, corporation, and turnover taxes for August and September, 1924;[l] other guarantees continue.	Monthly guarantee extended to September 30, 1925;[n] also 2,100 mil. RM from income, corporation, and turnover taxes guaranteed for 1925-26 and 1926-27; and turnover alone must equal state and local percentage (i. e., 30% or 35%) of 1,500 mil. RM; other guarantees continued.[m]

Tax	1927	1930
Income and corporation taxes	In determining origin, discontinued assigning 1/4 to place of residence and 1/10 to head office.[o]	Same.
Turnover tax	30% distributed as before.[p]	Same.
Land purchase tax	Same.	Same.
Inheritance and merger taxes	Merger: 50% to communes in proportion to losses from closing of plants.[r]	Discontinued September 30, 1930.[t]
Beer tax	Percentage of collections same, but maxima increased: Bavaria 45 mil. RM; Württemberg 8.6 mil.; Baden 5.8 mil.[o]	Special same; 16 2/3% of remainder returned to states on basis of collections.[s]
Motor vehicle tax	96% distributed, 1/4 in proportion to population, 1/4 collections, 1/2 area; all must be used for highways; local share to be used only for main highways.[q]	Same.
Betting tax	Same.	Same.

* For notes to Chart 3 see page 316.

Chart 3: PROVISIONS FOR DISTRIBUTION OF REICH TAXES TO STATE
AND LOCAL GOVERNMENTS, 1920-35 *—Continued

Tax	1927	1930
Stock exchange, mineral water, and meat taxes	. . .	Mineral water: 96% distributed to states, 1/3 on basis of collections, 2/3 population; all redistributed to communes on bases chosen by state.*s*
Guarantees and special provisions	In place of 1919 guarantee, income and corporation tax distribution must equal 25% more than income, corporation, and capital yield taxes for 1919-20, plus average yield of inheritance tax for 1912-16. In so far as turnover tax distributions exceed 1919 distributions these may be counted.*p* In place of 1925 guarantee, 2,600 mil. RM guaranteed from income, corporation, and turnover taxes for 1927-28 and 1928-29. At least 450 mil. RM to be distributed on turnover tax base. Excess over 2,400 mil. RM to be applied to reduction of real taxes under amount fixed by law of March 31, 1927. Per capita guarantee continued with limitation that such reimbursement is not to exceed 1/3 of state share on collection base.*o*	Additional tax on single persons and on income in excess of 8,000 RM not distributed. For this purpose 77 mil. RM withheld from wage tax and 67.8 from assessed income tax.*s* Excess over 1,300 mil. RM withheld from wage tax to meet deficit for pensions and health insurance.*u* Yield of wage tax in excess of 1,502 mil. RM withheld up to 30 mil. RM for unemployment relief.*v* 120 mil. RM withheld from three taxes for Reich in so far as taxes exceed 4,530 mil. RM in 1929-30 only.*u* Guarantees continued.

Tax	1931	1933
Income and corporation taxes	Same.	Same.
Turnover tax	Same.	Same.
Land purchase tax	Same.	Same.

* For notes to Chart 3 see page 316.

Chart 3: PROVISIONS FOR DISTRIBUTION OF REICH TAXES TO STATE
AND LOCAL GOVERNMENTS, 1920-35 *—Continued

Tax	1931	1933
Inheritance and merger taxes	...	...
Beer tax	Same.	Same.
Motor vehicle tax	Same as before, except that area on which 1/2 is distributed is weighted according to population density (if density is less than 5/6 of average area reduced to 5/6; if density is double average, area is doubled).*w*	Same.
Betting tax	Same.	96% distributed. All totalizator tax to state of business for breeding. 1/3 of bookmaker tax to state of business, 2/3 in proportion to population; for general use.*x*
Stock exchange, mineral water, and meat taxes	Discontinued December 8, 1931.	...
Guarantees and special provisions	Distribution on turnover tax base reduced from 450 to 375 mil. RM, 12 mil. deducted from turnover and 88 mil. from income and corporation tax distributions, as saving from salary reduction; per capita guarantee continued; 77 mil. RM withheld from wage tax, 120 mil. from assessed income tax as estimated amount of surtax. 50 mil. RM distributed from Reich funds to states in proportion to real tax reductions; 1926 guarantee repealed.*w*	7% deduction from wage tax and 16½% from assessed income tax as estimated amount of surtax.*v* States and communes guaranteed 160 mil. RM from motor vehicle tax which had been reduced. State and local governments reimbursed for tax reductions (28 mil. RM for beer tax, 1932 and 1933; 50 mil. RM for real tax, 1932 and 1933; 20 mil. RM for agricultural unification and 16.7 mil. RM for exemptions of houses). Turnover tax and 1920 guarantees, and deductions for salary decreases continued.*z*

* For notes to Chart 3 see page 316.

CHART 3: PROVISIONS FOR DISTRIBUTION OF REICH TAXES TO STATE
AND LOCAL GOVERNMENTS, 1920-35 *—Continued

Tax	1935
Income and corporation taxes	75% of that part of yield which is shared, distributed as before up to 1,100 mil. RM income tax and 240 mil. RM corporation tax. If 75% exceeds these sums, 33 1/3% of the excess distributed in the same manner, 33 1/3 to Reich, 33 1/3 to equalization fund for needy state and local governments.*aa*
Turnover tax	30% shared as before up to 573 mil. RM. If 30% exceeds this sum, excess distributed in same manner as excess income tax.*aa*
Land purchase tax	Same.
Inheritance and merger taxes	. . .
Beer tax	Same.
Motor vehicle tax	66 2/3% distributed as before.*bb* Guaranteed 90 mil. RM, of which 10% goes to equalization fund; to be used 4/5 for first class roads and 1/5 for second class roads.*cc*
Betting tax	Same.
Stock exchange, mineral water, and meat taxes	Meat: 96% to states, ½ in proportion to yield of 1933 state tax, ½ in proportion to yield of 1934 Reich tax.*dd*
Guarantees and special provisions	Beginning April 1, 1935, all guarantees for special taxes, except motor vehicle tax, abandoned.*ee* Reich deducts 26% of income tax as estimated amount of surtax over 8,000 RM and taxes for unemployment relief and promotion of marriage, before apportioning state and local share. Per capita guarantee limited to 1/5 of state yield. Other guarantees continued.*ff*

a State of origin determined by pay rolls, gross receipts, invested capital, and domicile.

b *Landessteuergesetz,* March 30, 1920, effective April 1, 1920.

c Law of December 24, 1919.

d Law of September 12, 1919, effective October 1, 1919.

e Law of September 10, 1919.

f Laws of March 27, 1919, April 1, 1919, and June 24, 1919.

g Effective April 1, 1921.

h *Finanzausgleichsgesetz* of June 23, 1923, effective April 1, 1923.

i Law of April 8, 1922, effective July 1, 1922.

j Had been distributed by law of April 8, 1922, 50% to state where business was done; 2/3 to be used for horse breeding.

k *Steuernotverordnung* of February 14, 1924, effective February 1, 1924.

l Law of November 10, 1924.

m Law of August 10, 1925, effective October 1, 1925.

[n] Law of March 26, 1925.

[o] Law of April 9, 1927, effective April 1, 1927.

[p] Law of April 27, 1926, effective April 1, 1926.

[q] Law of May 15, 1926, effective June 15, 1926.

[r] Law of March 31, 1926, effective April 1, 1926.

[s] Law of April 15, 1930, effective April 1, 1930.

[t] Law of September 30, 1930.

[u] Law of June 29, effective April 1, 1929.

[v] Decree of July 26, 1930, effective in part September 1, and in full October 1, 1930.

[w] Decree of December 1, 1930, effective April 1, 1931.

[x] Law of April 10, 1933, effective May 1, 1933.

[y] These deductions were 72 and 60 million RM, respectively, in 1932.

[z] Laws of March 18, 1933, May 30, 1933, and December 21, 1933.

[aa] Law of February 26, 1935, effective April 1, 1935. The state share has been further limited for 1936 (Law of March 30, 1936) in that the states are to receive no share in any excess over 1,220 million RM for the income tax, 262.5 million RM for the corporation tax, and 630 million RM for the turnover tax.

[bb] Law of March 26, 1934.

[cc] Law of February 28, 1935.

[dd] Law of March 24, 1934.

[ee] In 1934 these were 100 million RM for real tax and 33.3 million RM for exemptions of houses.

[ff] Law of October 16, 1934. Per capita guarantee was further limited by law of March 30, 1936.

CHART 4

PROVISIONS FOR DISTRIBUTION OF REICH AND STATE TAXES TO
LOCAL GOVERNMENTS *

PRUSSIA, 1924

Tax	State Provisions for Distribution
Income and corporation taxes	50.5% to local divisions: 38% to communes, 2.5% to provinces, 2.5% to rural circles, on basis of origin; 2% to school equalization fund; 5.13% to provinces, distributed 2/3 in proportion to population (reducing Berlin population 1/2 and increasing *Grenzmark* population 3x), 1/6 in proportion to area, 1/6 in proportion to highway mileage; .37% to rural circles in proportion to *Dotationen* of 1919, of which 1/4 goes to *Gutsbezirke* in proportion to population.[a] Communes receiving less than 80% of 1911 per capita income tax from this distribution receive the difference from a fund deducted from communes receiving more than 200% of 1911 per capita; 90% of excess is deducted from these.[b]
Turnover tax	60% to local divisions: 1/10 to rural circles on simple population base; 9/10 to communes on weighted population base.[c]
Land purchase tax	100% to circles where collected, together with privilege of levying surtax.[d]
Motor vehicle tax	100% to provinces: 20% for Rhine Province, Westphalia and Wiesbaden; remainder distributed 1/2 in proportion to area, 1/2 in proportion to population.[e]
Beer and mineral water taxes	. . .
Rentals tax	50% for building, shared by state and circle and spent where collected. 25% to state and 25% to circles for general use. Latter distributed, 3% to occupied territory, 20% where collected, and 77% in proportion to population.[f]
Real estate and business taxes	Local surtaxes or independent taxes. Surtaxes may not exceed 100% for real estate and 200% for business, without special permission.

PRUSSIA, 1931

Tax	State Provisions for Distribution
Income and corporation taxes	10 million RM deducted for communes bordering on city-states before division between state and local governments and distributed to such communes in proportion to yield of income and corporation taxes.[g] 50.5% to local divisions distributed as in 1924 with the following exceptions: from

* For notes to Chart 4 see page 332.

CHART 4: PROVISIONS FOR DISTRIBUTION OF REICH AND STATE TAXES
TO LOCAL GOVERNMENTS *—Continued

Tax	State Provisions for Distribution
	the communes' share distributed on the basis of origin, any sum by which the commune share of the turnover tax falls short of 148.5 million RM is deducted and distributed on the turnover tax base:[h] from the same share for all communes with a population over 2,000 is deducted 3,000 RM per local police officer. The latter is distributed to communes with local police in proportion to the number of officers. From the same share for communes with state police and a population in excess of 2,000 is deducted 1/3 of the cost of state police. This is levied against such communes, 1/2 in proportion to origin and 1/2 in proportion to population.[i] From the commune share of the corporation tax is deducted half of the excess over the average per capita share for communes with such excess and all over 10 RM per capita.[j] Also, in place of the 80% guarantee the amount received by each commune is adjusted before final distribution for the relative guarantee, which weights the base for each commune which would receive less per capita through an unweighted distribution than its pre-war revenues from income taxes.[k]
Turnover tax	55% to local divisions, 1/10 to rural circles, 9/10 to communes. Distribution in proportion to population weighted 1x (for first 2,000 inhabitants) to 2.25x (for inhabitants in excess of 50,000). This weighted population is again weighted 1/100 for every 1/10 of 1 per cent that children of school age exceed the average percentage of children of school age for communes of the same size.[k]
Land purchase tax	Same as 1924.
Motor vehicle tax	100% to provinces. Percentage to each province fixed by law. Distribution within province according to annual plan determined by province committee, with consideration for through highway mileage. To be used for highway support.[h]
Beer and mineral water taxes	50% of beer tax and 100% of mineral water tax added to commune share of income and corporation taxes and distributed as these are distributed.[h] Mineral water tax discontinued 1931.
Rentals tax	57.2% to circles: 40.5% for housing and 16.7% for general use. Housing share returned to place where collected. General share returned, 64.4% in proportion to population, 30% where collected, 1.4% to border communes, and 4.2% to communes with exceptional amount of unemployment. If

* For notes to Chart 4 see page 332.

CHART 4: PROVISIONS FOR DISTRIBUTION OF REICH AND STATE TAXES
TO LOCAL GOVERNMENTS *—Continued

PRUSSIA, 1931

Tax	State Provisions for Distribution
Rentals tax —Continued	local housing share is not needed for that purpose, sum up to 1/4 may be applied to general purposes. State may take over any of remaining share not needed for housing.[l]
Real estate and business taxes	Same as 1924.

PRUSSIA, 1935

Tax	State Provisions for Distribution
Income and corporation taxes	45% to local divisions: 35% to communes, 2.5% to provinces, 2.5% to rural circles, on basis of origin; 5% to school equalization fund.[m] Distribution of commune share modified, as before, for turnover tax guarantee, police compensation, and relative guarantee.
Turnover tax	Same as 1931, except that 54 million RM is deducted from local share for equalization fund.[n]
Land purchase tax	Same as 1924.
Motor vehicle tax	4% deducted for maintenance of bridges. Remaining 96% distributed: 4/5 to governments maintaining first class highways, in proportion to mileage, population, and area (at discretion of ministers of interior and finance); 1/5 to governments maintaining second class highways in proportion to mileage.[o]
Beer and mineral water taxes	Same as 1931.
Rentals tax	Circles receive 47% of remainder after state has deducted 37.5 million RM. Circles receive 15% of their share in proportion to collections. From remainder 65% or 102 million RM (whichever is larger) is deducted for reimbursement for losses from reduction of real estate taxes and for equalization fund for communes with heavy welfare burden.[p] Remainder is distributed to circles in proportion to population weighted for the number in excess of the average, of social insurance annuitants and those impoverished by inflation.[q]
Real estate and business taxes	Same as 1924.

* For notes to Chart 4 see page 332.

CHART 4: PROVISIONS FOR DISTRIBUTION OF REICH AND STATE TAXES
TO LOCAL GOVERNMENTS *—Continued

BAVARIA, 1931

Tax	State Provisions for Distribution
Income and corporation taxes	The share of each circle and commune is estimated separately by applying to the income and corporation taxes originating in the commune the percentage represented by circle and commune income, property and capital earnings taxes for 1912 to 1919 to the total of such taxes. Thus the percentage for each circle and commune remains constant, but the percentage of the tax going to all local governments varies as the proportion originating in the different communes varies. Before this is returned to local governments 6% is deducted from circle share for equalization fund, and the state may take excess over 50% of total state and local share allotted to any commune. The state may also take whatever is needed up to 10% of commune share for those communes that obtain nothing under above distribution. Share of income tax distributed to state on turnover tax base treated as turnover tax, and shares received under the minimum per capita guarantee paid to equalization fund.
Turnover tax[r]	Allotted to communes on simple per capita basis but the entire share of the communes over 2,000 population and the share of the communes under 2,000 population up to 30 pf. per capita goes to equalization fund.
Land purchase tax	Distributed to communes where land is located. Communes also have surtax privilege.
Motor vehicle tax	Distributed 2/5 to communes and 3/5 to districts in proportion to need for highway aid as determined by a state committee.
Mineral water tax	Distributed to those communes with more than the average proportion of unemployed in proportion to the number of unemployed.
Beer tax	None.
Rentals tax	One-third of rate levied for general use to communes where collected.

SAXONY, 1931

Tax	State Provisions for Distribution
Income and corporation taxes[s]	9% of state and local share to districts, half according to origin, half in proportion to population. 41% to communes. From the latter, 1/3 of the cost of teachers' salaries, paid by

* For notes to Chart 4 see page 332.

Chart 4: PROVISIONS FOR DISTRIBUTION OF REICH AND STATE TAXES
TO LOCAL GOVERNMENTS *—Continued

saxony, 1931

Tax	State Provisions for Distribution
Income and corporation taxes[s] —Continued	the state, is first deducted. From the remainder, half of the corporation tax is distributed according to origin; the other half is added to the income tax and distributed 3/5 according to origin of the income tax and 2/5 in proportion to population.[t] 3% to equalization fund.
Turnover tax	Distributed to communes, 3/5 according to origin of income tax, 2/5 in proportion to population.
Land purchase tax	To communes where land is located. Communes also have surtax privilege.
Motor vehicle tax	9/10 of local share to districts in proportion to yield of draught animal tax of 1925.[u] 1/10 to highway equalization fund. To be used for highway support.
Mineral water tax	All to equalization fund.
Beer tax	None distributed.
Rentals tax[v]	None of state tax for general use distributed. All of state tax for housing to communes where collected. Districts and communes also have surtax privilege, districts for general use, and communes for housing and general. Latter, 5/6 for housing, goes to communes where collected except for deduction of 25% of housing share for housing equalization fund. Share of very small communes goes to district.

baden, 1931

Tax	State Provisions for Distribution
Income and corporation taxes	3.5% of local share of income, corporation, and turnover taxes to circles in proportion to their share in the income and corporation tax in 1924. Remainder to communes, after deduction of 500,000 RM for equalization fund. Distributed 66% to communes with more than 9,000 population, 12% to communes with 3,000 to 9,000 population, and 22% to communes with less than 3,000 population. Distribution within the group, 70% according to origin of income and corporation taxes, 30% in proportion to population.
Turnover tax	Same as income and corporation tax.
Land purchase tax	To communes where land is located. Communes also have surtax privilege.

* For notes to Chart 4 see page 332.

CHART 4: PROVISIONS FOR DISTRIBUTION OF REICH AND STATE TAXES
TO LOCAL GOVERNMENTS *—Continued

Tax	State Provisions for Distribution
Motor vehicle tax[w]	None.
Mineral water tax	To communes in proportion to population.
Beer tax	None.
Rentals tax	To communes where levied. Approximately half of local share for housing.

WÜRTTEMBERG, 1931

Tax	State Provisions for Distribution
Income and corporation taxes	1/3 less 2,760 thousand marks to communes, distributed 9/10 according to origin, 1/10 in proportion to school children. Origin weighted in workers' communes. 2,760 thousand marks, together with 1,240 thousand marks from state share, to equalization fund. Share of income tax distributed to state on turnover base treated as turnover tax.
Turnover tax	Distributed to communes in proportion to permanent population.
Land purchase tax	To communes where land is located. Communes also have surtax privilege.
Motor vehicle tax	None.
Mineral water tax	Distributed to communes, together with beer tax, to the amount of 75 pf. per capita, plus 1% of the previous year's assessment for the land tax.
Beer tax	See mineral water tax.
Rentals tax	Communes have independent tax for general purposes and surtax at least 15% of which must be devoted to housing.

THURINGIA, 1931

Tax	State Provisions for Distribution
Income and corporation taxes[x]	5% of local share distributed to rural circles, 3/4 according to origin and 1/4 in proportion to population. From remaining local share, 3/10 of cost of teachers' salaries and half of cost of school materials is deducted. From the remainder each city circle receives its share according to origin. 1/5 of what is left is then deducted for the equalization fund. Remaining 4/5 is distributed to five groups of communes (grouped according to population) according to origin.

* For notes to Chart 4 see page 332.

CHART 4: PROVISIONS FOR DISTRIBUTION OF REICH AND STATE TAXES
TO LOCAL GOVERNMENTS *—Continued

THURINGIA, 1931

Tax	State Provisions for Distribution
Income and corporation taxes[x] —Continued	Within each group the distribution is made to individual communes, 2/3 according to origin, and 1/3 in proportion to population. Share of income tax distributed to state on turnover tax base treated as turnover tax.
Turnover tax[x]	Distributed to communes in proportion to weighted population, the weight varying from 1x for communes under 1,000 to 2x for city circles. 1/5 of the share belonging to communes other than city circles is deducted for circles and distributed 2/3 in proportion to population and 1/3 according to origin of income and corporation taxes. Remaining commune share distributed in proportion to weighted population.
Land purchase tax	To circle where land is located. Circles also have surtax privilege.
Motor vehicle tax	None.
Mineral water tax	1/4 to city circles, 3/4 to other communes, in proportion to welfare expenditures in excess of average.
Beer tax	None.
Rentals tax[y]	58% to circles and 42% to communes where collected. Communes over 5,000 population get housing share (62%) of circle share.

HESSE, 1931

Tax	State Provisions for Distribution
Income and corporation taxes[z]	Local share of turnover tax added to local share of income and corporation taxes. From local share 150,000 marks are deducted as compensation for reduced interest on loans for welfare expenditures and 1.25% for equalization fund for welfare. Remainder is allocated to circles, half according to origin of income and corporation taxes, half according to commune income taxes in 1913 and 1914. Proportion assigned to circles and provinces determined by ratio of circle assessments to total state and local income taxes in 1913 and 1914. Division between province and circle left to discretion of minister of interior. Commune share distributed half according to origin and half according to commune income taxes in 1913 and 1914. Share of income tax distributed to state on turnover tax base treated as turnover tax.

* For notes to Chart 4 see page 332.

CHART 4: PROVISIONS FOR DISTRIBUTION OF REICH AND STATE TAXES
TO LOCAL GOVERNMENTS *—Continued

Tax	State Provisions for Distribution
Turnover tax	Local shares of turnover tax distributed with income and corporation taxes.
Land purchase tax	To communes where land is located. Communes also have surtax privilege. When land is in an independent *Gemarkung* tax goes to circle.
Motor vehicle tax	After deductions for state-supported bridges, distributed to provinces for highway maintenance at discretion of minister of interior, but with due consideration for population, highway mileage, and collections.
Mineral water tax	All to equalization fund for welfare expenditure.
Beer tax	None.
Rentals tax	Communes have independent tax. Tax on new buildings must be used for housing. Use of other optional.

MECKLENBURG-SCHWERIN, 1931

Tax	State Provisions for Distribution
Income and corporation taxes	Communes receive that proportion of tax that direct personal taxes of commune bore to direct personal taxes of state in 1919. Maximum 40% and minimum 20% of total. From this is deducted 25% of teachers' salaries (but not more than 40% of local share).
Turnover tax	To communes in proportion to population.
Land purchase tax	To independent cities in proportion to population. Remainder, 2/3 to administrative districts and 1/3 to remaining cities and certain communes in proportion to population. State surtax distributed with other. No local surtax.
Motor vehicle tax	Shared by state and administrative districts in proportion to mileage of secondary highways supported by each. Communes may share if they are maintaining important improved highways. For highway support.
Mineral water tax	2/3 to welfare districts in proportion to publicly supported unemployed, to be redistributed to communes at discretion of district official. 1/3 to equalization fund.
Beer tax	None.
Rentals tax[aa]	30% of tax for general use to cities where collected, and 10% to districts outside independent cities. Housing levy goes 1/13 to minister of agriculture and 12/13 (to cities over 8,000), 6/13 (cities 4,000-8,000), or 4/13 (cities under 4,000), to cities where collected. Remainder to minister of interior.

* For notes to Chart 4 see page 332.

CHART 4: PROVISIONS FOR DISTRIBUTION OF REICH AND STATE TAXES
TO LOCAL GOVERNMENTS *—Continued

OLDENBURG, 1931 [bb]

Tax	State Provisions for Distribution
Income and corporation taxes	To communes according to origin. If commune share of income, corporation and turnover taxes combined comes to more than 2.4 million marks, excess is deducted for equalization fund for school expenditures and loans without interest.[cc dd] Share of income tax distributed to state on turnover tax base treated as turnover tax.
Turnover tax	Half distributed to communes in proportion to population, half to districts in proportion to origin of income and corporation taxes. District retains 2/3 of this and distributes the remainder to communes according to origin of income and corporation taxes.[ee] For share to equalization fund see income and corporation taxes.[ff]
Land purchase tax	Local share to commune where land is located in Oldenburg section; half to commune and half to district where land is located in Lübeck and Birkenfeld sections. Communes and districts may levy surtaxes.
Motor vehicle tax	All to districts where collected in Lübeck and Birkenfeld sections. Half to districts in proportion to highway mileage in Oldenburg section. For highway support.
Mineral water tax	To communes in proportion to population.
Beer tax	None.
Rentals tax	Communes do not share in state tax but may levy surtaxes. Tax on new buildings for housing. Use of other not specified.

BRUNSWICK, 1931

Tax	State Provisions for Distribution
Income and corporation taxes	17% of total state and local share to city of Brunswick, 8.5% to other cities, 5% to rural communes, 6% to circles. City and commune share divided, 40% according to origin, 40% in proportion to population, 20% in proportion to preceding year's welfare expenditures. Circle share divided 25% according to origin, 25% in proportion to population, and 50% in proportion to preceding year's welfare expenditures. In determining origin, if corporation tax of commune exceeds income tax, excess is not considered. If commune share exceeds needs, it may be reduced as much as half. May also be reduced if commune is not utilizing its own resources.

* For notes to Chart 4 see page 332.

Chart 4: PROVISIONS FOR DISTRIBUTION OF REICH AND STATE TAXES
TO LOCAL GOVERNMENTS *—Continued

Tax	State Provisions for Distribution
Turnover tax	1/3 of local share to circles and 2/3 to communes (Brunswick counting as both circle and commune). Distributed among circles and communes according to weighted population, the weight varying from 1 for communes with less than 1,250 inhabitants to 1.9 for Brunswick.
Land purchase tax	1/3 of local shares to circles and 2/3 to communes (Brunswick counting as both). Distributed where land is located.
Motor vehicle tax	1/5 of local share to Brunswick, 4/5 to circles in proportion to highway mileage. To be used for highway maintenance.
Mineral water tax	15% to Brunswick, 15% to other cities, 20% to rural communes, 50% to equalization fund. Distributed within groups in same manner as income and corporation taxes.
Beer tax	None.
Rentals tax	5% of yield in cities to cities for general purposes. 2 1/2% of total yield to equalization fund.

ANHALT, 1931

Tax	State Provisions for Distribution
Income and corporation taxes	150,000 RM deducted from local share for equalization fund. Remainder distributed according to origin except that when corporation tax share exceeds what communes would get on per capita basis, half the excess goes to equalization fund, and when it exceeds 10 RM per capita all of excess goes to equalization fund. Equalization fund used to guarantee communes a fixed per capita sum from this source varying from 12 RM for communes with less than 2,500 inhabitants to 20 RM in large cities. Share of income tax distributed to state on turnover tax base treated as turnover tax.
Turnover tax	To communes in proportion to population.
Land purchase tax	Commune share, including surtax, distributed in proportion to population.
Motor vehicle tax	Distributed to circles at discretion of state officials for highway support.
Mineral water tax	Distributed with beer tax. Half the local share goes to circles for highway maintenance, 1/5 to each circle. Half to welfare districts according to need.
Beer tax	Same as mineral water.

* For notes to Chart 4 see page 332.

CHART 4: PROVISIONS FOR DISTRIBUTION OF REICH AND STATE TAXES
TO LOCAL GOVERNMENTS *—Continued

ANHALT, 1931

Tax	*State Provisions for Distribution*
Rentals tax	Local share to communes where collected, to be used 51% for housing, 49% for general purposes.
Land, building, and business taxes	The circles receive 33 1/3% of the yield of the state land value tax, and the communes receive 50% of the yield of the state building tax in proportion to collections.

LIPPE, 1931

Tax	*State Provisions for Distribution*
Income and corporation taxes	1/10 of local share to equalization fund, 9/10 to city and rural communes according to origin. Communes give 1/6 of their share to school districts, distributed in proportion to school children. Must also share with village in accordance with need as indicated by population, industrial condition, and average income for 1912 to 1914. State withholds 1/4 of share assigned to equalization fund. Equalization fund distributed according to need. Communes are guaranteed average income for years 1912 to 1914. 20% of share received from Reich under per capita guarantee added to local share.
Turnover tax	Half the local share distributed according to origin of income tax, half in proportion to population. 4/10 of rural commune share withheld by state. From remainder 1/3 is to be distributed to villages in proportion to population.
Land purchase tax	Half the yield, including surtax, distributed to communes where land is located.
Motor vehicle tax	To communes in proportion to population and highway mileage.
Mineral water tax	To communes in proportion to population.
Beer tax	None.
Rentals tax	To communes where collected; 1/4 to be used for general purposes, 3/4 for housing. 1/5 of housing share to equalization fund for equalizing housing costs.

* For notes to Chart 4 see page 332.

CHART 4: PROVISIONS FOR DISTRIBUTION OF REICH AND STATE TAXES
TO LOCAL GOVERNMENTS *—Continued

MECKLENBURG-STRELITZ, 1931

Tax	State Provisions for Distribution
Income and corporation taxes	To communes according to origin. Rural communes receive only half their share, the remaining half being kept by district. Communes guaranteed 1913 income tax yield.
Turnover tax	To communes in proportion to population. Districts withhold 1/5 of rural commune shares for equalization fund for needy communes.
Land purchase tax	To communes where land is located. Communes also have privilege of surtaxes.
Motor vehicle tax	None.
Mineral water tax	None.
Beer tax	None.
Rentals tax	To communes where collected, 85.2% for housing, remainder for general purposes.

SCHAUMBURG-LIPPE, 1931 ^{gg}

Tax	State Provisions for Distribution
Income and corporation taxes ^{hh}	Local share to communes according to origin. Circles withhold 8% of commune share for their own use. They must, however, devote at least 10% of this to aid needy communes. The communes' half of school costs is also deducted from their share before it is distributed. Sums received under per capita guarantee distributed with the rest. Share of income tax distributed to states on turnover base treated as turnover tax.
Turnover tax	2% of total to city of Bückeburg and 6% to city of Stadthagen.
Land purchase tax	To communes where land is located. Both circles and communes have surtax privilege.
Motor vehicle tax	From total yield 17% and 25%, respectively, to two circles; 3% and 5%, respectively, to two cities.
Mineral water tax	Applied to reduction of commune share of school costs.
Beer tax	None.

* For notes to Chart 4 see page 332.

CHART 4: PROVISIONS FOR DISTRIBUTION OF REICH AND STATE TAXES
TO LOCAL GOVERNMENTS *—Continued

SCHAUMBURG-LIPPE, 1931 *99*

Tax	State Provisions for Distribution
Rentals tax	Communes receive 52.5% of total: 37.5% for housing to communes where collected; 15% for general purposes distributed 1/2 in proportion to population and 1/2 in proportion to collections.

HAMBURG, 1931 [44]

Tax	State Provisions for Distribution
Income and corporation taxes	In cities, 75% according to origin (100% to Geesthacht); in rural communes, 50% according to origin. Share of income tax distributed to state on turnover tax base treated as turnover tax.
Turnover tax	In cities, 75% in proportion to population (100% to Geesthacht); in rural communes, 50% in proportion to population.
Land purchase tax	In cities, 75% to city in which land is located (100% to Geesthacht); in rural communes, 50% to commune where land is located. State and commune have surtax privileges.
Motor vehicle tax	None.
Mineral water tax	None.
Beer tax	None.
Rentals tax	Communes receive none of tax on improved agricultural real estate, but all of tax on new buildings. This is distributed where collected for housing purposes. Half the tax on other property goes to communes where collected for general use. Communes also have surtax privileges.
Land, building, and business taxes	In addition to certain surtax privileges, city communes receive 80% of the collections from the state land tax, Geesthacht 100%, rural communes 30%, *Landherrenschaften* 20%. City communes receive 75% of the collections from the state business tax, Geesthacht 100%, rural communes 30%, *Landherrenschaften* 20%.

BREMEN, 1931

Tax	State Provisions for Distribution
Income and corporation taxes	To communes according to origin. Circles can levy on communes up to 1/5 of their share for redistribution to needy communes.

* For notes to Chart 4 see page 332.

CHART 4: PROVISIONS FOR DISTRIBUTION OF REICH AND STATE TAXES
TO LOCAL GOVERNMENTS *—Continued

Tax	State Provisions for Distribution
Turnover tax	To communes in proportion to population.
Land purchase tax	To communes where land is located. In addition to half the regular tax they receive 3/4 of state surtax.
Motor vehicle tax	Circles and cities receive share in proportion to area (area counted 3x for state, circle, and city), for highway maintenance.
Mineral water tax	None.^{jj}
Beer tax	None.
Rentals tax	All to cities where collected, and outside cities, to circles. At least 20% to be used for housing.
Land, building, and business taxes	Rural communes receive 75% of the state business tax levied within their jurisdiction. No local business tax is levied.

LÜBECK, 1931

Tax	State Provisions for Distribution
Income and corporation taxes	To communes according to origin.
Turnover tax	To communes in proportion to population.
Land purchase tax	None.
Motor vehicle tax	None.
Mineral water tax	None.
Beer tax	None.
Rentals tax	No provisions for distribution. Actually about 1/6 for building.
Land, building, and business taxes	Communes receive a small share of the state land tax. The communes themselves do not levy such a tax.

* For notes to Chart 4 see page 332.

^a Laws of April 1, 1924, and June 19, 1924. The local share was fixed at 50%, law of January 13, 1921; 61.75%, law of October 30, 1923; 57.5%, law of April 1, 1924; and 50.5%, law of June 19, 1924.

^b Laws of October 30, 1923, June 19, 1924, and May 28, 1925.

^c Law of April 1, 1924.

^d Law of October 30, 1923.

^e Law of May 15, 1924.

^f April 1, 1924. This was changed three times within the year.

^g Law of July 8, 1927.

^h Law of July 19, 1930, effective April 1, 1930.

ⁱ Law of August 2, 1929, effective April 1, 1930.

^j Law of April 1, 1929.

^k Law of November 27, 1925.

^l Law of October 8, 1931.

^m Law of March 17, 1934.

ⁿ Law of March 20, 1934, effective April 1, 1934. By law of April 6, 1936, excess over 150 million RM goes to equalization fund.

^o Local units are for the most part provinces, in some instances circles, and communes where such highways pass through a city. Law of March 11, 1935.

^p Reduced to 100 million RM by law of April 6, 1936.

^q Laws of March 17, 1934, and December 22, 1934.

^r By law of June 23, 1934, 900,000 RM of local share to be distributed on per capita basis. Remainder to be used for communes with unusual welfare burdens. This sum was 1,200,000 RM in 1932 and 600,000 RM in 1933. By law of February 8, 1936, per capita distribution fixed at 50 pfennigs.

^s By law of February 12, 1935, state retains from commune share a sum equal to 700 RM per kilometer of highway taken over by the state from the communes.

^t By law of March 4, 1936, the state deducts from each commune's share 700 RM per kilometer of first class road taken over by the state.

^u By law of March 12, 1936, distributed in proportion to mileage of second class roads.

^v Division of rentals tax has been revised annually since 1931. For 1934 none was applied to housing, but 4.9% to fund for amortization and interest on housing loan. 49.8% was retained by the state, 21.5% was given to communes and 10.8% to *Bezirke* for general purposes, and 13% to the equalization fund.

^w By law of July 26, 1935, communes supporting through highways receive a share in the sum of 245,000 RM.

^x For 1934-35 communes share of (1) income tax was set at 2,070,000 RM, (2) corporation tax at 725,000 RM and (3) turnover tax at 1,500,000 RM. Any excess went to equalization fund for needy circles and communes. By law of May 11, 1935, the income from these three taxes in excess of 1/3 of the 1934-35 yield goes to equalization fund.

^y By law of April 17, 1935, 13% goes for building and 8.7% for general use. Half this latter sum is paid to circles. In the case of rural circles, communes receive 28.5% and the circle 15% of collections.

^z By law of April 11, 1932, 8% of commune share of income and corporation taxes (increased to 10% by law of July 5, 1935) and all of commune share of turnover tax in excess of 3.3 million marks to equalization fund.

^{aa} By law of March 29, 1932, state 62%, communes 34%, equalization fund 3%, minister of interior for maintenance of old dwellings 1%. Where commune is subject to *Amt*, division is 28% to city, 6% to *Amt*; outside cities, all to *Amt*.

ᵇᵇ By law of March 8, 1934, meat tax goes to school equalization fund. By law of January 26, 1934, districts in Oldenburg section (which have been reduced from 12 to 6) get 2/15 of state share of turnover tax, ½ of state share of land purchase tax, including surtax and that part of motor vehicle tax determined by proportion of highway mileage supported. Have, in addition, rights to local income. Function of these districts to equalize. By law of February 22, 1935, 4/7 of corporation tax in the whole state, 3/7 of the personal income tax in Oldenburg and Lübeck and 4/7 in Birkenfeld to communes; all of motor vehicle tax to state.

ᶜᶜ By law of March 29, 1932, and September 28, 1932, school equalization fund receives income and corporation taxes received under guarantee, and one-third of turnover tax if necessary. May draw on all three taxes further, if needed, at discretion of state officials.

ᵈᵈ Lübeck fund is limited to 100,000 RM and Birkenfeld fund to 130,000 RM.

ᵉᵉ All returned in proportion to income and corporation taxes, April 1, 1933; old provisions restored, June 27, 1933.

ᶠᶠ State officials may deduct from turnover tax before distribution for communes with pressing need. Law of August 9, 1932.

ᵍᵍ State meat tax (January 2, 1934): 12% returned to cities and circles where collected for cost of local administration (reduced to 3% by law of April 18, 1934). If communes aid circles, receive 2% (reduced to 1½% by law of April 18, 1934).

ʰʰ By law of June 7, 1935, 30% to circles. Of this 36,000 RM is applied to tax reductions and the remainder is distributed, 3/5 in proportion to collections and 2/5 in proportion to population.

ⁱⁱ Meat tax introduced by law of June 5, 1932. Communes to retain 15% of collections.

ʲʲ Returned to communes where collected in 1932.

CHART 5

STATE GRANTS-IN-AID FOR ELEMENTARY SCHOOLS IN THE GERMAN STATES, 1930-31 [a]

PERCENTAGE OF EXPENDITURE

State	Salaries and Pensions	Building Costs	Trans-portation	Supplies
Prussia	25[b]	Depends on need[l]	100	Depends on need
Bavaria	100	m	Depends on need	Depends on need
Saxony	66 2/3[c]	m	66 2/3	Depends on need
Württemberg	20-55[d]	Depends on need	Depends on need	None
Bade	100	Depends on need	100	None
Thuringia	70[c]	m	70	50[o]
Hesse	100[e]	Variable sum	100	Variable sum
Mecklenburg-Schwerin	75[f]	m	None	None
Oldenburg	[g]	Depends on need	100	None
Brunswick	100	Depends on need	100	None
Anhalt	100	50	100	Depends on need
Lippe	100[h]	Depends on need	100	100
Mecklenburg-Strelitz	100[i]	Varies with district	Depends on need	None
Schaumburg-Lippe	50	Depends on need	Depends on need	None
Hamburg	100[j]	100[n]	None	100[n]
Bremen	25-100[k]	25-100[k]	25-100[k]	25-100[k]
Lübeck	100	100	None	None

[a] Data from *Einzelschriften*, Nos. 6 and 17, except where otherwise noted.

[b] Allowing one teacher to 60 pupils. Special aid to poor districts in addition.

[c] Local share deducted from local share of income and corporation taxes. State contributes 100% to pensions. Also special aid to poor districts.

[d] Varies from 55% in small districts to 20% in large cities. Also special aid to poor districts and a share in income and corporation taxes distributed in proportion to school children.

[e] State pays all salaries but levies sum equal to 200 RM per teacher on communes.

f More, if 40% of local share of income and corporation taxes does not cover local share of salaries.

g Depends on need. Beginning in 1935, a fixed sum per elementary school teacher is also paid.

h For minimum salary scale only. Special aid for poor districts.

i Some cities required to reimburse state for 50%.

j For minimum salary scale only in some districts.

k Varies in different communes.

l Size used as basis of need.

m Only as part of aid to poor districts for all expenditures.

n In more important districts. In rural areas district itself contributes a part.

o Also special aid to poor districts.

CHART 6

STATE AND LOCAL GRANTS-IN-AID FOR HIGHWAYS IN THE GERMAN STATES, 1930-31 *[a]

STATE AID		LOCAL AID
From Motor Vehicle Tax[b]	*From Other Sources*	
PRUSSIA		
4% for bridge maintenance, if tolls were levied in 1926-27. 96% to provinces; exact proportion to each province fixed by law.	*Dotation:* 5.5% of income and corporation taxes, distributed 14/15 to provinces, 1/15 to rural circles. Use not specified. Distributed to provinces, 2/3 according to weighted population, 1/6 area, 1/6 highway mileage. Distribution to rural circles as in 1919 (earlier *Dotation* had been subdivided among circles at discretion of provinces, i. e., amount, but not method, of distribution fixed by law).[c]	Circles receive distributions from motor vehicle taxes received by provinces, the amount being determined each year by provincial committees, consideration being given to mileage of through highways. Circles receive indefinite aids from provinces, and communes receive indefinite aids from provinces and circles in accordance with need, as measured by tax burden and highway mileage maintained.
BAVARIA		
27% to districts, 18% to communes, in accordance with highway expenditures and financial need.[e]	6% of local share of income and corporation taxes withheld for equalization and redistributed 5/10 to communes, 4/10 to districts, 1/10 to circles, in accordance with need for welfare and highways.[d]	. . .
SAXONY		
45% to districts in proportion to yield of draft animal tax in 1925-26 (any deficit to be made up from state's 50%). 5% to construction fund to aid local roads.[f]	Aid to communes with special financial need, for construction and maintenance.	Communes recompensed for half the cost of through roads by districts.

* For notes to Chart 6 see page 339.

CHART 6: STATE AND LOCAL GRANTS-IN-AID FOR HIGHWAYS IN THE
GERMAN STATES, 1930-31 *[a]—Continued

STATE AID		LOCAL AID
From Motor Vehicle Tax[b]	*From Other Sources*	
	WÜRTTEMBERG	
No fixed proportion, but about half goes to *Amtskörperschaft* and communes as highway aids for construction and maintenance.	. . .	. . .
	BADEN	
. . .	Fixed *Dotation* to circles for construction and maintenance. Aid to needy circles and communes for construction. Aid to cities for maintenance of state roads within city limits.	Circle aids needy communes for construction.
	THURINGIA	
No fixed proportion, but certain sum placed in budget each year for circles and communes, not to exceed 50% of cost of maintenance.	. . .	Circle aids needy communes.
	HESSE	
All but a small sum reserved for public bridges distributed to provinces in proportion to population, highway mileage and tax revenues, for maintenance.	*Dotation* of 1 million RM annually to provinces in approximately equal parts for maintenance. 3/8 of cost of provincial road construction.	Communes receive aid from provinces for construction and maintenance of through highways.
	MECKLENBURG-SCHWERIN	
50% distributed to *Amt* and state in proportion to mileage of main highways, for maintenance.	*Dotation* of 1 million RM annually as compensation for former highway toll, distributed to *Amt* and cities in proportion to highway mileage, for maintenance. Construction aid to *Amt* and communes for main highways, 11,000 RM per km.	. . .

* For notes to Chart 6 see page 339.

STATE AID		LOCAL AID
From Motor Vehicle Tax[b]	*From Other Sources*	
	OLDENBURG	
Half the Oldenburg share to *Amt* and communes in proportion to through highway mileage, for maintenance.	Birkenfeld: aid to communes for construction and maintenance of local roads. Lübeck: aid to communes for construction of local roads. Oldenburg: aid to *Amt* and communes up to 25% of cost of constructing main roads.	...
	BRUNSWICK	
10% to city of Brunswick; 40% to circle in proportion to highway mileage for maintenance.	...	Circle aids needy communes for construction and maintenance.
	ANHALT	
100% to circles for construction and maintenance; distribution determined by state officials following hearings.	1/3 of beer and mineral water taxes to circles (1/5 to each of 5 circles) for construction and maintenance. Aid to circles for construction.	Aid from circles to communes for construction and maintenance of especially costly highways.
	LIPPE	
40% to *Amt* and city in proportion to population and highway mileage for construction and maintenance.	...	...
	MECKLENBURG-STRELITZ	
...	11,000 RM per km. to communes for main highways for construction. Variable aids to communes for local highways depending on cost.	...

* For notes to Chart 6 see page 339.

CHART 6: STATE AND LOCAL GRANTS-IN-AID FOR HIGHWAYS IN THE GERMAN STATES, 1930-31 *[a]—Continued

STATE AID		LOCAL AID
From Motor Vehicle Tax[b]	*From Other Sources*	
	SCHAUMBURG-LIPPE	
42% to circles; 8% to cities (fixed sums set for each circle and city) for highway maintenance.	Optional aids to circles for construction.	Circle aids needy communes for construction.
	HAMBURG	
. . .	. . .	. . .
	BREMEN	
66 2/3% distributed to circles and cities, in proportion to area, for maintenance.	. . .	. . .
	LÜBECK	
. . .	Aid to communes in form of materials for main highways and special aid to needy.	. . .

[a] Data from *Einzelschriften* Nos. 6, 17, and 19, except where otherwise noted.
[b] By laws of February 12 and 28, 1935, states are guaranteed 90 million reichsmarks from the motor vehicle tax, distributed to them, and to be distributed by them to the authorities maintaining the highways, 80% for first class roads in proportion to population, area, and highway mileage, and 20% for second class roads in proportion to mileage.
[c] K. Stephan, *Das kommunale Finanz- und Steuerrecht in Preussen*, Berlin, 1926, pp. 72-73.
[d] *Finanz-Archiv*, XLV, 341-44.
[e] By law of February 29, 1936, 73% to state, 6% to communes supporting first class roads, 20% to districts and communes for second class roads.
[f] By law of March 12, 1936, distributed in proportion to mileage of second class roads.

CHART 7

STATE GRANTS-IN-AID FOR WELFARE AND SPECIAL LOCAL WELFARE REVENUES IN THE GERMAN STATES, 1930-31 [a]

State	Source	Basis of Distribution
Prussia	8% of local share of rental tax.[b]	2% to poor border circles; 6% to circles with exceptional relief burdens.[b]
Bavaria	(1) 6% of local share of income and corporation taxes, supplemented by deductions from the shares of certain communes and by part of the turnover tax. (2) All of mineral water tax. (3) Emergency rentals tax.[c]	(1) To circles in inverse proportion to the ratio of their tax income to uncovered welfare expenditures, and to districts in proportion to need for welfare and highways. (2) To communes where unemployment is above the average. (3) To circles for unemployment relief.
Saxony	(1) Local additions to rental tax. (2) 3.25 million RM from general revenues.	(1) At discretion of local authorities. (2) At discretion of state officials.
Württemberg	4 million RM from income and corporation taxes.	At discretion of state officials.
Baden	Not to exceed 6 million RM from general revenue.	In proportion to local welfare expenditures.
Thuringia	General revenue.	At discretion of state officials.
Hesse	12% of rental tax, all of mineral water tax, 1 1/4% of income, corporation, and turnover taxes.[d]	To welfare districts for needy rent payers at discretion of state officials.
Mecklenburg-Schwerin	All of mineral water tax.	2/3 to communes in proportion to unemployed; 1/3 to communes at discretion of state officials.
Oldenburg	General revenue.	At discretion of state officials.
Brunswick	None.	. . .
Anhalt	Business tax.	At discretion of state officials.

CHART 7: STATE GRANTS-IN-AID FOR WELFARE AND SPECIAL LOCAL
WELFARE REVENUES IN THE GERMAN STATES, 1930-31 [a]—Continued

State	Source	Basis of Distribution
Lippe	None.	. . .
Mecklenburg-Strelitz	None.	. . .
Schaumburg-Lippe	None.	. . .
City-states	None.	. . .

[a] Outdoor relief only. In some states where no special welfare aid is given, state aid is given to poor districts for general use. Data from *Einzelschriften* Nos. 6, 17, and 19, except where otherwise noted.

[b] These percentages have been changed from time to time. In addition to this aid, the state has undertaken to meet 20% of local welfare expenditures, beginning in 1932, from general revenues (*Der Städtetag*, February, 1933).

[c] Law of August 26, 1931, for 1931 only.

[d] By law of April 11, 1932, 8% of commune share of income and corporation taxes, and all of commune share of turnover tax in excess of 3.3 million RM, to equalization fund.

CHART 8

CHRONOLOGICAL SUMMARY OF GRANTS-IN-AID TO LOCAL AUTHORITIES IN ENGLAND AND WALES [a]

Date Introduced	Function	Basis of Distribution
1831	Highways	Fixed sum for repairs of Berwick bridge in compensation for transferring cost from Civil List to Berwick Corporation.
1833	Police	Expenditure for Metropolitan Police in excess of yield of 6d. rate, but not to exceed £60,000.
1835	Administration of justice	50% of cost of prosecution at Assizes and Quarter Sessions. £30,000 to cover cost of removal of prisoners to place of trial.
1839	Police	Estimated cost of duties transferred from national administration to Metropolitan Police.
1845	Welfare	50% of salaries of poor-law union medical officers. All the poor-law teachers' and industrial trainers' salaries, apportioned according to number of children and grade of certificate held by teachers. All the poor-law auditors' fees.
	Administration of justice	All the cost of prosecution. Fixed sum for maintenance of prisoners in county and borough jails.
1846	Administration of justice	All support of central criminal court.
1852	Administration of justice	All salaries of clerks of assize and clerks of the peace, substituted for abolished fees.
1854	Administration of justice	All (later 50%) the cost of juvenile offenders sent to reformatories and industrial schools by order of a magistrate. (Most of such schools were, and are, private.) Later classified as Education Grant.
1856	Police	25% of pay and clothing cost of county and borough police.
1857	Police	Sum equal to yield of 2d. rate for Metropolitan Police. (Local levy limited to 6d.)
1865	Fire	£10,000 to Metropolitan Fire Brigade.
1867	Health	Fees of public vaccinators paid in proportion to successful vaccinations.
1868	Police	Sum equal to yield of 2¼d. rate for Metropolitan Police. (Local levy limited to 6¾d.)

[a] This summary is intended to include all important grants introduced during the period covered and small grants which have continued for a long period of time. No attempt has been made to include minor grants which have been in effect for short periods only. The table has been compiled from data in H.C. 168, C. 9528, Cd. 7315, Cd. 7316, Cmd. 3157, and, for recent years, from the actual laws.

CHART 8: CHRONOLOGICAL SUMMARY OF GRANTS-IN-AID TO LOCAL AUTHORITIES IN ENGLAND AND WALES—Continued

Date Introduced	Function	Basis of Distribution
1870	Education	For elementary schools, distributed on basis of examination results (later on basis of average daily attendance). In addition, deficiency grant where yield of 3d. rate is less than £20, or less than 7s. 6d. per child.
1872	Health	50% of salaries of medical officers of health and inspectors of nuisances.
1874	Welfare	4s. per week per capita for pauper lunatics.
	Police	50% of pay and clothing cost of county and borough police.
	Not allocated	Compensation for loss of rates on government property.
1875	Health	Fixed sum per item for registration of births and deaths, amounting to 60% of cost to local government, stereotyped at 1888-89 amount.
1876	Education	Special aid to sparsely populated areas.
	Police	25% of rate charge and 25% of pay and clothing cost for Metropolitan Police.
1877	Administration of justice	All of support of prisoners.
1878	Police	Sum equal to yield of 4d. rate for Metropolitan Police. (Local levy limited to 5d.)
1882	Highways	25% of cost of main roads.
1887	Highways	50% of cost of main roads.
1888	Not allocated	40% of probate duties and all of certain licenses paid to Local Taxation Account. Probate duties distributed to counties in proportion to discontinued grants. Licenses returned where collected. From sums thus received counties pay subordinate divisions amount of discontinued grants, set aside sum of discontinued police grant for that purpose, and presumably apply any "free balance" to road costs, and relief of rates.
	Police	Transferred to Local Taxation Account.
	Health	Transferred to Local Taxation Account.

CHART 8: CHRONOLOGICAL SUMMARY OF GRANTS-IN-AID TO LOCAL
AUTHORITIES IN ENGLAND AND WALES—Continued

Date Introduced	Function	Basis of Distribution
1888	Welfare	Transferred to Local Taxation Account, and stereotyped, except for pauper lunatic grant, at 1887-88 expenditures.
	Highways	Discontinued.
1889	Agriculture	Discretionary grants for agricultural education, fixed later (1916) by administrative regulations at 66 2/3% of operating expense and 75% of capital expenditure.
1890	Not allocated	Excess over £300,000 from surtaxes on beer and spirits distributed to counties and county boroughs in proportion to distribution of probate duties. May be used for rate reduction or technical education.
	Police	£300,000 from new assigned revenues for police pensions, half to Metropolitan Police, half to other police.
	Agriculture	Fixed sum for compensation of owners of cattle killed by government order. Later fixed at 75% of cost. (Local governments had paid entire cost and continued to be responsible for any deficit.)
1891	Education	10s. per scholar to schools that reduce fees by that amount.
1896	Not allocated	Fixed sum equal to losses from derating agricultural land 50%, returned in proportion to losses as estimated on basis of preceding year's rates.
1897	Education	In addition to 1870 deficiency grant, 4d. per child for every 1d. per £ by which rate exceeds 3d. per £ but not more than 16s. 6d. per child.
1898	Welfare	Fixed sum per inmate of homes for inebriates.
1899	Not allocated	Sum equal to 50% of rates on clerical tithes; revised 1925.
1902	Education	In place of 1897 grant, 4s. per child plus 1½d. per child for each 2d. per child by which a 1d. rate falls short of 10s. per child. Other grants continued. Residue of whisky money allocated to higher education.
1905	Unemployment	Discretionary grants for projects for unemployed.
1906	Education	Temporary aid for districts where education rate exceeds 18d. Aid equals 75% of excess.

CHART 8: CHRONOLOGICAL SUMMARY OF GRANTS-IN-AID TO LOCAL
AUTHORITIES IN ENGLAND AND WALES—Continued

Date Introduced	Function	Basis of Distribution
1908	Agriculture	Discretionary grants for small holdings and allotments.
	Not allocated	Certain licenses from Local Taxation Account transferred to county administration. Fixed sum as compensation for cost of collection.
1909	Police	Additional grants of £100,000 for special services to Metropolitan Police.
	Highways	Motor vehicle license money for Local Taxation Account limited to 1908-09 receipts and cost of collection. Discretionary grants for roads provided from remainder. Maintenance grants first fixed by administrative regulation at 50% for Class I roads and 25% for Class II roads; increased later to 60% and 50%, respectively; construction grants vary with individual projects. Discretionary grants to unclassified roads.
	Agriculture	Discretionary grants for drainage projects.
1910	Education	Fixed grant of £807,000 for higher education in place of whisky tax surplus.
1911	Health	50% of expenditures for treatment of disease.
	Not allocated	Amount of liquor licenses and customs and excises paid to Local Taxation Account limited to 1908-09 amount.
1912	Health	Discretionary grant for medical service in schools.
1913	Welfare	Fixed sum for care of mentally deficient.
1915	Health	50% of maternity and child-welfare costs.
1916	Health	75% of expenditure for venereal disease.
	Welfare	50% of expenditure for mentally deficient. Pauper lunatic grants stereotyped at 1914-15 level in London and 1915-16 level outside London.
1918	Police	50% of all net expenditure, including pensions for Metropolitan and other police.
	Education	In place of former elementary education grants: (1) 36s. per child in average daily attendance. (2) 60% of teachers' salaries. (3) 50% of special services.

CHART 8: CHRONOLOGICAL SUMMARY OF GRANTS-IN-AID TO LOCAL AUTHORITIES IN ENGLAND AND WALES—Continued

Date Introduced	Function	Basis of Distribution
1918	Education	(4) 20% of remaining expenditures. (5) From these combined the product of a 7d. rate is deducted. (6) To this enough is added to bring total to 50% of approved expenditure. (7) Special 1906 grant for highly rated areas continued. For higher education 50% of expenditure substituted for fixed grant. Additional aid for social and physical education.
	Registration of electors	50% of cost of registering voters and printing registers.
1919	Agriculture	100% of cost of county agriculture committees. Afforestation grant up to £4 per acre depending on nature of work.
	Housing	Deficit in excess of yield of 1d. rate for approved housing plans.
	Education	50% of certain expenditures of provincial museums.
1920	Health	50% of cost of port sanitary authorities; 100% of cost of examining aliens.
	Unemployment	Grants for sewers, drainage, and other improvements, for unemployment relief. Fixed at 60% of wages (1924, 75%; 1931, 50%); 50% of interest for 5 years on loans for revenue-producing schemes (1924, 15 years, 1931, 10 years, or 25% for 30 years); 65% of interest and sinking fund charges for half the period of the loan, but not more than 15 years, for non-revenue-producing schemes (1924, 75%; 1931, 25% for 30 years).
	Welfare	50% of capital costs and capitation grant for teachers for care of blind.
1921	Unemployment	50% of cost of administration of choice-of-employment schemes; discretionary grants, usually 75%, of cost of juvenile unemployment centers. (Revised 1934.)
	Health	For care of tuberculosis, 50% of approved expenditure, compensation for former insurance funds, capital grant of £180 per bed (but not to exceed 60% of cost).

CHART 8: CHRONOLOGICAL SUMMARY OF GRANTS-IN-AID TO LOCAL
AUTHORITIES IN ENGLAND AND WALES—Continued

Date Introduced	Function	Basis of Distribution
1923	Housing	£6 per house per year (reduced to £4 for houses completed after September 30, 1927); for slum clearance 50% of loan charges.
	Not allocated	Compensation for derating of agricultural land from one-half to one-fourth of value, in proportion to loss.
1924	Housing	£9 per house per year; £12 10s. in rural districts (reduced to £7 10s. and £11, respectively, for houses completed after September 30, 1927).
1925	Administration of justice	50% of cost of probation of offenders.
1926	Housing	50% of estimated loan charges for rural houses.
	Agriculture	Land drainage grants limited to 33 1/3% of cost; later increased to 50% if using labor from depressed areas. Annual losses on allotments and small holdings already acquired; 75% of losses on new acquisitions.
1929	Not allocated	Abolished Local Taxation Account. Derated agricultural property 100%; transport, manufacturing, and mining real estate 75%. Block grant equal to losses from derating and discontinued grants plus £5,000,000 distributed partly according to losses, partly according to weighted population formula.
	Police	No change.
	Education	No change.
	Health	Port sanitary authorities grant continued from national revenues; vaccination, medical officers of health, and sanitary inspectors grant transferred to county revenues; other grants discontinued, except part of maternity and child-welfare grant (for training of midwives and health visitors).
	Welfare	Discontinued.
	Highways	Grants for Class I and Class II roads continued except in London and county boroughs; others discontinued.
	Other specific functions	No change.
	Improvements	New grants for loans for public utility improvements.

CHART 8: CHRONOLOGICAL SUMMARY OF GRANTS-IN-AID TO LOCAL
AUTHORITIES IN ENGLAND AND WALES—Continued

Date Introduced	Function	Basis of Distribution
1930	Housing	£2 5s. per annum per person displaced, for slum clearance.
1931	Education	Elementary: (1) 45s. per child in average daily attendance; (2) 50% of teachers' salaries; (3), (4), and (5), same; (6) abolished; (7) increased.
	Housing	Additional rural housing subsidy. Amount discretionary.
1933	Housing	50% of losses on guarantees to private building associations for approved projects. No further commitments under 1924 act.
	Welfare	For counties and county boroughs where relief expenditures exceed yield of 2s. rate, that proportion of £440,000 that excess bears to total excess, but not to exceed yield of 1s. rate.
1934	Welfare	National government assumes entire cost of support of able-bodied subject to contributions from local authorities fixed at 60% of their 1932-33 expenditures for this purpose.
1935	Improvements	Discretionary grants up to £1,000,000 for rural water supply.
	Housing	For relief of overcrowding. Amount varies with cost of site. Minimum £6 per flat.
1936	Education	50% of approved expenditure for building.

TABLE 30

TAX REVENUES ADMINISTERED BY REICH, STATE, AND LOCAL UNITS,
1913-14 AND 1925-26 TO 1934-35 [a]

Year beginning April 1	FOR ALL UNITS		FOR REICH		FOR STATE AND LOCAL	
	By Reich	By State and Local Units	By Reich	By State and Local Units	By Reich	By State and Local Units
Million Reichsmarks						
1913..................	...	4,046	...	1,631	...	2,415
1925..................	7,372	3,206	4,731	...	2,640	3,206
1926..................	8,011	3,668	5,312	...	2,698	3,668
1927..................	9,468	4,077	6,357	...	3,111	4,077
1928..................	10,065	4,231	6,568	...	3,497	4,231
1929..................	10,055	4,269	6,686	...	3,369	4,269
1930..................	9,028	4,454	5,978	...	3,050	4,454
1931..................	8,021	4,165	5,774	...	2,247	4,165
1932..................	6,803	3,559	5,138	...	1,665	3,559
1933..................	6,846	3,735	5,042	...	1,804	3,735
1934..................	8,223	3,611	5,862	...	2,361	3,611
Percentage Distribution						
1913..................	...	100.0	...	100.0	...	100.0
1925..................	69.7	30.3	100.0	...	45.2	54.8
1926..................	68.5	31.5	100.0	...	42.4	57.6
1927..................	69.9	30.1	100.0	...	43.3	56.7
1928..................	70.4	29.6	100.0	...	45.3	54.7
1929..................	70.2	29.8	100.0	...	44.1	55.9
1930..................	67.0	33.0	100.0	...	40.6	59.4
1931..................	65.8	34.2	100.0	...	35.1	64.9
1932..................	65.7	34.3	100.0	...	31.9	68.1
1933..................	64.7	35.3	100.0	...	32.6	67.4
1934..................	69.5	30.5	100.0	...	39.5	60.5

[a] Data compiled from publications of *Statistisches Reichsamt*.

TABLE 31

DISTRIBUTION OF SHARED TAXES AMONG REICH, STATE, AND LOCAL GOVERNMENTS, 1925-26 TO 1934-35

Taxes	1925-26	1926-27	1927-28	1928-29	1929-30	1930-31	1931-32	1932-33	1933-34	1934-35
All Units of Government										
Total	4,337.4	4,068.9	4,891.0	5,518.7	5,408.4	4,994.8	4,303.7	3,498.2	3,583.0	4,666.9
Income and corporation [a]	2,458.1	2,636.1	3,275.2	3,722.4	3,579.6	3,170.0	2,635.1	1,580.1	1,520.7	2,061.0
Turnover	1,403.3	882.5	878.8	1,002.4	1,023.7	1,002.5	985.2	1,337.7	1,516.2	1,872.5
Land purchase	90.5	91.4	124.4	119.0	110.5	83.0	71.2	59.9	51.7	62.8
Beer	256.0	240.8	360.2	396.7	411.8	457.9	366.3	314.4	242.1	267.6
Motor vehicle	58.0	104.6	156.2	177.1	204.5	203.5	186.8	165.3	211.6	145.4
Betting	31.4	30.6	34.2	32.3	33.2	30.1	27.2	23.1	23.9	25.9
Merger	40.1	82.9	62.0	68.8	45.1	32.8	19.4	17.4	16.6	28.9
Mineral water	...	...	...	...	...	15.0	12.5	0.3	0.2	202.8 [b]
Reich										
Total	1,697.3	1,378.3	1,779.7	2,021.6	2,038.9	1,944.2	2,056.1	1,800.1	1,778.7	2,320.1
Income and corporation	418.0	645.0	799.6	911.6	927.5	873.4	1,075.0	613.6	510.4	723.6
Turnover	1,003.5	425.8	614.4	700.1	709.2	697.4	707.9	936.5	1,082.0	1,318.3
Land purchase	1.2	1.1	1.5	1.5	1.4	1.2	0.9	0.7	0.7	0.8
Beer	231.0	218.1	301.0	337.5	352.4	335.0	247.6	225.7	159.5	177.3
Motor vehicle	2.3	4.2	6.2	7.3	8.4	8.4	7.7	6.6	9.3	51.3
Betting	1.2	1.2	1.3	1.3	1.3	1.2	1.1	0.9	1.0	1.1
Merger	40.1	82.9	55.7	62.3	38.7	27.0	15.5	15.8	15.6	28.4
Mineral water	...	...	...	...	...	0.6	0.5	0.3	0.2	19.3 [b]
State										
Total	1,269.6	1,298.6	1,491.7	1,667.4	1,600.8	1,483.7	1,129.8	849.8	853.8	1,257.4
Income and corporation	1,007.6	988.0	1,211.6	1,368.6	1,292.3	1,136.1	801.1	506.7	491.6	655.0
Turnover	177.4	219.3	133.3	151.0	153.8	150.3	148.6	201.8	214.1	269.6
Land purchase	12.6	11.7	15.9	15.6	14.8	12.4	9.4	8.6	9.0	33.7
Beer	25.0	22.7	59.2	59.2	59.4	109.5	102.3	75.3	70.5	77.0
Motor vehicle	18.8	29.6	41.2	44.1	49.9	48.0	45.0	36.6	47.3	21.5
Betting	28.2	27.3	30.5	28.9	29.2	26.5	23.9	20.8	21.3	23.3
Merger	...	...	...	...	1.4	0.9	-0.5	...	...	177.3 [b]

Local

Total	1,244.4	1,267.7	1,477.1	1,649.8	1,594.9	1,412.6	1,009.4	772.7	869.5	981.1
Income and corporation	924.5	899.7	1,139.3	1,280.8	1,205.9	1,026.9	670.2	404.6	460.8	605.4
Turnover	211.3	224.1	123.3	142.3	151.4	145.0	119.0	185.5	205.0	266.2
Land purchase	72.5	74.9	102.4	98.0	90.7	66.4	58.8	49.6	40.5	26.1
Beer and mineral water	...	...	...	...	...	26.0	26.6	12.4	11.0	12.1
Motor vehicle	36.1	69.0	106.1	122.5	142.6	143.5	130.6	119.0	151.2	70.8
Merger	...	...	6.0	6.2	4.3	4.8	4.2	1.6	1.0	0.5

Hanseatic Cities

Total	126.1	124.3	142.5	179.9	173.8	154.3	108.3	75.6	81.0	108.3
Income and corporation	108.0	103.4	124.7	161.4	153.9	133.6	88.8	55.2	57.9	77.0
Turnover	11.1	13.3	7.8	9.0	9.3	9.8	9.7	13.9	15.1	18.4
Land purchase	4.2	3.7	4.6	3.9	3.6	3.0	2.1	1.0	1.5	2.2
Beer and mineral water	0.8	...	...	...	...	1.8	1.8	1.0	1.1	1.2
Motor vehicle	...	1.8	2.7	3.2	3.6	3.6	3.5	3.1	3.8	1.8
Betting	2.0	2.1	2.4	2.1	2.7	2.4	2.2	1.4	1.6	1.5
Merger	...	...	0.3	0.3	0.7	0.1	0.2	...	...	6.2 b

a Including special levies not shared with state and local governments from 1931-32 on. b Meat tax.

TABLE 32

AMOUNT OF REICH REVENUE RETURNED TO STATES WHERE COLLECTED COMPARED WITH AMOUNT DISTRIBUTED ON OTHER BASES, 1925-26 TO 1934-35 [a]

Fiscal Year Beginning April 1	MILLIONS OF REICHSMARKS RETURNED						PERCENTAGE RETURNED	
	Total	Where Collected [b]	ON OTHER BASES				Where Collected	On Other Bases
			Total	Shared Taxes [c]	Grants [d]	Guarantees [e]		
1925......	2,928	2,395	533	238	250	45	81.7	18.3
1926......	3,191	2,272	919	429	296	194	71.2	28.8
1927......	3,344	2,560	784	536	232	16	76.6	23.4
1928......	3,775	2,938	837	541	278	18	77.8	22.2
1929......	3,624	2,765	859	564	254	41	76.4	23.6
1930......	3,343	2,450	893	562	293	38	73.3	26.7
1931......	2,925	1,753	1,172	540	615	17	59.9	40.1
1932......	2,675	1,245	1,430	395	1,010	25	46.5	53.5
1933......	2,752	1,321	1,431	483	932	16	52.0	48.0
1934......	2,975	1,887	1,088	475	597	16	63.4	36.6

[a] Data compiled from publications of *Statistisches Reichsamt*.

[b] All income and corporation taxes after deducting guarantees; 1/3 of turnover tax; all land purchase tax and beer tax; 1/2 the betting tax; 1/4 of motor vehicle tax from 1926-27 on.

[c] 2/3 of turnover tax; all the motor vehicle tax until 1926-27 and 3/4 beginning 1926-27; all the merger tax; 1/2 the betting tax.

[d] Includes 36.8 million RM turnover tax guarantee and 187.3 turnover tax guarantee for 1925 and 1926, respectively. The remainder is for the per capita guarantee which comes from the Reich share of the income and corporation taxes.

[e] Prior to 1931 most of this was for police subventions. In 1931 and 1932 this includes welfare subventions of 233.8 million RM and 705.1 million RM for unemployed supported by communes. The police subvention is distributed per capita. The subvention for unemployed is distributed on the basis of population weighted for the size of the commune and the percentage of unemployment. Indemnities for the reduction of real estate and beer taxes are also included in this item from 1930 on.

TABLE 33

AMOUNT OF REICH TAXES REDISTRIBUTED BY STATES TO LOCAL GOVERNMENTS, AND EXTENT TO WHICH THEY WERE RETURNED ON BASIS OF COLLECTIONS, 1931-32 [a]

State	Amount of Reich Taxes Received (In millions of reichsmarks)	Amount of Reich Taxes Redistributed (In millions of reichsmarks)	Percentage Redistributed	Amount Distributed Where Collected (In millions of reichsmarks)	Percentage Distributed Where Collected
Prussia	1,336.2	718.8	53.8	290.1	40.4
Bavaria	273.1 [b]	77.4 [b]	28.4	43.3	55.9
Saxony	205.0 [b]	106.2 [b]	51.8	47.8	45.0
Württemberg	100.2 [b]	35.4 [b]	35.3	17.4	49.1
Baden	76.0	23.1	30.4	7.1	30.7
Thuringia	46.6	16.3	35.0	1.2	7.4
Hesse	40.6 [b]	15.8 [b]	38.9	4.9	31.0
Mecklenburg-Schwerin	23.3 [b]	5.7 [b]	24.4	...	...
Oldenburg	16.9 [b]	9.3 [b]	55.0	4.4	47.3
Brunswick	16.2	6.3	38.9	1.0	84.1
Anhalt	12.1 [b]	5.3 [b]	43.8	3.0	56.6
Lippe	4.7 [b]	1.9 [b]	40.4	0.7	36.8
Mecklenburg-Strelitz	3.1	0.7	23.9	0.6	86.7
Schaumburg-Lippe	1.4	0.4	27.6	0.2	55.0
Total	2,155.5	1,022.7	47.4	421.8	40.9

[a] Compiled from *Statistik des deutschen Reichs*, Vol. CDXL.

[b] Includes equalization funds in so far as these are specifically from Reich taxes. It is not always possible to determine the exact amount of equalization funds obtained from Reich taxes, but since these funds are largely from this source it is believed that a more accurate picture of these tax distributions can be obtained by including these funds even though the estimate introduces a small margin of error.

TABLE 34

PERCENTAGE DISTRIBUTION OF NET EXPENDITURES AND TAX REVE-
NUES AVAILABLE FOR REICH, STATE, AND LOCAL GOVERNMENTS,
1913-14 AND 1925-26 TO 1934-35 [a]

Year Beginning April 1	NET EXPENDITURE					TAX REVENUES AVAILABLE				
	Total	Reich	State	Local	Hanseatic Cities	Total	Reich	State	Local	Hanseatic Cities
1913...............	100.0	39.9	23.5	33.2	3.4	100.0	40.3	19.3	37.1	3.2
1925...............	100.0	41.0	23.3	33.0	2.7	100.0	44.7	22.7	30.3	2.3
1926...............	100.0	44.5	21.1	31.9	2.5	100.0	45.5	21.4	30.7	2.4
1927...............	100.0	45.7	20.4	31.2	2.7	100.0	46.2	20.9	30.3	2.6
1928...............	100.0	47.7	19.3	30.4	2.6	100.0	45.9	20.5	30.8	2.8
1929...............	100.0	45.4	19.5	32.3	2.8	100.0	46.8	20.0	30.7	2.7
1930...............	100.0	46.3	18.6	32.2	2.8	100.0	44.3	20.8	32.1	2.7
1931...............	100.0	45.0	18.9	33.3	2.8	100.0	47.3	19.9	30.2	2.6
1932...............	100.0	45.6	18.8	32.8	2.8	100.0	49.6	19.9	28.3	2.2
1933...............	100.0	No data published				100.0	47.6	19.7	30.4	2.3
1934...............	100.0	No data published				100.0	48.2	18.8	30.8	2.2

[a] Computed from data in publications of *Statistisches Reichsamt.*

TABLE 35

TAX REVENUES FOR STATE AND LOCAL USE ADMINISTERED BY REICH, STATE, AND LOCAL GOVERNMENTS, RESPECTIVELY, 1913-14 AND 1925-26 TO 1934-35 [a]

Year Beginning April 1	FOR STATES		FOR LOCAL UNITS		FOR HANSEATIC CITIES	
	By Reich	By State and Local Governments	By Reich	By State and Local Governments	By Reich	By State and Local Governments
Millions of Reichsmarks						
1913.............	...	782	...	1,503	...	131
1925.............	1,270	1,126	1,244	1,960	126	120
1926.............	1,306	1,194	1,268	2,316	124	157
1927.............	1,492	1,262	1,477	2,613	142	202
1928.............	1,667	1,270	1,650	2,747	180	215
1929.............	1,601	1,260	1,595	2,795	174	214
1930.............	1,484	1,321	1,412	2,921	154	211
1931.............	1,130	1,297	1,009	2,672	108	195
1932.............	850	1,200	740	2,199	75	160
1933.............	854	1,230	869	2,346	81	159
1934.............	1,257	1,030	981	2,762	108	156
Percentage Distribution						
1913.............	...	100.0	...	100.0	...	100.0
1925.............	53.0	47.0	38.8	61.2	51.3	48.7
1926.............	52.5	47.5	35.5	64.5	44.2	55.8
1927.............	54.2	45.8	36.2	63.8	41.5	58.5
1928.............	56.8	43.2	37.5	62.5	45.5	54.5
1929.............	56.0	44.0	36.2	63.8	45.0	55.0
1930.............	52.9	47.1	32.5	67.5	42.4	57.6
1931.............	46.5	53.5	27.5	72.5	35.7	64.3
1932.............	41.5	58.5	25.1	74.9	31.9	68.1
1933.............	41.0	59.0	27.0	73.0	33.8	66.2
1934.............	55.0	45.0	26.4	73.6	40.9	59.1

[a] Data compiled from publications of *Statistisches Reichsamt.*

TABLE 36

COMPARISON OF EXPENDITURES, TAXES, AND TAX RATES IN TWELVE GERMAN CITIES [a]

	MEDIAN		GROUP A									GROUP B		
	Group A	Group B	Cologne	Frankfurt-am-Main	Düsseldorf	Stuttgart	Münster	Potsdam	Breslau	Duisburg-Hamborn	Gelsenkirchen	Hindenburg	Herne	Offenbach
Population, 1933 (thousands)	...	...	750	555	499	403	122	74	625	440	332	130	99	81
Per capita yield of income and corporation taxes 1932-33 [b] (reichsmarks)	110.5	57	94	127	115	133	78	106	68	72	45	34	46	83
School children per 1,000 inhabitants, 1932-33	129	179	146	128	130	124	140	116	128	175	189	184	183	136
Number of persons receiving out-door relief per 1,000 inhabitants, March 31, 1933	81	142	91	91	80	82	52	73	143	140	115	83	155	171
Index of need, 1932 [h]	54	170	76	52	54	47	72	54	123	133	206	233	224	109
Net expenditures per capita (reichsmarks): [c] 1928-29	149	104	152	176	151	111 [d]	118	147	140	133	99	61	109	90 [d]
1932-33	115	130	134	133	119	108 [d]	90	112	135	151	110	72	125	170 [d]
Net expenditures per capita for other purposes than welfare, 1932-33 (reichsmarks)	69	92	76	72	67	55	52	71	92	112	79	55	96	120
Net welfare expenditures per capita, 1932-33 (reichsmarks) [c]	52	35	58	61	52	53	38	41	43	39	31	17	29	50
Percent of net expenditures for welfare, 1932-33	43	27	43	46	44	49	42	36	32	26	28	24	23	30
Total welfare expenditures per capita, 1932-33 (reichsmarks)	68	91	72	78	64	71	46	56	93	88	67	40	97	122

	41	30	43	46	44	46	72	83	74	80	79	80	43	79
Percent of total welfare expenditures met from local taxes and surpluses[c]	41	30	43	46	44	46	72	83	74	80	79	80	43	79
Tax rates on land:[e]														
1928-29	ʲ	200	250	205	200[i]	225	150	150	ʲ	195	200	250	205	195
1932-33	ʲ	400	500	375	300	500	224	300	ʲ	225	265	325	400	265
Tax rates on business:[g]														
1928-29	ʲ	600	750	600	650[i]	490	400	400	ʲ	430	400	525	600	400
1932-33	ʲ	640	390[i]	600	540	459[i]	500	540	ʲ	455	540	540	540	540
Reich tax distributions per capita (reichsmarks):														
1928-29	40	25	24	32	30	31	34	26	34	33	48	33	30	34
1932-33	15	9	9	13	11	9	8	6	13	9	8	9	10	8
Percent of net expenditures covered by Reich tax distributions:														
1928-29	43.4	23.0	40.2	31.9	22.2	22.3	23.1	21.7	30.6	21.5	26.9	21.1	27.4	22.4
1932-33	8.6	7.2	12.3	11.6	7.0	6.7	7.2	7.1	11.8	7.6	6.2	6.5	7.9	7.1
Per capita local taxes, 1932-33 (reichsmarks)[f]	41	33	25	31	38	64	35	45	55	55	69	58	35	55

[a] Data largely from *Statistisches Jahrbuch der deutschen Gemeinden*; supplemented by *Statistisches Jahrbuch für das deutsche Reich*; *Statistik des deutschen Reichs*, 387; and unpublished data from *Statistisches Reichsamt*.

[b] 1932 yield on base fixed in 1931.

[c] That part of the expenditures falling on tax resources including Reich tax distributions and surpluses from industries.

[d] The net expenditures of Stuttgart and Offenbach are not strictly comparable with the Prussian cities since the division of support of schools and other functions between state and local governments differs in the different states.

[e] On improved land.

[f] Rate not comparable with Prussian cities.

[g] On yield.

[h] Calculated by finding ratio of school children per 1,000 and persons receiving public relief per 1,000 to average proportion of these two relatives and dividing the resulting relative for such city by the relative of ability obtained by taking the ratio of income and corporation taxes per capita for each city to the average per capita taxes. Thus a city with 10% more than the average of relief cases and school children and 10% more than the average of tax yields would rate 100, whereas the city with 10% more than the average of relief cases and school children and 10% less than the average of tax yields would rate 122.

[i] For Duisburg. Rates for Hamborn, which was combined with Duisburg between 1928 and 1932, were 250% for the land tax and 625% for business.

[j] Reduced by *Osthilfe* from 540% in the case of Breslau and from 600% in the case of Hindenburg.

TABLE 37

EXPENDITURES OF REICH, STATE, AND LOCAL GOVERNMENTS FOR SELECTED YEARS, 1913-14 TO 1932-33 [a]

IN MILLIONS OF REICHSMARKS

	1913-14	1925-26	1928-29	1930-31	1931-32	1932-33
All governments						
Total.....................	5,437	11,728	16,968	17,060	14,358	12,358
Military.................	1,738	625	809	739	686	701
Domestic war burden......	41	1,968	2,304	1,970	1,789	1,540
Reparations..............	...	750	2,178	1,812	556	176
Police...................	199	665	803	781	705	674
Education................	1,046	1,933	2,577	2,550	2,093	1,885
Welfare..................	420	1,913	2,735	3,758	3,942	3,715
Housing.................	1	757	977	859	363	154
Highways................	469	837	1,067	1,059	868	691
Debt service [b]...........	470	193	810	713	873	670
Other...................	1,053	2,087	2,708	2,818	2,483	2,152
Reich						
Total.....................	2,170	4,806	8,099	7,903	6,463	5,559
Military.................	1,738	625	809	739	686	701
Domestic war burden......	41	1,968	2,304	1,970	1,789	1,540
Reparations..............	...	750	2,178	1,812	556	176
Police...................	...	194	204	197	192	192
Education................	4	26	37	33	27	24
Welfare..................	55	453	976	1,546	1,669	1,496
Housing.................	−1	20	21	87	8	61
Highways................	48	158	192	183	166	148
Debt service [b]...........	218	111	612	531	538	490
Other...................	67	501	766	805	832	731
State						
Total.....................	1,280	2,733	3,271	3,182	2,717	2,306
Police...................	88	267	351	307	261	254
Education................	404	1,029	1,310	1,346	1,139	1,082
Welfare..................	51	292	189	163	136	119
Housing.................	[c]	240	263	181	131	39
Highways................	79	95	119	110	90	76
Debt service [b]...........	153	26	103	139	162	133
Other...................	505	784	936	936	798	603
Local						
Total.....................	1,804	3,876	5,158	5,497	4,782	4,150
Police...................	97	177	214	241	223	202
Education................	599	806	1,133	1,070	850	714
Welfare..................	290	1,090	1,471	1,923	2,006	1,960
Housing.................	2	450	627	533	201	52
Highways................	319	547	712	718	585	451
Debt service [b]...........	50	49	59	...	121	...
Other...................	447	757	942	1,012	796	771
Hanseatic cities						
Total.....................	183	314	441	478	396	343
Police...................	14	27	34	35	29	26
Education................	38	71	98	102	77	65
Welfare..................	24	79	99	125	131	141
Housing.................	[c]	46	66	57	23	2
Highways................	23	36	43	47	27	16
Debt service [b]...........	48	7	36	43	52	46
Other...................	36	48	65	69	57	47

[a] Net expenditures, to be met from taxes and surplus earning of industry. Expenditures from grants-in-aid are credited to the jurisdiction making the grant; expenditures from shared taxes are credited to the jurisdiction making the expenditure. Data from *Statistisches Jahrbuch für das deutsche Reich* and *Einzelschriften* 10 and 20 and *Statistik des deutschen Reichs*, Vol. CDXL.

[b] Includes total debt service for Reich and states and Hanseatic cities, but only that part of the debt service of local governments which cannot be assigned to specific functions.

[c] Less than one-half million marks.

TABLE 38

EXPENDITURES OF REICH, STATE, AND LOCAL GOVERNMENTS FOR
SELECTED YEARS, 1913-14 TO 1932-33

PERCENTAGE DISTRIBUTION ACCORDING TO FUNCTIONS

	All Governments	Reich	State Governments	Local Governments	Hanseatic Cities
1913-14					
Total..................	100.0	100.0	100.0	100.0	100.0
Military............	31.9	80.0	...	...	...
Domestic war burden.	0.8	1.9	...	...	...
Reparations.........	...	...	...	...	...
Police..............	3.7	...	6.9	5.4	7.7
Education..........	19.3	0.2	31.6	33.2	20.8
Welfare.............	7.7	2.5	4.0	16.1	13.1
Housing............	0.3	—0.6	...	0.1	...
Highways...........	8.6	2.2	6.2	17.7	12.6
Debt service........	8.6	10.0	12.0	2.8	26.2
Other..............	19.1	3.8	39.5	24.8	19.7
1925-26					
Total..................	100.0	100.0	100.0	100.0	100.0
Military............	5.3	13.0	...	...	...
Domestic war burden.	16.8	41.0	...	...	...
Reparations.........	6.4	15.6	...	...	...
Police..............	5.7	4.1	9.8	4.6	8.6
Education..........	16.5	0.5	37.6	20.8	22.6
Welfare.............	16.4	9.4	10.7	28.1	25.1
Housing............	6.5	0.4	8.8	11.6	14.6
Highways...........	7.2	3.3	3.5	14.1	11.6
Debt service........	1.6	2.3	0.9	1.3	2.3
Other..............	17.8	10.4	28.7	19.5	15.3
1928-29					
Total..................	100.0	100.0	100.0	100.0	100.0
Military............	4.8	10.0	...	...	...
Domestic war burden.	13.6	28.5	...	...	...
Reparations.........	12.8	26.8	...	...	...
Police..............	4.7	2.5	10.7	4.1	7.8
Education..........	15.1	0.5	40.0	22.0	22.2
Welfare.............	16.1	12.0	5.8	28.5	22.4
Housing............	5.7	0.3	8.1	12.3	14.9
Highways...........	6.3	2.4	3.6	13.8	9.9
Debt service........	4.8	7.6	3.2	1.1	8.1
Other..............	16.0	9.4	28.6	18.2	14.7
1930-31					
Total..................	100.0	100.0	100.0	100.0	100.0
Military............	4.3	9.4	...	...	...
Domestic war burden.	11.6	25.0	...	...	...
Reparations.........	10.6	22.9	...	...	...
Police..............	4.6	2.5	9.7	4.4	7.3
Education..........	15.0	0.4	42.3	19.5	21.3
Welfare.............	22.1	19.6	5.1	35.0	26.2
Housing............	5.0	1.1	5.7	9.7	11.9
Highways...........	6.2	2.3	3.5	13.1	9.9
Debt service........	4.2	6.7	4.4	...	9.0
Other..............	16.5	10.2	29.4	18.4	14.4

TABLE 38: EXPENDITURES OF REICH, STATE, AND LOCAL GOVERN-
MENTS FOR SELECTED YEARS, 1913-14 TO 1932-33—Continued

PERCENTAGE DISTRIBUTION ACCORDING TO FUNCTIONS

	All Governments	Reich	State Governments	Local Governments	Hanseatic Cities
1931-32					
Total.................	100.0	100.0	100.0	100.0	100.0
Military.............	4.8	10.6	...	...	...
Domestic war burden.	12.5	27.6	...	...	...
Reparations.........	3.9	8.5	...	...	...
Police..............	4.9	2.9	9.6	4.7	7.2
Education..........	14.6	0.4	41.8	17.8	19.5
Welfare.............	27.5	25.8	5.0	42.0	33.1
Housing............	2.5	0.1	4.8	4.2	5.7
Highways...........	6.0	2.6	3.3	12.2	6.9
Debt service........	6.1	8.3	6.0	2.5	13.1
Other..............	17.3	12.9	29.4	16.6	14.4
1932-33					
Total.................	100.0	100.0	100.0	100.0	100.0
Military.............	5.7	12.6	...	...	...
Domestic war burden.	12.5	27.7	...	...	...
Reparations.........	1.4	3.2	...	...	...
Police..............	5.5	3.5	11.0	4.9	7.6
Education..........	15.3	0.4	46.9	17.2	19.0
Welfare.............	30.1	26.9	5.2	47.2	41.1
Housing............	1.2	1.1	1.7	1.3	0.6
Highways...........	5.6	2.7	3.3	10.9	4.7
Debt service........	5.4	8.8	5.8	...	13.4
Other..............	17.4	13.1	26.1	18.6	13.7

TABLE 39

EXPENDITURES OF REICH, STATE, AND LOCAL GOVERNMENTS FOR
SELECTED YEARS, 1913-14 TO 1932-33

PERCENTAGE DISTRIBUTION ACCORDING TO JURISDICTIONS

	All Governments	Reich	State Governments	Local Governments	Hanseatic Cities
1913-14					
Total.................	100.0	39.9	23.6	33.2	3.4
Military.............	100.0	100.0	...	...	...
Domestic war burden.	100.0	100.0	...	...	...
Reparations.........	100.0	100.0	...	...	...
Police..............	100.0	...	44.2	48.6	7.2
Education..........	100.0	0.4	38.7	57.3	3.6
Welfare.............	100.0	13.1	12.1	69.0	5.8
Housing.............	100.0	−100.0	14.3	178.6	7.1
Highways...........	100.0	10.3	16.9	68.0	4.9
Debt service.......	100.0	46.3	32.7	10.7	10.3
1925-26					
Total.................	100.0	41.0	23.3	33.0	2.7
Military.............	100.0	100.0	...	...	...
Domestic war burden.	100.0	100.0	...	...	...
Reparations.........	100.0	100.0	...	...	...
Police..............	100.0	29.2	40.2	26.6	4.1
Education..........	100.0	1.4	53.3	41.7	3.7
Welfare.............	100.0	23.7	15.3	56.9	4.1
Housing.............	100.0	2.7	31.8	59.5	6.1
Highways...........	100.0	18.9	11.3	65.5	4.3
Debt service.......	100.0	57.4	13.2	25.6	3.8
1928-29					
Total.................	100.0	47.7	19.3	30.4	2.6
Military.............	100.0	100.0	...	...	...
Domestic war burden.	100.0	100.0	...	...	...
Reparations.........	100.0	100.0	...	...	...
Police..............	100.0	25.4	43.6	26.6	4.3
Education..........	100.0	1.4	51.0	43.8	3.8
Welfare.............	100.0	35.7	6.9	53.8	3.6
Housing.............	100.0	2.1	26.9	64.2	6.8
Highways...........	100.0	18.0	11.1	66.8	4.1
Debt service.......	100.0	75.5	12.8	7.3	4.4
1930-31					
Total.................	100.0	46.3	18.6	32.2	2.8
Military.............	100.0	100.0	...	...	...
Domestic war burden.	100.0	100.0	...	...	...
Reparations.........	100.0	100.0	...	...	...
Police..............	100.0	25.3	39.4	30.9	4.4
Education..........	100.0	1.3	52.7	42.0	4.0
Welfare.............	100.0	41.2	4.3	51.2	3.3
Housing.............	100.0	10.2	21.1	62.1	6.6
Highways...........	100.0	17.3	10.4	67.8	4.5
Debt service.......	100.0	74.5	19.5	...	6.0

Table 39: EXPENDITURES OF REICH, STATE, AND LOCAL GOVERN-
MENTS FOR SELECTED YEARS, 1913-14 TO 1932-33—Continued

PERCENTAGE DISTRIBUTION ACCORDING TO JURISDICTIONS

	All Governments	Reich	State Governments	Local Governments	Hanseatic Cities
1931-32					
Total.................	100.0	45.1	18.9	3.33	2.8
Military.............	100.0	100.0	...	...	...
Domestic war burden.	100.0	100.0	...	...	...
Reparations.........	100.0	100.0	...	...	...
Police..............	100.0	27.2	37.0	31.7	4.1
Education...........	100.0	1.3	54.4	40.7	3.7
Welfare.............	100.0	42.4	3.3	50.9	3.3
Housing.............	100.0	2.3	36.2	55.3	6.3
Highways............	100.0	19.2	10.3	67.4	3.2
Debt service........	100.0	61.7	18.6	13.9	5.9
1932-33					
Total.................	100.0	45.0	18.7	33.6	2.8
Military.............	100.0	100.0	...	...	...
Domestic war burden.	100.0	100.0	...	...	...
Reparations.........	100.0	100.0	...	...	...
Police..............	100.0	28.5	37.7	30.0	3.9
Education...........	100.0	1.3	57.4	37.9	3.4
Welfare.............	100.0	40.3	3.2	52.8	3.8
Housing.............	100.0	39.6	25.3	33.8	1.3
Highways............	100.0	21.4	11.0	65.3	2.3
Debt service........	100.0	73.1	19.9	...	6.9

TABLE 40

DIVISION OF SUPPORT OF ORTSPOLIZEI BETWEEN STATE AND LOCAL GOVERNMENTS, 1931-32 [a]

PERCENTAGE

State	STATE ORTSPOLIZEI		LOCAL ORTSPOLIZEI	
	State Support	Local Support	State Support	Local Support
Prussia...................	66 2/3	33 1/3	66 2/3	33 1/3
Bavaria...................	50 [b]	50	...	100
Saxony...................	60	40	...	100
Württemberg..............	c	c	...	100
Baden....................	40	60	...	100
Hesse....................	d	d	e	e
Mecklenburg-Schwerin......	100	...	...	100
Oldenburg................	100	...	...	100
Brunswick................	f	f	...	100
Anhalt...................	100	...	...	100
Lippe [g].................	33 1/3	66 2/3	...	100
Mecklenburg-Strelitz......	...	...	...	100
Schaumburg-Lippe.........	100	...	...	100
Hamburg.................	100	...	...	...
Bremen..................	100 [h]	h	...	100 [i]
Lübeck..................	100	...	...	...

[a] In Thuringia the security police are *Landespolizei*. Hence this state has been omitted.

[b] State pays all in *ausmarkischen Bezirken*.

[c] Local government makes contribution in proportion to population. Per capita levy varies with city and is fixed by law.

[d] Local government makes contribution of 1,200 marks per officer.

[e] In certain cities in occupied territory state makes same contribution as to state police.

[f] Only city with state police, Brunswick, makes a special contribution.

[g] The state has since taken over all police in Lippe, December 21, 1933, but the communes still contribute the largest part of their support. By law of March 31, 1935, communes and circles meet all the salaries and 75% of other costs for the *Schutzpolizei* and a smaller part of the cost of other police.

[h] In Bremen 100%. Bremerhaven makes a special contribution.

[i] Administration police only.

TABLE 41

PERCENTAGE OF NET STATE AND LOCAL EXPENDITURES FOR DIFFERENT FUNCTIONS MET BY GERMAN STATE GOVERNMENTS, 1931-32 [a]

State	Education [b]	Police	Highways	Welfare	Housing	All Functions
Prussia................	50.0	54.7	0.4	4.0	27.4	30.9
Bavaria...............	78.4	59.6	21.1	10.8	7.3	51.1
Saxony...............	60.8	45.3	31.4	7.5	92.8	42.3
Württemberg..........	58.8	43.3	31.1	18.4	64.8	42.5
Baden................	69.4	52.7	30.5	14.5	100.0	41.5
Thuringia.............	63.1	42.3	40.2	13.8	26.9	51.4
Hesse.................	79.8	55.5	8.4	16.3	57.5	42.6
Mecklenburg-Schwerin...	81.7	54.7	53.1	17.0	0.5	54.3
Oldenburg.............	43.7	69.0	26.1	5.8	8.2	36.5
Brunswick.............	79.1	69.6	31.5	8.7	61.6	51.3
Anhalt................	82.8	30.2	2.1	12.8	77.8	45.9
Lippe.................	91.8	39.9	26.6	9.2	66.1	53.8
Mecklenburg-Strelitz....	94.5	61.5	79.9	29.2	...	65.8
Schaumburg-Lippe......	41.5	55.9	37.3	11.1	0.1	42.0
Hamburg..............	98.4	99.9	88.7	97.9	96.7	97.9
Bremen...............	93.2	98.6	78.6	91.8	97.7	95.8
Lübeck................	100.0	100.0	96.8	99.6	100.0	99.6
All states [c]...........	57.3	53.8	10.5	35.7	39.6	36.2

[a] *Statistik des deutschen Reichs*, Vol. CDXL.
[b] Excluding church.
[c] Excluding city-states.

TABLE 42

AMOUNT OF GRANTS COMPARED WITH AMOUNT OF NATIONAL AND LOCAL TAX INCOME FOR SPECIFIED YEARS FROM 1842-43 TO 1933-34 [a]

Year	UNITED KINGDOM			ENGLAND AND WALES		
	MILLIONS OF POUNDS		Percent of Tax Revenue to Grants	MILLIONS OF POUNDS		Percent of Rates and Grants From Grants
	National Tax Revenue	Grants		Local Rates and Grants	Grants	
Pre-war						
1842-43	50.2	0.6	1.3	9.1	0.2	2.7
1852-53	53.0	1.3	2.8	10.5	0.6	5.4
1872-73	65.9	2.4	3.7	19.7	1.1	5.6
1887-88	75.7	5.1	6.8	31.5	4.3	13.6
1891-92	75.3	10.9	14.5	37.3	8.8	23.6
1903-04	129.1	19.2	14.9	69.0	16.1	23.3
1913-14	163.0	27.1	16.6	94.4	23.1	24.5
Post-war						
1918-19	784.3	34.3	4.4	115.9	31.2	27.0
1919-20	999.0	56.3	5.6	155.6	50.0	32.1
1920-21	1,031.7	71.3	6.9	219.6	67.8	30.9
1921-22	856.7	88.2	10.3	249.5	78.6	31.5
1922-23	774.7	87.6	11.3	234.1	76.8	32.8
1923-24	718.1	90.7	12.6	223.2	79.9	35.8
1924-25	689.7	94.2	13.7	224.8	82.8	36.8
1925-26	684.5	97.5	14.3	234.0	85.4	36.5
1926-27	663.9	100.7	15.2	247.3	88.3	35.7
1927-28	693.4	104.5	15.1	258.1	91.4	35.4
1928-29	685.3	108.3	15.8	259.8	93.8	35.9
Local Government Act of 1929						
1929-30	676.6	125.3	18.5	270.6	114.3	42.3
1930-31	704.2	155.1	22.1	288.6	138.7	48.1
1931-32	733.0	151.4	20.7	283.8	135.5	47.9
1932-33	725.0	145.0 [b]	20.0	272.9	126.6	46.4
1933-34	709.1 [c]	147.1 [b]	20.7	279.5 [c]	131.8 [c]	47.2

[a] *Statistical Abstract of the United Kingdom.*
[b] Partly estimated.
[c] *Rates and Rateable Values,* 1933-34, and *Finance Accounts of the United Kingdom,* 1933-34.

TABLE 43

AMOUNT OF GRANTS-IN-AID FOR SPECIFIED YEARS FROM 1842-43 TO 1934-35: ENGLAND AND WALES

YEAR BEGINNING APRIL 1

Grants	1842 d	1872 d	1887 e	1891 f	1903 f	1913 g	1923 g	1928 g	1930 h	1932 h	1934 i
	Millions of Pounds										
Total	0 2	1.1	4.3	8.8	16.1	23.1	79.9	93.8	138.7	126.6	132.6
Specific.......	0.2	1.0	4.1	6.2	13.3	19.8	73.2	85.4	88.5	78.3	84.0
Police.......	0.1	0.5	1.4	2.0	2.3	2.9	8.7	10.3	10.4	10.1	10.5
Education...	...	m	1.3	2.3	8.3	14.0	38.8	41.7	43.9	38.8	39.8
Welfare.....	...	0.2	0.7	1.6	2.3	2.0	2.2	2.2	0.1	m	m
Health......	...	m	0.1	0.1	0.2	0.4	3.3	4.2	1.3	1.6	m
Highways...	...	...	0.5	...	..:.	0.6	11.0	14.3	19.2	13.6	14.1 i
Housing.....	...	...	...	...	...	...	7.4	10.7	11.9	12.7	13.8
Other.......	0.1	0.3	0.1	0.2	0.1	0.1	1.7	2.1	1.6	1.5	5.8 k
General.......	m	0.1	0.2	2.6	2.8	3.3	6.7	8.4	50.2	48.3	48.6
Government property a.	m	0.1	0.2	0.2	0.5	0.8	1.8	2.0 i	2.0 i	1.9 i	1.8 i
Agricultural derating b.	...	....	...	...	0.7	1.2	3.1	3.5	m	m	m
Free balance I. T. A.c..	...	...	...	2.4	1.6	1.3	1.8	2.9	3.1	1.4	1.4
Exchequer grant.....	...	...	...	...	...	...	...	...	45.0	45.0	45.4

Percentage Distribution

	1842	1872	1887	1891	1903	1913	1923	1928	1930	1932	1934
Specific.....	93.5	94.4	95.9	70.6	82.5	85.9	91.6	91.1	63.8	61.8	63.5
General.....	6.5	5.6	4.1	29.4	17.5	14.1	8.4	8.9	36.2	38.2	36.5

a Compensation in lieu of rates on general property.
b Under acts of 1896 and 1923, not including share allocated to specific functions.
c Includes receipts from licenses not under Local Taxation Account.
d C. 9528, op. cit., p. 24.
e H. C. 168, op. cit.
f Cd. 7316, op. cit.
g Statistical Abstract of the United Kingdom.
h Annual Local Taxation Returns.
i Finance Accounts of the United Kingdom.
j Civil Estimates.
k Grants from public works not segregated to distinguish health and other grants.
l For 1933-34.
m Less than 50,000 pounds.

TABLE 44

NET EXPENDITURES OF LOCAL GOVERNMENTS, 1928-29 AND 1932-33: ENGLAND AND WALES [a]

	TOTAL		LONDON [c]		ADMINISTRATIVE COUNTIES		COUNTY BOROUGHS		MUNICIPAL BOROUGHS		URBAN DISTRICTS		RURAL DISTRICTS		POOR-LAW UNIONS		MISCELLANEOUS UNITS	
	1928-29	1932-33	1928-29	1932-33	1928-29	1932-33	1928-29	1932-33	1928-29	1932-33	1928-29	1932-33	1928-29	1932-33	1928-29	1932-33	1928-29	1932-33
In millions of pounds																		
Total	258.0	270.0	41.6	40.2	60.7	91.6	67.2	89.0	17.1	20.7	20.4	20.4	15.8	6.6	33.0	...	2.1	1.3
Police	20.7	20.8	5.0	5.0	8.5	8.5	6.3	6.4	0.9	0.9	...	...	...	...	...	...	b	...
Education	77.8	80.4	12.7	11.8	29.3	30.7	25.9	27.6	5.9	7.0	3.9	3.3	...	...	...	...	0.1	0.1
Welfare	39.2	37.3	9.4	6.2	1.2	16.2	0.8	15.0	b	b	...	...	...	...	27.7	...	...	0.1
Housing	12.6	15.7	1.1	1.3	b	b	4.9	5.7	1.7	2.1	3.3	3.8	1.6	2.8	...	...	b	...
Highways	47.8	49.0	3.9	3.6	17.6	28.2	9.9	10.7	2.8	2.8	4.2	3.3	9.3	...	...	...	...	0.1
Other	59.8	66.7	9.5	12.4	4.1	8.0	19.3	23.6	5.8	7.9	9.0	10.0	5.0	3.7	5.3	...	2.0	1.0
Percentage to different functions																		
Total	100.0	100.0	100.0	100.0	100.0	100.0	100.0	100.0	100.0	100.0	100.0	100.0	100.0	100.0	100.0	100.0	100.0	100.0
Police	8.1	7.7	12.0	12.4	14.0	9.3	9.5	7.1	5.1	4.4	...	...	...	...	...	...	0.5	...
Education	30.2	29.8	30.6	29.3	48.2	33.5	38.6	30.9	34.4	33.8	19.0	16.0	...	...	...	...	4.9	6.8
Welfare	15.2	13.8	22.7	15.3	1.9	17.7	1.2	16.8	0.1	0.2	...	...	...	...	84.1	...	...	6.1
Housing	4.9	5.8	2.6	3.1	0.1	0.1	7.2	6.4	9.8	10.0	16.3	18.5	10.3	42.9	...	...	...	...
Highways	18.5	18.1	9.4	8.9	29.0	30.8	14.8	12.3	16.5	13.3	20.6	16.3	58.5	...	...	...	1.0	10.4
Other	23.1	24.8	22.8	30.9	6.7	8.7	28.7	26.5	34.1	38.3	44.0	49.2	31.3	57.1	16.0	...	93.6	76.7

[a] Net expenditures include all those not met from rates and grants.

[b] Less than 50,000 pounds.

[c] Including County of London, City of London, Metropolitan Boroughs, and that part of Metropolitan Police District within County of London. Remainder of police district expenditures apportioned to administrative counties and county boroughs, respectively, in proportion to rates collected in these.

TABLE 45

PERCENTAGE OF NET EXPENDITURES OF LOCAL GOVERNMENTS MET FROM GRANTS, 1928-29 AND 1932-33: ENGLAND AND WALES [a]

YEAR BEGINNING APRIL 1

	TOTAL		POLICE		EDUCATION		WELFARE		HOUSING		HIGHWAYS	
	1928	*1932*	*1928*	*1932*	*1928*	*1932*	*1928*	*1932*	*1928*	*1932*	*1928*	*1932*
Total...............	35.3	46.2	49.4	48.4	53.6	48.2	9.4	0.1	76.6	81.3	28.7	27.8
London...........	27.1	31.1	49.1	45.8	47.7	37.1	3.8	...	64.4	63.4	10.9	12.2
Administrative counties........	55.8	54.7	50.6	51.3	56.9	52.3	22.3	0.1	36.4	35.6	43.5	37.9
County boroughs..	36.5	40.3	49.1	48.2	52.9	48.0	21.4	0.2	70.8	75.7	17.0	14.7
Municipal boroughs	33.5	47.3	37.7	37.0	53.3	47.0	...	...	80.1	82.0	19.4	13.5
Urban districts....	31.7	57.0	...	...	57.0	54.3	...	...	88.7	88.7	20.4	11.9
Rural districts.....	31.4	65.9	...	...	...	...	...	...	76.4	90.9	27.4	...
Poor-law unions...	9.8	...	...	...	...	...	10.3	...	...	...	...	...
Miscellaneous districts........	47.2	23.9	100.0	...	100.0	100.0	100.0	3.7	...	...	...	77.5

[a] Grants include those for capital expenditures and those for general purposes. Compensation for losses in rates on government property is not included because the amounts received by different types of districts is not available. This accounts for the substantial difference between the totals here and those in Table 21 for the same years. The other differences are the result of a change in classification between 1928-29 and 1932-33 in the *Local Taxation Returns*. The 1928-29 figures in this table are from the *Local Taxation Returns* for that year. The 1928-29 figures in Table 21 are from an unpublished summary prepared by the Ministry of Health which conforms to the 1932-33 classification.

TABLE 46

CHANGES IN FINANCIAL POSITION OF SELECTED MUNICIPAL
BOROUGHS AND URBAN AND RURAL DISTRICTS,
1928-29 AND 1932-33: ENGLAND AND WALES [a]

	PERCENTAGE OF RATE AND GRANT EXPENDITURES FROM GRANTS		RATEABLE VALUE PER CAPITA (IN POUNDS)		RATES IN THE POUND (IN SHILLINGS)		PER CAPITA RATE AND GRANT EXPENDITURE (IN SHILLINGS)	
	1928-29	*1932-33*	*1928-29*	*1932-33*	*1928-29*	*1932-33*	*1928-29*	*1932-33*
Boroughs								
Okehampton.......	1	148	3.6	5.6	11.3	7.2	18	13
Godmanchester....	41	114	5.2	3.4	12.8	9.3	27	19
Hartlepool........	44	81	3.9	2.9	20.0	16.0	69	68
Jarrow...........	48	69	4.0	3.5	21.3	19.7	80	81
Whitehaven.......	55	66	4.3	3.9	17.3	12.7	65	69
Port Talbot.......	34	63	4.2	3.7	23.5	19.0	71	66
Montgomery......	6	51	5.8	3.6	12.5	16.3	24	27
Bexhill...........	14	41	12.5	13.8	8.2	8.3	75	78
Hove.............	20	39	11.4	15.2	10.8	8.0	82	75
Wimbledon.......	19	30	9.5	11.7	11.2	8.7	70	66
Richmond.........	16	28	10.8	13.3	11.0	8.6	82	76
Urban Districts								
Roxby-cum-Risby..	42	162	6.6	3.2	10.7	...	47	22
Billingham........	18	120	16.4	9.3	12.3	13.5	51	52
Wantage..........	55	103	4.5	5.7	8.3	7.5	23	27
Newburn..........	61	92	4.4	3.8	12.7	8.7	49	50
Rishworth........	...	82	13.9	9.5	9.0	10.5	25	27
Tilbury...........	65	66	5.1	4.4	16.4	17.3	118	130
Abertillery........	46	58	4.1	3.3	24.7	24.8	82	92
Weybridge........	9	58	12.1	12.5	10.3	6.0	49	43
Frinton-on-Sea.....	5	49	14.9	19.8	14.1	10.5	107	126
Mallwyd..........	13	48	2.8	1.7	15.9	13.0	7	28
Gellygaer.........	15	42	3 6	3.2	34.9	23.8	46	45
Bedwellty.........	17	42	5.5	3.1	23.5	24.3	44	48
Esher and the Dittons...........	4	38	12.7	13.5	11.0	8.4	52	43
Coulsdon and Purley	14	31	11.8	12.9	10.5	9.3	58	50
Sutton and Cheam.	6	30	11.2	10.8	8.3	8.8	37	41
Rural Districts								
Hastings..........	50	[b]	9.6	9.0	7.4	3.7	51	...
Llanwrthwl........	16	1,401	23.4	22.0	8.1	8.3	20	6
Stockton..........	28	294	14.2	6.8	12.4	10.3	56	8
Codnor Park and Shipley.........	40	124	13.5	5.7	6.9	7.2	21	17
Sibsey............	41	61	3.7	1.7	16.1	7.5	68	7
Tregaron..........	29	60	2.1	1.3	16.8	12.6	22	4
Sunderland........	27	59	3.6	3.1	20.8	14.6	46	28
Llantrisant........	35	53	4.4	3.1	24.0	26.3	70	44
Cardigan..........	50	47	2.9	1.9	17.8	12.8	40	10
Auckland.........	20	30	2.9	2.3	22.1	17.5	20	12

[a] Data from records of Ministry of Health.
[b] Income for special purposes exceeded total expenditures.

BIBLIOGRAPHY

BIBLIOGRAPHY[1]

General Problem of the Relation of Central and Local Finance

Adarkar, B. R., Principles and Problems of Federal Finance, London, 1933.

Grice, J. Watson, National and Local Finance, London, 1910.

Hensel, A., Finanzausgleich im Bundesstaat, Berlin, 1922.

German System

Public Documents

Reichsgesetzblatt.

Statistisches Reichsamt, Verwaltungsaufbau, Steuerverteilung und Lastenverteilung im deutschen Reich, Einzelschrift No. 6, 1929.

—— Ausgaben und Einnahmen der öffentlichen Verwaltung im deutschen Reich, 1913-14, 1925-26 und 1926-27, Die, Einzelschrift No. 10, 1930.

—— Finanzausgleich im deutschen Reich, Der, 2 Vols., Einzelschriften Nos. 16, 17, 1931.

—— Steuerverteilung und Steuereinnahmen im deutschen Reich, 1928-29 bis 1930-31, Einzelschrift No. 19, 1931.

—— Ausgaben und Einnahmen der öffentlichen Verwaltung im deutschen Reich, 1928-29, Die, Einzelschrift No. 20, 1931.

—— Kommunale Finanzwirtschaft, 1913-14 und 1925-26 bis 1928-29, Statistik des deutschen Reichs, CCCLXXXVII, 1931.

—— Ausgaben und Einnahmen der öffentlichen Verwaltung im deutschen Reich, 1931-32, Die, Statistik des deutschen Reichs, CDXL, 1934.

—— Statistisches Jahrbuch für das deutsche Reich.

—— Wirtschaft und Statistik.

[1] This bibliography is not comprehensive. Only those titles which the author has found most useful have been included. The German literature on problems of central and local finance is very extensive. More than one thousand titles were found in the course of this study. The English literature, on the contrary, is very limited and confined almost entirely to official sources. A complete bibliography of the German literature through 1930 is to be found in *Statistisches Reichsamt, Einzelschrift No. 16.*

Reichssparkommissar, Gutachten über die Staatsverwaltung des Volksstaates Hessen, 1929.
—— Gutachten über die Landesverwaltung Lippes, 1930.
—— Gutachten über die Landesverwaltung Württembergs, 1930.
—— Gutachten über die Verwaltung der Stadt Mannheim, 1933.
—— Gutachten über die Verwaltung der Stadt Stuttgart, 1932.
—— Gutachten über die Verwaltung des Kreises Iserlohn. Sonderheft der Monatszeitschrift Reich und Länder, May, 1934.
Prussia, Denkschrift des preussischen Landtags, No. 2275, 1928-29.
—— Zeitschrift des preussischen statistischen Landesamts.

General Treatises

Delpech, H., Les Aspects d'un fédéralisme financier. L'Exemple Allemand, Paris, 1933.
Gerloff, W., Finanz- und Zollpolitik des deutschen Reiches, Jena, 1913.
Gerloff, W., und Meisel, F., eds., Handbuch der Finanzwissenschaft, Tübingen, 1929, 3 Vols.
Jessen, A., Der deutsche Finanzausgleich in Theorie und Praxis. Vierteljahresschrift für Steuer- und Finanzrecht, 1932.
Kaufmann, R. von, Die Kommunalfinanzen, Leipzig, 1906.
Lichtenstein, H., Die Finanzwirtschaft der deutschen Grossstädte von 1925 bis 1931, Jena, 1933.
Mann, F. K., Deutsche Finanzwirtschaft, Jena, 1929.
Markull, W., Kommentar zum Gesetz über den Finanzausgleich, Berlin, 1923.
Most, O., und Bühler, O., Die Finanzlage der Ruhrgebietsstädte, Jena, 1931, 1932, 2 Vols.
Popitz, J., Der künftige Finanzausgleich, Berlin, 1932. This is the most comprehensive and authoritative work on the subject.
Stephan, K., Das kommunale Finanz- und Steuerrecht in Preussen, Berlin, 1926.
Suren, F. K., Preussischer Finanzausgleich, Berlin, 1927.
Wagner, A., Finanzwissenschaft, Leipzig, 1901.

Periodicals, Year Books, and Other Serial Publications

Denkschrift des deutschen Städtetages.
Finanz-Archiv.

Gemeindetag, Der. Formerly Der Städtetag. Official publication of the organization of municipal officials, Der Gemeindetag.

Reich und Länder.

Schriftenreihe des deutschen Städtetages.

Statistisches Jahrbuch der deutschen Gemeinden. Published by Der Gemeindetag.

Vierteljahresschrift für Steuer- und Finanzrecht.

ENGLISH SYSTEM

Public Documents

Command papers

Royal Commission on Local Government, Evidence, C. 9528, 1899.

Royal Commission on Local Taxation, Final Report, Cd. 638, 1901.

Departmental Committee on Local Taxation, Final Report, Cd. 7315, 1914.

——— Appendix to Final Report, Cd. 7316, 1914.

Commission on National Expenditure, First Report, Cmd. 1581, 1922.

Royal Commission on London Government, Report, Cmd. 1830, 1923.

Board of Education, Memorandum on the Grant System, Cmd. 2571, 1926.

Ministry of Health, Proposals for Reform in Local Government, Cmd. 3134, 1928.

Government Grants to Local Authorities, Cmd. 3157, 1928.

Committee on Local Expenditure for England and Wales, Report, Cmd. 4200, 1932.

Ministry of Labour, Reports of Investigations into the Industrial Conditions in Certain Depressed Areas, Cmd. 4728, 1934.

House of Commons reports

Report on County Rates, H.C. 542, 1834.

Report on Local Taxation, H.C. 168, 1893.

Miscellaneous

Central Valuation Committee, Report on Rating and Valuation Acts, 1925 to 1932, 1934.

Civil Estimates.

Finance Accounts of the United Kingdom.

Ministry of Health, Rates and Rateable Values; England and Wales. Annual.

Ministry of Health, Annual Report.
———— Annual Local Taxation Returns. England and Wales.
Statistical Abstract of the United Kingdom.

General Treatises

Century of Municipal Progress, A, 1835-1935, London, 1936.
Finer, H., English Local Government, London, 1933.
Gunston, D. W., and Peto, G., Rating Relief, London, 1929.
Webb, Sidney, Grants in Aid, London, 1920.

Miscellaneous

Association of Municipal Corporations, Reform in Local Government
    and in the Financial Relations between the Exchequer and Local
    Authorities, 1928.
Institute of Municipal Treasurers and Accountants, Lectures and other
    publications.
Preston Borough Treasurer, Rates Levied in Various Towns, 1934-35.